ASIAN POLITICAL, ECONOMIC AND SECURITY ISSUES

ECONOMIC CRISIS AND VULNERABILITY

THE STORY FROM SOUTHEAST ASIA

ASIAN POLITICAL, ECONOMIC AND SECURITY ISSUES

Additional books in this series can be found on Nova's website under the Series tab.

Additional E-books in this series can be found on Nova's website under the E-books tab.

GLOBAL RECESSION - CAUSES, IMPACTS AND REMEDIES

Additional books in this series can be found on Nova's website under the Series tab.

Additional E-books in this series can be found on Nova's website under the E-books tab.

ASIAN POLITICAL, ECONOMIC AND SECURITY ISSUES

ECONOMIC CRISIS AND VULNERABILITY

THE STORY FROM SOUTHEAST ASIA

TULUS TAHI HAMONANGAN TAMBUNAN

Nova Science Publishers, Inc.
New York

Copyright ©2012 by Nova Science Publishers, Inc.

All rights reserved. No part of this book may be reproduced, stored in a retrieval system or transmitted in any form or by any means: electronic, electrostatic, magnetic, tape, mechanical photocopying, recording or otherwise without the written permission of the Publisher.

For permission to use material from this book please contact us:
Telephone 631-231-7269; Fax 631-231-8175
Web Site: http://www.novapublishers.com

NOTICE TO THE READER

The Publisher has taken reasonable care in the preparation of this book, but makes no expressed or implied warranty of any kind and assumes no responsibility for any errors or omissions. No liability is assumed for incidental or consequential damages in connection with or arising out of information contained in this book. The Publisher shall not be liable for any special, consequential, or exemplary damages resulting, in whole or in part, from the readers' use of, or reliance upon, this material. Any parts of this book based on government reports are so indicated and copyright is claimed for those parts to the extent applicable to compilations of such works.

Independent verification should be sought for any data, advice or recommendations contained in this book. In addition, no responsibility is assumed by the publisher for any injury and/or damage to persons or property arising from any methods, products, instructions, ideas or otherwise contained in this publication.

This publication is designed to provide accurate and authoritative information with regard to the subject matter covered herein. It is sold with the clear understanding that the Publisher is not engaged in rendering legal or any other professional services. If legal or any other expert assistance is required, the services of a competent person should be sought. FROM A DECLARATION OF PARTICIPANTS JOINTLY ADOPTED BY A COMMITTEE OF THE AMERICAN BAR ASSOCIATION AND A COMMITTEE OF PUBLISHERS.

Additional color graphics may be available in the e-book version of this book.

Library of Congress Cataloging-in-Publication Data

Hamonangan Tambunan, Tulus Tahi.
 Economic crisis and vulnerability : the story from Southeast Asia / Tulus Tahi Hamonangan Tambunan.
     p. cm.
 Includes bibliographical references and index.
 ISBN 978-1-61324-240-7 (hardcover)
 1. Southeast Asia--Economic conditions. 2. Financial crises--Southeast Asia. 3. Financial crises--Indonesia. I. Title.
 HC441.H346 2011
 330.959'053--dc22
                                                  2011009051

Published by Nova Science Publishers, Inc. † New York

Contents

Preface		vii
Chapter 1	Introduction	1
Chapter 2	Economic Crisis: Theory and Evidence	7
Chapter 3	Impacts on Households Incomes and their Crisis-coping Measures	61
Chapter 4	Impact on Micro, Small and Medium Enterprises	93
Chapter 5	Regional Vulnerability to Economic Crisis: An Analysis with Indonesia Data	153
References		227
Index		243

PREFACE

This book is about economic crisis and vulnerability with reference to some countries in East Asia. The main reason that this book focuses on Indonesia is simply because since 1990 until recently, Indonesia has been hit by two big economic crises. The first one was a regional economic crisis in Southeast Asia during the period 1997-98. The crisis was triggered by a sudden capital flight which led to currency crises and ended up as financial/economic crises in Indonesia, Thailand, the Philippines and South Korea. The economy of these countries had plunged into a deep recession in 1998. Among these countries, Indonesia was the most severely affected with the economic growth of minus 13.7 percent in 1998. Output in almost all sectors dropped significantly, e.g. construction - 39.8 percent, banking -26.7 percent, trade, and hotel and restaurant -18.9 percent, manufacturing industry -12.9 percent and transport and communication -12.8 percent. Among these crisis-affected countries, Indonesia was also the only country which had policy and social crises at the same time. As the result of these multi-crises, the recovery process in Indonesia went very slowly, while South Korea and Thailand, for instance, already showed signs of recovery in 1999.

The second crisis was the global economic crisis in the period 2008-09. The crisis which started in 2007 as a financial crisis in the United States (USA) and then spread worldwide, has been called by many economists as the most serious economic or financial crisis since the great depression in the 1930s. Its global effects include the failure of key businesses, declines in consumer wealth estimated in the trillions of U.S. dollars, substantial financial commitments incurred by governments, and a significant decline in economic activity. The crisis rapidly developed and spread into a global economic shock, resulting in a number of bank failures, declines in various stock indexes, and large reductions in the market value of equities and commodities. In Asia, most countries, including China, India and Indonesia were affected by the crisis. While many Asian developing countries only saw moderate deceleration in their economic growth in 2008, as the crisis intensified and export demand began to slow sharply in 2009 from the US, for the European Union and Japan, a substantial decline in domestic economic activities took place in many of these countries in 2009.

Indonesia, with this crisis experience twice, shows that the country's economy is vulnerable to economic shocks. There are reasons for that. First, the Indonesian economy is more open now as compared to, say, three decades ago. Second, though at a decreasing rate, Indonesia's dependence on exports of many primary commodities is still high, and world prices of these commodities are often unstable. Third, the country has become increasingly dependent on imports of a number of food items such as rice, food grains, cereals, wheat, corn, meat, dairy, vegetables and fruits, or even oil. Fourth, more Indonesian working populations, including women, went abroad as migrant workers, and hence livelihoods in many villages in Indonesia have become increasingly dependent on remittances from abroad. With this awareness of potential crises that Indonesia will almost certainly face in the near future, having an early warning system for economic crisis is important, and this is one issue addressed in this book.

Another important fact from the Indonesian experience with crises is that the impacts varied by region. During the 1997/98 crisis, although Indonesia's economic growth was negative, many provinces still had positive growth rates. During the 2008/09 global economic crisis, the world demand for many commodities declined, some of which were among Indonesia's key export commodities. Within Indonesia, only provinces producing and exporting the crisis-affected commodities were directly affected by the declined world demand. For this type of crisis, some regions in the country are more vulnerable than other regions. Thus, this fact suggests that in analyzing the impact of an economic crisis on a country or a region, the type of crisis is important as the starting point of the analysis. Different types of crises have different transmission channels and hence different impacts. This implies that in a huge country like Indonesia with many islands and regions (i.e. provinces, districts and subdistricts), and many production centers of a wide range of world tradable commodities sited in different regions, the level of vulnerability to an economic shock varies by region, and within a region, by household. Analytical framework of economic vulnerability with the focus on the regional and household levels is another issue addressed in this book.

This book consists of five chapters. Chapter I discusses types of economic crisis and transmission channels. It also discusses the Indonesian experience with the two crises, i.e. 1997/98 and 2008/09. Evidence of the impacts of the crises on such as economic growth, poverty, unemployment, and trade are presented in this chapter. Chapters II and III examine the impact of the two crises on small and medium enterprises (SMEs) and households, respectively. As a comparison, the chapter also provides some recent evidence of the impact of the crises on SMEs in some other Asian developing countries. Chapter IV deals with an analytical framework of economic vulnerability focusing at regional and household levels. It proposes indicators to be used to monitor the level of vulnerability at those two levels. It also presents data for some indicators at the provincial level in Indonesia. Chapter V is about the construction of an economic crisis early warning system (ECEWS). For this purpose, it discusses an ECEWS for a currency crisis by using Indonesia data during the 1997/98 crisis period.

Chapter 1

INTRODUCTION

In the past 15 years or so, many countries in Southeast Asia have experienced two subsequent economic crises; although the seriousness of the impact of those two crises on domestic economy varied by country. The first one was the Asian financial crisis that started in the second half of 1997 and reached its climax during the middle of 1998. This crisis was considered merely as a regional economic crisis since it was not only initially emerged in Southeast Asia but it also hit only countries in the region. The crisis was triggered by a sudden capital flight out from Thailand which led to a significant depreciation of its currency, bath, against the U.S dollar. Soon after, capital in huge amounts also fled out from Indonesia, South Korea and the Philippines, leading to a big fall in their currencies. Indonesia was the most impacted country by the crisis, which resulted in a negative economic growth rate at 13 percent, which led poverty rates to increase significantly.

The second one occurred during the period 2008-2009. This crisis is generally referred to as a global economic crisis since its impact was much wider than that of the 1997/98 crisis. The crisis started first in the United States (U.S) in 2007 as a serious financial crisis. This crisis has been called by many economists as the most serious economic or financial crisis that the U.S. ever experienced since the Great Depression in the 1930s. Its global effects include the failure of key businesses, declines in consumer wealth estimated in the trillions of U.S. dollars, substantial financial commitments incurred by governments, and a significant decline in economic activities in many countries. The crisis then rapidly developed and spread into a global economic shock, resulting in a number of bank failures, declines in various stock indexes, and large reductions in the market value of equities and commodities. In Asia, most countries, including China, India and Indonesia were also affected by the crisis. While many Asian countries only saw moderate deceleration in their economic growth in 2008, as the crisis intensified and export demand began to slow sharply in 2009 from the U.S, the European Union (EU) and Japan, a substantial decline in domestic economic activities took place in many of these countries in 2009.

This book is about those two crises. However, since there are many works done on the 1997/98 Asian financial crisis already, published either as books or articles in various international journals, whereas, there are not many published works on the 2008/09 global economic crisis, this book discusses the first crisis only briefly. Regarding the 2008/09 crisis, by country, the focus of the discussion in this book is on selected developing countries in Southeast Asia, and it examines empirically the impact of the crisis on limited issues, ranging from economic growth, sectoral output growth, employment, poverty, trade, remittance, capital inflows, and development of micro, small and medium enterprises (MSMEs). In addition, the book also gives special attention to how the crisis-affected households coped with the 2008/09 crisis. After the discussions on the impact of the 2008/09 crisis, this books ends with a special discussion on how and with what to measure vulnerability of a country or a region to an economic crisis with Indonesia as the case study.

Specifically, this book is organized in five chapters, including this Chapter I on introduction. Chapter II deals with the theoretical as well as empirical sides of the two crises, but with the focus on the 2008/09 crisis with the reason already given above. It consists of two main sections. The first section provides a theoretical discussion on how different types or sources of economic crises may have different transmission channels, different outcomes, and different impacts on sectors, households and vulnerable groups, and hence on the economy as a whole. It discusses the most important types of economic crises that the world or many countries have ever experienced in the past 50 years, and their transmission channels through which the crises affected the economy of a particular country, namely production crisis, banking crisis, currency crisis, trade crisis, and foreign capital/investment crisis. It also suggests key indicators for monitoring for each of the types of economic crises. For instance, for the production crisis, the main indicators are employment by sector and region, output by sector and region, inflation, income by sector and region, and poverty by sector and region.

Then, section two of Chapter II examines empirically the impact of the 2008/09 crisis on the economy of selected countries in Southeast Asia, including Indonesia, Malaysia, Thailand, Philippines and Singapore. But first, the section deals briefly with the 1997/98 Asian financial crisis. It hit many countries in East and Southeast Asia, especially Indonesia, Thailand, Singapore, Malaysia Philippines and South Korea. However, the impact varied by country, and Indonesia together with South Korea were among the most severely affected ones. The Indonesian economy, for instance, had plunged into a deep recession in 1998 with overall growth at minus 13.7 percent. This was much higher than the highest positive economic growth ever achieved during the Soeharto era (1966-1998). The crisis also led to a significant drop in income per capita and poverty rate to increase in the country. While the 1997/98 Asian financial crisis affected only a small number of Asian countries, the 2008/09 global economic crisis hit many countries in the region, as well as in other parts of the world. The crisis impacted through various channels, i.e. exports, investment (including foreign direct investment/FDI), and remittances. However, the most important channel for most of the affected countries was export. The impacted countries saw serious declines in their exports for various commodities, especially for the U.S market.

One interesting point discussed in this section is about differences between the two crises. The key difference was the fact that during the latest crisis, countries such as Thailand, Philippines and Indonesia which were seriously hit by the first crisis, had shown some resilience towards the 2008/09 crisis. They managed to have positive overall economic growth rates in 2008 and 2009; though the rate varied by country. Since Indonesia was the worst country affected by the 1997/98 crisis, during the 2008/09 crisis, the Indonesian economic performance was closely monitored by banks such as the World Bank and the Asian Development Bank. Indonesia not only managed to keep positive economic growth rates but poverty rates in the country also did not increase during the 2008/09 crisis; instead, surprisingly, it declined. As discussed in this section, there were two main factors that may explain the better economic performance than was expected of Indonesia and other countries in the region during the latest crisis, namely the relatively healthy state of their banking sector/financial systems prior to the crisis and the fiscal and monetary stimuli that had been quickly provided by governments and central banks in those countries.

Chapter III examines the impact of the 2008/09 crisis on households incomes and explores their crisis-coping measures. As a world demand or export crisis, theoretically, it would affect household incomes through both direct and indirect channels. The direct channel (i.e. direct effects) is the impact on households directly linked to crisis-affected firms. Whereas, the indirect channel (i.e. indirect effects) is the impact of the decline in production or export of the crisis-direct affected firms on household incomes in other firms through local/regional income multiplier effects. The impact of the crisis on other firms (or sectors) would take place through three transmission channels, i.e. production, consumption, and investment-saving.

Due to data limitation and lack of field studies in other countries in Southeast Asia, this chapter covers only Indonesia. It is divided into two main sections with the first section discussing briefly findings from various surveys/crisis monitoring activities conducted by a number of organizations, including the World Bank in Indonesia, during the crisis period. The main aim of those survey activities was to examine the impact of the crisis at the sectoral and household levels. In general, the surveys found several interesting facts, e.g. many households during the crisis period experienced a drop in head of household working hours that adversely affected their incomes, little change in the unemployment or labor force participation rates for heads of households, the proportion of households having difficulty meeting the increased daily consumption costs and its impact on households real financial conditions is significantly different between poor and non-poor households, female headed households recovered more quickly than their male counterparts, and regions experienced the impact of the crisis differently, both in labor market indicators and household hardship indicators. In addition, there are at least two more interesting facts from one of the surveys. First, extreme coping mechanisms, even among the poor households during the crisis period, such as sending their children into the labor force (having children drop-out or absenteeism from school) to boost failing household incomes and significant cut in their education and health expenditures have not been apparent in both rural and urban areas. Second, not all provinces in Indonesia were affected by the crisis, or not all of the crisis-affected provinces showed similar outcomes. Some provinces were largely unaffected, some saw a deterioration in conditions but had recovered quickly, while others saw continued or lagged deterioration.

In addition to the findings of those surveys/crisis monitoring activities, the second section presents a case study aimed at assessing the impact of the crisis on households incomes and to explore their crisis-coping mechanism in the Indonesian furniture industry. The case study is based on a household survey which had been conducted during July-August 2009, covering 50 households. The households were randomly selected with the following composition by region: 20 households in Cirebon district in the province of West Java, and 11 and 18 households in Jepara district and Solo district, respectively. Both districts are in the province of Central Java. These three regions are among production centers of furniture in Indonesia. Although households as respondents were randomly selected, the survey covered only households with the heads or other members who were still working in or have been laid off from enterprises making furniture during the survey period. The findings of the survey may suggest that many households affected by the 2008/09 crisis took some measures, including made adjustments on their expenditures to cope with it. But they would try what ever they could not to reduce their expenditures for the education of their children, even in a hardship condition as they experienced during the 2008/09 crisis.

Chapter IV deals with MSMEs, which aims to answer the following main research question: how is the resilience of MSMEs to an exogenous economic shock/crisis? For this purpose, the chapter assesses the impact of the 1997/98 Asian financial crisis and the 2008/09 global economic crisis on these enterprises in selected developing countries in Asia where data/information is available. The rationale of this assessment is that although there are already many studies on the impacts of the two crises (expecially of the first one) on economic areas, such as economic growth and export, and on social areas such as employment, migrant workers, farm household's incomes, education and health, however, not many studies have been done on the impact of the crises, especially the 2008/09 crisis, on MSMEs. The chapter starts first with a brief examination of the current state of the performance of the enterprises in Indonesia and some other countries in the region. It also discusses the main constraints facing them. Then, in the next section, it provides a theoretical explanation on how an economic crisis may affect MSMEs. Finally, the chapter comes with some evidence on the effects of the 1997/98 and 2008/09 crises on MSMEs in a number of countries in the region. Differently than the 2008/09 crisis, the 1997/98 Asian financial crisis provides more evidence on the resilience of MSMEs to an economic crisis. The evidence comes mainly from studies in Thailand and Indonesia. The Thai case comes with the following key findings: (i) MSMEs were more severely hit by the crisis than large enterprises (LEs), but, differently than their larger counterparts, these smaller enterprises managed to recover in a relatively short period; (ii) many of MSMEs were struggling with financial difficulties because of high interest rates and unavailability of other financial sources; (iii) MSMEs have been particularly affected later on when the crisis has peaked and extended to many sectors, especially manufacturing industry. They have all been subjected to reduced output, consumption, employment and investment; and (iv) in export-oriented and strongly connected with foreign partners, MSMEs suffered less and even gained thanks to devaluation and support from foreign partners.

While, the Indonesian case shows the following key findings: (i) although many MSMEs were also seriously hit by the crisis, in overall, they were relatively better off than LEs; (ii) in different industries or sectors, MSMEs had different experiences with the crisis because individual entrepreneurs, though producing the same products or in different industries/sectors, faced different internal and external conditions, e.g. constraints, challenges and opportunities; (iii) MSMEs which could make quick and right adjustments to the crisis were more resilience than those which were slower in response to the crisis; and (iv) world trade-linked (for inputs as well as output) and bank credit depending MSMEs were more affected by the crisis than local markets-oriented and self-funding-based MSMEs.

With respect to the 2008/09 global economic crisis, since the export market was the main important transmission channel through which it affected domestic economy, the most affected MSMEs in countries like Indonesia, China, Malaysia, Philippines, India, Singapore and Vietnam were the export-oriented ones. Especialy in labor-incentive manufacturing industries, e.g. textile, garment, toys, food and beverages, footwear, electronics, and furniture, many exporting MSMEs had to stop or reduce their productions as world demand for their goods dropped significantly. Also, many MSMEs-producing items for the tourist sector were seriously impacted by the demand slump caused by the crisis. Many workers in these enterprises, especially women, have been affected in a number of ways such as layoffs of fixed as well as contract workers; reduction of work days or hours; and freezes on the minimum wage.

The final part of this chaper presents and discusses findings of a field survey on MSMEs in the furniture industry in Central Java, Indonesia. Among various Indonesian key export commodities affected by the 2008/09 crisis was furniture, and the industry is traditionally dominated by MSMEs. In 2009, as the world demand for Indonesia- made furniture declined due to the crisis, the industry had to lay off nearly 35,000 workers in the early part of that year. In the second quarter of 2009, the export value of Indonesian furniture to a number of countries was found to have declined by 30 percent, and many MSMEs in the industry had to stop, or to cut their productions, or, as an alternative way, to reshift their market orientation towards domestic buyers.

After examining the impacts the 1997/98 crisis and the 2008/09 crisis on economic growth, income per capita, unemployment, poverty, households incomes, and MSMEs, in various countries in Southeast Asia, it becomes obvious that those countries are vulnerable to any economic crises and within a country, it was found some regions (e.g. province or district) were more affected than the others. Therefore, the final part of this book, Chapter V, discusses the importance of having knowledge about the vulnerability of a region, which can be at country level or at provincial or district level, to an economic crisis. The chapter also proposes a range of indicators which can be used to monitor the level of economic vulnerability. As empirical examples, this chapter uses provincial data in Indonesia.

Chapter 2

ECONOMIC CRISIS: THEORY AND EVIDENCE

II.1. TYPES OF ECONOMIC CRISIS AND TRANSMISSION CHANNELS

This Chapter provides a theoretical discussion on how different types or sources of economic crisis may have different transmission channels, different outcomes, and different impacts on sectors, households and vulnerable groups, and hence, on the economy as a whole.[1] Therefore, it is important, especially for policymakers and economic development planners, to understand the various transmission channels of different crises and their different impacts on sectors and households or vulnerable groups. Such knowledge will assist policymakers with the development of a crisis and vulnerability monitoring system, the identification of appropriate indicators to monitor the impact of an economic crisis on the poor and vulnerable groups, and to develop an early warning system.

II.1.1. Types of Economic Crisis

An economic crisis can be originated from outside or inside a particular country or region. From inside, for instance, a sudden, large drop in output of a particular commodity (e.g. harvest failures due to a natural disaster), while, from outside as in the 2008/2009 global economic crisis (except for the U.S., it was originated from inside). Economic crises from different origins have different transmission processes, and, depending on the nature and the extent of linkages with the rest of domestic economy, may have different overall impacts. The following subsections discuss the most important types of economic crisis that the world or many countries have ever experienced in the past 50 years.

---

[1] There are two different natures of an economic crisis by the process of becoming a crisis. An economic crisis can outbreak unexpectedly, which is usually regarded as an economic shock. For instance, the first oil crisis in 1974 or the 1997/98 Asian financial crisis. Although the degree of shock of the 1974 oil crisis was much higher than that of the 1997/98 crisis, because in the latter crisis there were already some signals that some countries in Asia were about to face a crisis in the coming months. In Indonesia, one of the signals was the weakening of the rupiah which begun already in the second half of 1997, started first slowly but continued day by day until it reached the deepest level in 1998 (the year that the crisis reached its climax). Whereas, a foreign debt crisis is certainly not a shock, since it is the result of an accumulation of foreign debt that normally takes many years before it becomes a crisis.

Production Crisis

Production crisis is among types of economic crisis from internal sources. It can be in the form of a sudden drop in domestic production of an agricultural commodity such as rice. It then will result in income decline of rice farmers and agricultural laborers. In regions (e.g. provinces) where rice production is the key economic sector, not only in the form of output share in the formation of total gross regional product (GRP), but also as the largest source of regional employment or income, a significant number of rural households will lose their incomes as a result of it. If rice is also used as the main raw material by other sectors such as food processing industries, then the production and hence employment and income in those related sectors will drop also. The latter is an indirect effect of the rice production crisis. Overall, the level of poverty in the regions will increase. If no imports compensate the drop in the local productions of rice as well as outputs in the other rice-related sectors, the local market will face an excess demand which will generate a higher inflation rate. The higher inflation deteriorates further the real income in the regions. Another important effect is that the drop in rice production and zero import of rice will cause a food shortage with serious consequences such as social unrest and political instability.

In this type of economic crisis, the key transmission channels are price (inflation) and employment, and the most vulnerable groups are the rice farmers/farm households, agricultural workers and their families in the rice sector and, to a lower degree, employees and their families in the related sectors.

Banking Crisis

The direct or immediate impact or the first phase of the effect of a banking crisis is the income or employment decline in the banking sector. As the second phase of the effect, it may affect companies depending much on bank credits for financing their operations. The companies are affected because no credit is no longer available or interest rates on credit increases due to excess demand in the money/credit market. During the 1997/98 Asian financial crisis, for instance, many big companies in Indonesia were forced to stop their businesses or to reduce their production because the national banking sector collapsed. The proses of this kind of crisis will lead further to lay offs of many workers, or, ultimately, depending on the linkages of the affected companies with the rest of domestic economy, it will result in the increase of unemployment or poverty (Figure II.1).

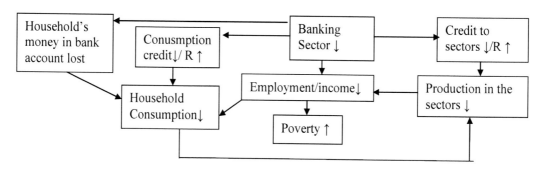

Figure II.1. Domestic Banking Crisis and Its Impact on Poverty.

Households are also affected by this crisis. There are two types of impacts on households and two types of affected households. First, wealthy households: their money (savings) in bank accounts will be lost. In many countries, the government gives some saving security quarantee, but only up to a certain limit. Thus, very rich depositors will loss more than low or middle class depositors. Second, non-wealthy households: their expenditure will decline because they cannot borrow money (consumer credits) anymore from banks, or the lending interest rate is too high.

In this type of economic crisis, the most important transmission channels are credit flows, interest rate, output and employment. The immediate vulnerable group is not the poor as in the case of agricultural production crisis discussed before, but mostly the middle to upper income classes, such as bank shareholders and their employees. Depending on what economic sectors or industries are heavily financed by bank, the next vulnerable group can be the poor (especially if the agricultural sector depends much on bank credits), or middle- to high-income classes such as employees in automotive, electronics, and other sophisticated goods industries since companies in these industries usually depend on bank financing.

Currency Crisis

With respect to currency crisis, i.e. depreciation of a national currency, the direct impact will be on local firms doing international trade (i.e. export and import) and international financial transactions. In the international trade, export will respond differently than import will. By assuming other factors are constant, export, and hence, production and employment or income in the exporting firms/sectors and their backward and forward linked firms or sectors will increase, as the depreciation will improve their price competitiveness in foreign values. Of course, it will depend on domestic production capability to respond to this particular foreign market opportunity. On the import side, the price in national currency of imported goods (i.e. raw materials/inputs and consumption/final goods) will go up, *ceteris paribus*. As a direct response to this, two possibilities may happen. First, import declines which leads to the decrease in domestic productions (in the case of imported raw materials/inputs) and hence, unemployment will increase. Second, imports may stay constant. In the case of imported inputs for domestic industries/sectors, this will cause domestic production cost to go up and, finally, it will result in higher domestic inflation. The net result on poverty will depend on whether the total export (positive) effects are larger than, equal to, or smaller than the total import (negative) effects of the crisis (Figure II.2).

However, the decline in import may also have a positive effect as it may encourage domestic import-substitution productions, although it will take time, depending on domestic production capability and other domestic supporting factors[2]. If this happens, then the overall impact can be positive, namely the sum of the export increase effects and the domestic production increase effects.

Regarding international financial transactions, local firms mostly affected by this kind of crisis are those which have huge foreign debts. In the case of Indonesia, for example, when its currency, rupiah, depreciates against, say, the US dollar, Indonesian foreign indebted local companies will face serious financial difficulties or even they can collapse because the

---

[2] Generally, it is easier to do for consumption goods than in the case of imported intermediate or capital goods. Domestic import-substitution productions of the latter goods are more complex, and thus the process will be more difficult to carry on for many developing countries.

cost in rupiah of having foreign loans will increase. If these companies stop their production, then other related firms may also have to stop or reduce their production and, thus in overall, unemployment and poverty will increase.

The key transmission channels in this case are changes in export, import, employment/income, and inflation. The most vulnerable group is on the import side. But, it will depend on what sectors are mostly affected by higher import costs (in national currency) and their response to the increased import costs: whether they keep the import volume the same as before the depreciation took place and without any labor adjustment (e.g. lay offs or less working hours), or they reduce their imports.

Trade Crisis

With respect to economic crises originating from outside sources, there are two main channels, namely trade and investment/capital, and in trade there are two sub-channels, i.e. exports and imports (for both goods and services). Regarding the export channel, for instance, exports of goods, a crisis can happen either because of significant declines in world prices or drops in world demands for key commodities. As an example, suppose that the world prices or demands for Indonesian key exports of agricultural commodities decline, then farm/agricultural incomes in the country will decline. This process however will not stop here. As with other cases discussed before, there is a multiplier effect: declines in farm incomes will reduce consumption as well as intermediate demands within the rural areas, and as a result, rural income will decline or rural poverty will increase.

In this case, the most important transmission channels are changes in output and employment. The most vulnerable groups are farmers and exporting companies, including their employees and their families. In a 2009 report from the World Bank and the ASEAN Secretariat, it was predicted that the 2008/09 global economic crisis in Indonesia was most likely to be felt only among a few regions that produce commodities such as estate crops, for which world prices have dropped significantly.[3] Regions where export-oriented factories, such as garment factories, are located (e.g. Bandung in the West Java province, and Greater Jakarta) were also more likely to feel the impact (World Bank and ASEAN, 2009).

For export of services, a crisis arises when, for instance, the number of foreign tourists declines sharply or a significant drop in remittance receipts from overseas migrants. According to the same report, the crisis has been transmitted to ASEAN economies[4] through several transmission channels, and among the most important ones were fewer tourist arrivals [5] and reduced remittance receipts from overseas migrants.[6]

---

[3] According to the same report, the average prices of crude petroleum, copper, palm oil, coffee, and rice have fallen by 25-50 percent since the beginning of the crisis, although prices of major commodities have started to rebound since the first quarter of 2009. As stated further in this report, ASEAN countries exporting primary commodities have experienced significant declines in their export values for such commodities. For example, Myanmar has experienced a drop in its export values of natural gas due to decreasing global demand and falling commodity prices. The export value of natural gas to Thailand, its biggest trade partner, was estimated to drop by 50 percent year-on-year (World Bank and ASEAN, 2009).

[4] Association of Southeast Asian Nations (ASEAN) comprises of Brunei Darussalam, Cambodia, Indonesia, Lao People's Democratic Republic, Malaysia, Myanmar, Philippines, Singapore, Thailand, and Viet Nam.

[5] Official data from the ASEAN Secretariat shows that during the first seven months of 2009, foreign tourist arrivals fell by around 14 percent in Indonesia and 20 percent in Vietnam, compared with the same period in 2008. In Cambodia, the number of tourists dropped by almost 2.2 percent in the first two months of 2009 compared to 2008 (World Bank and ASEAN, 2009).

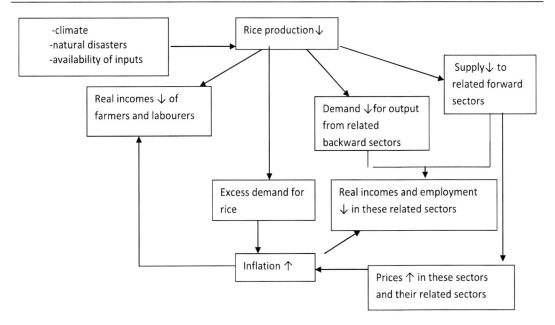

Figure II.2. National Currency Crisis and Its Impact on Poverty.

With respect to import, a significant increase in world price or a sudden and huge drop in world stock for a worldwide tradable commodity can become a serious economic crisis for importing countries if for them, it is a crucial commodity. For instance, rice and oil, which are also key commodities for the poor. The increase of oil prices in the world market leads to the increase of domestic prices of fuel, electricity, and fertilizers as well as the costs of domestic productions of many goods. For instance, in 1974, the sudden unexpected decision made by the organization of petroleum exporting countries (OPEC) to increase their price of oil as their collective response to the Arab-Israel conflict was a big crisis for all oil importing countries, especially the developed economies such as the US and European countries which, in that time, were yet very depending on oil from the Middle East. With no change in total oil import, as this commodity was the key source of energy, this 'first oil crisis' had led the energy costs and hence, domestic production costs to increase in the oil importing countries and resulted in a world hyper-inflation. At least, theoretically, in this kind of crisis, the impact can be relatively small if oil importing countries make an adjustment by subsidizing oil with alternative energies or by improving efficiency in the use of oil in their domestic production. The result of this adjustment was then evident in the second 'oil crisis' by the end of the 1970s or early 1980s, when the worldwide impact of this second oil crisis was much smaller than that of the first one.

In this case, most important transmission channels are changes in output, inflation and employment. The most vulnerable groups are, first, companies depending much on oil as

---

[6] According to a World Bank estimation, during the crisis period, international remittances have fallen by 7-10 percent (World Bank, 2009c). In Indonesia, Koser (2009) estimates that remittances have declined to US$3 billion in 2009, from US$6 billion in 2007; while, Titiheruw et al (2009) show, using Bank Indonesia data, that total remittance flows to Indonesia until the last quarter of 2008 were higher than in previous years. A qualitative assessment of migrant workers from the Philippines by the Philippines Central Bank also suggests that the frequency and size of remittances sent home were declined, though the overall remittance growth in the country during the whole year of 2009 was predicted to remain positive (BSP, 2009).

energy or raw materials and their employees (and their families), and, second, through domestic production and consumption/income linkages, other related companies or sectors, including their employees and their families.

Foreign Capital/Investment Crisis

Finally, a decline in foreign investment or a sudden 'foreign capital flight' in a huge amount may also cause a crisis for the host country. The process is as simple as the following: less foreign investment, especially foreign direct investment (FDI), less domestic production, lower productivity, and ultimately less employment and more poverty. On the other hand, a huge capital flight will cause a significant depreciation of currency of the host country with further effects, as already shown in Figure II.2.[7]

In this case, the most important transmission channels are domestic production and employment. The most vulnerable groups can be both the poor and the non-poor, depending on what sectors/industries are most impacted. If foreign investments are mainly in domestic capital intensive industries or in extractive activities using few local employees and having few or no linkages with other domestic labor intensive industries (i.e. the foreign investment based-domestic industries depend much on imported inputs), then the impact on the poor is likely to be weak. More skilled or middle to high income rather than unskilled or low income employees will be affected. On the contrary, if foreign investments are in the agricultural sector such as in crude palm oil or in food industries using local agricultural commodities as their main raw materials, then the effect on the poor (e.g. farm incomes and incomes of agricultural laborers) will be significant.

II.1.2. Key Transmission Channels and Monitoring Indicators

In summary, from all types of economic crisis discussed above, it can be seen that the levels of inflation and employment or unemployment are the key determinants of poverty, or they can be considered as the key transmission channels of the effect of an economic crisis on poverty. Unemployment (employment) is a negative (positive) function of output or gross domestic product (GDP), and inflation depends negatively on GDP (or positively on consumption). GDP is a function of, among other variables, investment (including FDI) and trade balance. The latter is influenced by exchange rates and other factors.

Table II.1 proposed a list of main transmission channels for each of the discussed types of economic crisis. The channels can be ranked as the first channels (*), i.e. the first revealed effects of a crisis, the second channels (**), the third channels (***), and so on. When an economic crisis occurs, its effects may take place through more than one channel simultaneously, depending on the type of the crisis. The table also suggests main important indicators for monitoring the poverty impact of each of the discussed types of economic crisis.

---

[7] Within ASEAN, during the 2008/09 global economic crisis, some member countries experienced a decline in FDI. For instance, in Cambodia, FDI decreased by nearly 50 percent in the first quarter of 2009 compared to the same period in 2008, resulting in a significantly lower investment in the construction sector. Thailand also faced a contraction in FDI in the first quarter of 2009 at almost 22 percent (year-on-year). While, in Indonesia, based on official data from Indonesian Investment Coordination Board (BKPM; www.bkpm.go.id), no indication that FDI has dropped during the crisis period.

Table II.1. Main Transmission Channels and Proposed Main Indicators for Crisis Monitoring by Type of Economic Crisis

Type of crisis	Main Transmission Channels	Main Indicators for Crisis Monitoring
Production crisis	Employment/income* Inflation*	Employment by sector and region Output by sector and region Inflation (CPI) Income by sector and region Poverty by sector and region
Banking crisis	Credit* Interest rate* Output** Employment/income***	Employment by sector and region Output by sector and region Income by sector and region Poverty
Currency crisis	Export* Import* Output** Employment/income*** Inflation***	Export by sector and region Import by sector and region Output by sector and region Empoyment by sector and region
Export crisis	Output* Employment/income**	Export by sector and region Employment by sector and region Output by sector and region Income by sector and region Poverty
Import crisis	Output* Employment/income** Inflation**	Output by sector and region Employment by sector and region Income by sector and region Poverty
Foreign investment/capital crisis	Output* Currency depreciation* Employment/income** Inflation**	Output by sector and region Employment by sector and region Income by sector and region Poverty

II.2. EMPIRICAL ANALYSIS

In the past 15 years or so Southeast Asian countries have experienced two big economic crises. The first one was the 1997/98 Asian financial crisis and the second one was the 2008/09 global economic crisis. This second one is referred to as a global economic crisis since its impact was much wider than that of the 1997/98 crisis. The latter crisis affected only East and Southeast Asia. The following sections discuss each of these crises. Since many works have already been done on the 1997/98 crisis, but few yet on the 2008/09 crisis, this section focuses on the 2008/09 crisis. The 1997/98 crisis is discussed only briefly.

II.2.1. 1997/98 Asian Financial Crisis

Transmission Channels

The 1997/98 crisis was triggered by a sudden capital flight out of Thailand which led to the country's currency crisis (i.e. huge depreciation of bath against the US dollar) and ended up as a big financial/economic crisis in the country. Soon after, capital in huge amounts also fled out of Indonesia, South Korea and the Philippines, leading to a big fall in their currencies. Thus, for those countries, the 1997/98 crisis was a currency crisis. Other countries in the region such as Malaysia and Singapore were also affected, though less severely.

Rupiah, Indonesia's currency, for instance, depreciated day by day and reached a total fall of more than 500 percent between August 1997 to May 1998. Through the rupiah depreciation and higher interest rates (as the monetary authority's direct response in that time in order to stop capital flight), the crisis hit first, or more directly, middle and high income groups such as current employees in the financial/banking and large-sized companies. While, micro, small and medium enterprises (MSMEs), mostly undertaken by the low income population or poor households and are found in the informal sector (especially micro and small enterprises (MSEs)), were more resilient since they are generally more flexible in changing activities, and less dependent on imported inputs (thus, less affected by the rupiah depreciation) as well as on credits from banks (thus, less affected by the increase in interest rate).[8] In other words, due to the nature of the crisis, and the difference in nature between the formal and the informal sector, the first sector was more severely affected than the second one. The informal sector or many economic activities of the poor had even experienced employment growth as many laid off employees from the collapsed formal large-sized firms, including many banks, moved to the informal sector looking for alternative jobs or changed their consumption habit towards cheaper goods, including cheaper foods. That is why during the crisis, open unemployment rate in Indonesia did not increase significantly as was generally expected. However, after several months, domestic prices on final and intermediate goods started to increase significantly which reduced domestic demand and pushed up further domestic production costs, which, at last, also affected the informal sector. The increase in domestic inflation, and added by new emerging poor individuals (i.e. laid off workers in firms in the formal sector adversely affected by the crisis), had then caused the significant increase in poverty in 1998.

Impact

The 1997/98 crisis hit many countries in East and Southeast Asia, especially Indonesia, Thailand, Singapore, Malaysia Philippines and South Korea. However, the impact varied by country. Indonesia, together with South Korea, were the most seriously affected ones. The Indonesian economy had plunged into a deep recession in 1998 with overall growth at minus

---

[8] Often stated in the literature that one comparative advantage of MSMEs is their flexibility relative to their larger counterparts. In Berry *et al.* (2001,2002), these enterprises are construed as being especially important in industries or economies that face rapidly changing market conditions, such as the sharp macroeconomic downturns. These enterprises work as a shock-absorber of business cycle. Other studies on MSMEs in Indonesia during the crisis such as Thee (2000) and ADB (2002) found that Indonesian MSMEs weathered the crisis well and grew at a faster pace than the rest of the economy, as a number of them turned to exports due to the favorable exchange rate. MSME exports grew by 3.6 percent in 1998 and 5.8 percent in 1999, or their share in total exports doubled between 1996 and 2000. In contrast, exports by large exporters declined by 0.8 percent in 1998 and by 7.5 percent in 1999.

13.7 percent (Figure II.3). This was much higher than the highest positive economic growth ever achieved during the Soeharto era (1966-1998), or even until the present day. The worst declines were in the construction sector (-39.8 percent), financial sector (-26.7 percent), trade, and hotel and restaurant (-18.9 percent). Other sectors, which had large contractions, were manufacturing (-12.9 percent) and transport and communication (-12.8 percent). Mining and other services sectors experienced a contraction of about 4.5 percent. The agricultural and utility sectors still experienced positive growth at about 0.2 percent and 3.7 per ent, respectively (Feridhanusetyawan, et al., 2000). The crisis also led to a significant drop in income per capita (Figure II.4).

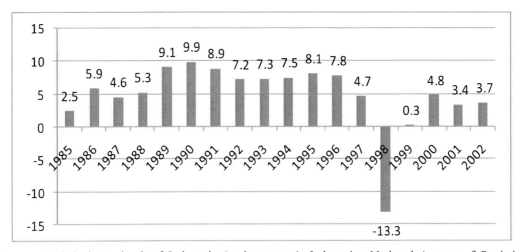

Source: Statistical Yearbook of Indonesia (various years), Indonesian National Agency of Statistics (BPS) (www.bps.go.id).

Figure II.3. Indonesian GDP Growth rate during the 1997/1998 Crisis.

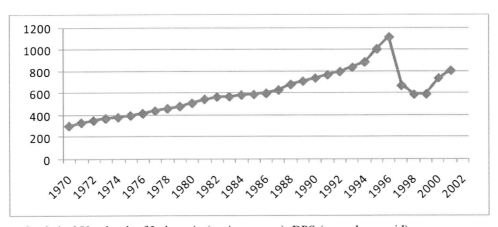

Source: Statistical Yearbook of Indonesia (various years), BPS (www.bps.go.id).

Figure II.4. Development of Indonesian Income per Capita during the 1997/98 Crisis Period (US dollar).

As discussed before, theoretically, the depreciation of national currency can have negative or positive net effects on poverty. The net effect can be negative or positive or zero. In Indonesia, for instance, the reality shows that during the crisis period, the poverty rate increased significantly (Figure II.5), which may suggest that the rupiah depreciation was more negative rather than positive for the Indonesian economy. The increase in poverty was consistent with almost 13 percent output contraction experienced by the manufacturing industry. In fact, many domestic industries used heavily imported inputs for their exported goods. So, the rupiah depreciation prevented them from gaining better world price competitiveness. Also, many big companies, known as conglomerates, collapsed because they could not pay back their foreign debts.

The situation became worst as the national banking sector also collapsed and as a result. Local firms could not continue doing international trade (export and/or import) because it was hard, if not impossible, for them to get international trade finance from their banks. Usually, local companies doing export or/and import can use various types of international finance from local commercial banks, and the three most important types are letter of credit (LC), domestic bank credit, and trade credit. LC is specifically designed to facilitate international trade. The function of this mechanism is both to provide finance and provide assurances about payment to the exporting enterprises. If an irrevocable LC is issued, the exporter receives payment when it provides the specified documents to the advising/confirming bank. However, LC requires confidence and liquidity to be maintained at various points along the chain of payment from the importer, to the issuing bank, to the advising/confirming bank and to the exporter. Because the national banking sector in Indonesia collapsed, banks in foreign countries did not accept the LC issued by Indonesian banks.

Domestic bank credit or trade credit is usually used by exporters to cover their pre-shipment or post-shipment costs. Such funding is similar to the provision of working capital in general, although it may be less risky to the extent that it is loaned against specific purchases and assets. Financial outflows during the 1997/98 crisis reduced liquidity in the domestic banking system. Whereas, international banks operating in the domestic market reduced credit in order to cut the exposure of parent banks. Also, shortages of foreign currency prevent banks in the affected countries (i.e. Indonesia, Thailand, South Korea and the Philippines) lending the foreign exchange needed for the import of inputs or export freight charges.

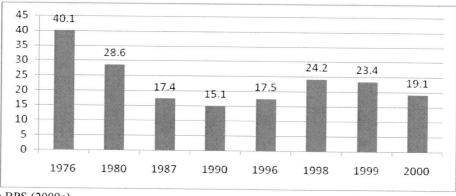

Source: BPS (2009c).

Figure II.5. Poverty rate in Indonesia During the 1997/98 Asian Financial Crisis.

In addition to the above impacts, there is some evidence showing that the 1997/98 crisis also harmed human development in the affected countries in various ways, not only increasing poverty, but also reducing the quality and supply of education and health services. Chhibber, at al. (2009) report that the crisis decreased enrollment rates among children aged 8-13 years and increased enrollment rates among children aged 14-19 years. These changes were small, just one percentage point of enrollment. The impact on school enrollment, however, varied by region within the studied countries, suggesting that different regions in a country may have had experienced differently with the crisis. A 1999 report issued by the Australian Agency for International Development (AusAID) also showed that the crisis had numerous adverse health impacts in Indonesia, including (AusAid, 1999):

(1) 20 and 25 percent decline in personal and government expenditures, repectively, on primary care from 1996 to 2000. The use of health services for primary care also declined;
(2) 25 percent decline in purchases of medicines;
(3) declines in DTP3 immunization rates from 92 to 64 percent and polio rates from 97 to 74 percent. Vitamin A supplementation also fell. The declines most likely occurred among the poorer populations;
(4) 18 percent decline in the lowest wealth quintile in child visits to health facilities (vs. 7 percent decline in highest wealth quintile);
(5) 15.4 percent decline in lowest wealth quintile in contacts with outreach workers (vs. 9.7 percent in highest wealth quintile);
(6) a halt in the 1990s downward trend in infant mortality; and
(7) mortality increases in 22 of 26 provinces between 1996 and 1999.

The report also shows that while malnutrition did not widely increase among Indonesian children, the nutritional status of adults substantially worsened during the crisis period. In that time, the Indonesian government and its donor partners, mainly the Asian Development Bank (ADB), responded to the crisis with a set of social-safety net measures, known in Indonesia as *Jaring Pengaman Sosial* (JPS). The initial objective of JPS was to mitigate the effects of the crisis on the health of the poor by maintaining spending on primary health care and the quality of services provided to the poorest sectors of the community. However, after the crisis, JPS has become an important policy measure to mitigate the financial burden of the poor. In addition to JPS, the government and non-governmental organizations (NGOs) also distributed free food and food at subsidized prices to counteract shortages which occurred during the crisis period. However, according to the report, these health and food support efforts did not prove very effective (AusAid, 1999).

II.2.2. 2008/09 Global Economic Crisis

The 2008/2009 crisis, started first in 2007 as a financial crisis in the US and spread worldwide, has been called by many economists as the most serious economic or financial crisis since the great depression in the 1930s. Its global effects include the failure of key businesses, declines in consumer wealth estimated in the trillions of U.S. dollars, substantial financial commitments incurred by governments, and a significant decline in economic activity. The crisis rapidly developed and spread into a global economic shock, resulting in a number of bank failures, declines in various stock indexes, and large reductions in the market value of equities and commodities.

In Asia, most countries, including China, India and Indonesia were affected by the crisis. Based on a report on the current outlook for the Asian economy from the International Monetary Fund (IMF) issued in April 2009, the economic growth in the region as a whole was predicted to drop to around 1.4 percent in 2009. This was a serious pessimistic prediction as compared to the economic growth rate of 5.1 percent in 2008 or much higher at 8 percent in 2007. While many Asian developing countries[9] only saw moderate deceleration in their economic growth in 2008, as the crisis intensified and export demand began to slow sharply from the US, the EU and Japan, a substantial decline in domestic economic activities took place in many of these countries from the last quarter of 2008 to 2009 (IMF, 2009).

Transmission Channels

The crisis impacted many countries through various channels, i.e. exports, investment (including FDI), and remittances. However, the most important channel for most of the affected countries was export, as also stated in the *Asian Development Outlook 2009* from the Asian Development Bank (ADB): *the main channel by which the global financial crisis and economic slump spread to developing Asia was the collapse of demand in major global markets, hitting the region's exports. With a large proportion of regional trade in parts and components supporting supply chains, imports also buckled. The more open economies of East Asia and Southeast Asia—such as Hong Kong, China; Republic of Korea (henceforth Korea); Malaysia; Singapore; Taipei,China; and Thailand—were hardest hit, and their economies contracted significantly ...* (ADB 2009a, page 2).

Consequently, the impact of the crisis on export, production, workers and their families in these countries was widespread. Retrenchments mounted in many export-oriented manufacturing industries across the region, while working time fell along with increased downward pressure on wages. In response, millions of workers migrated back to rural areas and shifted to informal and vulnerable employment. In response to the crisis, many of the affected countries in the region, as with many crisis-affected countries in other parts of the world, have reacted with both market-based and regulatory policies to mitigate the negative impacts of the crisis on their economies.[10]

---

[9] In ADB, Asian developing countries are stated as developing Asia which refers to its 44 developing member countries.

[10] In Asia, many affected countries in that time have opted for more international trade restrictions, often taking advantage of the flexibility on the use of contingent measures in the multi-lateral trading rules. In Indonesia, for example, while it is an open economy, there has also been a tendency toward creeping protectionism, especially through the use of non-tariff barriers (NTBs). More than one-half of Indonesia's tariff lines in that period required special import permits. Many of these permits existed for health and safety purposes (e.g., quarantine rules) but they provided a wide scope for border officials to use discretionary judgment. Nearly one-third of import containers were subject to physical inspection (red lane) versus less than 10 percent under international good practice. Many new import permits have been created, such as the special import registration number (NPIK) and a new requirement that imports of electronics, garments, footwear, toys and shoes hold a Limited Importer license and undergo pre-shipment inspections at the port of loading. While the purpose was often to combat smuggling, these regulations pushed up the costs of inputs needed by domestic industries, such as those manufacturing computers, office instruments, and hand phones, thereby reduced the competitiveness of Indonesian-made products not only in the export market but also in domestic market against cheaper products, especially from China which have been expanding rapidly in the Indonesian market in the last 10 years. But, this

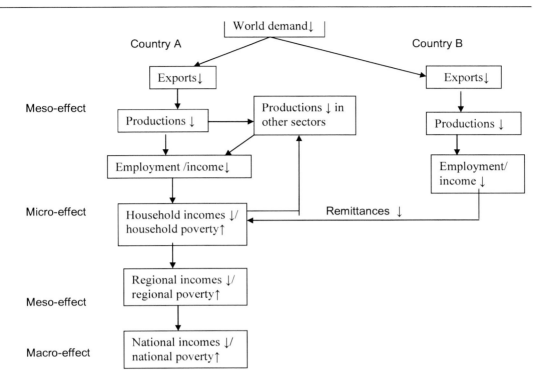

Figure II.6. The 2008/09 Global Economic (World Demand) Crisis and Its Impact on Poverty.

While export was the most important transmission channel for most of the affected countries, the 2008/09 crisis for those countries was primarily a world demand crisis. Theoretically, as illustrated in Figure II.6, this kind of shock will affect those countries, first, through its effects on their domestic firms exporting products which face less world demands. It leads further to less production and employment in these firms and also in other backward as well as foward production-related industries/sectors (meso-level effects). The employment reduction causes a decline in incomes of many individuals or households (micro-level effects). Lower individual or household incomes will result further in lower market demands for goods and services and hence, production cuts in many industries/sectors, leading to more unemployment and households with lower incomes, and so on.

In large countries like China, India and Indonesia which consists of many regions (i.e. provinces, districts and subdistricts), the impact may vary by region, or even the impact in some regions within a country may be more severe than at the national level. For instance, within a country, if the decline in average income per person or household in a region, where most export-oriented manufacturing industries are located, is higher than in the rest of the country and the proportion of the affected individuals or households in that particular region is significantly large, then the total income in that region will decline faster than that in the rest of the country (meso-level effects).

Within Southeast Asia, Indonesia and the Philippines are two countries (country A in Figure II.6) which have huge number of workers working abroad; mostly in some Middle

tendency toward more protectionism in fact has already been appeared some years before the 2008/2009 global crisis. There is no evidence, therefore, that these protectionism measures have to do with the crisis (Tambunan,

East countries (country B). At least theoretically, if the 2008/09 crisis also affected those Middle East countries, then remittance inflows to Indonesia and the Philippines would decline, and hence, incomes in many regions where most of the international migrant workers came from in those two countries would drop further. Finally, the national incomes or the economic growth rates in Indonesia and the Philippines would decrease (macro-level effects).

Within a country, if one region was affected by the crisis, and that region is not so important for the national economy based on the contribution of the region's economy to the country's GDP or total employment, then the effect at the national level may be insignificant, even if the impact for that particular region was not small. In Indonesia, for instance, Java is very important as the country's GDP and total population are concentrated in this island. It means that even a small impact of a global economic crisis, as that in 2008/09, will produce a serious shock for the national economy.

Thus, depending on (1) the importance of the affected commodities in total export of the particular country, and (2) within the particular country, the importance of the economy of the region where the firms producing such commodities are located, and the backward and forward production linkages of the firms with the rest of the country's economy, the impact or outcome of the 2008/09 crisis on the country's economy and hence, poverty can be significant or insignificant. Therefore, in analyzing the impact of a global economic crisis, such as the 2008/09 crisis, on national economy and poverty or vulnerable groups, the main questions that should be taken into consideration are the followings:

1. What export commodities have been hit by the crisis?
2. Within the particular country, in what regions firms/sectors producing such commodities are located?
3. How are the linkages of the firms/sectors with the rest of the economy?
4. What types of workers in the firms/sectors are mostly affected?

Theoretical illustration in Figure II.6 does not include investment effect, although it was said before that investment, especially FDI, was among the important transmission channels of the impact of the 2008/09 crisis. As stated in the Asian Development Outlook 2009, beyond the trade channel, the impact of the 2008/09 crisis on private investments was also severe. FDI and other financial forms inflows from major industrialized countries into the region slowed sharply in the midst of the financial panic after September-October 2008. The credit squeeze was also reflected in elevated spreads of Asian bonds. In some Asian countries, however, the investment effect of the crisis was insignificant (ADB, 2009a).

From the above theoretical discussion, it can thus be concluded that the 2008/09 crisis was significantly different than the 1997/98 crisis, at least in two respects. First, the 2008/09 crisis was an external shock, while the 1997/98 crisis had internal origin. Second, the 2008/09 crisis was a world demand crisis caused by the drop in incomes from many developed countries like the US, the EU and Japan, whereas the 1997/98 crisis was initially a national currency crisis caused by capital flights, followed by a national banking crisis and ended up as an economic crisis.

2009a).

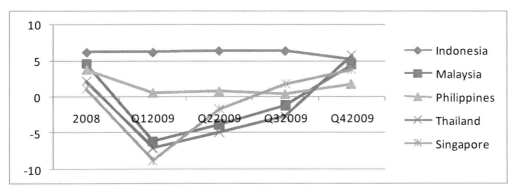

Source: World Bank database (country indicators) (http://web.worldbank.org/ WBSITE EXTERNAL/COUNTRIES/).

Figure II.7. Economic Growth Rate in Selected ASEAN member countries, 2008 and 2009 (% change year-on-year).

Impact

Economic Growth

Many Asian developing countries were affected by the 2008/09 crisis, though not in the beginning. Based on quarterly data on the economic growth rate in Southeast Asia for the period 2008 and 2009, countries like Thailand, Malaysia, Singapore, Philippines and Indonesia still showed some resilience towards the crisis. They managed to have positive overall economic growth rates in 2008; though the rate varied quarterly and by country. Within the group, Indonesia had the highest rate at around 6.1 percent. However, as shown in Figure II.7, in the first quarter of 2009, they experienced deteriorating economic performance, except Indonesia. Singapore suffered the most and recorded -8.9 percent in real GDP growth rate (year-on-year basis) in the first quarter of 2009. This is not surprising at all, given the fact that as a tiny economy, Singapore is fully integrated with the global market for goods, services and finance. Consequently, its economy is fully sensitive to any external economic shocks. The country's economy then started to recover with positive growth again in the third quarter of 2009. Similar with Singapore was Thailand, which has also been seriously hit by the crisis since the third quarter of 2008 and the economy contracted by 7.11 percent in the first quarter of 2009. Thailand achieved positive growth again in the last quarter of 2009. Malaysia, which experienced a slightly positive growth of around 0.1 percent in the last quarter of 2008, also suffered economic contraction by 6.20 percent in the first quarter of 2009. Meanwhile, Indonesia and the Philippines managed to keep positive growth, although at declining rates during the crisis period. In the first quarter of 2009, Indonesia achieved 6.2 percent growth, but in the last quarter it was lower at 5.2 per ent.

What was surprising was that, while the economy of other countries in the group was deteriorated significantly, especially during the first months in 2009, Indonesia had not only positive but also slightly higher GDP growth rates during the second and third quarters of that year. In overall, however, the growth rate of the Indonesian economy was at around 4.5 percent, which was much lower as compared to 2007 and 2008 (Figure II.8). This may suggest that the Indonesian economy was also affected by the crisis, but nevertheless, Indonesia was able to keep positive economic growth rates during the crisis period.

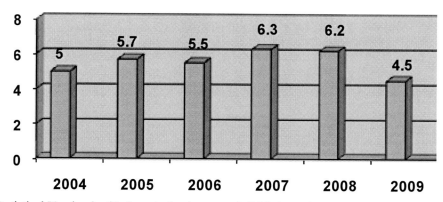

Source: Statistical Yearbook of Indonesia (various years), BPS (www.bps.go.id).

Figure II.8. Indonesian Annual Economic Growth 2004-2009 (%).

Furthermore, as shown in Table II.2, there were other few countries in the region, such as China, India, Pakistan and Banglades which also managed to mitigate the impact of the crisis on their domestic economy. Interestingly, the table shows that within the developing world, countries in Asia and the Pacific region performed much better than those in other parts of the world during the crisis. Of course, many explanations are possible, including that the variation in the impact of this kind of crisis on domestic economy is strongly related to the degree of integration of the particular country with the world economy. Rapidness and effectiveness of crisis-coping policy measures in the particular country may also play an important role.

The Indonesian ability to keep positive (though lower) economic growth rates during the 2008/09 crisis was mainly because of positive growth rates of domestic (demand-side) components of GDP growth, especially government and private consumptions (Figure II.9). Government consumption increased by 18.0 percent during the first half (H1) of 2009, or almost four times as fast as in 2008. According to the ADB report, *Asian Development Outlook 2009* (ADB, 2009a), this significant increase was a result of pay increases for civil servants and the election-related spending (parliamentary elections were held in April and presidential elections in July 2009), and an improvement in the disbursement rate of budgeted outlays. While private consumption, which accounted for approximately 60 percent of GDP, made the biggest contribution to GDP growth on the demand side during the crisis period. It grew by 5.4 percent in the H1 2009, only slightly below the 2008 rate, which may indicate some impact of the crisis on the demand-side of the Indonesian economy. As explained further in the ADB report, domestic consumption growth received a lift from slowing inflation, good harvests that supported farm incomes, and election-related spending. Also, the government provided cash transfers to 18.5 million poor households in the first two months of 2009 and lowered some taxes as part of a fiscal stimulus package aimed at mitigating the impact of the crisis on domestic economic activities. Nevertheless, tighter credit which led to higher interest rates hurt domestic sales of consumer durables such as motor vehicles (ADB, 2009a).

Table II.2. Economic Growth in the Developing World by Region, 2007-2010

	2007	2008	2009	2010[*]
East Asia and Pacific	11.4	8.0	6.8	8.1
-PRC	13.0	9.0	8.4	9.0
-Indonesia	6.3	6.2	4.5	5.6
-Thailand	4.9	2.2	-2.7	3.5
Europe and Central Asia	7.1	4.2	-6.2	2.7
South Asia	8.5	5.7	5.7	6.9
-India	9.1	6.1	6.0	7.5
-Pakistan	5.7	2.0	3.7	3.0
-Bangladesh	6.4	6.2	5.9	5.5
Latin America and Caribbean	5.5	3.9	-2.6	3.1
Middle East and North Africa	5.9	4.3	2.9	3.7
Sub-Saharan Africa	6.5	5.1	1.1	3.8

[*] forecast by the World Bank.
Source: World Bank (2010).

Gross domestic capital formation or fixed investment (GDI) also grew positively, but at a very low rate, around 0.9 percent in the H1 2009, after experienced double-digit positive rates since mid-2007. ADB data shows that investment in buildings increased by 6.3 percent but investment in machinery and equipment fell by slighly more than 10 percent. Table II.3 shows that during the crisis period, the percentage share of GDI in Indonesian GDP did not fall; on the contrary, it even increased. While in other ASEAN member countries (where data was available), i.e. Thailand, Singapore, Philippines and Malaysia, the ratios declined; though at different rates.[11]

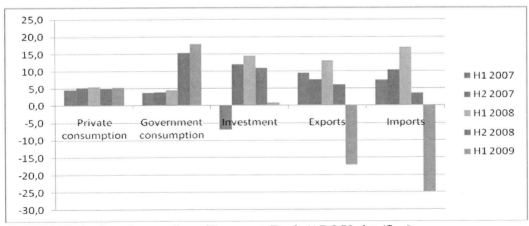

Source: ADB database (www.adb.org/Documents/Books/ADO/Update/figs/).

Figure II.9. Growth of GDP Demand-side Components in Indonesia, H1 2007-H1 2009.

---

[11] In ADB, GDI is defined as the sum of gross fixed capital formation plus changes in inventories. Gross fixed capital formation is measured by the total value of a producer's acquisitions, less disposals, of fixed assets in a given accounting period. Additions to the value of non-produced assets, e.g., land, form part of gross fixed capital formation. Inventories are stocks of goods held by institutional units to meet temporary or unexpected fluctuations in production and sales (ADB, 2010)..

Table II.3. Gross Domestic Investment in ASEAN, 2005-2009 (% of GDP)

Member countries	2005	2006	2007	2008	2009
Brunei Darussalam	11.4	10.4	13.0	13.7	-
Cambodia	18.5	20.6	20.8	18.5	-
Indonesia	25.1	25.4	24.9	27.8	31.0
Lao People's Dem. Rep.	-	-	-	-	-
Malaysia	20.0	20.5	21.7	19.1	14.0
Myanmar	-	-	-	-	-
Philippines	14.6	14.5	15.4	15.2	14.0
Singapore	19.9	20.3	20.7	30.1	27.6
Thailand	31.4	28.3	26.4	28.9	21.9
Vietnam	35.6	36.8	43.`1	41.1	-

Source: ADB database (www.adb.org/Documents/Books/ADO/Update/figs/).

With respect to bank credits for businesses, borrowing from banks for investment also contracted during the same period. This may reflect, on one hand, that many firms' unwillingness to expand their production due to the market being unsecure in that time, and, on the other hand, the tighter bank credit. Regarding this latter, since the 1997/98 crisis, when many banks in Indonesia were forced to close down due to their extremely high non-performing loans (NPL), commercial banks in Indonesia now are extra careful in lending credits to business community, especially in the time of an economic crisis like in 2008/09.

With respect to external demand-side components of Indonesia's GDP growth, the growth rates for both imports and exports (for goods and services) were also negaive in the H1 2009. The decline in export was mainly because world prices declined for some commodities and the slump in global trade; whereas the drop in imports was caused by lower degrees of domestic consumer optimism (generally measured by the Consumer Confidence Index) on the state of the national economy and lower industrial demand for imported capital and intermediate goods, products components, tools, and other inputs. Official data shows that imports contracted faster than exports, thereby generated positive net exports, which also contributed to maintained positive GDP growth rate during the crisis period.

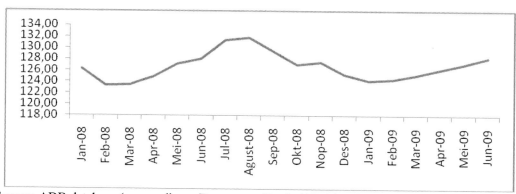

Source: ADB database (www.adb.org/Documents/Books/ADO/Update/figs/).

Figure II.10. Manufacturing Production Index in Indonesia, 2008-2009 (2000=100).

Table II.4. Indonesian GDP Growth by Sector 1995-2009 (% y-o-y)

Sector	1995	2000	2007	2008	2009
Agriculture	4.4	2.3	3.5	4.8	4.1
Mining	6.7	5.3	1.9	0.7	4.4
Manufacturing Industry	10.8	5.5	4.7	3.7	3.5
Electricity, Gas & Water Supply	15.9	9.6	10.3	10.9	13.8
Construction	12.9	5.8	8.5	7.5	7.1
Trade, Hotel & Restaurant	7.9	8.5	8.9	6.9	1.1
Transportation and Communication	8.5	8.7	14.0	16.6	15.5
Finance	11.0	5.7	8.0	8.2	5.0
Services	3.3	2.4	6.4	6.2	6.4
GDP	8.2	5.4	6.3	6.0	4.5

Source: BPS (www.bps.go.id) and Sadewa (2010).

Sectoral Output Growth

On one hand, as discussed before, the 2008/09 was a world demand crisis, and, on the other hand, different sectors of the economy have different degrees in the relationship with the world economy. Some sectors are more export-oriented than others. Some sectors have high import dependence, while some others are fully closed, i.e. supply their products only to local/domestic markets and use local inputs. So, from the production/supply side, different sectors may experience different impacts of the crisis. To see this, Table II.4 shows Indonesian GDP growth rate by sector for the period before the 1997/98 crisis, between the two big crises and during the 2008/09 crisis. As can be seen, before the 1997/98 crisis, the Indonesian economy was booming with the growth rate of GDP at around 8 percent in 1995. One year before the global economic crisis, the Indonesian economy was not so bad, although the growth rate was still lower than the pre-1997/98 crisis level. During the 2008/09 crisis, all sectors managed to maintain positive growth although some at decreasing rates.

With respect to the manufacturing industry, the production index (2000=100) in Indonesia declined from the maximum level at 131.83 in August 2008 to 124.17 in January 2009, and then started to increase again (Figure II.10). This curve may suggest that the impact of the crisis on industrial production in Indonesia was only short lived. One possible reason was the role of domestic market. With a huge population on one side, and high real income per capita which did not decline during the crisis, on the other side, domestic market has played an important role as the last resort for domestic export-oriented firms. Indeed, during the crisis, the Indonesian government has tried with tax and some other forms of fiscal incentives included in its fiscal stimulus packages launched during the crisis period to shift the focus of crisis-affected export-oriented industries from external toward internal markets.

Regarding other Asian developing countries, Figure II.11 shows that the so-called newly industrialized economies (NIEs) such as Hong Kong China, Taipei China, South Korea and Singapore suffered most from the collapse of world demand for industrial products, and had the most severe contractions in domestic industrial production as many firms drew down inventories and shuttered production. According to ADB, 2009a), the costs of the crisis beared by these countries were much larger than during the 1997/98 Asian financial crisis. It was mainly because they are more global rather than regional market oriented, while the 1997/98 Asian financial crisis was a regional economic crisis which mainly affected East and Southeast Asia.

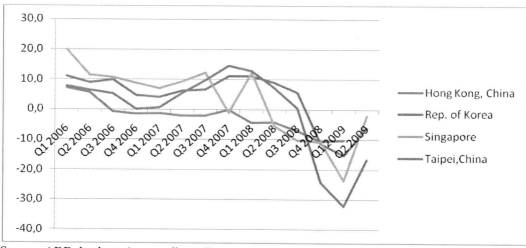

Source: ADB database (www.adb.org/Documents/Books/ADO/Update/figs/)

Figure II.11. Quarterly Growth of Industrial Production in NIEs, 2006-2009 (%).

Furthermore, Table II.5 provides data on the annual growth rate of value added in industry in the region. In this case, industry is comprised of manufacturing, mining and quarrying, construction, and utilities. As can be seen, although at a decreasing rate, Indonesian industry had managed to maintain positive growth rates during the crisis period. Besides Vietnam (which had also the same experience as Indonesia) and Lao People's Democratic Republic (which had not only positive but even a significant increase in the growth rate of industrial value added), other ASEAN member countries experienced negative value added/output growth rates of their industrial sector. For the Lao performance, no special explanation is given by either ADB or World Bank. However, given the fact that Lao is a small and landlocked country and it is a more domestic rather than export-oriented economy, it is most likely that the country was not affected at all by the crisis.

Table II.5. Growth Rate of Value Added in Industry in ASEAN, 2005-2009 (% per year)

Member countries	2005	2006	2007	2008	2009
Brunei Darussalam	-1.8	2.9	-5.6	-5.4	-
Cambodia	12.7	18.3	8.4	4.0	-13.0
Indonesia	4.7	4.5	4.7	3.7	3.5
Lao People's Dem. Rep.	10.6	14.2	4.4	10.2	17.3
Malaysia	3.4	4.5	3.0	0.9	-7.1
Myanmar	-	-	-	-	-
Philippines	3.8	4.5	6.8	5.0	-2.0
Singapore	8.1	10.7	7.1	-1.0	-.1.1
Thailand	5.4	5.6	5.9	3.3	-4.3
Vietnam	10.7	10.4	10.2	6.1	5.5

Source: ADB (2010).

Trade

In the trade area, especially export, the 2008/09 crisis has caused the fall in world demand for manufacturing exports from many developing countriers, including in Asia. The Asian Development Outlook 2009 Update from ADB shows that NIEs were among many countries in the region which suffered most from the collapse of world demand and had the most severe contractions in their industrial production (Figure II.12). The negative growth rate in imports of goods and services quickly matched the rate of decline in exports as supply chains reacted to the fall of demand in major industrial economies, especially the USA, Japan and countries in the Eurozone. This NIEs' experience with the crisis was anticipated as among Asian developing countries, they, together with China, have higher degrees of trade and investment integration with the world and and extremely high export dependence while other Asian developing countries, including Indonesia and India, are relatively small economies in terms of shares of global GDP and trade. For other countries in the region which are rich in natural resources, they also suffered from export declines, but mainly due to the decline of world prices for some commodities which were among their key exports (ADB 2009a).

Exports, especially manufactured goods, in some ASEAN member countries also suffered from the decline of world demand, which have contracted even since October 2008. In January 2008, for instance, manufacturing exports in Malaysia and Thailand have fallen by 34 and 41 percent, respectively. Indonesia's export grew by 34 percent (year-on-year) in January 2008, but fell by about the same percentage in January 2009. The Philippines's exports also fell significantly by around 40 percent per month since the end of 2008. Singapore's exports also grew by -26 percent in April 2009 (Table II.6). As a further consequence, many firms in these countries reduced their production which led to many factory closures.

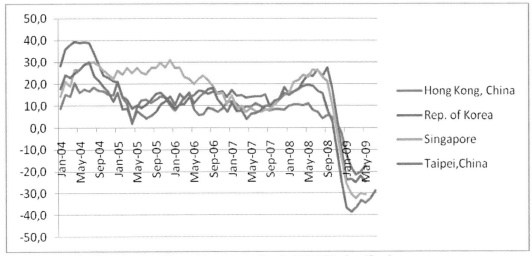

Source: ADB database (www.adb.org/Documents/Books/ADO/Update/figs/)

Figure II.12. Export Growth of NIEs, Jan.2004-May 2009 (%, 3-moths moving average).

Table II.6. Year-on-Year Export of Manufactured Goods of Selected ASEAN Member Countries, April 2008-April 2009

Period	Indonesia	Malaysia	Philippines	Singapore	Thailand	Vietnam
2008						
April	22.5	20.9	4.9	16.4	16.6	29.1
May	31.6	22.9	2,4	12.5	12.5	32.1
June	34.1	18.6	9,2	10.9	20,6	34.1
July	24.8	25.3	4.4	15.2	39.7	47.1
August	29.9	10.7	6.6	7.7	5.2	36.8
September	29.0	15.0	1.3	11.4	18.2	8.6
October	4.7	-2.6	-14,4	-4,3	2.4	20.1
November	-1.8	-4.9	-11.4	-11.9	-20.1	-6.3
December	-18.7	-14.9	-40.3	-20.4	-11.5	4.3
2009						
January	-35.0	-27.8	-40.6	-37.8	-24.6	-25.5
February	-32.3	-16.0	-39.0	-23.7	-6.6	32.3
March	-27.9	-15.6	-30.8	-20.7	-16.6	13.0
April	-22.6	-26.3	n.a	-26.0	-16.1	-16.1

Source: CIEC Data Company Ltd.provided by Atje and Kartika (2009).

A preliminary assessment by the World Bank and the ASEAN Secretariat in 2009 shows that in the first seven months of that year, manufacturing exports declined by 30 percent in Vietnam and in Indonesia by almost 40 percent, compared to the same period in 2008. Their most severely affected exports by the fall of world demand were textile and garments, food and beverages, and furniture. The Philippines also experienced a significant decline in its exports, recorded as much as 60 percent, in the first quarter of 2009. The country's most affected exports were semiconductors and electronics. In Malaysia, the most affected export-oriented industries were those manufacturing metal products, non-electrical machinery, and industrial equipments. The decline of exports and hence, output in these industries made a significant contribution to the the total output contraction in the Malaysian manufacturing industry, which was minus 14.5 percent (year-on-year) in the second quarter of 2009, compared with minus 17.9 percent in the first quarter of the same year. In Singapore, among its total exported goods, electronics exports were the most severely affected by the crisis which contracted by 14 per ent around mid-2009, after a 15 percent decline in the previous month (year-on-year) (World Bank and ASEAN, 2009).

Based on data from Economic Intelligence Unit Country Database-October 2009, a UNDP's regional study reports that exports slumped quite sharply in almost all Asian developing economies, including China, Indonesia, India, Hong Kong China, Taipei-China, Pakistan, Malaysia, Philippines, Singapore, and South Korea, from September 2008 to January/February 2009, turning negative across the region. According to Titiheruw, et al (2009), there were two main reasons for the decline in Indonesian exports: (1) drops in commodity prices since mid-2008, and (2) weakened world demand after September 2008.

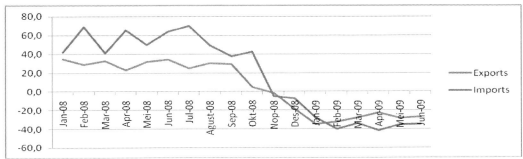

Source: ADB database (www.adb.org/Documents/Books/ADO/Update/figs/)

Figure II.13. Export and Import Growth in Indonesia, Jan.2008-Jan.2009 (%).

Imports also fell, usually following the decline in exports by a few months. Since imports have collapsed more dramatically than exports, trade balance has improved in many countries. Within Asian developing countries, exports in low income countries were able to hold up somewhat better than those of higher income/emerging economies in the developed markets (e.g. the US, Japan and Eurozone countries) because of many factors, including product mix (Chhibber, at al., 2009).

However, since February/March 2009, exports and imports in many Asian developing countries started to recover, though in the beginning, the process was slow. With respect to Indonesia, for instance, its total trade (exports and imports) declined significantly during September/October 2008 and January/February 2009, and then started to recover (Figure II.13). But, the recovery of export has been mainly due to the increase in world prices for some primary commodities. While, with respect to manufacturing industry, Indonesian export growth rate until June 2009 was still negative compared to the same period in 2008; although some goods already started to have positive growth rates (Table II.7).

Table II.7. Export Growth by Selected/Key Manufactured goods, 2008-2009 (January-June; % change year-on-year)

Commodity	Growth Performance (%)
Crude palm oil (CPO)	-43.66
Steel, machines and automotive	-24.68
Textile and garments	-12.39
Rubber	-44/75
Electronics	14.08
Pulp and paper	-23.95
Wood, including furniture	-26.58
Food and beverages	-25.83
Leather, including footwear	-14.14
Plastic	-19.51
Tobacco	8.22
Fertilizer	-26.01
Gold and silvers	38.30
Cosmetics	5.69
Total exports of manufactured goods	26.77

Source: database from Ministry of Trade (www.depdag.go.id).

Most of these industries are labor intensive and some of them are dominated (in number of units) by MSMEs such as wood (including furniture), textile and garments, food and beverages, and leather industries. Consequently, slowed down production in these industries may have significant impact not only on employment but also poverty. Many reports during the crisis period indicated that laid-off employees in 2009 were coming mainly from those industries (Djaja, 2009).[12]

Some of the most severely affected export-oriented industries such as textile and garments, footwears and furniture are closely connected in regional and global value chains through trade and production systems in countries like Japan and the US and key European countries, i.e. Germany, France and United Kingdom (UK).[13] Therefore, these industries are very vulnerable to global external shocks like the 2008/09 crisis (i.e. unexpected decline in the world demand).

Overall, only few ASEAN member countries managed to have a positive trade balance in 2008 and 2009 and even the surplus increased in 2009, which contributed to the surplus in their current account balance (Table II.8). According to ADB country data, Indonesia's current account balance (not shown in this table) increased significantly from only US$ 125 million (or 0.0 percent of GDP) in 2008 to US$10,582 million (2.0 percent of GDP) in 2009. As with the trade surplus, Indonesia's current account surplus was predicted to decline to US$ 8,930 million (1.4 percent of GDP) in 2010. Current account balances of Malaysia and Singapore also increased significantly during the same period (ADB, 2009).

The impact of the crisis on exports was considered very seriously by governments in many Asian developing countries, especially in ASEAN member countries, as exports have been playing a major role in their economic growth performance. Even many of these countries are highly reliant on exports to earn foreign currency to finance their imports and domestic development. In Indonesia, with the experience of the 1997/98 crisis that high foreign debt had contributed partly to the accumulation of the crisis, since then the government has been giving efforts more seriously than ever to promote export and FDI to replace the role of foreign debts in the post-1997/98 crisis in financing national economic development.

---

[12] Official data from the Department of Manpower and Transmigration in Indonesia issued in December 2008 shows that the number of workers already laid-off was 17,488 and the number of laborers that were expected to be laid-off soon was 23,927. According to the data, Jakarta, the capital city of Indonesia, recorded the highest number with 14, 268 laid-off laborers and 9,757 laborers that were planned to be laid off from a total of 60 companies in the manufacturing industry, such as textile and garments, furniture and other wood based products, and metal and steel industries. In the second place was the Riau province with 837 laid-off's laborers and 8,720 laborers that were planned to be laid-off, mainly from the pulp and paper industry. The record of people out of work in the provinces in Kalimantan was also high, and mainly were low-skilled workers in the estate plantation and wood industries. In that time, there was a strong indication on a massive return of workers to Java as a result of falling commodity prices which forced plantation companies in Kalimantan and Sumatra to scale down their work force. The other sources of laborer's lay-offs were coming from the food and beverages, electronics, and construction industries (Djaya, 2009). It cannot be sure, however, whether all of these laid-off workers happened (or planned to be laid-off) mainly due to the 2008/2009 crisis (less order, lower demand, etc) or the lay-offs were already planned months before the crisis occurred (or even already planned in 2007) for other reasons (e.g. less production due to increasing imports or competition).

[13] In Indonesia (as in many other Asian developing countries), in these export oriented industries, many MSMEs are involved in subcontracting production arrangements with LEs, either domestic or foreign companies. In addition, workers in these industries are served by many informal and formal establishments such as transportation and food and catering, among others.

Table II.8. Trade Balance in ASEAN, 2005-2009 (US$ million)

Member countries	2005	2006	2007	2008	2009	2010*
ASEAN	74,332	107,913	114,334	80,714	105,898	90,962
-Brunei Darussalam	4,834	6,041	5,677	8,104	-	-
-Cambodia	-1,008	-1,078	-1,343	-1,802	-1,541	-2,272
-Indonesia	17,532	29,661	32,753	22,916	35,199	34,556
-Lao People's Dem. Rep.	-573	-456	-835	,1177	-975	-999
-Malaysia	34,034	37,428	37,141	51,167	40,149	38,126
-Myanmar	1,574	2,266	924	506	284	-269
-Philippines	-7,773	-6,732	-8,391	-12,85	-8,878	-10,599
-Singapore	36,432	42,565	46,065	26,559	30,549	32,878
-Thailand	-8,254	994	12,782	108	19,416	9,376
-Vietnam	-2,439	-2,776	-10,438	-12,782	-8,306	-9,836

*ADB's prediction.
Source: ADB (2010).

Based on data from the ASEAN Secretariat and ADB, in percentage of GDP in 2008, manufacturing exports in Singapore and Malaysia, comprised of more than 140 percent and nearly 70 percent, respectively. In Cambodia and Thailand in the same year, the ratio was around 0.5, and more than 0.3 in the Philippines and Vietnam, In Indonesia, the percentage was much lower at around 12 percent. If exports of other sectors, including services were included, then in Singapore, total exports accounted for around 243.3 percent, Malaysia 103.6 percent, and Indonesia was the lowest in the region at 29.8 percent of GDP. In other parts of Asia, the highest ratio was in Hong Kong, China at 212.5 percent and the lowest was Nepal at 12.2 percent (Figure II.14). Functioning as regional hubs for export, automatically, both Singapore and Hong Kong, China will have export to GDP ratio more than one (1).

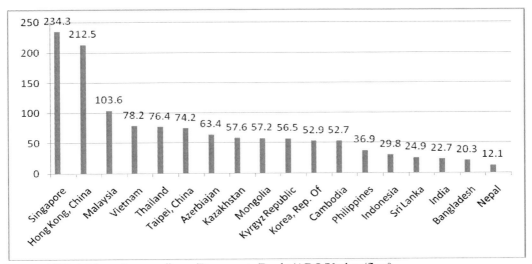

Source: ADB database (www.adb.org/Documents/Books/ADO/Update/figs/).

Figure II.14. Exports of Goods and Services in Selected Asian Developing Countries, 2008 (% of GDP).

Remittance

Based on the World Development Indicator database (www.worldbank.org/data), in the past, remittances have proven to be a relatively stable source of private foreign currency inflows (Figure II.15) than many other non-trade sources to many developing countries, particularly in Asia. Many country studies cited by ADB (2009a) show that remittances foster macroecnomic stability by supporting domestic demand in the recipient countries, suggesting that there is a strong positive link between remittances and economic growth. In countries like Indonesia and the Philippines, livelihoods in many villages are very dependent on the continuation of remittances inflows. The remittances are the main source of income in these villages, suggesting a strong negative link between remittances and poverty and income inequality. The remittances also promote human capital development by increasing the capacity of households to spend on education, health, and nutrition. Therefore, although remittances entail economic and social costs, they are considered by the governments in those countries as a very important engine of economic growth and poverty and income inequality reduction, especially in relatively less developed or poor regions. They not only provide credit-constrained or poor households means to smooth domestic consumption but they can be used as funds for local investment and thus generate local economic activities.

According to *Asian Development Outlook 2009,* from 1990 to 2008, the coefficient of variation of remittance flows to developing countries was 0.77 compared to 0.80 for FDI, 1.34 for private debt, or 1.17 for portfolio equity flows (lower values indicating more stable flows). The stability of remittance flows can counter the effects of falling FDI, foreign debt, and equity flows during an economic slowdown in the recipient country (ADB, 2009a). Based on this calculation and many country studies about the importance of remittances in Asia, ADB states that *millions of dollars of remittances to households in Asia can make a significant dent in poverty. Encouraging the use of remittances not only for consumption but also for investment in areas such as health and education can enhance domestic demand and boost economic growth, as well as develop human capital, contributing to long-term growth. In addition, remittance-boosted household consumption will generate extra demand in the receiving economy* (ADB, 2009a, p.7)

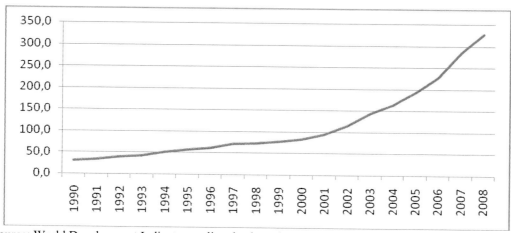

Source: World Development Indicators online database (www.worldbank.org/indicator).

Figure II.15. Remittances to Developing Countries 1990-2008 (US$ billion).

Table II.9. Migration Status of Asian Developing Countries

Net Labor Sending	Bangladesh, Cambodia, China, Indonesia, Lao PDR, Myanmar, Nepal, Philippines, Sri Lanka, Vietnam
Labor Sending and Receiving	India, Malaysia, Pakistan, Thailand
Net Labor Receiving	Brunei Darussalam, Hong Kong China, Japan, Middle East, Republic of Korea, Singapore, Taiwan China

Source: Ghosh (2007) and Chhibber,et al (2009).

Within developing countries, developing Asia is a major provider of foreign workers and beneficiary of remittances. The region received more remittances than any other part of the world in 2008, and remittance flows to the region have become an increasingly important source of foreign exchange. Even in Indonesia, for instance, the government has become more serious in supporting local unemployed/poor people to work abroad not only as a source of their incomes but also as a source of foreign exchange, to replace foreign debts in financing national economic development. Based on official estimates provided by central banks from many individual developing countries in Asia, ADB shows that in total, international remittances to the region multiplied about 18 times in the last two decades from around $9.3 billion in 1988 (about 1 percent of regional GDP) to approximately $162 billion in 2008 (about 2 percent of regional GDP). The amount varies, however, not only by individual country but also by subregion, i.e. Central, South, Southeast and East (ADB, 2009a). More interestingly is that the region has evolved into not only a source of but also a host to migrant workers. Recent trends reveal that Asian migrants are no longer restricting themselves to jobs in industrial-countries, and intra-migration among Asian developing countries, especially in Southeast and East Asia, has become more pronounced (ADB 2008). For instance, there have been more flows of migrant workes from Indonesia to Malaysia, Singapore and the Middle East, or from Sri Lanka to the Philippines, or from the Philippines to Hong Kong China, than flows from these countries to the US, Japan, Australia, or Eurozone countries.

As recorded by Chhibber, et al. (2009), short-term migration increased rapidly in the past two decades, and most of it has been within the Asian continent, reflecting many factors, such as the significance of labor-scarce oil-exporting countries in the Middle East (particularly, Arab Saudi and Kuwait) and more export-oriented/industrialized countries (e.g. Malaysia, Hong Kong, China) and the differential levels of economic development that different countries have reached within the region (i.e. more industrialized countries need more workers than countries with low levels of industrialixation). Based on a number of country studies, Table II.9 provides information on the major flows of migrant workers within Asian developing countries. As can be seen, most of them are net labor-sending countries. These are labor surplus economies either because their level of industrialization is low combined with a decreasing role of agriculture in labor absorption (e.g. Bangladesh, Lao PDR, Myanmar, Nepal) or they are highly populated countries (i.e. China and Indonesia). Migrant workers have provided crucial foreign exchange for these countries and have been a major contributor to their balance of payments stability, and have played a significant role in domestic consumption. In Indonesia and the Philippines, as discussed, local economic acitivities in many villages can keep running only because of the sustained inflows of remittances. These are villages which lack infrastructure, rather isolated from urban areas, and have no modern businesses. Their local economic activities consists mainly of MSMEs or informal sector.

The Asian Development Outlook 2009 Update shows that in addition to trade and financial linkages, migration or remittances were the third area hit by the 2008/09 crisis. The crisis has slowed remittance flows to the developing world. Remittances to all developing countries grew by only an estimated 15 percent in 2008, compared with 25 percent in 2007 and 15 percent on average annually in the decade before that (ADB, 2009a). The World Bank forecasted a decline of 7–10 percent in remittances in 2009 (Ratha et al. 2009a).[14] However, in 2010 onwards, remittances are expected to recover, and will reach worldwide around 425 billion US dollars or 322 billion US dollars in developing countries as a whole in 2010 (Table II.10).

From Indonesia, as a case study, according to ILO (2009), the number of workers abroad had been on an upward trend until the crisis deepened in mid-2009. In 2007, 697,000 workers legally emigrated in search of employment, while there may have been at least twice that number of illegal migrants. Overall, it was estimated that the number of Indonesian overseas migrant workers, including undocumented migrant workers, stood at 5.8 million in December 2008. Around 65 percent of them, including many of the female migrants, were domestic workers, deployed in 41 countries. Plantations (especially palm oil) and construction (mainly building and roads) sites are common workplaces for Indonesian migrant workers, i.e. Malaysia and the Middle East, respectively. Some Indonesian workers are employed in the manufacturing sector, especially in the electronic industry (e.g. Taiwan China and Hong Kong China).

Using data from Bank Indonesia (BI), Yudo et al. (2009) show that with geographical proximity, cultural and linguistic similarities, and traditionally existing Indonesian migrant networks, about half of total Indonesian overseas workers are found in Malaysia. Malaysia also hosts a sizable number of Indonesian illegal workers (ILO, 2009). The others work in the Middle East, especially in Saudi Arabia (30 percent) and the rest in Singapore, Hong Kong (China), Taiwan (China), and the United Arab Emirates. Therefore, as shown in Table II.11, based on 2008 data, Malaysia contributed the biggest share of remittance inflows from Indonesian overseas workers, accounting for around US$578 million (36 percent), followed by Saudi Arabia at US$547 million (34 percent), Hong Kong at US$115 million (7 percent) and Taiwan at US$95 million (6 percent).

Table II.10. Remittances Flows by Region, 2006-2011 (billion US$)

Region	2006	2007	2008	2009	2010*	2011*
World	317	385	444	420	425	441
Develping Countries	235	289	338	317	322	334
East Asia and Pacific	58	71	86	85	85	89
South Asia	43	54	73	72	73	76
Europe and Central Asia	37	51	58	49	51	53

* Prediction.

Source: ADB (2009c, page 7) and Ratha et al. (2009a, page 10).

---

[14] See, among many others, World Bank (2008b) and Chhibber, et al. (2009).

Table II.11. Indonesian overseas workers' remittances, 2008 (US$million)

Period	Country of origin			
	Malaysia	Saudi Arabia	Hong Kong	Taiwan
2007	2.60	1.70	0.42	0.36
2008				
– first quarter	0.64	0.57	0.11	0.09
– second quarter	0.64	0.57	0.11	0.10
– third quarter	0.62	0.56	0.14	0.10
– fourth quarter	0.58	0.55	0.12	0.10

Source: Yudo et al. (2009).

Yugo et al (2009) also give some estimations showing that total remittances inflows from overseas Indonesian workers declined slightly from approximately US$1.589 billion in the end of first quarter of 2009 from US$1.61 billion in December 2008. But, during the same period, the number of Indonesian workers departed overseas increased with 258,000 workers by the end of December 2008 or around 54 percent as compared to the end of September 2008 with 168,000 workers. However, Indonesian workers who went abroad in 2008 were less than in 2007 (Figure II.16). No further information is provided by this study on the main reason of this fact. The question is: was the less number of Indonesian overseas workers in 2008 compared to 2007 mainly because of the crisis? Was the slight decline in remittances inflows discussed above was also caused by the crisis?

Based on national data presented in the appendix of a 2010 ESCAP's (2010) report, total remittances by Indonesian workers abroad have increased in the past few years from around 651 million US$ in 1995 (or about 0.3 percent of gross national income (GNI)) to around 6 billion US$ in 2007 (1.4 percent of GNI)(Table II.12). While, according to ILO (2009), total remittances sent home by Indonesian overseas workers were estimated to have reached USD 12 billion in 2008, and according to Koser's (2009) estimates, remittances sent to Indonesia declined to US$3 billion in 2009.

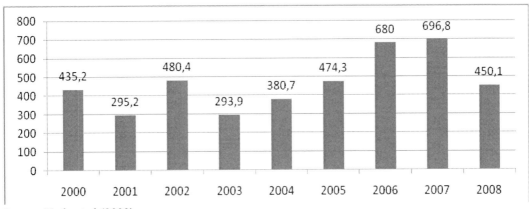

Source: Yudo et al.(2009).

Figure II.16. Total Number of Indonesian Overseas Workers, 2000-2008 (000 persons).

Table II.12. Overseas Workers' Remittances in ASEAN, 1995-2007

Member countries	Millions of US$			Percentage of GNI		
	1995	2000	2007	1995	2000	2007
Brunei Darussalam	-	-	-	-	-	-
Cambodia	10	100	184	0.3	3.2	2.5
Indonesia	651	1,190	6,004	0.3	0.9	1.4
Lao People's Dem. Rep.	-	-	-	-	-	-
Malaysia	81	77	-	1.0	1.1	-
Myanmar	432	5,161	13,266	0.6	6.4	8.4
Philippines	-	-	-	-	-	-
Singapore	-	-	-	-	-	-
Thailand						
Vietnam						

Source: ESCAP (2010).

Chhibber, et al. (2009) explain the reason that the impact of the crisis on remittances flows, that is when economic activities slow or contract leading to less need or demand for labor in destination countries, migrant workers are the first to be laid off and, although not all, many of them went home. This is even more likely since migrant workers from developing countries are low educated and a lot of them have been explicitly short-term in terms of meeting specific labor shortages in the host countries. It will depend, however, on what sectors the migrant workers are employed and whether the sectors are seriously hit by a crisis while migrant female workers working as domestic helpers, as many Indonesian young unmarried as well as married women do in Malaysia and Singapore, are unlikely to be affected by the 2008/09 crisis.

However, surprisingly, based on estimations shown before, remittance flows to Indonesia did not decline significantly during the crisis period, as generally expected. From the estimated figures provided by Yugo et al. (2009), the decline can be considered relatively small. The same evidence is also found from several other country studies[15] that relied strongly on remittances. In other words, although there is some evidence of decelerating remittances, overall flows remained resilient. Even in countries like Bangladesh, India, Pakistan, Philippines, Nepal and Sri Lanka remittance inflows have actually increased rather than declined during that period. In the Philippines, for instance, official data indicates that remittance flows were still increasing slightly, at an annual rate of around 2 percent during the period 2008-2009 (Chhibber, et al., 2009).

According to Chhibber, et al. (2009), to some extent, this theoretically unexpected trend is not really surprising, or it can happen because, as they state, *even if the crisis leads to large-scale retrenchment of migrant workers who are forced to come home, they would obviously return with their accumulated savings. In such a case, there could even be a (temporary) spike in remittances rather than a continuous or sharp decline because of the crisis. Eventually, as the adverse conditions for overseas employment further aggravate, this would then lead to a decline in remittance inflows. Intra-Asian migration may be affected by*

---

[15] The studies include, among others, Chhibber, et al. (2009), ADB (2009a,c), and Ratha, et al. (2009a,b).

migration policies instituted by some governments in the wake of the crisis, such as moves by Republic of Korea, Malaysia and Thailand to restrict work permits for migrants (page 35).In addition to the above explanation, Chhibber, et al. (2009) give other possible explanations (page 36):

1. male migrants are dominant in the manufacturing and construction sectors, while women migrants are concentrated in the service sectors, such as the care economy broadly defined (including activities such as nursing and domestic work) and "entertainment". Production activities and hence, their related employment and incomes are much more linked to the business cycle in the host economy. Job losses in the North during the crisis have been concentrated in construction, financial services and manufacturing, all dominated by male workers. By contrast, the care activities dominantly performed by women workers tend to be affected by other variables such as demographic tendencies, institutional arrangements, and the extent to which women work outside the home in the host country so employment in such activities is often relatively invariant to the business cycle, or at least responds to a lesser extent. This, in turn, means that source countries that have a disproportionately higher share of women out-migrants (such as the Philippines and Sri Lanka) would tend to experience a less adverse impact in terms of downturn of remittances;
2. female migrants are far more likely to send remittances home, and typically send a greater proportion of their earnings back so given the fact that male migrants are less likely to send remittaces home, their declining incomes during the crisis have not been widely evident;
3. many migrants may be unwilling to return home to possibly even more fragile and insecure employment conditions in the home country (many developing countries have been even worse hit by the crisis). The unwillingness to return may be even stronger when they have already developed some local social networks that allow them to survive for a period while they look out for other employment. The return migration, on the other hand, would be dominated by the worst hit workers, who, in turn, were expected to be the undocumented, irregular or illegal migrants who are mostly in low-wage and low-skilled occupations, and do not qualify for any kind of official support such as welfare benefits or social security from the host country.

ADB (2009c) also has a similar thought that the insignificant drop in remittance flows during the crisis period may be due to the following three main reasons. First, most overseas foreign workers worked in countries or sectors that were less affected by the crisis. Second, most workers did not return and preferred temporary unemployment abroad (while waiting for new employment opportunities) as the labor markets in their home countries did not provide them with adequate job opportunities. Or, third, displaced migrant workers repatriated their savings as remittances. In such cases, the impact of the crisis on remittance flows may be felt later once individuals' savings are depleted.

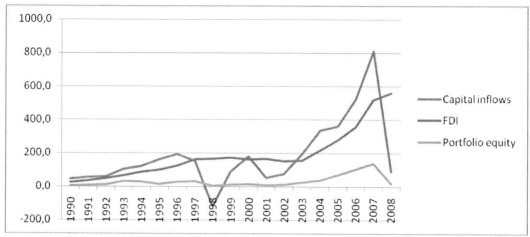

Source: ADB database (www.adb.org/Documents/Books/ADO/Update/figs/), and International Monetary Fund online database (www.imf.org/country-data).

Figure II.17. Capital Inflows to Asian Developing Countries, 1990-2008 (billion US$).

Capital Inflows

Based on country data provided by ADB (2009a) and the International Monetary Fund (IMF), in developing Asia, capital inflows, consisting of long-term investment (i.e. FDI), short-term investment (e.g. portfolio equity), and loans, into the highly integrated economies (e.g. People's Republic of China; Hong Kong China; India; Indonesia; Republic of Korea; Malaysia; Philippines; Singapore; China Taipei; Thailand; Cambodia; and Vietnam) were interrupted in 2008 as the crisis deepened. As might be expected, portfolio and other short-term capital flows, including bank loans, accounted for most of the decline, which was particularly notable in Hong Kong China; India; Korea; and Taipei China while, as shown in Figure II.17, in 2008, total FDI inflows into Asian developing countries' highly integrated economies kept increasing, especially to China the inflows continued at high rates, although at a declining pace. Other countries like Republic of Korea; Philippines; Singapore; and China Taipei, where electronics manufacturing and exports in general were hit hard by the 2008/09 crisis experienced slowdown in FDI from the last quarter of 2008 up to the first quarter of 2009. In 2009, China and many other Asian developing countries also experienced a slowdown in their FDI inflows. With respect to ASEAN, as shown in Table II.13, FDI inflows to all member countries, except Singapore and the Philippines, also dropped.

However, the decline of FDI (in growth rate or in value/unit) shown in Table II.13 may have not been fully caused by the crisis. Normally, when there is an economic crisis, short-term investment/capital flows will react first, and sometimes overreact while fixed or long-term investment, as it is less mobile than short-term investment, is usually less sensitive to a crisis like the one in 2008-09, which was generally expected as a short-term phenomenon. Even if sectors of destination are hit hard by a crisis (i.e. market demand for the sectors' output declines), long-term investment inflows will only slow down, as long as the declined demand is only short-lived. In other words, the crisis may have no a significant influnce on FDI decisions, One important similarity that emerges from comparing the 1997/98 crisis and the 2008/09 crisis is that FDI flows are more resilient to economic shocks than other forms of capital flows. The experience with these two crises show that short-term capital flows like portfolio investment and bank loans declined sharper and were higher volatility than FDI flows. As shown in ADB (2009a), the resilience of FDI flows relative to that of short-term capital flows is indicated by the coefficient of variation (the standard deviation divided by the mean); the coefficient of variation associated with FDI flows was by far lower than that for other forms of capital flows, especially during the two crisis periods.

It is well accepted that, different than short-term capital flows such as portfolio investment and bank loans, FDI is determined by many internal, long-term factors in the host country such as infrastructure, availability of raw materials and skilled workers, market size (determined by both population and real income per capita), political and social stability, trade regime (i.e. open economy or export orientation versus protectionism), and investment policies generating incentives to FDI. This view is supported by ADB (2009a), in which its estimation results show that in terms of attracting FDI inflows, internal factors dominate. Before the 1997/98 crisis, Indonesia was among the most favorable destinations in Southeast Asia for FDI. However, after that crisis, Indonesia has been losing its position in competing with other countries in the region (e.g. Vietnam, Malaysia, Singapore and Thailand) to attract FDI, exactly because Indonesia has serious problems with those mentioned FDI internal determinants, especially a lack in infrastructure and logistics, human resources, law enforcement, and political and social stability.

Employment

The most obvious and direct impact of a big economic crisis like the 2008/09 crisis or the one in 1997/98 on households is the negative effect on employment and hence, household incomes. In fact, the experience of the two crises show that employment losses have tended to be more severe than aggregate output (GDP) losses, largely because the worst affected sectors have been those that are export-oriented and more labor intensive, such as textile and garment, food and beverages, wood (including furniture), and leather products industries. According to the Asian Development Outlook 2009, unemployment in many Asian developing countries has risen during the 2008/09 crisis, particularly in the more export-dependent economies of Hong Kong, China; Singapore; and China Taipei. It was generally expected that the recovery in employment will be both more delayed and less dynamic than the recovery in GDP output. However, the ADB report concludes that the prospects for labor market improvement seem favorable as industrial production, especially those which are more domestic rather than external market oriented, continues to accelerate (ADB,2009a).

Table II.13. FDI in ASEAN, 2005-2009 (US$ million)

Member countries	2005	2006	2007	2008	2009
Brunei Darussalam	176	70	260	237	-
Cambodia	375	475	820	815	593
Indonesia	8,337	4,914	6,929	9,318	5,300
Lao People's Dem. Rep.	500	650	770	906	681
Malaysia	4,065	6,060	8,460	7,240	1,607
Myanmar	-	-	-	-	-
Philippines	1,854	2,921	2,916	1,544	1,948
Singapore	15,458	29,055	35,777	10,912	16,346
Thailand	8,048	9,460	11,330	8,570	6,148
Vietnam	1,430	1,757	6,550	9,279	6,900

Source: ADB (2010).

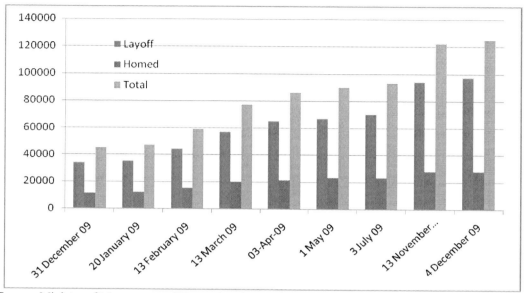

Source: Ministry of Manpower and Transmigration, and BPS (www.bps.go.id/sakernas).

Figure II.18. Number of Laid off and homed workers in the formal sector, 31 December 2008-4 December 2009.

In Indonesia, for instance, government (BPS) estimates show a steady increase of workers dismissal and homed in the formal sector during the end of December 2008 and early December 2009 (Figure II.18). While, according to ILO (2009), slowed economic growth caused by the crisis has prompted a steep fall in the growth of wage employment, which grew about 1.4 percent during the period February 2008-February 2009, compared to 6.1 percent during the same period in the previous year. Based on government data, the ILO study reports that employment in the tradable sectors grew by a mere 1.1 percent during the period February 2008-February 2009, compared to 4.0 percent growth rate in the non-tradable sectors which are not fully/directly linked with the global economy.

According to the Jakarta Post (cited from ILO,2009, page 8), the Ministry of Manpower and Transmigration reported in that time that job reductions already exceeded 51,000, while the Indonesian Employers Association (ASPINDO) reported over 237,000 layoffs between October 2008 and March 2009, with the textile and garments industries, accounting for 100,000 of the retrenchments; palm oil plantations 50,000; the automotive and spare parts industry 40,000; construction 30,000; and the footwear industry, 14,000. Subcontracted, casual and temporary workers in export-orientated industries were the hardest hit. According to ASPINDO, 90 to 95 percent of those who lost jobs were casual or subcontract workers.

By sector or industry, the textile and garment (TG) industry was among the most affected by the crisis. As cited from a report by the SMERU Research Institute (2009b), in 2009, at the national level, the production of the industry fell by 10 percent. According to the Indonesian Textile Producers Association (API) in that time, the possibility of dismissals of workers could involve 100,000 people, from around 1.2 million workers employed (or around 12.7 percent of the total workforce in the manufacturing industry). Most of the affected TG industries are located throughout Java, and the province of West Java is the center of Indonesian TG industries with more than 700 factories, employing around 700,000 workers.

In this province, the most affected TG industries were found in Bandung and Cimahi. According to API, because of the crisis, the production costs have risen by 25 percent, following the increase in the price of imported raw materials as a consequence of the depreciation of the rupiah against the US dollar in the beginning of the crisis period. Thus, the industries had the same experience as during the 1997/98 Asian financial crisis. According to API's estimates, more than 40 TG industries in this region have laid-off several thousand temporary workers, while approximately other 100,000 workers faced the threat of losing their jobs. In one industrial area in the district of Bandung (Dayeuhkolot Industrial Bonded Area (KBI)), lay offs of thousands of contract workers in the TG industries started already since October 2008. This decision was made as an effort to increase efficiency and to stem the effects of the crisis. The Dayeuhkolot KBI in that time employed approximately 18,000 permanent and 4,900 contract workers, and in that time there was a plan to dismiss 1,810 of the permanent workers, and lay off another 855 temporary workers. Also, it was planned not to extend the contract of all contract workers.

In some other districts in the West Java province, many TG industries also experienced difficulties during the crisis period. For instance, in Purwakarta, one company whose whole output was exported to the US had suffered serious losses due to the termination orders worth US$2 million. As a consequence, he has planned to dismiss up to 6,536 workers. In Bekasi, 11 TG companies were also found to have this experience and had planned to lay off 3,000 workers. In the province of Central Java, it was estimated that around 400,000 workers in the industry could lose their jobs. Several TG companies in important cities like Solo, Semarang, Boyolali, and Kendal had already dismissed hundreds of workers since October 2008 as a consequence of the cancellation of orders from the US and some other countries. One TG company in Boyolali was found to have laid off 848 workers as a consequence of less orders from the US, South Korea, Turkey and some other Western European countries (SMERU, 2009b).

In Jakarta, there were also many TG companies which were threatened with closure. They included 16 companies employing 9,800 workers in the Nusantara Bonded Zone (KBN) which exported TG to the USA which was found to have stopped their activities, and all their workers were dismissed (SMERU, 2009b).

Many cases of the increase in unemployment caused directly or indirectly by the crisis in other industries are also provided by the SMERU's (2009b) report from its media-monitoring, direct observations and interviews. For instance, the shoe industry in Surabaya (East Java) experienced a decline in export by 50 percent and many workers faced the threat of losing their jobs after completed remaining orders from 2008. In Serang (West Java), it was found that in October 2008, the shoe industry had already dismissed 450 employees.

Other industries which were also seriously hit by the crisis were the paper and pulp (PP), and electronics industries. In the second half of 2008, the PP industry in the province of Riau was found to have dimissed 500 workers and laid off another 500 temporary workers. In Bandung (West Java), it was found one electronic company producing small outline Ics, plastic-leaded chip carries and transistor outlines had closed its activities. In addition, SMERU reports that between 2008 and mid-2009, 18 companies in Serang and Tangerang in the province of Banten, stopped production and dismissals of 16,407 workers had taken place (SMERU,2009b).

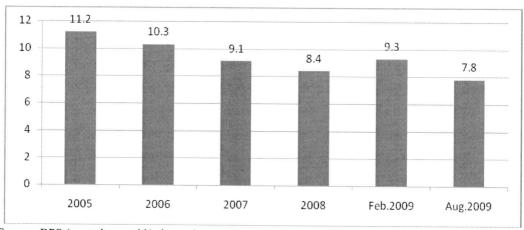

Source: BPS (www.bps.go.id/sakernas).

Figure II.19. Open Unemployment Rate, 2005–2009 (%).

With all of those stories, it can be expected that the level of open unemployment in Indonesia during that crisis period would certainly increase significantly. But, surprisingly (or maybe not at all), the official estimation from BPS does not fully support this theoretical thought although it increased in early 2009 but then declined again, as shown in Figure II.19. The main explanation for this is that Indonesia (as developing Asian countries in general) has large informal employment and higher rates of petty self-employment. Thus, based on this fact, another theoretical expectation is that impact of the crisis on employment in Indonesia will be reflected in greater disguised unemployment, more casual work and lower wages incomes rather than in the increase of open unemployment. According to ILO (2009), this growth of employment in the informal economy has been the most significant impact of the crisis on Indonesia's labour market.

As a comparison, Figure II.20 shows changes in unemployment rates in other selected Asian developing countries between the third quarter (Q3) of 2008 and the latest. The Philippines (PHI) has the smallest percentage point of change in the group (with the latest data Q2 2009), followed by Thailand (THA) (April-June 2009); Sri Lanka (SRI) (Q1 2009); Korea (KOR) (May-July 2009); Malaysia (MAL) (Q1 2009); Chna Taipei (TAP (May-July 2009); and Hong Kong, China (HKG) (May-July 2009). Whereas, Singapore (SIN) has the highest percentage point of change for the period Q3 2008-Q2 2009.

Even though total unemployment is falling as shown in Figure II.19, many cases discussed before indicate that the crisis has still caused reductions in the demand for particular types of worker in certain sectors or Industries. In this respect, by using data from three waves (February 2008, August 2008 and February 2009) of the Indonesian Labor Force Survey (SAKERNAS), [16]McCulloch and Grover (2010) have tried to find out what were the

---

[16] SAKERNAS is conducted by BPS every year, and the main part of it takes place every August. The August 2008 survey covers 931,890 individuals from 291,689 households across the country. This large sample is designed to provide estimators which are representative at the district level. The February surveys cover a random subset of the August sample. In 2008 and 2009, it sampled 218,833 individuals (69,114 households) and 291,689 individuals (68,535 households), respectively. The February surveys are representative at the provincial level. The surveys are stratified into rural and urban samples. The census blocks in each stratum are geographically ordered within each district and the districts are geographically ordered within each province, so that systematic sampling provides implicit stratification by province and district. Samples are clustered at the household level.

main reasons of those who have stopped working during the crisis period. Normal expectation was that they did so because of labor demand reasons (e.g. being fired or made redundant, or the firm that they were working for downsized or went bankrupt as a result of a drop in demand) relative to labor supply reasons (e.g. the worker disliking the pay or conditions of employment). The findings are presented in Table II.14 which shows the change in the reasons for finishing a job between August 2008 and Feburary 2009 (no question was asked during the February 2008 survey). As can be seen, the labor demand reasons for stopping working appear to dominate the cause of the increase in workers who have lost their jobs during the crisis period: the increase in the share of workers ending work or changing jobs as a result of being fired or made redundant is statistically significant, and a large increase in the share of those doing so because of their firms scaling down or going bankrupt.

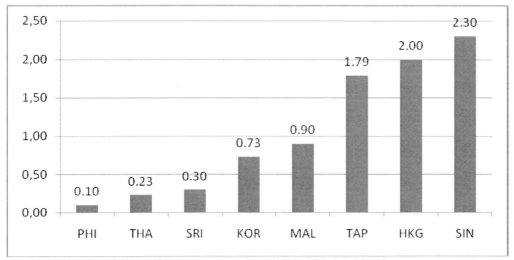

Source: ADB database (www.adb.org/Documents/Books/ADO/Update/figs/).

Figure II.20. Unemployment Rates in Other Asian Developing Countries, Q3 2008 and latest (%).

Table II.14. Reasons for Ending Employment in Indonesia, August 2008 and February 2009

Reason	August 2008	February 2009
Fired/made redundant	0.050	0.060 ***
No demand or firm went bankrupt	0.141	0.177 ***
Income too low	0.205	0.195 *
Unsuitable work environment	0.093	0.094
Contract finished	0.157	0.165
Other	0.353	0.310 ***

Note: asteriks in February 2009 column indicate statistically significant changes from August 2008; * = significant at 10%; ** = significant at 5%; *** = significant at 1%.
Source: McCulloch and Grover (2010).

All estimators take into account stratification and clustering and use sample weights to calculate population estimates (McCulloch and Grover (2010).

Poverty

Another serious concern during the crisis period was the impact on poverty and inequality, mainly because the economic booms enjoyed by many developing countries in the pre-2008/09 crisis were characterized by increasing income inequality and therefore the persistence of poverty in these countries. Unlike the 1997/1998 crisis, the latter crisis which led to a global economic recession and hence, a drop in world demand for many commodities produced by developing countries was predicted to have a less impact on the extreme poor (based on the world-bank definition, i.e. those living under the US$1.25 international poverty line), but a greater effect on those who were not poor but very vulnerable to poverty. In particular, this was the case for the workers and households who have risen just barely above the poverty line in recent years due to sustained economic growth, enhanced market integration and new formal employment opportunities and were very vulnerable to falling back into poverty as a result of the crisis. They were mainly unskilled workers employed as contract workers in export-oriented and labor-intensive industries, e.g. textile and garments, food and beverages, leather products and wood products (including furniture).

In ASEAN, although the crisis had serious impacts on the welfare of millions of people in the region (though the impact varied by country), it did not reverse the progress achieved by member countries in reducing poverty in the pre-2008/09 crisis. Since 1990, the share of the region's population living in absolute poverty (less than US$1.25/day) has declined from 55 percent to less than 10 percent of the population. The 1997/98 crisis did have effects on the pace of poverty reduction, but it was only temporary. However, at the time of the 2008/09 crisis, the speed with which ASEAN member countries would be able to recover from the crisis was questionable (ASEAN-World Bank, 2009). Even the World Bank (2009f) estimated that the speed of the process of poverty reduction in the region would diminish (Figure II.21), although it may vary by country, depending on a number of factors, including effectiveness of poverty-reduction policies and fiscal policies in stimulating domestic demand.

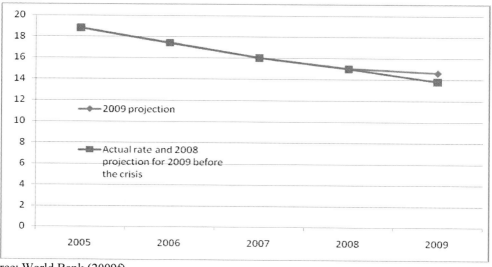

Source: World Bank (2009f).

Figure II.21. Poverty Reduction Process in ASEAN During the Crisis Period.

Table II.15. Poverty in Indonesia, 1976-2008

Year	Number of Poor (million)			Percentage of poverty (%)		
	Urban	Rural	Total	Urban	Rural	Total
1976	10.00	44.20	54.20	38.79	40.37	40.08
1980	9.50	32.80	42.30	29.04	28.42	28.56
1984	9.30	25.70	35.00	23.14	21.18	21.64
1987	9.70	20.30	30.00	20.14	16.14	17.42
1990	9.40	17.80	27.20	16.75	14.33	15.08
1996	9.42	24.59	34.01	13.39	19.78	17.47
1998	17.60	31.90	49.50	21.92	25.72	24.23
1999	15.64	32.33	47.97	19.41	26.03	23.43
2000	12.30	26.40	38.70	14.60	22.38	19.14
2001	8.60	29.30	37.90	9.76	24.84	18.41
2002	13.30	25.10	38.40	14.46	21.10	18.20
2003	12.20	25.10	37.30	13.57	20.23	17.42
2004	11.40	24.80	36.10	12.13	20.11	16.66
2005	12.40	22.70	35.10	11.68	19.98	15.97
2006	14.49	24.81	39.30	13.47	21.81	17.75
2007	13.56	23.61	37.17	12.52	20.37	16.58
2008	12.77	22.19	34.96	11.65	18.93	15.42
2009	11.91	.20.62	.32.53	10.72	17.35	14.15
2010[*]	11.10	19.93	31.02	9.87	16.56	13.33
2011	..	..	..	..	..	11.42[**]

[*] March; [**] World Bank's estimates (World Bank, 2009d).
Source: BPS (www.bps.go.id).

In Indonesia, based on BPS data, in the aftermath of the 1997/98 crisis, poverty increased dramatically from around 17.47 percent in 1996 to about 24.23 percent in 1998, when the crisis reached its climax. However, in 1999, poverty started to decline gradually, though first very slightly, up to 2005. In 2006, due to the high increase in world fuel prices, and as Indonesia has become increasingly dependent on imports of oil, the poverty rate increased again, on average between 1.8 percentage points per year or about 4.2 million people fell into poverty between the period of 2005-2006. Only after some policy adjustments and macroeconomic stabilization, the poverty rate started to decline again in 2007. In relative terms, the poverty rate in 2007 was the same as that before the 1997/98 crisis. However, in absolute terms, the number of those living under the current poverty line was still higher than that in the pre-1997/98 crisis period. Although the difference varies by year, the poverty rate in urban areas is always lower than that in rural areas. According to World Bank's most recent estimates, the poverty rate in the country is likely to continue to fall to 11.4 percent in early 2011(Table II.15). This suggests that the 2008/09 crisis would not lead to an increase of the poverty rate in Indonesia (as compared to the 1997/98 crisis).

Two other indicators often used for measuring the seriousness of poverty or the current economic condition of the poor are the Poverty Gap Index (PGI) and Severity Index or Distributionally Sensitive Index (DSI). PGI is a measure of the average gap or 'distance' between expenditure of the poor and poverty line. The higher the gap, the worse the economic condition of the poor. It reveals the size of the lump-sum subsidy that would be required for those living below the current poverty line to escape from poverty. Meanwhile, DSI to some extent shows the distribution of expenditure among the poor. Tables II.16 and II.17 show BPS calculations of PGI and DSI, respectively, in Indonesia. As can be seen, although both indicators show a decline in urban and rural areas during the reviewed period, urban areas appeared to be better off than rural areas in terms of their PGI, and were more or less of a similar condition with the rural areas in terms of their DSI. This suggests that the economic growth after the 1997/98 crisis up to 2008 tended to favor urban households more than those in rural areas. This, of course, is not surprising at all as inequality in economic development in favor of urban economy and population is a key feature of developing countries.

While some sectors/subsectors were negatively affected by the crisis, there were two factors which may play important roles in reducing the net poverty effects of the crisis. First, the growth of the informal sector which absorbed many displaced workers and/or provided extra/secondary incomes to people who were still working in the formal sector but with lower incomes/wages. As shown before, despite the crisis, the official unemployment rate in Indonesia declined instead of increased because the informal sector absorbed many laid off workers and therefore, reduced the likelihood of them falling into poverty. Second, many existing poverty alleviation programs from the government may also have played a crucial role in offsetting the net poverty effects of the crisis. In one of its series of studies on the impact of the crisis on Indonesian economy, World Bank argues that poverty reduction in Indonesia, despite the crisis, is likely to be supported by the planned expansion of the National Program for Hopeful Family (PKH), focusing on education and health, the National Program for Community Empowerment (PNPM), focusing on own business development/creation by women, and other targeted poverty reduction policies currently under development. In the first 100 days of the current president SBY second cabinet, the government also plans various other policy measures that may accelerate poverty reduction indirectly (World Bank, 2009d).

The Indonesian government and the World Bank have made three scenarios with respect to the likely effects of the crisis on poverty in Indonesia (Table II.18). The first is the 'without crisis' scenario, where economic growth reaches 6 percent per year. The second is where the 2008/09 crisis affects the domestic economy without the government doing anything (crisis without fiscal stimulus and other crisis-response policies). The third is where the crisis affects the country but the government inserts a stimulus and other policies to cushion the impacts. Table II.18 may suggest that government interventions directed towards poverty are important, at least, to prevent poverty from increasing.

Table II.16. Poverty Gap Index in Indonesia by Region, 1999-2008

Year	Urban	Rural	Total
1999	3.52	4.84	4.33
2000	1.89	4.68	3.51
2001	1.74	4.68	3.42
2002	2.59	3.34	3.01
2003	2.55	3.53	3.13
2004	2.18	3.43	2.89
2005	2.05	3.34	2.78
2006	2.61	4.22	3.43
2007	2.15	3.78	2.99
2008	2.07	3.42	2.77

Source: BPS (www.bps.go.id).

Table II.17. Distributionally-Sensitive Index in Indonesia by Region, 1999-2008

Year	Urban	Rural	Total
1999	0.98	1.39	1.23
2000	0.51	1.39	1.02
2001	0.45	1.36	0.97
2002	0.71	0.85	0.79
2003	0.74	0.93	0.85
2004	0.58	0.90	0.78
2005	0.60	0.89	0.76
2006	0.77	1.22	1.00
2007	0.57	1.09	0.84
2008	0.56	0.95	0.76

Source: BPS (www.bps.go.id).

Unfortunately, until recently, the Indonesian government has not issued national data on the impact of the crisis on education and health. However, given the fact that the poverty rate continued to decline despite the crisis, and the government response to the crisis this time was much better than during the 1997/98 crisis, it can be expected that the impact of the 2008/09 crisis on education and health in Indonesia is insignificant, although the impact may vary by region and sector.

II.3. CRISIS-MONITORING ACTIVITIES IN INDONESIA

Although at the national level, as shown before, the impact of the 2008/09 crisis was insignificant, especially compared to the 1997/98 crisis, at the meso (province/district/village) and micro (household) levels, the story might be different. With respect to the sectoral effect, the 2008/09 crisis was primarily a world income/demand crisis which led to the decline of exports of various commodities in many developing countries, then, theoretically, export-oriented sectors or subsectors would be the first sectors directly hit by the crisis, followed by other related sectors through production and consumption linkage. As shown before in Table II.4, although all sectors (except trade, hotels and restaurants) managed to have positive growth in 2008 and 2009, some of them experienced decreasing rates of growth. It is hard, however, to conclude that the negative growth experienced by trade, hotels and restaurants and the decreasing positive growth rates faced by agriculture, manufacturing industry, finance, and services were caused mainly by the 2008/09 crisis. Other internal factors may have also played a role simultaneously.[17]

Nevertheless, the manufacturing industry was likely to be the most affected sector for two main reasons. First, many Indonesian exports of manufactured goods, especially furnitures and textiles, have experienced a decline in world demand in 2008 and 2009 (while, there is not enough evidence on the impact of the crisis on exports from agriculture and mining). Second, theoretically, when a country's economy is hit by a crisis which leads to a decline in its income per capita, imports of unnecessary goods (e.g. furniture, cloths, footwears,

---

[17] A factor analysis may be needed to estimate the contributions of individual theoretically expected factors..

electronics, etc) will be the first to be adjusted, not imports of basic goods (rice or other agricultural commodities, and oil and gas).

With respect to the regional impact, theoretically, it can be expected that the most affected regions would be those where their key sectors (i.e. having the largest contributions to regional GDP (say, GRP) and employment and the largest production linkages with the rest of the regions' economy) were seriously affected by the crisis. If the crisis-affected sectors are not the key sectors, the overall impact on the region's economy would be insignificant. Or, alternatively, the most affected regions would be those which have been depending significantly on remittances from abroad, and during the crisis, many of its migrant workers returned home because their host countries were also adversely affected by the crisis.

No official data from BPS or other government departments is available yet to show the affected regions by the crisis. However, BPS data on annual GRP growth rates may help assess the regional impact, as shown in Table II.19. It is generally expected that as clusters of export-oriented industries, especially furnitures, textile and leather products are mainly in Java, Java provinces (or districts within Java) would be more affected than the rest of Indonesia, and it should be reflected by lower GRP growth rates in Java than in outside Java provinces (not shown in Table II.19). Surveys' findings from many crisis-monitoring activities, which will be discussed briefly below, may also give some evidence about the impact at the district level. For instance, based on quarterly change in labor market conditions and household hardship between April and July 2009, the survey's finding from the World Bank shows that the most affected regions were Lampung, West Nusa Tenggara, and Central Java (World Bank, 2010b).

Finally, with respect to the household effect, theoretically, the most affected households would be those who have worked in or earned incomes from sectors affected by the crisis. For instance, the furniture industry was also affected by the crisis, and thus many employees as well as employers in this industry would also be affected; they could come from poor or non-poor households, or from rural or urban areas. A study from SMERU/IDS (which will be discussed later on) shows that in rural areas where the local community depends on rubber plantations and coal exploration to make a living, the fall in the prices of these commodities, as well as the decrease in the world demand for these commodities, have caused a decline in the income of farmers, laborers, local transportation drivers, and workers in other supporting sectors. The study also shows that in urban areas adjacent to the industrial park, the decrease in the demand for automotive, electronic, and consumer goods has led to a reduction in working hours at the factories, reduction of additional benefits, temporary layoff of permanent workers and terminations of jobs for contracted workers (IDS, 2009).

Table II.18. Impact of 2008/09 Crisis on Poverty Rates in Indonesia (three scenarios)

Scenario	Poverty rate projection (%)	
	Government	World Bank
Without crisis	12.68	13.10
Crisis without policies	13.34	13.90
Crisis with policies	12.93	13.80

Source: Bappenas (www.bappenas.go.id) and World Bank (2008, page 3).

Table II.19. Annual GRP Growth Rates in Provinces in Indonesia
(%, constant market prices 2000)*

Province	2004	2005	2006	2007	2008
Nangroe Aceh Darussalam	1.76	1.22	7.70	7.23	1.88
North. Sumatera	6.00	5.52	6.26	6.89	6.40
West Sumatera	5.47	5.73	6.14	6.34	6.36
Riau	9.01	8.54	8.66	8.25	8.06
Jambi	6.48	6.25	8.35	6.58	7.36
South Sumatera	6.79	6.91	7.31	8.04	6.34
Bengkulu	5.38	5.82	5.95	6.03	4.93
Lampung	5.76	4.61	5.31	6.14	5.33
Bangka Belitung	4.34	4.60	4.80	5.37	5.03
Riau islands	7.42	7.08	7.23	7.55	7.22
DKI Jakarta	5.70	6.06	5.96	6.46	6.19
West. Jawa	5.08	6.23	6.31	6.86	5.97
Central Jawa	4.90	5.00	5.32	5.97	5.33
D. I. Yogyakarta	5.12	4.73	3.70	4.31	5.02
East. Jawa	5.84	5.84	5.79	6.04	5.86
Banten	5.63	5.88	5.57	6.04	5.82
Bali	4.62	5.56	5.28	5.92	5.97
West Nusa Tenggara	6.07	1.71	2.77	4.91	2.63
East Nusa Tenggara	5.34	4.36	5.08	5.15	4.81
West Kalimantan	4.79	4.69	5.23	6.02	5.42
Central Kalimantan	5.56	5.90	5.84	6.06	6.16
South Kalimantan	5.85	5.29	5.05	6.08	6.37
East Kalimantan	7.44	8.07	12.62	9.56	6.88
North Sulawesi	3.82	5.39	5.69	6.47	7.56
Central Sulawesi	7.15	7.19	7.22	7.25	7.42
South Sulawesi	5.27	6.05	6.73	6.35	7.79
Southeast Sulawesi	7.51	7.31	7.68	7.96	7.27
Gorontalo	6.93	7.19	7.30	7.51	7.76
West Sulawesi	6.00	6.30	6.90	7.43	8.54
Maluku	4.44	5.08	5.56	5.74	4.23
North. Maluku	4.71	5.10	5.48	6.01	5.98
West Papua	6.29	6.83	7.36	8.61	8.68
Papua	-22.53	36.40	-17.14	4.34	-1.49

* Not including oil and gas.
Source: BPS (www.bps/go.id/pdrb).

In relation to the national effect, if the economy of the affected region has only a small contribution to Indonesia's GDP or if total exports of the affected sector are only from a small fraction of the country's total exports, then the impact of the crisis experienced by the sector or region will not be recorded significantly in the Indonesia's GDP or total export growth.

Therefore, the impact of an economic crisis at the macro level can be different than that at the meso- or micro-level. During 2009, various agencies, research institutes and development partners in Indonesia such as the World Bank, SMERU Research Institute,

OXFAM, JICA and many others have conducted global crisis monitoring activities by collecting data/information at provincial, district, village, sectoral, and household levels (Table II.20) through various ways, such as surveys, direct observations, interviews, media monitoring, and focus group discussions (FGD).

Table II.20. Sector, Region, Household and Employment by Type Covered by the Crisis-Monitoring Activities

Institute/ organization	Covered Units			
	Sector	Region	House-hold	Employment/ occupation
WB-BPS	Some sectors	471 districts, 33 provinces	14,130 hhs	Formal/informal workers
JICA-CASEPS	Agriculture (e.g rice, cabagge, shallot, tobacco, coffee, and weakly cacao), non-agriculture	30 villages in 3 provinces (CJ, SS, Lampung)	300 hhs	Farmers, domestic migrant workers, agricultural workers, self-employment, part-/full-time workers, skilled/unskilled workers.
SMERU-IDS	Rubber plantation, coal, supporting industries, automotive, electronics, consumer goods industries	2 rural villages, 1 urban village, SK, WJ	Na*	Farmer, agricultural laborers, drivers, industrial contracted & permanent workers
SMERU-BAPPENAS	TPI, automotive, electronic; handicraft, fishery, fish processing industries, timber & wooden products, including furniture, plantation (palm oil, cacao, coffe, rubber, copra, corn cassava), , mining (coal, iron, metal, nicle, bauxit, aluminium, marmer), tourism	Bekasi, WJ (Bandung), NTB (West Lombok), Riau (Kampar), CJ (Jepara), EJ (Malang), NS (Bitung), S.Sumatra, Bandar Lampung.	Na	Farmers/plantation owners, migrant workers, small producers by gender, factory workers, contract laborers, child workers,
AKATIGA-OA		NTT; NTB	Na	Migrant workers
UGM-GRIPS	Agriculture, mining, manufacturing, services, transportation	Medan, Tangerang, Samarinda, Makassar	Na	Migrant workers, casual workers, permanent jobs, self-employment, unpaid family workers

* Not specifically mentioned.

The overall finding from all of those crisis-monitoring activities gives two important facts. First, many households were affected by the crisis, and many of them took crisis-coping measures to mitigate the impact. Second, the experienced impacts vary, however, by sector as well as region (for a more detailed discussion, see Chapter III).

II.4. RECOVERY AND GOVERNMENT EFFORTS

In the Asian Development Outlook (ADO) 2009 Update (ADB, 2009a), it states the following: *despite a notable slowdown in its economic expansion relative to potential, developing Asia is leading the recovery from the global downturn. Its growth is underpinned by the relatively healthy state of its financial systems prior to the financial crisis; by the fiscal and monetary stimuli that have been quickly provided by governments and central banks across the region; and by the rapid turnaround in its larger, less export-dependent economies* (page1). In this annual report, Indonesia is stated as among the meant Asian countries leading the recovery while based on ADO 2010, Indonesian economy is expected to grow at 5.5 percent in 2010, which is slightly higher than in 2009, and 6.0 percent in 2011 (Table II.21). As can be seen, within ASEAN, Indonesia has the highest predicted growth after Vietnam and Lao PDR. However, in Asia as a whole, People Republic of China and India are still the leading countries. These most recent predictions about the Indonesian economic growth reflect a more optimistic view about the country's ability to recover, as compared to previous predictions not only by ADB but also by many other organizations (Figure II.22).

Table II.21. GDP Growth Rates per year in Selected Asian Developing Countries in 2009-2011 (%)

Countries	2009	2010[*]	2011[*]
Brunei Darussalam	2.3	2.3	-
Cambodia	4.0	3.5	-
Indonesia	5.0	5.5	6.0
Lao PDR	5.7	5.7	-
Malaysia	4.4	5.3	5.0
Philippines	3.5	3.8	4.6
Singapore	3.5	6.3	5.0
Thailand	3.0	4.0	4.5
Vietnam	6.5	6.5	6.8
China, People Rep.	8.0	9.6	9.1
Hong Kong, China	3.0	5.2	4.3
Taipei, China	2.4	4.9	4.0
India	6.5	8.2	8.7
Developing Asia	5.2	7.5	7.3

[*] ADB's prediction.
Source: ADB (2009a, 2010).

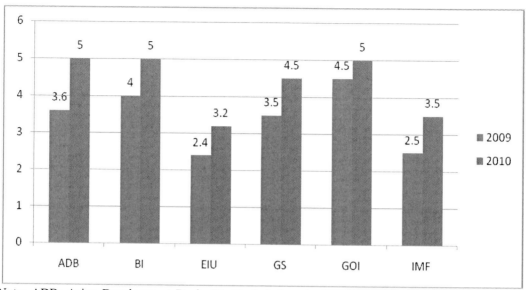

Note: ADB: Asian Development Bank; BI: Bank Indonesia; EIU: Economic Intelligence Unit; GS: Goldman Sachs; GOI: Government of Indonesia; IMF: International Monetary Fund
Source: ILO(2009).

Figure II.22. Previous Predictions of Indonesian Economic Growth from Various Selected Organizations (as of May 2009).

Table II.22. Current Account Balance as % of GDP in Selected Asian Developing Countries, 2007-2011

Countries	2007	2008	2009	2010	2011
Brunei Darussalam	39.6	54.0	35.0	33.0	31.0
Cambodia	-8.2	-12.2	-10.7	-16.3	-17.0
Indonesia	2.4	0.0	2.0	1.4	0.6
Lao PDR	-17.2	-15.4	-11.8	-10.0	-11.0
Malaysia	15.7	17.6	16.7	14.0	13.8
Myanmar	0.6	-2.5	-1.0	-1.8	-2.1
Philippines	4.9	2.2	5.3	3.3	3.2
Singapore	27.6	19.2	19.1	18.0	21.0
Thailand	6.3	0.5	7.7	4.0	2.0
Vietnam	-9.8	-11.8	-7.4	-7.6	-5.5
China, People Rep.	10.6	9.4	5.8	5.7	5.3
Hong Kong, China	12.3	13.6	8.7	7.6	7.2
Taipei, China	8.4	6.2	11.2	8.2	6.7
India	-1.3	-2.5	-1.9	-1.5	-2.0
Developing Asia (Average)	6.5	5.4	4.9	4.1	3.6

Source: ADB database (www.adb.org/Documents/Books/ADO/Update/figs/

With respect to current account balances, the most recent ADB's estimates predict that Indonesia's current account balance, as percentage of GDP, in 2010 will be slightly lower than that in 2009 and it will go down further to less than one percent of GDP in 2011 (Table II.22). In many developing countries, including Indonesia, the key element of the current account balance is the trade balance, and the way to increase trade surplus (export less import) and hence, current account surplus, is by increasing export and/or reducing import. Exactly for this matter, Indonesia has been facing two serious problems since the end of the 1997/98 crisis, and the problems are most likely to continue in the near future. First, on the export side, for many manufactured goods such as textile, garments, leather products and rattan-and wood-based furniture, Indonesia seems to losing the battle especially with China, while at the same time, there are many domestic constraints that make Indonesia difficult to upgrade the producing capacity of its export-oriented industries and to improve the quality of its exports. Secondly, on the import-side, due to the lack of domestic production capacity and low competitiveness, Indonesia has been depending increasingly on many imported goods, not only for basic needs but also capital and intermediate goods for domestic production activities.

This optimistic prediction for Indonesian economy in 2010 is not without a strong reason, that is the government response to the crisis, which was quicker and better than during the 1997/98 crisis period. The government had learned good lessons from the 1997/98 crisis. Even, the "Bank Century" case (despite of its political effects) can also be seen as a response of the government to the 2008/09 crisis based on lessons learned from the 1997/98 crisis that not helping trouble banks by bailing-out will only enhance the crisis. In addition to the bail-out of Bank Century, the Indonesian Central Bank (Bank Indonesia/BI) also took several measures such as (Yudo et al., 2009): (1) reducing the volatility of the exchange rate by measured interventions in the foreign exchange markets and developing foreign exchange swaps transactions with banks; (2) providing more flexibility for banks to manage liquidity, including (a) postponing implementation of accounting regulations related to fair valuation of banks' assets, particularly the marking-to-market rules on banks' SUN (government's debt certificate) holdings, (b) lowering foreign exchange reserve requirement from 3 to 1 percent, (c) reducing the effective rupiah reserve requirement rate from 9.01 to 7 percent, comprising of 5 percent statutory reserve (must be placed in the central bank's account) and 2.5 percent secondary reserve in the form of BI Certificates or government bonds or other excess reserves, (d) extending the foreign exchange swap tenure from 7 days to one month, and (e) proposing (together with the Ministry of Finance) amendments to BI Laws to provide banks with a short-term liquidity facility upon encountered liquidity problems, with government securities/bonds and other credit assets; and (3) maintaining financial system stability, by proposing amendments (together with the Ministry of Finance) to the Law on the Deposit Insurance Corporation to increase coverage of the deposit guarantee to Rp 2 billion.

The government also launched a fiscal stimulus package worth Rp. 73.3 trillion (USD 7.3 billion, or approximately 2.4 percent of Indonesian GDP). The package consisted of three main components, and the biggest one was tax rebate, i.e. tax cut for companies, workers and individuals Rp. 43.0 trillion and tax subsidies and import duties exemption Rp. 13.3 trillion. The tax rebate was expected to prevent massive layoffs by easing the burden on crisis-affected companies. The second largest component of the package was for infrastructure projects (including the improvements of roads, ports, bridges and irrigation systems) and empowerment programs (including housing development program) for people living in rural areas, worth Rp Rp.12.2 trillion. The last component was diesel and electricity subsidies as well as loans for rural empowerment worth Rp 4.8 trillion. In combination with the cut in interest rates, the government also expected that the package will bolster private consumption and achieve private consumption growth of between 4 and 4.7 percent, and in total, 3 million jobs will be created. From the infrastructure projects alone, the government expected it would absorb 1.6 million workers (ILO, 2009).

The importance of a fiscal stimulus package on GDP economic growth can be empirically estimated using simple time series analysis. Recently, Ducanes, et al (2006), quoted from World Bank (2010c), have estimated the effectiveness of fiscal policy reflected in government expenditure, both via discretionary policy and automatic stabilizers, for a number of developing countries, including Indonesia, using structural macro-econometric model simulations. They evaluated the effectiveness of a discretionary policy based on the size of the short-term and medium-term fiscal multipliers under three scenarios: (i) an untargeted increase in government expenditure , (ii) a targeted increase in government expenditure (i.e. investment spending), and (iii) and a tax reduction. Their estimations for Indonesia are the following. For the first scenario, short-term fiscal multiplier is 0.22, meaning that every 10 percent increase in government expenditure will generate only 2.2 percent increase in GDP. For the second scenario, medium-term fiscal multiplier is 0.76. For the third scenario, the tax reduction multiplier is 0.16.

The World Bank (2010) also has its own analysis on the effectiveness of government spending on the GDP growth in Indonesia with the estimated model: $\Delta GDP_t = c + a \Delta GE_{t, t-1, t-2, t-3, t-4} + b \Delta GDP_{t-1} + d \Delta GR_{t, t-1}$, where c is a constant, GE is the relevant government spending component with respected quarterly lag (e.g., t, t-1), and GR is government revenue. Preliminary results indicate that an increase in government spending supports GDP growth in Indonesia. Under several specifications, it is found that a 10 percentage point increase in central government spending is associated with GDP growth by between minimum 0.2 and maximum 0.26 percentage points.[18] Thus, based on these two estimations, it can be said that the fiscal stimulus or the increased government spending during the crisis period has at least kept (if not accelerated) a positive growth rate of GDP in Indonesia during the crisis period.

The importance of these policies is also stated in the ADB's 2009 regional economic outlook report: *... many regional governments' quick and decisive response to the weak global environment prevented a freefall in developing Asia's economic growth. Tax cuts, greater public spending, targeted assistance, and easy monetary policies boosted consumption and investment. The regional economy is now poised to achieve a V-shaped rebound. The larger economies provided much of the impetus for the region's transition to recovery. In addition, stronger financial systems in the region than elsewhere at the onset of the financial crisis underpinned the region's resilience to the global downturn* (ADB 2009a, page 2).

In addition to the package, the government also increased the salaries of civil servants (including retired civil servants) and members of the military and the police by as much as 15 percent and offer a one-month bonus as well as distribute direct cash transfers of Rp 100,000 (US$8)/month to 18.2 million targeted households for two months (Yudo, et al., 2009).

---

[18] See further World Bank (2009a).

Table II.23. Import Duty Exemption

NO.	Industry	Import duty Subsidy (Rp millions)
1.	Ballpoints	25,390
2.	Heavy equipment raw materials and components	220,560
3.	Low capacity thermal power plant raw materials and components	14,037
4.	Dairy raw materials (skim and full cream milk powder)	256,680
5.	Methyltin mercaptide additive materials	1,488
6.	Automotive manufacturing raw materials and components	795,200
7.	Electronic components	323,400
8.	Telematics (fiber optics and telecommunications components)	70,000
9.	Shipbuilding raw materials and components	226,600
10.	Additive materials for sorbitol production	1,058
11.	Raw materials and equipment for film production	25,000
12.	Electricity	14,000
13.	Medical equipment	11,400
14.	Aircraft	416,000
	TOTAL	2,400,813

Source: Tambunan (2009a).

In the trade area, the government also took trade-related measures conducted according to WTO rules (Yudo, et al., 2009). By the end of 2008, the Ministry of Trade announced that five categories of goods (food and beverages, garments, electronic goods, shoes and toys) should only be imported through five major seaports: Jakarta, Medan, Semarang, Surabaya and Makassar. On tariff policies, the Ministry postponed implementation of the 2009 tariff harmonization program for 324 tariff lines which were still applied in 2008. There were some temporary tariff increases for some imported products which are also produced domestically with the aim to prevent declining competitiveness of Indonesian industries. While, at the same time, the Ministry reduced the tariff on some other imported primary and intermediary products not produced domestically. In addition, a regulation on the Indonesia Export-Import Bank (*UU Lembaga Pembiayaan Ekspor Indonesia*/LPEI) was launched and some measures were introduced to strengthen the institution of ASEI (Indonesian Export Insurance).

The Ministry of Trade, together with the Ministry of Industry, tried to explain the above policy measures by stating that in the short run, economic policy would need to focus on domestic demand as a necessary response to the crisis. It was expected in that time, however, that the crisis would be a short-term phenomenon, and soon the global economy would recover, and exports would increase again. Therefore, the ministries have emphasized that Indonesia needs to position itself to take advantage of the future recovery by improving the competitiveness of domestic production during the crisis period (Tambunan, 2009a).

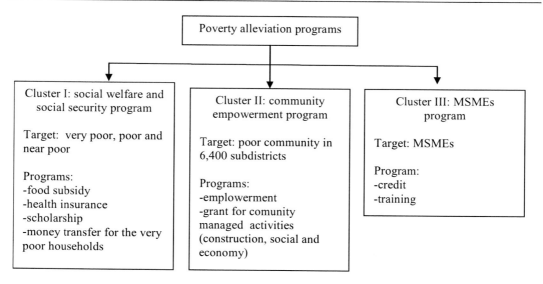

Source: Murniningtas (2009), Riyadi and Murniningtyas (2010).

Figure II.23. Poverty Reduction Programs During the Crisis Period.

Although the short-run crisis-response policy was inward looking, the Indonesian government did not tend to indulge in more protection, which stifles efficiency and innovation and perhaps retribution by other countries, but to improve competitiveness and to increase production capacity of Indonesian industries through various measures such as reducing barriers to domestic trade by streamlining local regulations and licenses, cutting logistics costs, investing in infrastructure, and improving standards and product quality, and maintaining an open and competitive trade and investment regime, by reducing non-tariff barriers (NTBs) and logistics costs. These measures were taken simultaneously with measures to boost domestic demand through fiscal simulation packages.

To promote growth in the real sector during the crisis period, the government has adopted a more 'liberal' than 'protectionism' step by allocating a fiscal stimulus through tax cuts for food staples, agriculture and manufacturing, including value added tax (VAT) exemption for 17 industries. In addition, the government provides import duty relief for 9 industries. Allocations of the two stimuli prescribed in Minister of Finance regulations total almost Rp 12 trillion (Table II.23).

In further actions, the government has issued Government Regulation No.62 of 2008 concerning Amendment of Government Regulation No.1 of 2007 concerning Income Tax Relief for Investment in Designated Business Lines and/or Designated Regions. The amendment encompasses several improvements in provisions of income tax relief for investments. Under Government Regulation No. 62 of 2008, tax relief on investment has been expanded to include 8 (eight) new lines of businesses as follows: livestock farming; processing of forestry products from timber estates; low rank coal mining development and extraction; geothermal energy production; dairy and dairy food industries; oil refineries; construction of a mini-scale natural gas refining and processing plant; synthetic fiber manufacturing. In addition to these industries/sectors, six new business lines are also eligible for tax relief when operating in designated regions: food crop cultivation; horticulture development; leather, leather goods and footwear manufacturing; electrical accumulator and solid battery manufacturing; and fishing boat building and repair industry (Tambunan, 2009a).

This positive growth stimulated by such quick and right policies has no doubt strengthened the public trust, including from the business community, on the government's ability to do better and have a quicker recovery than during the 1997/98 crisis. High public trust in combination with government's efforts to maintain relatively high levels of infrastructure spending in 2010 and the modest global rebound are expected to generate better economic growth in 2010.

Specifically in the poverty area, in the adjusted State Budget 2009, the government included social protection and poverty alleviation programs, and some had been launched during the 1997/1998 crisis. These include (Yudo, et al, 2009): (1) subsidies, (2) social safety net programs such as JPS-BK (healthcare), BKM (students' special assistance) and BOS (school operational assistance), and food assistance (rice for the poor/OPK), and (3) labor-intensive projects such as PNPM Mandiri (independent people's empowerment program). For fiscal year 2009, the government allocated Rp. 66 trillion to reduce poverty, up from Rp. 58 trillion disbursed in fiscal year 2008. Of that total, Rp. 15 trillion went to the PNPM, Rp. 12 trillion to the OPK and Rp. 11 trillion to the BOS. The PNPM program was expected to cover 6,408 sub-districts and 78,000 villages in 2009, absorbing 3 to 4 million workers.

In addition, the government work plan for 2009 had focused on the Welfare Improvement and Poverty Reduction program. To carry out this work plan, the government had set up three development priorities, which were: (1) promoting basic public services and rural development; (2) encouraging inclusive growth; and (3) improving anti-corruption efforts, bureaucratic reform and strengthening democratization. In regard to promoting basic public services for the poor and rural development priorities, the activities covered: (1) developing and improving social protection systems for the poor; (2) expanding community-based development programm; and (3) improving micro, small and medium enterprises (MSMEs).

Figure II.23 shows the comprehensive national poverty reduction programs introduced in 2008/09 which might have played an important role in mitigating the impact of the crisis on poverty in Indonesia. The programs were divided into three clusters, namely social welfare and social security; community empowerment; and support to MSMEs.

Theoretically, as illustrated in Figure II.24, if those two interventions (fiscal stimulus and poverty alleviation programs) are well-implemented, they may not only minimize but can also offset the negative impacts of the 208/09 crisis on poverty. Even the net result can be a poverty reduction despite the crisis. The process of the positive impact of the fiscal stimulus package on poverty will go through two stages. First, it will affect the formal sector: higher domestic demand leads to more production and more employment, and, as a result, lower poverty. Second, through domestic/local production and consumption/income linkages, the increases in production, employment and incme in the formal sector will generate a growth source for production and employment in the informal sector. Thus, the overall employment (in both formal and informal sectors) will increase and, as the final result, poverty will decrease. On the other hand, business promotion programs for the poor like the PNPM may boost production in the informal sector which is important to absorb many displaced workers from the formal sector during the crisis, which will help mitigate the impact of the crisis on poverty.

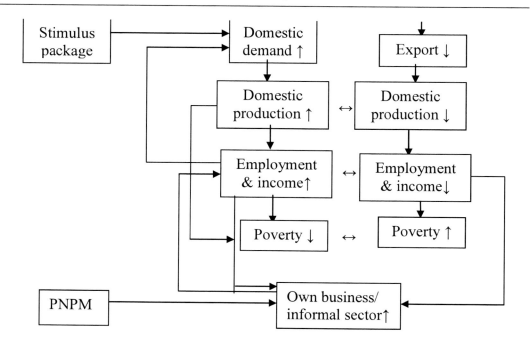

Figure II.24. Impact of Government Interventions on Poverty during the 2008/09 Crisis.

II.5. WHAT MADE THE DIFFERENCE?

By now it is well-known that among many Asian countries, Indonesia was not only weathering the 2008/09 global economic crisis better, but it was also much different than during the 1997/98 Asian financial crisis. The World Bank concluded the following: *One year after the global financial crisis and economic downturn, Indonesia's economy appears to be broadly back on track. Economic activity has been picking up, inflation has remained moderate, financial markets have risen, and the newly re-elected government, having established the strong fundamentals that supported Indonesia through the global crisis, appears to be now gearing up for new investments in Indonesia's physical infrastructure, human services and institutions of state. Indonesia seems well-positioned to get back on its pre-crisis growth trajectory, with the possibility of further acceleration and more inclusive growth* (World Bank, 2009d, page iv).

The question now is what made the difference? Was that because the Indonesian government's response this time was more quick or was better prepared than during the 1997/98 crisis, or something else? According to many discussions[19] reports, there are a number of reasons:

---

[19] See World Bank, (2009b, 2010c) Djaja (2009), Zavadjil (2009), and ADB (2009a, 2010).

(1) from a regional perspective, the Indonesian economy performed well in the years before 2008 (with one of the best growth rates in Asia after the 1997/98 Asian crisis up to 2008, particularly during the period 2005-2008)[20];

(2) the banking sector remains in good health (which was not the case in the years before the 1997/98 Asian economic crisis), although bank lending growth reduced in line with the slowing economy;

(3) consumer prices kept stable, allowing Bank Indonesia (BI) to loosen monetary policy (which is important to keep consumption growth);

(4) Indonesia's external position remained sound, the country's significant external financing obligations are being met, and foreign exchange reserves have risen slightly;[21]

(5) Indonesia's public finances are strong (which was not the case during the 1997/98 Asian crisis), allowing policy makers to quickly move to offset the global downturn's effects on Indonesia with a fiscal stimulus;

(6) also based on the experience of the 1997/98 crisis, cautious policies by Indonesia's government[22], banks,[23] and corporations,[24] over the past decade have resulted in low debt levels and limited refinancing needs. This served the country especially well in late 2008 and early 2009, when liquidity tightened around the world;

(7) compared with some Asian countries, Indonesia is a relatively "closed economy";[25]

(8) consumers kept spending despite the fact that banks tightened credits in late 2008. Much of this spending might also be related to the election related activities; and

---

[20] Sustained high rates of annual economic growth over several years is not a guarantee that a country will not experience a big crisis in the near future. Until early 1997, Indonesia had annual growth rates of on average 7 percent. But, unexpectedly, by the end of that year, the Indonesian economy was hit by the biggest crisis, at least since its independence in 1945.

[21] According to Zavadjil (2009), Bank Indonesia (BI) had built-up adequate foreign exchange reserves, equivalent to almost 200 percent of short term debt on a remaining maturity basis, which provided a good cushion against capital outflows in the second half of 2008. With these reserves, BI was not only able to intervene in the market to limit the fluctuation of the rupiah, and thus prevent a major decline in confidence, but the rupiah was also free to fluctuate to absorb the impact of the capital outflows.

[22] Zavadjil (2009) explains that careful fiscal management policies adopted by the Indonesian government in the post-1997/98 Asian economic crisis period reduced the public debt ratio to around 33 percent by the end of 2008, which was amongst the lowest in the G20, and had the prospect of further decline. Consequently, the government was in a position to increase the deficit from roughly 0.1 percent of GDP in 2008 to as much as 2.5 percent in 2009, raising the growth rate by 0.5-1.0 percentage points according to IMF estimates. Moreover, as he argues, if global economic conditions deteriorate again, Indonesia has the option of pursuing more stimulus.

[23] Indonesia's banks were able to maintain ample liquidity and capital buffers. In 2008, the capital adequacy ratio was around 17 percent (compared with the Basel requirement of 8 per cent). Also, banks hold about 23 percent of their assets in BI paper or government bonds, considerably above international norms. Thus, the overall loan to deposit ratio was about 75 percent, i.e. banks were mainly financed by deposits rather than the interbank market and/or foreign loans which proved much more unstable sources of funds during the crisis (Zavadjil, 2009).

[24] The bulk of Indonesia's corporations were in relatively good shape, in line with the rest of emerging Asia (Zavadjil, 2009). This was very different with the 1997/98 Asian crisis. Currency and maturity mismatches were one of the key causes of the 1997/98 crisis.

[25] In his study, Djaja (2009) shows that the share of Indonesia's exports to GDP was 29.4 percent in 2007. The figure in the next three quarters of 2008 was 30.0 percent on average. About 85 percent of goods and services produced by Indonesian economy were used domestically in 2005, while only about 15 percent went to foreign buyers. This indicates that Indonesia is not so strongly integrated with the rest of the world, at least from an export point of view. With such low exports, a sudden drop in world income and hence in world demand for Indonesian exports will not affect significantly domestic production.

(9) based on the experience of the 1997/98 Asian crisis, this time the Indonesian government was quicker and more active in response with appropriate measures to the crisis, e.g. by providing the stimulus through fiscal and monetary policies.

Specifically, the Asian Development Bank gives its own reasons that Indonesia was more resilient than other countries during the 2008/09 crisis (ADB, 2010b, page 7):

(1) the impact of a spike in risk aversion was muted by steady policy responses in Indonesia and the stabilizing impact of coordinated global counter-measures on global financial markets;
(2) the income impact of the fall in commodity prices was mitigated by the fact that the preceding years had seen record high prices for these same commodities, allowing rural households to build up a savings buffer to help them smooth out consumption spending;
(3) because the global recession was of relatively short duration, the lagged effects of the financial crisis were avoided;
(4) the government's good housekeeping of previous years provided it with the space to take swifter and more effective policy responses than in previous episodes of external shocks; and
(5) the balance sheets of the banking, corporate, and household sectors were much stronger.

Chapter 3

IMPACTS ON HOUSEHOLDS INCOMES AND THEIR CRISIS-COPING MEASURES

III.1. TRANSMISSION CHANNELS

Theoretically, the 2008/09 crisis as a world demand or export crisis would affect household incomes through both direct and indirect channels. Through direct channels the impact on households is linked directly to crisis-affected firms, either as employers/owners or employees. Whereas, through indirect channels (i.e. indirect effects) the impact of the decline in production or export of the crisis-direct-affected firms on household incomes in other related firms via local/regional income multiplier effects. Thus, households who have no direct income links with the firms directly hit by the crisis may also experience drops in their incomes if the crisis-direct-affected firms have strong links with the rest of the local/regional economy. Especially if crisis-direct-affected firms in a region are the main engine for the growth of the regions' economy/income through regional/local economic linkages, the crisis-direct impacting the firms would also become a crisis for other linked (directly and indirectly) economic activities in the region. The impact of the crisis on other firms (or sectors) will take place through three transmission channels, i.e. production, consumption, and investment-saving (Figure III.1).

With respect to the production linkage effect: the decline in production in the crisis-direct affected firms would reduce intermediate demands from the firms to other firms in backwards/upstream sectors producing raw materials and other inputs as well as intermediate supply from the firms to other firms in forward/downstream sectors producing finished goods. It also would reduce demands from the crisis-direct affected firms for services such as marketing, distribution, communication and transportation provided by other firms. Consequently, households depending on incomes from those firms linked to the crisis-direct affected firms would also suffer reductions in their incomes. The production linkage effects, and hence, the multiplier effects of the crisis, would be greater if the crisis-direct affected firms do not import raw materials or other inputs from outside the region.

With respect to the consumption linkage effect: households suffering income loss from the crisis-direct affected firms would reduce their consumption (or some components of it) as the result of their crisis-coping measures. It means that demand for consumption goods and services would decline and hence, local production of those goods and services would also decline (with the assumption that no imports of consumption goods take place). Consequently, revenues and employment in firms producing those goods and services would also drop, with further results, decline more in local production, and the process would keep going on and on. Thus, the household incomes decline in the crisis-direct affected firms would create a negative multiplier income effect on the local economy, which by definition is a sum of direct and indirect effects of the household income decline in the first group of firms. Here, the income multiplier effect would be greater if all consumption goods and services are local production.

With respect to investment-saving linkage effect: less revenues in crisis-direct affected firms and less income earned by employees in the enterprises would reduce total investments and household savings in the particular region. Total investment consists of investment by the crisis-direct affected firms and other firms in other sectors and by households. Less investment by the crisis-direct affected firms means less production or no production expansion of the enterprises whereas, less investment by other enterprises in other sectors means less production in the other sectors as well thus, in overall, less total production or income growth in the region while less household savings would result at the end in less bank credit supply and investment in the region since no funds in local banks or other financial institutions would available to be used as credits for businesses or consumption purposes. Here also, the effects would be greater if no capital out-and inflows take place, meaning that firms' revenues and households' savings are invested locally and business and consumption credits are from internal sources.

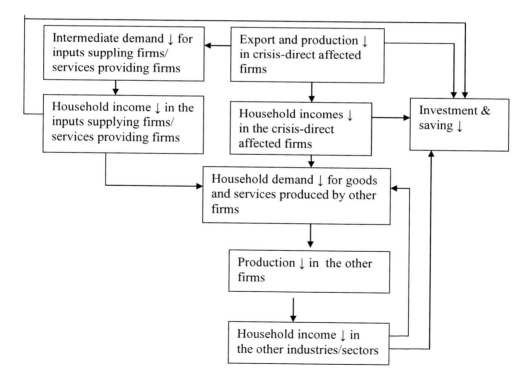

Figure III.1. Direct and Indirect Effects of Household Incomes Decline of Employees and Employers in the Crisis-Direct Affected Firms.

Table III.1. Changes in Weekly Working Hours Experienced by the Head of the Surveyed Households (HH) in Indonesia during the Crisis, May-November 2009

Classification	May to August	August to November	May to November
National	-1.3	0.6	-0.8
Rural	-1.5	1.1	-0.5
Urban	-1.1	0.0	-1.1
Non-poor	-1.3	0.3	-1.0
Poor	-1.5	1.8	0.3
Head of HH:			
Male	-1.4	0.4	-1.0
Female	-1.1	2.4	1.2

Source: World Bank (2010c).

III.2. EVIDENCE FROM VARIOUS SURVEYS/CRISIS MONITORING ACTIVITIES IN INDONESIA

III.2.1. WB-BPS (Crisis Monitoring and Response System/CMRS)

With the unpleasant experience of the 1997/98 crisis when the Indonesian government in that time was really not prepared and thus was seriously failed to response quickly and effectively, and with the prevailing Indonesian economic condition by the end of 2008, the Indonesian government has established a Crisis Monitoring and Response System (CMRS) to understand how the crisis is transmitted to households, how households are responding, and what their socio-outcomes are. The initiative was carried out by the Indonesian National Planning Agency (Bappenas) and National Statistics Agency (BPS) in partnership with the World Bank Office Jakarta, with financial support from the Australian Government Overseas Aid Program (AusAID) (World Bank, 2009b,c).

For this purpose, the World Bank has developed an analytical framework which has 5 subsequent processes: crisis, effect on the labor market, effect on household economics, coping mechanisms, and outcomes. Start from process 1, the crisis has immediate/direct effects on the labor market (process 2), which reflected in the forms of labor force reduction, increase in unemployment, reduction in working hours, and reduction in wages/income. The affected labor market then affected household economics (process 3) in the forms of reduced household income, more difficulties meeting everyday living expenses, and higher costs for food, transport, education and health. The affected households then took crisis-adjustment measures (process 4) and the coping mechanisms range from entering the labor force or opening own businesses in the informal sector, lowering consumption or changing consumption structure, financial solution (e.g. using savings to meet living expenses), to receiving government assistances. Finally, the outcomes (process 5) of the crisis and coping measures, e.g. school dropout or absenteeism, increase in poverty or become poor, and deterioration in health condition (WorldBank, 2009b).

Thus, based on the analytical framework, with respect to the transmission channels, three possible changes were monitored and analyzed: employment by sector, region (urban-rural; district (*kabupaten/kota*); and provinces), and channel (i.e. wages, working hours); prices of staple foods and other commodities; and government spending in ministries and by types. Prices of a number of staple foods had been included in the analysis due to the fact that since July 2009, households have faced increasing food prices (although there was no strong evidence that the increase of food prices was related to the crisis). This has made considerable pressure on household expenditures, particularly for the poor, for whom food represents almost 75 percent of their consumption. With respect to the impact, three issues were addressed: the response of households to the crisis, their adopted coping mechanisms, and the development outcomes of the crisis.

The World Bank has identified/developed a total of 31 indicators to monitor, addressing the transmission mechanisms, coping strategies, readiness for response, and outcomes, and identified potential data sources. The indicatos were aggregated into three indices: labor market, household economics, coping strategies, and indicators relating with important components of the national and provincial pictures. Data for some of these 31 indicators was gathered from existing sources, while data for other indicators were collected via a quarterly, nationwide, district-level household survey (World Bank, 2010b,c).

The main objective of the CMRS was to generate data indicating the impact of the crisis in Indonesia over the course of three quarters beginning April 2009 through three rounds of data collection. More specifically, the CMRS focused on identifying and quantifying negative changes in the situation of households on a quarterly basis. The aim was to produce quarterly national and provincial estimates of the 31 indicators and their changes, to identify districts that appear to have become at risk socio-economically due to the effect of an economic crisis such as the 2008/09 crisis (World Bank, 2010b).

The CMRS used both existing data from BPS (and other official sources) such as existing survey data on wages and administrative data on key health indicators, and new data in its assessment. But, the most important component of CMRS was the CMRS household survey, which was a new quarterly household survey conducted by the BPS (World Bank, 2010b). The CMRS survey consisted of four rounds. The first round was conducted in August 2009, alongside the National Labor Survey (SAKERNAS), and November 2009. The third and final round of the survey began in February 2010 (alongsisde SAKERNAS). Per round, it covers 471 districts (i.e. Kabupaten/Kota) in 33 provinces. Per district, it covers 30 households.[1] Thus, in total there were 14,130 households in the sample plus 2,826 government health care institutes (471 at district level/*Dinas Kesehatan*, and 2,355 at subdistrict level/*Puskesmas*) Each round has the same household (panel sampling). Given the limited time and resources, only head of household labor market outcomes were asked in the CMRS survey, using the same questions as SAKERNAS uses (World Bank, 2010b).

Their most important findings of the first two rounds are the following (World Bank, 2010b):[2]

1) many households during mid-2009 experienced a drop in head of household working hours that adversely affected their incomes. From May to the begining of August 2009, weekly working hours fell by approximately 1.3 hours on national average, and it occurred slightly more in rural areas than urban ones. Working hours were also down year-on-year to August 2009, compared to SAKERNAS data for August 2008,

---

[1] Lot Quality Assurance Sampling (LQAS) was used to select the households This is a sampling method which can only be used for a very small sample size (World Bank, 2009a,b; BPS, 2009).

and relatively flat for the period February-August 2009.[3] This decline cannot be explained by seasonality alone; there were many other determinants, and the crisis was one factor among them. At constant wages, this decline represents almost a 5 percent drop in household income and a majority of the sampled households perceived their incomes to be lower to some extent than three months ago. This 5 percent decline was broadly similar for poor and non-poor households in the sample. However, the effect on household real financial condition may be significant different between poor and non-poor households. For non-poor households, this 5 percent decline was not seen as a big shock, but poor households may have experienced it as a significant adverse outcome of the crisis, especially since it occurred at the same time with the increasing food prices. By late 2009, however, working hours had partially recovered and households in the sample no longer reported having difficulties in meeting their consumption costs (Table III.1). Within the sampled households, female headed households recovered more quickly; they regained more hours than male heads;

2) the proportion of households having difficulty meeting daily consumption costs increased by approximately 3 percent during the same period. But, when poor and non-poor households are examined separately, the proportion of poor households has been found to have increased faster, namely by almost 6 percent. In response to higher food prices[4] and lower income, many households, especially amongst the poor, substituted their staple food (mainly rice) for one of lower cost or quality items, or substituted their main food accompanying rice (generally a protein such as meat or fish). This coping strategy was twice as common in rural than in urban households, probably, as one explanation, because low cost foods were more available in rural than in urban areas. As compared to households headed by males, those headed by females experienced more difficulties in meeting their consumption needs (Figure III.2) and were more likely to substitute staple food items and main food accompanying rice. This may not come as a surprise, especially in developing countries such as Indonesia where, in general, women have more difficulties finding well paid employment opportunities than their male counterparts. Furthermore, no households across poor and non-poor and in both rural and urban areas have been found to have reduced rice consumption to deal with increasing difficulties in meeting everyday living expenses. This change in households' spending on food may be a consequence of the crisis, but it is difficult to disentangle from other possible causes (e.g., seasonality or events such as national elections in 2009);

3) what is more interesting from the survey is that extreme coping mechanisms, even among the poor, such as sending their children into the labor force (having children

---

[2] For more detail, see World Bank (2010c).

[3] SAKERNAS data also shows that working hours for heads of households were relatively the same between February and August 2009 (0.2 hours difference), whereas they were 0.8 hours increase between February and August 2008. See World Bank (2009c).

[4] Several months before the crisis, the price of a number of basic commodities such as rice, sugar, cooking oil, etc. had already increased due to the increase of fuel price, although the rate of the increase varied by provinces or even districts within provinces or sub-districts within district, due a number of factors, including transportation costs, accessibility and stock. In many villages even before the crisis, a number of food items as well as energy sources, such as kerosene and gas in the size of 3 kg, aside from being expenses, were also unavailable in the market which caused higher prices.

drop-out or absenteeism from school) to boost failing household incomes and significant cuts in their education and health expenditures have not been apparent in both rural and urban areas. The proportion of households having at least one child working across rural and urban areas remained unchanged between April and July 2009, although the proportion of households with child workers were more than twice as high in rural than in urban areas. Their healthcare and education affordability also remained more or less constant. Similarly, transportation expenditures were also unchanged;

4) there was little change in the unemployment or labor force participation rates for heads of households. In other words, no heads of households in the sample were found to had been laid off and also no evidence on the change in the proportion of poor as well as non-poor households across urban and rural areas with members working. Nor was there a change in the proportion of poor and non-poor households in both rural and urban areas with a female member working;

5) around 5 percent of households indicated some outward migration over the survey period, more from rural households than urban ones. About 1 percent of households indicated inward migration, and this result is roughly the same in rural as urban households. However, it is still not clear whether the found patterns of out-and inward migrations were a continued trend related to the crisis or can be considered as a normal trend (due to seasonality), since there is not enough data available to show the long-term trend of migration in 'normal' time;

6) many of the sampled households that experienced less income used savings or sold property and assets to meet living expenses, although the proportion was much lower for poor than non-poor households since the poor ones normally do not have the capacity to save and assets or property with high market values to sell. Also, many of the surveyed households have been found to borrow from relatives/family or friends/neighbors;

7) formal and informal nominal wages remained steady for most workers in both urban and rural areas. However, real wages decline caused by increased inflation, especially higher food prices, and the decline varied between rural and urban areas;

8) regions experienced the impact of the crisis differently, both in labor market indicators (head of working hours and unemployment) and household hardship indicators (including the subjective perceived change in household income compared to a quarter ago, the change in the proportion of households reporting difficulty meeting consumption costs, and the change in the proportion of households reporting substitution of a lower quality or cost food).[5] Some provinces were largely unaffected, some saw a deterioration in conditions from May to August 2009 but had recovered by November 2009, while others saw continued or lagged deterioration. The most affected provinces over the period May-November 2009 were Lampung,

---

[5] With respect to the labor market indicators, the quarterly provincial changes of the indicators were compared to the national average, and based on that, provinces were determined as reflecting the national impact (decline in head of working hours, little change in unemployment), a more adverse effect than the national impact (greater decline in head of working hours or increased unemployment), or small adverse effect. Regarding the household hardship indicators, the same method was applied and provinces were categorized as similar to the national impact (reduced household income, greater difficulty meeting consumption costs, increased substitution of lower quality or cost foods), greater than the national impact (a more adverse change on one more of the indicators), or lower than the national impact (less adverse changes) (World Bank, 2010b).

West Nusa Tenggara (NT) and Gorontalo, followed by North and West Sumatra, Kepulauan Riau, Banten, Bali, East Kalimantan and Central and South Sulawesi. The least affected over the six months were South Sumatra and Bengkulu (Figure III.3). Based on this, it is expected that different regions may be recovering from the crisis at different rates;

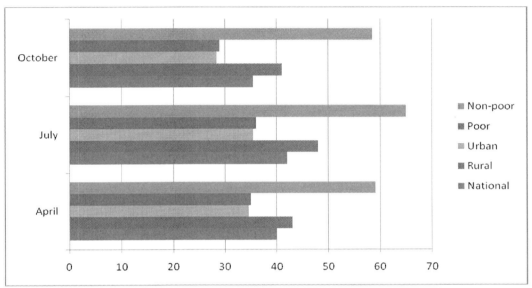

Source: World Bank (2010c).

Figure III.2. Difficulties in Meeting Consumption Costs of the Surveyed households in Indonesia during the Crisis, April-October 2009 (% of total surveyed households).

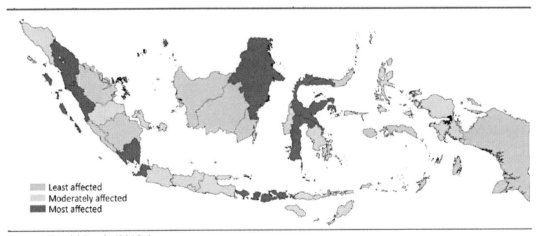

Source: World Bank (2010c).

Figure III.3. Provincial Variations Based on the Impact of the Crisis on the Surveyed HHs in Indonesia, May-November 2009.

III.2.2. JICA-ICASEPS (Financial Crisis Monitoring Survey)

Japan International Cooperation Agency Indonesian office (JICA-RI) conducted quarterly surveys in some rural villages in several provinces between June 2009 and December 2010 in collaboration with the Indonesian Center for Agriculture Socio Economic and Policy Studies, Ministry of Agriculture (ICASEPS). The main aim of the JICA-ICASEPS survey was to monitor and analyze the impact of the 2008/09 crisis on rural households in Indonesia. The survey mainly focused on labor, farmers, child schooling, income, and consumption expenditure of the households. The same sample of households was revisited every three months during that period. In June 2009, it covered 100 households in 10 villages in only two provinces: Central Java and South Sulawesi, and in October-November 2009, the survey's sample expanded to cover 300 households in three provinces: Central Java, South Sulawesi and Lampung.

The selected provinces and villages should have the following features: (i) rural economy characteristics (i.e. overall agrarian and produce/export agricultural commodities); (ii) infrastructure conditions (sufficient vs. insufficient); and (iii) spatial mobility (migration) of the people (high vs. low). Thus, Central Java was selected for its proximity to Jakarta and its better infrastructure condition, also for its more diversified composition of manufacturing industries, while the other two regions were selected for their variety in rural-based production activities (they do not have a strong base in manufacturing). In agricultural commodities, Central Java is among main production centers of rice, while the other two provinces depend much on estate crops and fishery (Subandoro and Yamauchi, 2009). The sample for June 2009 survey was derived from the survey 'Effects of Physical Infrastructure Development on Poverty Alleviation and Human Capital Outcomes in Indonesia' conducted in 2007 by JICA-RI in collaboration with IFPRI and ICASEPS (JICA-RI & ICASEPS, 2009, and Muto and Shimokoshi, 2009a,b).[6]

In order to refine the survey design and implementation plan of the quarterly surveys during that period, and also to conduct a quick survey on the effect of the crisis, JICA-RI together with ICASEPS had conducted a pre-test in June-August 2009.[7] In this pre-test, provinces chosen were Central Java and South Sulawesi with 5 villages per province with a total of 100 sample households (50 households per province).[8] Based on a panel dataset of 100 rural households in 10 villages in Central Java and South Sulawesi from the pre-test survey in June 2009 and the survey in 2007, Muto and Shimokoshi (2009a,b) made a rapid analysis, and their main important findings are the following:

(1) the majority of households were rice/paddy farmers, and the remaining households produced cabagge, shallot, tobacco, coffee, and weakly cacao. However, the

---

[6] The 2007 survey covered more than 200 households in 98 villages in 7 provinces (Lampung, Central Java, East Java, South Kalimantan, West Nusa Tenggara, North Sulawesi, and South Sulawesi). This 2007 survey was designed to overlap with villages in the 1994-5 National Farmer's Panel (PATANAS) survey conducted by ICASEPS to build household panel data (Muto and Shimokoshi, 2009b).
[7] Although this activity was technically a pre-test, it constituted an integral part of the monitoring of the effects of the crisis against poverty reduction (JICA-RI & ICASEPS, 2009).
[8] In the province of Central Java, the villages were Sitanggal, Mojo Agung, Kwadungan Gunung, Cepogo and Karang Wungu and the districts were Brebes (subdistrict: Larangan), Pati (Trangkil), Temanggung (Kledung), Boyolali (Cepogo), and Klaten (Karang Dowo). In the province of South Sulawesi, the villages were Teromu,

importance of each of these agricultural commodities varied by villages in the sample. For instance, in the Sitanggal village, the main agricultural commodities were paddy and shallot, while in Majo Agung village, they were cassava, sugar cane and paddy; both villages are in Central Java. During the survey period, those producing those commodities were found to have a hard time because the market prices for their products declined, although the declined prices varied among the regions due to a number of factors including transportation. However, there is no strong evidence that can be used to claim that the declined prices was strongly related to the crisis. A price declines can be simply a reflection of excess supply (with demand constants) or less demand (with no change in supply/production) in the market, and this can be attributed to many factors nothing to do with the 2008/09 crisis such as seasonal factors (depending on particular commodity) and short-term distortions in the production side (e.g. El Nino climate phenomenon);

(2) among the 100 sampled households, 39 experienced a decrease, while the remaining 61 households experienced an increase of total income per capita between between 2007 and 2009. The change in income per capita, however, varies by regions: those households with declining incomes were found more in Central Java, i.e. 28 households and 11 households in South Sulawesi. Many factors can be assumed to have attributed to the change and variation between the provinces, which may include province-specific trends and seasonality;

(3) main sources of incomes were agriculture (as farmers or laborer), non-agriculture (e.g. industry, transportation, trade and services), self employment (own businesses) and remittance (from other regions within Indonesia or abroad). Among these sources, agriculture was the dominant one, and total farm incomes mainly come from crop income, livestock/poultry, ponds/brackish water and fishery. But the share of this sector in total incomes of the sampled households declined overtime, and non-agricultural sectors have become more important in 2009. During the period 2007-2009, those households with decreasing incomes, on average, experienced a sharp drop in agricultural income at almost 97 percent. Employment income in non-agricultural sector also decreased but only around 8 percent. Although the proportion of remittance in total income of the sampled households having members worked abroad or in other provinces within the country is small on average, the share of this income source in households experiencing decline in their incomes in South Sulawesi had increased sharply, i.e 520 percent in real terms, resulting in 45.6 percent increase in total incomes in 2009. This comparison data survey between 2007 and 2009 suggests that the reduced households' total income was a result of losses in agricultural and non-agricultural employment incomes. However, it is hard to conclude whether the decline was related with the crisis. No evidence from the survey which shows main causes of the decline of agricultural and non-agricultural incomes from agricultural as well as non-agricultural sectors;

(4) with respect to the households with increased incomes were found more in South Sulawesi (39 households) than in Central Java (22 households). Those households, on average, experienced a sharp increase in agricultural incomes (466 percent) as

---

Pancakarsa, Kado, Pallameang, and Mattirotasi. The districts and subdistricts were East Luwu (Mangkutana), Tana Toraja (Rantepao), and Pinrang (Mattirosompe).

well as self-employment incomes (636 percent). The amount of remittance was also found to have increased. Incomes from non-agricultural employment increased very slightly during that period. Again, from the results, it is still difficult to say that the crisis was the main contributor to the increased incomes;[9]

(5) although the share of non-agricultural employment income in total incomes of the sampled households increased by almost 7 percent from 46 percent in 2007 to 49 per ent in 2009, the number of households engaged in this activity decreased by almost 29 percent from 35 to 25 percent, and the decrease was found larger in Central Java where manufacturing industries are more developed and diversified than in South Sulawesi where the economy is still dominated by agriculture. Based on this finding, Muto and Shimokoshi (2009b, page 3) suggests that non-agricultural employment activities were negatively affected by the crisis which reduced job opportunities in the proximity of Jakarta while Subandoro and Yamauchi (2009, pages 6-7) argue that *it is not possible to disentangle this change into factors that could be attributed to changes in export market conditions and/or province-specific trends (due to other reasons than manufacturing exports) with the data from two points in time... .* Thus, no strong evidence to support this view that the crisis had been the main cause;

(6) self-employment income not only increased sharply (as mentioned in point 4), but its share in total incomes also increased significantly by almost 80 percent from 15.7 percent in 2007 to 28.2 percent in 2009. The number of households in the sample engaged in this activity also increased, though only slightly at around 10.5 percent from 19 percent in 2007 to 21 percent in 2009. A number of micro enterprises (mainly from the category of self-emplotment activity, which is often called as "one-man" business unit: unit without workers/helpers, only rum by the owner) often increase during an economic downturn which reduces job opportunities in the formal sector, as unemployed individuals open their own businesses as a means to survive. Thus, the increases in incomes and number of households engaged in self-employment activities may support this view. As stated in the report (Muto and Shimokoshi, 2009b, page 4), *this suggests that self-employment income may have played a large role in increasing total income as a part of coping strategy.* However, it was found that the importance of this activity as a crisis-coping strategy varies by the studied regions; it seems to be stronger in Central Java where the share of self employment income increased nearly 227 percent from almost 22 percent to 72 percent between the studied period;

(7) around 14 percent of the sampled households received remittances, and majority of remittances were from domestic migrants sent to their parents or families. On average, the amount of remittances per capita increased by almost 12 percent from 12 percent in 2007 to 23 percent in 2009. In the past few years, the young and newly educated migrate has become an important part of long-term trend of migration (within Indonesia as well as abroad) in the surveyed regions, and this in fact, reflects

---

[9] Using data from this survey and with a simple model, Subandoro and Yamauchi (2009) found that change in total farm income has a negative and statistically significant effect on net remittance (i.e. the difference between remittances received from household/non-household members and contribution given (sending) to household/non-household members). This means that a lower total farm income increases net remittances. This result can be interpreted that when total farm is higher, less need for remittances or higher financial contribution to other member/non-member.

the national trend. However, of the sample there were also households (11 in Central Java and 8 in South Sulawesi) who experienced a drop in remittances over the two years. It was also found that 12 households with returning migrants, who returned between 2007 and 2009 (most of them returned during 2008), as compared to 23 households with continuing migrants. During the pre-test survey in June 2009, the heads of households with returning migrants were asked the reason for returning, and most answers were, as expected, 'lost job'. Whereas, with respect to the continuing migrants, it can be easily assumed that they continued to be employed (in formal or informal sector) or staying in urban areas while searching for a job. The returning migrants include highly educated young people, but mostly with less experience. On average, the returning migrants had education of 10.67 years, only slightly higher than the average education level of continuing migrants. However, the findings suggest that in Central Java, highly educated migrants but with less experience were more likely to return as compared to their counterparts in South Sulawesi. With respect to continuing migrants, on average, they had 10.26 years of education, and this level has been found to be similar among the two provinces. From the findings, education and experience seem to be very important in affecting the job status (full time/part time, seasonally, contract/permanent/based on orders, etc.) of the migrants, and in its turn, the job status appears to be a strong determinant distinguishing between returning and continuing migrants. It was found that about 33 percent of returning migrants were in full time job, compared to 73 percent of continuing migrants. The latter varied, however, between the two regions: in Central Java it was 87 percent and 66 percent in South Sulawesi. It can be assumed that the returning migrants were directly or indirectly affected by the slowdown of the urban economy caused by the crisis. But, again, no strong evidence to support this assumption because, even in a normal situation, many countries always experience increasing unemployment suggesting that besides economic growth, other factors, especially education and experience are also crucial determinants of employment opportunities;[10]

(8) based on residence location of migrants, they can be divided into two main types: domestic migrant and international migrants. The former type can be further distinquished into several components: within village, within sub-disctrict, within district, within province, and within Indonesia (outside the province). The main important destination for domestic migrants is Jakarta, while for international migrants, destnation is Arab Saudi, followed by Singapore, Malaysia and Hong Kong China. From the sample, the majority of migrants went outside the province; although the rate varied between Central Java and South Sulawesi. Working abroad seems not to be the first choice for most of the returning as well as continuing migrants, and this structure of migration by location of destination did not appear to change during the crisis period;

(9) in Central Java, the number of absent days from school during the last three months to June 2009 due to illness was greater in sampled households with decreasing incomes than those with increasing incomes, i.e. 2.17 days versus 1.45 days. In South

---

[10] The survey also found some households in the sample with members who started migration in between 2007 and 2009. Most of them migrated during 2008. Their average level of education was 9.22 years and they were

Sulawesi, it was greater in the case of remittance decreasing households than increasing ones, i.e. 2.17 days versus 0.16 days. This finding may support a general view that an economic crisis is associated with children health deterioration and school drop out or absenteeism through decreasing household incomes.

III.2.3. SMERU-IDS

In January 2009, the United Kingdom Department for International Development (DfID) commissioned the Institute of Development Studies (IDS) in Sussex University (United Kingdom) to conduct a rapid/pilot study of the impacts of the food, fuel and the 2008/09 crisis on poor developing countries. This approach was qualitative and participatory, and research took place in rural and urban communities in Bangladesh, Indonesia, Jamaica, Kenya and Zambia (IDS, 2009). This pilot study aimed to provide a qualitative assessment on how the 2008/09 crisis has affected the people's lives, particularly the poor, and how they cope with the crisis. Specifically, the study aimed to (i) provide a rapid report on the situation that can communicate to policymakers and a global audience the urgency of the impact of the crisis on poor communities in developing countries, and (ii) develop and test a methodological approach and tools that were used to extend qualitative monitoring in 2009. For the research in Indonesia, SMERU Research Institute was given the task (Fillaili, et al., 2009, McCulloch and Grover, 2010).

The impacts and responses assessed in this study include: (i) livelihoods and employment (migration and remittances, formal and informal sector employment, prices of production, inputs, and travel), (ii) household consumption, productive and human capital investment (health and education spending); (iii) inter-and intra-household relations and dynamics, social cohesion, and impacts on gender and inter-generational relations; (iv) official state, civil society or informal institutional social protection mechanisms (state safety nets, church or mosque charity, loans or grants provided by non-government organizations (NGOs), neighborhood, kin group or community support networks); and (v) perceptions and experiences of insecurity, including concerns about crime and social and political unrest (Fillaili, et al., 2009).

The study was based on two timed visits (Fillaili, et al., 2009). The first one was one week of field study in February 2009 in two villages, i.e. one rural village, Simpang Empat, in the district of Banjar in the province of South Kalimantan and one urban village Gandasari, in the district of Bekasi (just outside the capital city Jakarta) in the province of West Java. The second one was a 4 day visit to the same village in West Java in August 2009. The two villages were selected on the basis that they were likely to be affected by the crisis due to the following resons (McCulloch and Grover, 2010, page 6). With respect to Simpang Empat, most of its area is a rubber plantation, owned by local small-holder farmers. Most villagers support themselves by collecting rubber sap, as land owners, working on others' land, as farm laborers, or by working in coal exploration and as drivers in local transportation. Rubber and coal were among a number of agricultural and mining commodities which experienced a

---

significantly younger than the continuing migrants.

significant decline in their world market prices starting around October 2008. [11] As the decline was assumed to be related to the crisis, it was then expected that many villagers in Simpang Empat would be badly affected by the crisis.

The selection of Gandasari was simply because it is located near a big industrial park known as East Jakarta Industrial Park, home to over 170 mostly large Japanese, Korean and American automotive and electronic companies with a total employment of around 73,000 employees and with a lot of migrant workers from many other villages in various provinces (East, Central, and Wes Java, and Sumatra) who reside in the village. Automotive and electronic manufacturing industries were most severely affected by the crisis,[12] and thus ,in that time, it was expected that the migrant workers would be seriously affected by the crisis.

Three methods of collecting data/information of the impacts and responses were adopted during the field studies: (1) a series of in-depth interviews with formal village elites (heads and other officials), local informal leaders, local businessmen/ economic agents, local government officials (at district and subdistrict), program/assistance implementers (Indonesian government, international, local NGOs, etc.), and households; (2) focus group discussion (FGDs) at two levels: (a) village level with village elites, *dusun* representatives, village officials, community informal leaders, teachers, health cadres, etc.; and (b) community level (around 4 FGD per village) with crisis impacted groups (women and men, youth group and children); and (3) direct observations (transect walk) with the main aim to observe current living conditions, working environment, public facilities, and other relevant issues. Data/information collected includes: (i) changes in prices of consumables and products as well as in social and economic activities in the last year (2008), and the magnitude of the changes compared to conditions during the 1997/98 crisis; (ii) household responses and coping strategies; (iii) responses by the government, NGOs, and the community; and (iv) perceived impacts on social life, security, and intra-household relations (Fillaili, et al., 2009).

The most important findings from the field studies in these two villages (Fillaili, et al., 2009, McCulloch and Grover, 2010) are the following:

(1) in Simpang Empat village, where the local community has been heavily dependent on rubber plantations and coal exploration to make a living, the sharp fall in the prices of these commodities in the world market, accompanied with lower world demand for these commodities, have caused through production and demand linkage effects a significant decline in the incomes of farmers, laborers, traders, truck drivers, and workers in other supporting sectors. It was found that as the first impact of the decline in rubber prices, income of rubber farmers, both owners and workers, had declined sharply to a level which was only 30 to 40 percent of their pre-crisis income level. For instance, the average income for plantation owners per day and per ha young rubber tree was between Rp 75,000 and Rp 85,000 after October 2008 as compared to Rp 200,000 6 months ago. The income of a truck driver per rit for rubber was Rp 500.000 before and between Rp 100,000 and Rp150,000 after the

---

[11] For instance, the world price of rubber in rupiah was Rp 3,700/kg in 2005 and much higher in September 2008 at Rp 11,200/kg. In October 2008, it fell significantly to Rp2,500/kg and improved very slightly to Rp3,750/kg in January-February 2009 (Fillaili, et al., 2009).

[12] Official reports, quoted from Fillaili, et al. (2009) have stated that some companies have closed. Other companies were taking measures to improve efficiency, economizing production, reducing electricity use, reducing overtime

decline of rubber price while for coal truck drivers, on average, until September 2008, they received Rp 1,100,000 per trip, which then fell to Rp600,000, Rp400,000, and in February 2009 it was between Rp200,000 and Rp 250,000. Their trip also declined from on average two trips transporting coal per day to only one trip per every two days at the most;

(2) in Gandasari village, adjacent to the industrial park, the fall in the demand for automotive, electronic, and other consumer goods has led to a reduction in working hours at many factories, reduction of additional benefits/bonuses, temporary/permanent layoffs, and terminations of jobs for contracted workers. Overall, there was a reduction in employment and it was estimated that around 10 percent of permanent workers had been laid off and approximately 40 percent of contract workers were not having their contracts renewed again. This employment condition has had a serious impact on the local economy in the village: (a) many owners of dormitories had experienced a big loss in their incomes from renting rooms as many laid off workers went back to their home town or moved to another area to look for jobs (before the crisis, the level of occupancy in these dormitories reached 100 percent, but then dropped significantly during the crisis); (b) as the buying power of the community declined due to the laid offs of many workers, the profits from the stalls selling basic necessities also dropped by 50 to 70 percent compared to previous profits before October 2008; (c) incomes/profits of *ojek* drivers (informal local public transport by motorcycle or called motorcycle taxi) also declined from Rp80,000-Rp100,000 per day in May 2008 to Rp40,000-Rp50,000 per day in August 2008, and fell further to only Rp15,000 per day. Before the crisis, the total number of *ojek* in the village had reached 600 motorcycles, and it declined significantly after October 2008; and (d) demand for rental cars (to take workers to and from the factory) also declined gradually between May-October 2008 from on average six days to four days per week. The price for renting a car also declined by approximately 30 percent between July-October 2008;

(3) there little change in the workforce, especially in Simpang Empat village, because the type of work available during the crisis period was relatively consistent. In this village, despite the decline of rubber prices, most of the community did not try to do other jobs or look for new empoyment opportunities because, on one hand, they did not have other skills required by other jobs, while, on the other hand, there was no other options available for them. They still depend on rubber farming or coal mining. There were some households in the village who have diversified their income sources by doing other odd jobs, and many of them have left the village and migrated to other regions;

(4) in both villages, household responses to their declined incomes are similar, namely by changing their daily expenditure patterns and daily live behavior, although the intensity of the change varied by household within the village as well as between the two villages, depending on the seriousness of the decline experienced by individual households. For instance, many of the respondents stated that because of the crisis they cut down their expenditures on unnecessary non-food items such as clothes,

---

hours, and even laying off some workers, especially who did unimportant parts of the production or those who were employed based on short-term contracts.

shoes, and recreations. In Simpang Empat village, the impact seemed to be less serious than that in Gandasari village. However, as in Gandasari village, in Simpang Empat village, many households were found to have sold their valuable things such as jewelry and poultry, and borrowed money from various sources such as local stores/stalls, cooperatives, rubber intermediary traders, plantation owners, relatives, neighbors, informal money lenders, and banks. Many rubber plantation owners were also found to have taken some measures of economizing by reducing the use of fertilizers, pesticides and herbicides. They used to apply these items to their plantation twice a year, but not since the drop of rubber prices. However, despite all these changes, household living pattern in Simpang Empat village had not changed significantly as the consumption needs were still sufficiently fulfilled;

(5) from Simpang Empat village, the decline of household incomes in general, did not cause a reduction in the frequency and amount of meals eaten per day, but they tended to reduce the quality of their eaten foods. However, they managed to fulfill their nutritional intake. In Gandasari village, the picture is slightly different. Here, although the community's eating frequency also had not changed, many households were found to have changed and reduced the volume of their daily food consumption, especially side dishes, and the intensity of this crisis-adjustment strategy varied by different households according to type of employment (i.e. permanent employee, contract-based worker, motorcycle taxi driver, property-owner, car rental owner, farmer and trader);

(6) the health situation of the communities in the two villages has not been affected, but it was apparent that many people, especially the poor, have changed their health service seeking behavior, i.e. instead of going to a medical doctor/private clinics, they go to a community health center (*puskesmas*) that provides cheaper or free medical treatments, which is the result of the regional government policy set some years ago, supported by the central government policy in the form of national health insurance program for low-income communities;

(7) in Simpang Empat village, there have been no incidents of drop-outs from primary, junior, and senior high schools. Also, in Gandasari village, the impact of the crisis on the education of the children of the surveyed households is not evident. These findings were not surprising as they are in line with the national figure showing that the education sector in Indonesia has not been affected that much by the crisis. The report (Fillaili, et al., 2009) gives various reasons for that. First, when the crisis hit the country, students were already at the middle of the first semester, so they did not have to make any big spending such as the admission and school uniform fees. Second, the national government has run a school operational assistance (BOS) program, which exempts students from the school tuition and lends them study books. Besides receiving BOS, the schools also receive assistance from district governments in the form of basic education operational assistance (BOPD). Both of these programs have been found to be effective in reducing the education expenditure burdens of the poor, and have helped the smooth running of the schools'management. Nevertheless, there were some cases where households have changed their childrens' schools to more cheaper ones;

(8) there was no indication that the crisis has resulted in the involvement of school children in labor. The reason is because the crisis has not had an affect on education

of children as mentioned in point 6. All respondents stated explicitly that they would keep their children's attending school despite their financial hardship. For them, childrens' education is still a priority;

(9) there was no indication of an increase in women's participation in economic activities or even as migrant workers to other regions or abroad due to the crisis. According to many of the respondents, work opportunities were hard to find, even before the crisis. They said that the current recruitment system that uses outsourcing companies and the enforcement of the contract system is the main responsible to the difficulties in finding jobs, especially in the formal sector. Some of them said that during the 1997/98 crisis, work opportunities were still available, even in the formal sector it was much easier to find jobs. Thus, based on these explanations, it is hard to state that difficulties in finding work during the period 2008-2009 has to do directly with the crisis;

(10) in Simpang Empat village, household lives were still the same as before the crisis in that there were no cases where domestic violence happened as a result of the crisis. In Gandasari village, the picture was different. Since the crisis began, the social changes most felt by the community have been the increase in criminality and juvenile delinquency. According to the sampled households, problems with finding work, as well as the increase in unemployment due to the crisis were suspected to be two of the factors behind the increased criminal rate especially among youth. They have complained about the youth's behavior in their village such as drunkenness, thug-like activities, and theft, which, according to them, have become obvious since the crisis;

(11) activities such as participation in *arisan*, religious and other social activities declined in frequency. Social cohesion in the two villages was also found to have reduced which led to social exclusion.

III.2.4. SMERU-BAPPENAS

In addition to the above discussed surveys, with the support from the AusAID, SMERU research institute in collaboration with BAPPENAS have carried out a more comprehensive crisis monitoring activity from July 2009 to early 2010 to get a wider picture about the social-economic impact of the crisis. The monitoring was conducted through four activities: 1) media monitoring, (2) community study; (3) quantitative analysis; and (4) case study. Media monitoring has 2 rounds. The first round was conducted during July-September 2009 covered Bandung (West Javaprovince), West Lombok province (NTB), Kampar (Riau province), Jepara (Central Java province), Malang (East Java province) and Bitung (North Sulawesi province) and a number of sectors, including textile and garments (Bandung), fishery and fish processing industries (Bitung), palm oil plantations, and timber and wooden products (e.g. furniture). The second round was conducted during November-December 2009 in the same locations.

The case study was carried out every 4 months. The main aim of the case study was to get a general picture about the impact, implementation and the role of existing social protection programs and other policies to mitigate the impact of the crisis and to support the daily life of the affected households. The case study was conducted using a qualitative method through interviews with all key resource persons/institutes and selected households. The first case study was conducted during August-November 2009 to assess the role of existing social protection programs to mitigate the impact. The second case study was during January-April 2010 to assess the effectiveness of fiscal stimulus, especially labor-intensive programs.

The most important findings are the following(SMERU, 2009a,b,c, Fillaili, 2010):

(1) the most severely affected sectors have been rubber and oil palm plantations; mining, especially coal, iron, metal, nicle, bauxit, aluminium, and marmer; and manufacturing, particularly timber and wooden furniture, textile and garment, automotive, electronic, and handicraft. Households with members working in or having incomes from these sectors had a really hard time during the crisis period. However, some of these sectors have already shown signs of recovery by the end of 2009. The variety in the crisis-recovery process by sector or subsector was determined by differences in many factors, including adopted crisis-coping strategy, availability of capital to cope with the crisis, intensity of the impact on the sector/subsector, and government measures to support particular sector/subsector;

(2) sectors such as plantation, i.e. cacao, coffe, copra, corn, cassava; fish manufactuing industry, and tourism were less or temporarily affected. Many households in these sectors did not feel the impact of the crisis significantly. Some households experienced small and temporary decline in their incomes;

(3) the communities in the sampled regions affected by the crisis were not homogenous, and the severity of the effect felt was also not uniform. The most affected households were the poorest and those lived in industrializing regions or regions with high intensity of land conversion (palm oil plantation). Although the wealthy households, such as business operators, land/plantation/farm owners, and traders, also experienced many losses due to the crisis, most of them still have other resources or excess capital to cope with a downturn of their incomes/revenues. For poor households, especially the poorest ones, such as landless farm laborers, informal laborers doing odd jobs, and taxi motorcycle (*ojek*) drivers, the impact of the crisis was more severe as they have limited assets to cope with the crisis;

(4) The crisis has caused sources of income of women to decline or disappear. This happened especially in handicraft, furniture and garment industries, where the majority of their workers are female. However, many enterprises in these industries were not seriously affected by the crisis, and thus no lay offs of workers took place. In the case of plantation farming of rubber and oil palm, women from farm laborer families were forced to take up odd jobs with a low wage. As compared to their male counterparts, the crisis was felt more severely by women in coping with the crisis due to fact that women in their nature are less mobile and face more social restrictions to do other jobs or to go far from their homes to find other jobs;[13]

---

[13] See Tambunan (2009b) for a comprehensive study on women entrepreneurship in Asian developing Countries. According to the study, women's entrepreneurship in the region is affected by many factors. These factors can be direct or indirect factors. The direct factors include economic pressures and socio-cultural background. The indirect factors include government policies, and stable domestic socio-economic and political conditions. These two groups of factors are related to each other in shaping women's entrepreneurship. The direct factors are often discussed in the literature on women entrepreneurship development in the developing world, especially socio-

(5) for youth, the crisis has led to tighter competition in the labor market. For instance, in many villages in the West Lombok province, it was found that the cessation of pottery production caused many young people to lose their jobs. Previously, they had worked decorating and finishing the pottery. In the furniture industry in Jepara, in the province of Central Java, the youth faced a similar situation due to the crisis. In the oil palm plantation in Kampar, in the province of Riau, job opportunities for youth as daily workers also dropped significantly, and it had become a serious social problem in the region as it has led to an increase in criminal activity. During the peak of the crisis, many of these unemployed youth were becoming "ninjas" (a local term used to refer to masked thieves that stole oil palm or rubber lump from government owned oil palm or rubber plantations);

(6) in the formal sector, the affected industries adopted various coping strategies involving their labor policy. Usually, the first effort was to reduce working hours and cut back on overtime. For permanent staff, temporary lay offs were applied when production was stagnant. The first laborers to be dismissed were those recruited on a contract basis, mostly through an outsourcing company. Some of them did not have their contracts extended, while others had their contracts terminated before the contracted term was complete and did not receive any compensation. Contract workers were usually unemployed between jobs for approximately 1–2 months, but during the crisis, the time between jobs was longer. If these contract workers were lucky, they would get another job in 3–4 months;

(7) in plantation farming businesses, farm laborers who did not own land had been the most severely affected by the crisis because the land owners cut labor costs by firing laborers. The farm laborers were forced to look for other jobs; some tried to find their fortune by entering illegal businesses such as illegal mining; some migrated to other regions, gathered forest products from nearby forests because they were no longer available in the oil palm plantation areas that used to be forests, or did odd jobs with an unstable income;

(8) to cope with the difficult situation caused by the crisis and high inflation (caused initial by the increase in fuel price before the crisis), most households in the villages studied maintained their consumption level of staple food. Families tended to eat less protein or shifted to cheaper sources of protein, and also bought less prepared food. If available, they also collected more vegetables, fruits, and roots from surrounding areas, but during the crisis period, these foods were becoming difficult to find in industrial areas and oil palm plantations. They also purchased goods in smaller quantities or bought them on credit; and this has been supported by fresh food hawkers and local shops that allowed people to buy on credit;

---

cultural background. Among the many social and cultural backgrounds that affect women's entrepreneurship are religion, educational attainment and skills, age, ethnicity and customs, marital status, and geographical location. It is also generally stated that religion affects women entrepreneurs in selecting their type of economic activities. However, no one religion can be said to be more or less supportive of women's access to economic participation. It depends on the context in which religion is placed. In a given group of women in the same setting, however, the type of religious belief may affect why one set of women responds in one way and another does not. Muslim women, for instance, tend to select economic activities which are not forbidden in their religious teaching (e.g. working in pig raising or in alcoholic factories, etc.). For non-muslim women, as in the western countries, the types of business activities do not matter much.

(9) with respect to education, as in the other case studies/crisis-monitoring activities discussed earlier, drop out cases in primary schools were not found significantly. Although the crisis has meant that children get less pocket money from their parents, it has not caused them to be absent from school. Only from some villages in the sample, drop out cases were reported, mainly because the schools were located far from the village, and some poor families could not afford to cover transport and living costs during the peak of the crisis. In general, it can be concluded that the school operational assistance (BOS) program and local government assistance to schools revealed as a significant policy to help affected households/communities to keep their children going to schools at the time of the crisis;

(10) in general, the health condition of the communities in the sampled villages has not changed, although it was found some changes in health service seeking behavior. Many households did not or reduced the visit frequency to private clinics and midwives, even though these private health service providers have lowered their charges. More people were found to have self medicated and bought medicine from a drugstore. The visits to community health centers, on the other hand, have increased;

(11) in Malang (East Java), more than 40 percent of the households have member/s that have worked as migrant workers. It was found that the most affected migrant workers were those who worked in the electronic, automotive, and construction industries in South Korea and Malaysia. Those who worked as domestic workers and who worked in the Middle East have not been affected. Most of the affected migrants did not return home for two main reasons. First, most of them in that time were still working, but with shorter working hours or without the opportunity to work over time. Consequently, their income has dropped and so the remittance has also dropped by around 25 to 50 percent. Some of them have not had their contracts extended, but they were still waiting for the industry to recover because the companies where they worked have requested them to stay in the country and not go back to Indonesia. Second, many of these Indonesian migrant workers were illegal, so if they return home it would be difficult for them to leave again.

III.2.5. AKATIGA-OA

This study was based on a survey aimed to identify changes experienced by rural people in East Nusa Tenggara (NTT) and West Nusa Tenggara (NTB) between the period 1997-2009, with the focus on migration workers. The key question of the research is: has the 2008/09 global economic crisis affected migration workers in those two poorest provinces in Indonesia? Methodologically, the study used various approaches: qualitative research, secondary data (on economic and migration profiles) analysis, indepth interviews (with staffs from non-government organizations (NGO), international development agencies, and researchers at the national and local levels, and also with provincial and district government officials, a two month field survey of 24 both migrant and non-migrant households, and FGD with male and female groups.

The main important finding from this study is that the regions or households in the regions were not affected by the crisis (AKATIGA and Oxfam Australia, 2010). There are three main reasons for that. First, as explained before, the crisis was a world demand crisis which led to the decline in exports of several commodities. Thus, export decline was the most important transmittion channel of the 2008/09 crisis. As Indonesia also exports many of those crisis-affected export commodities, Indonesia was also affected by the crisis. But, factories or sectors producing those commodities are not located in NTT and NTB. Thus, there were no local firms or farms in these two provinces which collapsed or lost their incomes because of the crisis and no lay-offs of employees took place. It was apparently different with the 1997/98 crisis, which did significantly affect the two regions as the rate of inflation in that time increased significantly across the country. Besides the increased inflation rate, NTT and NTB (as many other parts of the country) in 1998 also faced serious food shortages due to several reasons, and the most important ones were long and extremely warm climate (El Nino phenomenon) which caused failure in harvest in many parts of the country and distortions in inter-islands food trade/distribution. Second, most migrants from NTT and NTB worked abroad in non-or less-affected countries like Malaysia and Middle East countries. Third, most households in NTT and NTB live in subsistence levels, not depending on market economy and the regions are not integrated with the global economy (AKATIGA, 2009).

III.2.6. UGM-GRIPS

Two researchers, i.e. Darmawan from the Gadjah Mada University/UGM (Indonesia) and Chikako Yamauchi from the Graduate Research Institute of Policy Studies (GRIPS) (Japan) did a research on the impact of the global crisis on labor market activities of rural-urban migrants in Indonesia. More specifically, it investigated changes in location and labor market activities for native and migrant households. The research question is: did initial condition matter, or whether individuals who were initially at a disadvantaged position (such as casual workers and migrants who recently came from rural areas) more likely to be negatively affected by the crisis? The main reason of doing this research was because aggregate figures on rural-urban migrant workers in Indonesia did not address this particular issue.

The study used panel data drawn from March-May of 2008 and March-May of 2009 rural-urban migration in Indonesia (RUMII) study. The data covers 4 major enclaves of rural-urban migrants: Medan, Tangerang, Samarinda, and Makassar. In this study, a migrant household is defined as the head of household who was born in a rural area and lived in a rural area for five consecutive years before he or she completed elementary school. The RUMI data is rich with socio-economic information of the sampled migrant households, which include labor force participation, industry and employment status for workers, monthly income, household per capita monthly expenditure, educational attainment, health condition, demographic structure of the household and migration history (i.e. non-migrant, lifetime migrant, and recent migrant).

The RUMI data covers 17620 households with the following migration status: 8739 non-migrants, 7568 lifetime migrants (more than 5 years), and 1313 recent migrants (5 years or less). In November and December 2008, this RUMI set of households was tracked by using the following procedures: (1) household/mobile phone, alternative contacts, (2) visits to the original address, (3) ask neighbors for new information if not found, and (4) call new number or visit new address. In 2008, 2364 households were interviewed and 2052 households in 2009, with the focus of the interview being on household heads' labor supply.

The study found that many heads of the interviewed migrant households shifted their jobs from tradable sectors (agriculture, mining, and manufacturing) to non-tradable sectors (e.g. services, transportation), and/or from permanent jobs in private firms in the formal sector to self-employment or unpaid family workers in the informal sector. A possible explanation for this is that labor demand in the formal/tradable sector (in firms affected by the crisis) may have declined because of the crisis. But, the study did not find direct evidence on the impact of the crisis on the well-being of the studied households. Even income of many household heads in the sample was found to have increased significantly. One possible explanation is that the household heads have increased the number of working hours, and/or, labor supply of other household members have also increased (Darmawan and Yamauchi, 2010).

III.2.7. Gap Analysis of the Crisis-Monitoring Activities

As discussed before, different ecomomic crises may have different impacts, different transmission indicators/channels, different crisis-coping measures, different outcomes, and different affected sectors or households or vulnerable groups. In the past 13 years, Indonesia has experienced two big economic crises, namely the 1997/98 Asian financial crisis which had limited effects mainly on Southeast Asia (though some parts of the world also felt the crisis through trade, investment and supply-chain with the region), and the 2008/09 global economic crisis. For Indonesia, the first crisis was the biggest one the country ever experienced since its independence in 1945, or even before that.

As discussed earlier, the 1997/98 Asian financial crisis had its origin in massive capital flight, which started in Thailand, which led to currency crises in some Southeast Asian countries (Thailand, Indonesia, South Korea and the Philippines) and ended as a big financial/economic crisis. Even in Indonesia, it was followed soon by a massive political and social crisis, and then, unexpectedly, a policy reform towards democratization. The evidence shows that the crisis hit the middle and high income groups more rather than the low income group or the poor. The formal sector was more severely affected than the informal sector by that crisis, because the first sector is more integrated than the informal one with the regional/global economy, or more firms in the formal sector than those in the informal one which use foreign currencies and/or depend on banks and other formal financial institutions.

For Indonesia, in analyzing the impact of this type of crisis at meso (sector) and micro (household) levels, the research questions should be the following: First, with respect to a currency (rupiah) crisis: what sectors/subsectors where many firms are dependent much on foreign currencies in their operations (e.g. export-oriented firms, import dependent firms, firms borrowed money from abroad, firms operate in tourism sector)? In which regions (e.g. province, district, subdistrict, village) are those firms located? How are the backward and forward production linkages between those firms and the rest of domestic economy? Second, with respect to a banking crisis, the key research question should be: what sectors where the majority of firms are dependent much on the banking sector for financing their businesses?

With respect to the 2008/09 crisis, for many countries, including Indonesia, it was generally regarded as a world demand crisis (especially from the US and other developed countries), which led to the decline of Indonesian exports of a number of commodities. Depending on the size of the declined world demand for these commodities and their backward and forward linkages (i.e. production, investment and consumption) with the rest of the Indonesian economy, the impact of the crisis on the Indonesian economy or poverty can be very serious or, on the contrary, it can be relatively small or insignificant. Therefore, in this respect, in analyzing the impact of this crisis, the main important research questions should be: which export commodities are most severely affected by the crisis? How are the linkages between these affected export commodities with the rest of the Indonesian economy? In which regions are those sectors producing the affected export commodities and their linked sectors located? How is the impact being transmitted to their workers and households and other related economic formal as well as informal activities?

All the crisis-monitoring activities/surveys discussed above have attempted to examine the impact of the 2008/09 global economic crisis on the Indonesian economy. Although these activities adopted different monitoring strategies or started from different analytical frameworks, they all gave a strong emphasis on unemployment and poverty and coping mechanisms taken by the affected households. Various issues were covered by these surveys, including agricultural and non-agricultural incomes, remittances/migrants, rural-urban households, child labor, formal/informal employment. Regarding the regional coverage, in overall, the surveys cover almost all areas within the country. Based on the summary of their findings discussed above, some important issues need to be taken into consideration for further research.

First, regarding the BPS/World Bank survey, there are some limitations with respect to the indicators proposed. A comprehensive list of indicators (31) is defeating the purpose of their monitoring activity. The future use of the indicators also depends much on the sustained availability of secondary data (e.g. from BPS) and the visibility to conduct a regular national survey similar to the WB/BPS survey to collect data for indicators which have no national data. Moreover, some of the indicators may have correlations with some others, so the 31 indicators need to be redefined or reselected. Concentration on fewer indicators dealing with key aspects of the crisis, instead, may give a clearer picture about the real impact of the crisis and will have less problem with data collection.

With respect to employment, the indicator framework does not give explicit attention to the vulnerability of weak worker groups such as female, low-educated and non-permanent/part-time/casual workers. At least it is not shown in its report (World Bank, 2010c). A study on the impact of the crisis on furniture enterprises in some regions in the West Java and Central Java provinces conducted by GTZ (Tambunan and Ardha, 2009) has found that these weak worker classes were the first victims of labor-adjustment measures adopted by the affected enterprises in coping with the crisis. More female/low-educated/part-time/casual than male/high educated/full time/permanent workers were laid off. SAKERNAS from BPS provides data on employment/unemployment situations in Indonesia by three aspects: level of formal eduation (i.e. no schooling, did not complete primary school, primary school, junior and senior high school, academy and university), gender (female versus male), and status or type of employment (casual, contract, temporary and permanent). which indicate that the annual percentage increase in employment/unemployment varies by these three aspects. Comparing the BPS/World Bank survey's results with SAKERNAS data would therefore provide a better picture about the real impact of the 2008/09 crisis on the employment situation in the country by different classes (education, gender, status, location, etc.). Thus, regarding the employment aspect of the crisis, the key question that the BPS/World Bank crisis-monitoring activity should answer is whether the effect of the crisis on employment varies by level of education, gender and status/type of emploment? This question is especially important when dealing with poverty, because, at least theoretically, laid-off highly educated employees, because of the crisis, have more opportunities to find a well-paid job, even during an economic crisis, than workers who have only primary school. Similarly, though officially there is no gender discrimination in Indonesia, females have more constraints than their male counterparts to find jobs. One hypothesis can be derived from this theoretical thought is that the more low-educated or female employees laid off during an economic crisis, the more likely that the crisis will have a significant impact on poverty, *ceteris paribus*, other poverty determinants are constant.

Moreover, the existing Labor Law in Indonesia gives more incentive to firms to hire new workers on a short-term contract base. Short-term based employment is therefore expected to increase faster than the permanent-based employment. The findings from the above mentioned GTZ study show that during the 2008/09 crisis, 'temporary' or 'contract' workers, rather than 'permanent' employees tend to be the first victim of the crisis-affected firms' labor-adjustment. So, it can be expected that in Indonesia as a whole, during the crisis, dismissal of contract employees was likely to increase faster than that of permanent employees. Therefore, the analytical framework adopted by the BPS/World Bank survey should also disaggregate the employment impact of the crisis by status, i.e. permanent vs. temporary/contract-based employment.

With respect to employment by sector, the BPS/World framework also covers agriculture. However, it is not clear whether in analyzing the impact of the crisis, the employment in the sector is disaggregated by subsector. SAKERNAS has data on employment by main occupation, including agriculture, animal husbandry, forestry workers, fishermen, and hunters. This level is, however, still too aggregate. Disaggregating agriculture by higher digits is therefore, needed and it is crucial for a number of reasons. First, some subsectors are open to the global economy through international trade (export and import), production (regional/global supply/value chain) and investment, while others are more domestic-oriented/isolated from the global economy. Consequently, the outcome of the impact may differ by subsector within the agricultural sector. Second, fishery is the very poor section of the Indonesian population. Based on data from BPS, distribution of poverty in Indonesia by sector (one digit level) shows that the majority of the poor are found in rural areas, and most of them work as farmers or laborers in the agricultural sector. Within the sector, fisheries are the most poor, in contrast to plantations which is the most wealthy subsector. There is, unfortunately, no evidence at the national level on how the impact of the crisis was on the fishery subsector, and especially on fisheries and their households.[14]

---

[14] Evidence available so far is only from SMERU Research Institute, although it is about the impact on the fishing industry, not on fisheries and their households, and only from one location, namely in the North Sulawesi town of Bitung, which is the center of the industry. As stated in its Mesia Monitoring publication, during the study, the industry has 20 canneries as well as businesses that preserve tuna. They employed around 50,000 workers. During the survey, it was found that workers in a number of fish factories were threatened with redundancy because exports of fish products had fallen by approximately 50 percent. One company that employed 300 workers and also 700 fishers who supply fish to the company was found to have been at a standstill since September 2008 because there have been no orders from Japan. The study also finds that activities in the fishing industry in this province decreased drastically between the period October-December 2008, which was claimed as a consequence of the crisis. The media-monitoring publication also states that according to the head of the Fisheries Agency for North Sulawesi, the drop of 40 percent in fish exports from 160,000 tons in 2007 occurred because of a decline in demand for fish in Japan; Republic of Korea; Hong Kong, China; the USA; and in a number of European countries. It stated further that the Agency has received information that dismissals of workers have already taken place (SMERU, 2009a,b,c).

Second, with respect to JICA's survey, it has made an effort to examine the impact of the crisis on rural economy or rural households in particular. The survey attempted to examine the impact not only on agricultural incomes (by subsectors, including crops, plantation, livestock, and fishery), but also on non-agricultural incomes by subsector/activity. To improve the quality of this survey, however, at least the following two issues should be taken into consideration. First, more isolated rural economies from urban areas (centers of economic and financial activities, public utilites and governmentr administration) may have different outcomes of the impact of a crisis than more 'open' rural economy closely located to big cities like Jakarta, Surabaya, Makassar and Medan. Second, agricultural commodities to be included in the survey should be distinguished between 'tradable' and 'non-tradable' commodities, because trade (exports and imports) and investment are two main important transmission channels of an economic crisis.

Finally, with respect to changes in employment as one of the framework's transmission indicators, most of the crisis monitoring activities (except WB-BPS) did not give serious attention to the informal sector, such as undocumented/non-registered firms, which are mainly micro enterprises (MIEs) and small enterprises (SEs), despite the fact that this category of enterprises is the majority (around 99 percent) of total enterprises in Indonesia. It would be interesting to see whether the informal enterprises were differently impacted than the formal ones by the crisis. Thus, any effort to assess the impact of an economic shock on employment should also include not only the formal but also the informal sector in the analysis, and the data collection vehicle should be a combination between a firm survey with an household survey. Thus, the respondent (informal workers and formal employees) is approached from two sides: from his/her household (household survey) and from his/her source (s) of income (firm survey). From household survey, the key question for the respondent should be: are you still working despite the crisis or have you been laid off? If the latter is the case, then the next question should be: has the crisis put you out of job? From the firm survey, the question for the owner should be: has your firm been affected by the crisis and, if yes, have you therefore laid off your workers? Thus, the combination between firm and household surveys acts as a cross-check mechanism to have a better picture about the real impact of an economic crisis on employment.

Two additional issues need to be taken into account in a crisis monitoring activity like the above discussed surveys. The first issue is about outlaying regions in Indonesia such as villages in Kalimantan in Indonesia, located along the borderline with Kalimantan in Malaysia; in Papua along the borderline with Papua New Guinea (PNG); and many small islands in the province of North Sulawesi close to the Philippines. Ideally, these much less developed/isolated/mostly poor regions in Indonesia should be equally covered and deeply examined in the survey for the following reason. Theoretically, it is possible that, because of their isolation or remoteness (at least from the Indonesian side), the regions were not so affected by the 2008/09 global economic crisis (there was also no evidence that the regions were severely affected by the 1997/98 Asian financial crisis). But, it is also possible that outlaying districts in the North Sulawesi province such as Talaud and Sangir islands, which are closer to the Philippines than to market centers in the South Sulawesi province (Makassar and Menado), are, in fact, not isolated at all since they are strongly linked with the markets in Mindanao, the Philippines (Talaud and Sangir import basic needs more from Mindanao or the Malaysia part of Kalimantan than from Java). Consequently, if the Philippine's economy is in a recession, the economy of these two islands can be impacted, although the Indonesian economy is in a good condition. The World Bank/BPS does cover all areas in Indonesia intentionally, but mainly the "well-known" areas which are accessible; while, almost all so-called outlying areas are "unknown" areas with no easy/formal transportation and communication links.

The second issue is about Indonesian overseas workers which should also be given more attention. The AKATIGA-OA survey has focused on this issue and SMERU has covered this matter as well in its crisis-monitoring activities. But because the survey's sample is small, not only in terms of the total number of respondents but also region (AKATIGA-OA covers only two villages and SMERU includes only one village in Malang, East Java), the survey's findings are far from enough to be seen as the representative of Indonesia as a whole regarding the impact of the crisis on Indonesian overseas workers, their related remittances flows, and their families' livelihoods.

Overall, despite some shortcomings discussed above, all of the crisis-monitoring activities provide some evidence about the impact of the crisis at meso and micro-levels which are not covered by macro-level BPS data. Such crisis monitoring activities are indeed needed during a crisis to function as the early or supplementary source of information of the impact of an economic crisis. Besides that, the surveys also offer two other things which may be useful for crisis monitoring activities in the future when new crises strike again. First, crisis-related indicators, such as the 31 indicators proposed by the World Bank/BPS. But, as discussed before, the indicators should be reduced/simplified to focus only on key issues. Second, methods of analysis used by SMERU, such as a combination between media monitoring, in-depth interviews, FGD at village and community levels, direct observations (transect walk), and quantitative analysis can be applied (with or without any modification) to other regions not covered by these surveys. The SMERU's used methods are comprehensive because indepth-interviews accompanied with FGD, media monitoring and direct observations will provide a "cross-check" to the gathered information (qualitative and quantitative).

III.3. CASE STUDY FROM INDONESIA: IMPACTS ON HOUSEHOLDS IN THE FURNITURE INDUSTRY

In addition to the findings of many surveys/crisis monitoring activities discussed above, for this chapter, a household survey has been conducted during July-August 2009, covering 50 households. The households were randomly selected with the following composition by region: 20 households in Cirebon (West Java province), and 11 and 18 households in Jepara and Solo, respectively; both in Central Java Province. These three regions are among production centers of furniture in Indonesia. Although households as respondents were randomly selected, the survey covered only households with the heads or other members who were still working in or have been laid off from enterprises making furniture during the survey period. The main aim of the survey was not only to assess the crisis' impact on households incomes, but also to explore their crisis-coping mechanisms.

III.3.1. General Picture of the Furniture Industry

Indonesia has a rich tradition in woodcarving. Wood furniture and handicraft are part of the Indonesian culture. Many people, especially in Java and Bali are known for their wood-carving skills. That is why the wood furniture business has long known to be the hereditary business in Indonesia. Handcrafted furniture produced by the country has gained worldwide recognition for its exquisite craftsmanship and innovative design. The intricate weaving and woodcarving, low minimum order requirements, and abundant supply of raw materials have made Indonesia one of the major sourcing centers for wooden furniture.

Although the Indonesian furniture is produced from a variety of raw materials, not only wood, but also rattan, swan, plastic, and even iron, wood furniture production and export have been the largest component. According to the Association of Indonesian Furniture and Handicraft (ASMINDO, 2007), wood furniture accounts for three-quarters of the Indonesian total furniture exports, followed by rattan (20 percent), metal, bamboo, plastic and other (5 percent). Wood furniture, together with other wood products, accounted for the lowest 1.3 percent to the highest 1.5 percent of GDP for the period 2004-2009. Annually, the Indonesian wood furniture industry requires timber 4.5 million m3. The main timber species for wood carving are teak, mahogany and sonokeling (*dalbergia latifolia*).[15]

Furniture, together with textile and garment, leather, and food and beverages are labor-intensive manufacturing industries and they have been a key source of wage employment, also for women in rural areas. This fact has made the government very serious in giving support to these industries because they are considered very important not only as a source of foreign currencies but also for employment creation and hence, poverty alleviation. With respect to the furniture industry, BPS data shows that it comprises more than 3,500 companies. The majority of the companies are MSMEs. Many of these enterprises established trading houses and production linkages in the form of subcontracting arrangements with large enterprises (LEs).[16] In Jepara, Roda *et al* (2007) identified a total of 15, 271 enterprises with the composition as follows: 14 091 MIEs and SEs, 871 MEs (medium enterprises), and 309 LEs. According to ASMINDO (2007), the furniture industry employs around four million workers, directly (i.e. working in the industry) and indirectly (i.e. working in supporting industries and other related sectors, e.g. trade and services). This means that the industry has provided living to a significant number of households in Indonesia.

In Indonesia, 14 out of 33 provinces in Java, Bali, Sumatera, Kalimantan, Sulawesi and Papua produce furniture products but for wood furniture, it is concentrated in Java. In Sumatera and Kalimantan, furniture is mainly produced from timber, swan and rattan. In Papua, there is only cluster of timber and swan furniture. Within Java, the wood furniture industry is concentrated in Central Java, notably Jepara, Klaten, Sukoharjo, Semarang City, and Solo, whereas, Cirebon, another important cluster of furniture industry, is known as the largest producer of rattan furniture. Almost half of the total national rattan production is based

---

[15] According to ASMINDO Secretariat, although Indonesia is the world's second largest timber producer, in the last few years, especially after the 1997/98 Asian financial crisis, the shortage of raw materials has become a serious constraint for the growth of the industry.

[16] The subcontracting system has caused the MSMEs in the furniture industry to expand rapidly, at least before the 2008/09 global economic crisis. It stimulated a so-called spin-off in which LEs/exporters also motivate their workers to become independent and work exclusively as subcontractors. Furthermore, contractors usually establish relationships with several subcontractors since the capacity of their subcontractors is usually small. For LEs, working with several subcontractors is also a strategy to reduce default risks (Andadari, 2008)..

in Cirebon. These clusters have grown and can be considered as successful since they link to international markets (Andadari, 2008).

Based on BPS data 2004, Central Java contributed approximately 26.5 percent of national production and about 27.8 percent of the employment in the wood furniture industry. Based on data from the Central Java Industrial and Trade Office for the period 1999-2006, the share of wood export in Central Java's total non-oil exports is fairly constant and highly substantial, i.e. 25-30 percent. Together with clusters of furniture in Surabaya, the most important furniture cluster in the East Java province, furniture clusters in Central Java account for about 40 percent of Java's total exports.

Among the furniture clusters in Central Java, Jepara is the most famous one, locally and worldwide. It is known as the center of Indonesian furniture production. The Jepara cluster has a special position in Central Java because it has the largest share in total production value of furniture in Central Java, and in other aspects, including numbers of employees, exporters, enterprises. Jepara had developed from a rural traditional cluster and began to grow rapidly when it was opened to foreign buyers by the end of the 1970s when foreign tourists started to visit the region (Andadari, 2008). Its reputation has attracted many related economic activities linked to wood production and processing, especially furniture making. Today, Jepara is a typical example of what is called an 'industrial district' in which growth in one sector (furniture manufacturing) has attracted thousands of MSMEs to the district. This, in turn, has created an opportunity for further subsidiary activities and industries.

Many studies on the Jepara furniture industry have been conducted in the past 10 years or more. Among them are Berry and Levy (1994), Schiller (2000), Roda, et al. (2007), Sandee *et al* (2000), Andadari (2008), and the most recent one, Purnomo, *et al.* (2009) who found that with the supports from foreign tourists, furniture producers in Jepara were able to improve their product quality and boost the growth of export significantly, particularly in the period of 1980's. According to them, the annual exports of Jepara furniture reached US$ 150 million, with furniture retailers in Europe, the US, Australia and Japan.

Roda et al. (2007) found that the concentration of industrial activity making a variety of furniture in Jepara has stimulated a substantial economic boom in the region and its surrounding areas and attracted local political supports. For example, the need for container trucks to export furniture led the previous *Bupati* (district administrator) to have some major roads in the district reclassified as 'provincial class' roads. This allowed container trucks to reach most parts of the district, stimulating economic growth by attracting more people and activities, generating new trade and industry, and elevating economic activity around Jepara to a new level. The minimum wage of workers is reputed to be significantly higher in Jepara than in the rest of the province (Schiller 2000).

The dynamic nature of the Jepara industrial complex also affects the Indonesian wood products chain, attracting timber produced from forests located throughout Central Java and beyond, including the outer islands. Thousands of trucks and pickups bring logs into the district from distant places, including state and community forest plantations. In addition to serving the huge domestic market in Indonesia, Jepara is well-connected to foreign markets in the USA, Europe, Japan, Hong Kong, Australia and elsewhere, and thereby acts as a bridge between local people, forests and these global markets (Roda et al., 2007).

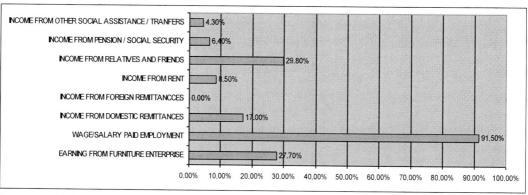

Source: Field Survey.

Figure III.4. Sources of Household Incomes and Assets of the Sampled Households in Total (% of total sampled households) (N=47).

As the center of Indonesian furniture production, the structure of the furniture industry in Jepara reflects the structure of the national furniture industry. Enterprises involved in the industry in Jepara can be categorized into three groups. The first consists of integrated enterprises, which produced essentially finished or pre-finished products from an input of unprocessed round-wood. The second group comprises those enterprises (log parks and sawmills) that specialize in the initial processing of the raw material to produce simple sawn timber for the third group. The third group is made up of workshops in which the input comprises sawn timber and various components, pieces, and sets of products at different stages of manufacturing, which are then assembled into a finished product (Roda et al., 2007).

III.3.2. Background Profile of the Surveyed Households

The majority of the sampled households on average have 3 members (30 percent), followed by households with 4 members (28 percent), where most of them are husband and wife with 1 or 2 children. About 49 percent of the sampled households have 2 female members and 29 percent have 1 female member. During the survey, it was found that only 24 households (less than 50 percent of the total sample) have all members working, whereas the majority (46 percent) only have 1 member workingfollowed by 42 percent with 2 members who worked during the previous week. While the other half (26 respondents) did not work for at least 1 hour during the previous week. Most of the members have been found to have formal jobs, such as teachers and employees in formal private enterprises. Out of 28 respondents, 46 percent have at least 1 member who worked in the formal sector while 39 per ent have 2 members worked in the formal sector. The highest level of education owned by members of the majority of the sampled households was secondary school, i.e. 38 respondents (76 percent), followed by primary school. For households members who have tertiary education, were mainly diploma certificates with the following composition: 11 respondents (22 percent) and vocational training with 8 respondents (16 percent).

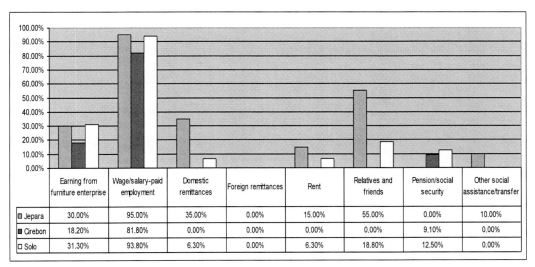

Source: Field survey.

Figure III.5. Sources of Household Incomes and Assets of the Sampled Households by Region (% of total sampled households) (N=47).

Of the total sampled households, 88 percent said that their members who work/worked in the furniture industry are the head of the household, while in the remaining 12 percent of the members who work/worked in the industry are their children. By region, it was found that in Cirebon, all of the surveyed respondents were households with the head who works/worked in the furniture industry, while in Jepara and Solo, the proportion is 85 and 83.30 percent, respectively.

In this survey, the respondents were given two questions: (1) do you have a family member who has recently been laid off from the furniture industry?; and (2) if you have a family member who is currently working in the furniture industry, has his/her employer reduced his/her working hours, his/her wages, or his/her bonuses? Three respondents answered 'no' to both questions, and thus they were not further included in the sample. Then, the remaining 47 respondents were asked about the most important sources of their income and assets. This question is important in order to assess the importance of the furniture industry as family income source.

The findings, as shown in Figures III.4 and III.5, indicate that in the three sampled regions, income from wage/salaried employment, either in the government sector as civil servants or in private enterprises, was the most important source of income for the majority of the respondents. The second important source of income was from relative and friends, with 14 respondents, mostly sited in Jepara. Income from household enterprise activities (MIEs or SEs) was given the third place. Since the majority of furniture producers in the three regions (or in Indonesia in general) are from the category of MIEs or SEs, the findings may suggest that income from furniture enterprises, either as employees or owners/producers, was not the most important source of income for the majority of the sampled households.

III.3.3. Impact of the Crisis on Incomes of the Sampled Households

In order to assess the impact of the crisis on income and consumption expenditures of the sampled households, during the survey they were asked how has the labor adjustment measures made in the crisis-affected furniture enterprises decreased their incomes since the end of the second quarter of 2008 until the present day (i.e. the survey period). It was found that the income of the majority of the respondents has dropped during that particular period, although the rate of decline varied by individual respondents, depending on their employment status and the seriousness of the impact faced by the enterprises. Of those who experienced a decline in their income, 20 respondents said that their income dropped by 50 percent. The smallest percentage, i.e. 10 percent, was experienced by only one respondent and the highest percentage, i.e. 100 percent, by two respondents. On average, the income has declined by 52.05 percent, and by region, Jepara has the highest percentage of income decreases (Figure III.6).

To explore the crisis-coping measures taken by the affected households in the form of daily expenditure adjustments, the sampled households were asked whether they have reduced their expenditures on things such as housing, food/nutrition, education, and others. The respondents who have reduced their expenditures were given two options, complete or partial reduction. The findings are presented in Table III.2. There are two ratios which are important to be examined, namely the ratio of complete to partial reduction as well as the ratio of those who have reduced their expenditure to those who have not. It reveals that both ratios vary by item of expenditure and region. From the category of those who did not make expenditure adjustments, the largest percentage is for education, whereas, the largest complete expenditure reduction is for entertainment and the largest partial expenditure reduction is for utilities/transport/communication. The findings may suggest that for the majority of the sampled households, education is very important for their children, it can be considered as a long crucial household investment. Therefore, whenever they could, they would not disturb the education of their children, even in a hardship condition as they experienced during the 2008/09 crisis.

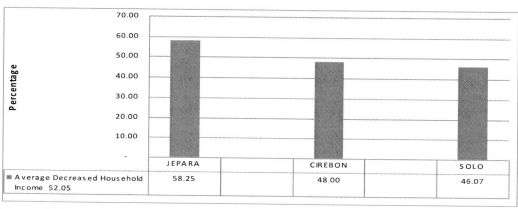

Source: Field Survey.

Figure III.6. The Average Percentage Decline in Income of the Sampled Households (N=47).

Table III.2. Impacts on Expenditures of the Sampled Housholds (N=47)

		All regions Total	%	Jepara Total	%	Cirebon Total	%	Solo Total	%
Reduce remittances received	No	18	39.10	15	75.00	2	18.20	1	6.70
	Yes Complete	10	21.70	2	10.00	4	36.40	4	26.70
	Yes Partial	18	39.10	3	15.00	5	45.50	10	66.70
Reduce expenditures on housing	No	19	41.30	18	90.00			1	6.70
	Yes Complete	11	23.90	1	5.00	6	54.50	4	26.70
	Yes Partial	16	34.80	1	5.00	5	45.50	10	66.70
Reduce expenditures on food / nutrition	No	7	15.20			4	36.40	3	20.00
	Yes Complete	6	13.00	4	20.00	1	9.10	1	6.70
	Yes Partial	33	71.70	16	80.00	6	54.50	11	73.30
Reduce expenditures on education	No	37	80.40	16	80.00	10	90.90	11	73.30
	Yes Complete	1	2.20			1	9.10		
	Yes Partial	8	17.40	4	20.00			4	26.70
Reduce expenditures on health	No	17	37.00	2	10.00	5	45.50	10	66.70
	Yes Complete	2	4.30			2	18.20		
	Yes Partial	27	58.70	18	90.00	4	36.40	5	33.30
Reduce expenditures on utilities /transport / communications	No	1	2.20			1	9.10		
	Yes Complete	8	17.40	1	5.00	6	54.50	1	6.70
	Yes Partial	36	78.30	18	90.00	4	36.40	14	93.30
Reduce expenditures on durable goods	No	2	4.30					2	13.30
	Yes Complete	20	43.50	3	15.00	7	63.60	10	66.70
	Yes Partial	24	52.20	17	85.00	4	36.40	3	20.00
Reduce expenditures on entertainment	No	1	2.20					1	6.70
	Yes Complete	34	73.90	17	85.00	8	72.70	9	60.00
	Yes Partial	11	23.90	3	15.00	3	27.30	5	33.30

Source: Field Survey.

III.4. OVERALL FINDINGS

This chapter discusses findings from many surveys which shows that many households in Indonesia were impacted by the 2008/09 global economic crisis, and many of them took special measures to cope with the crisis. However, the impact and hence, the crisis-coping measures vary by sector and region. As already discussed in Chapter II, the 2008/09 global economic crisis was a world demand crisis, i.e. world demand for some commodities declined and countries producing and exporting such commodities, including Indonesia, were automatically affected. At the sectoral level, export-oriented sectors or industries were hit most by the crisis as compared to domestic market/less export-oriented sectors or industries. At the regional level, within countries, regions where the crisis-affected commodities are produced were hit most. At the household level, households whose main sources of income are from the affected export-oriented sectors or industries were hit most.

However, the findings at micro-level discussed in this chapter may not tell the true story about the impact of the crisis on households. In other words, the hardships experienced by many households may not be fully or directly caused by the crisis for, at least, two main reasons. First, in some surveys, the hardships have been found to be caused by the increase in food prices. However, there is no strong evidence that the food price increase was related to or caused by the crisis. During the 1997/98 Asian financial crisis, food prices in Indonesia also went up, but it was mainly due to El nino phenomenon which caused a long dry season.

As the second reason, the hardships may not be directly caused by the crisis. For instance, many households during the surveys/monitoring activities were found to be laid off or to be experienced lower wages. These experiences are considered as the evidence on the impact of the crisis. It can be true or not true, or at least not as direct effects. As already explained theoretically, some households may have been affected not because they were employees in the crisis-affected export-oriented companies, but because they were working in firms which were affected by crisis-coping measures taken by the crisis-affected households., Expenditure adjustments made by these households as their strategy to cope with the crisis may have led to the decline in local demand for basic goods, and the latter, in turn, has caused troubles for many local firms producing such items.

Chapter 4

IMPACT ON MICRO, SMALL AND MEDIUM ENTERPRISES

IV.1. THE IMPORTANCE OF MSMEs

From a worldwide perspective, it has been recognized that micro, small and medium enterprises (MSMEs) play a vital role in economic development, as they have been the primary source of job/employment creation and output growth, not only in developing but also in developed countries. Based on a survey of country-studies in the 1990s, Tambunan (2009d) shows that 12 million or about 63.2 percent of total labor force in the US worked in 350,000 firms employing less than 500 employees, which is considered as MSMEs. They, often called the foundation enterprises, made up more than 99 percent of all business entities in the country, and they are the core of the US industrial base. MSMEs are also important in many European countries. In the Netherlands, for instance, they accounted for 95 percent or more of total business establishments. As in the US, also in other industrialized/OECD countries such as Japan, Australia, Germany, French and Canada, MSMEs are an important engine of economic growth and technological progress.

In developing countries, MSMEs also have a crucial role to play because of their potential contributions to employment creation, improvement of income distribution, poverty reduction, export growth of manufactured products, and development of entrepreneurship, manufacturing industry, and rural economy. Levy *et al* (1999) emphasize the extreme importance of the existence of MSMEs and their performance for the economic development of most less-developed countries. For this reason, the governments in these countries have been supporting their MSMEs extensively through many programs, with subsidized credit schemes as the most important component. International institutions such as the World Bank and the United Nation Industry and Development Organization (UNIDO) and many donor countries through bilateral co-operations have also done a lot, financially as well as technically, in empowering MSMEs in developing countries.

In Asian developing countries, MSMEs have made significant contributions over the years, measured in terms of their shares especially in: (a) number of enterprises; (b) employment; (c) production and value added (VA); (d) aggregate output (GDP); (e) enterprises set up by women entrepreneurs; and (f) regional dispersal of industry. According to Narain (2003), the contributions of these enterprises are vital in as much as they: (a) make up between 80 and 90 percent of all enterprises; (b) provide over 60 percent of the private sector jobs; (c) generate between 50 and 80 percent of total employment; (d) contribute about 50 percent of sales or VA; (e) share about 30 percent of direct total exports. In large countries like India, China and Indonesia, the present of MSMEs is also considered very important due to their potential contributions to employment creation, improvement of income distribution, poverty reduction, export growth of manufactured products, and development of entrepreneurship, manufacturing industry, and rural economy.

The importance of MSMEs is especially because of their characteristics, which include (Tambunan, 2008, 2009b): (1) their number is huge, and they are scattered widely throughout the rural areas and therefore, they may have a special 'local' significance for the rural economy; (2) as being populated largely by firms that have considerable employment growth potential, their development or growth can be included as an important element of policy to create employment and to generate income or to reduce poverty; (3) they use technologies that are more 'appropriate' as compared to modern technologies used by large enterprises (LEs) to factor proportions and local conditions in developing countries such as many raw materials are locally available but capital, including human capital, is very limited; (4) they finance their operations overwhelmingly by personal savings of the owners, supplemented by gifts or loans from relatives or from local informal moneylenders, traders, input suppliers, and payments in advance from consumers, and (6) although many goods produced by MSMEs are also bought by consumers from the middle and high-income groups, it is generally evident that the primary market for MSMEs' products is overwhelmingly simple consumer goods, such as clothing, furniture and other articles from wood, leather products, including footwear, household items made from bamboo and rattan, and metal products.

Given the importance of MSMEs as described above, it is no surprise that during the 1997/98 Asian financial crisis, as well as the 2008/09 global economic crisis, governments in the affected countries have given efforts to support the MSMEs in coping with the crises. In Indonesia, for instance, during the 2008/09 crisis, the government increased the fund to finance a special credit scheme, called People Business Credit, or known as KUR (*Kredit Usaha Rakyat*), to boost MSMEs production during the crisis. The government also tried to help export-oriented MSMEs facing the decline in world demand for their products to shift their market orientation toward the domestic market. To boost domstic demand, the government then launched packages of fiscal stimulus.

The aim of this chapter is to answer the following main research question: how is the resilience of MSMEs to an exogenous economic shock/crisis. For this purpose, the chapter assesses the impact of the 1997/98 Asian financial crisis and the 2008/09 global economic crisis on these enterprises in selected developing countries in Asia where data/information is available.

The rationale of this assessment is that although there are already many studies on the impacts of the two crises on economic areas such as economic growth and export, and on social areas such as employment, migrant workers, farm household's incomes, education and health, few studies have been done on the impact of the crises, especially the 2008/09 crisis, on MSMEs in Indonesia.

Table IV.1. Total Enterprises by Size Category in All Economic Sectors, Indonesia (000 units)

Size Category	2000	2001	2003	2004	2005	2006	2007	2008
MIEs & SEs	39,705.2	39,883.1	43,372.9	44,684.4	47,006.9	48,822.9	49,720.3	51,217.9
MEs	78.8	80.97	87.4	93.04	95.9	106.7	120.3	39.7
LEs	5.7	5.9	6.5	6.7	6.8	7.2	4.5	4.4
Total	39,789.7	39,969.97	43,466.8	44,784.14	47,109.6	48,936.8	49,845.02	51,262.0

Source: Ministry of Cooperative and SMEs (www.depkop.go.id) and BPS (www.bps.go.id).

IV.2. PERFORMANCE OF MSMEs AND THEIR CONSTRAINTS

What constitutes an MSME varies widely between countries, or even by different agencies/organizations within a country. MSMEs may range from a part time business with no hired workers or a non-employing unincorporated business, often called self-employed units, such as traditional business units making and selling handicrafts in rural Java in Indonesia, to a small-scale semiconductor manufacturers employing more than ten people in Singapore. They may range from fast growing firms, to private family firms that have not changed much for decades or stagnated. They range from enterprises, which are independent businesses, to those which are inextricably part of a large company, such as those,which are part of international subcontracting networks. The only true common characteristic of MSMEs is that they are 'not-large'; that is whether a firm is really an MSME or not is relative. Most enterprises from the MSME category are actually very small and about 70 to 80 percent of them employ less than five (5) people. There are only a very small percentage of firms, typically ranging from about 1 to 4 percent, which have more than 100 employees.

In Indonesia, there are several definitions of MSMEs, depending on which agency provides the definition. Nevertheless, Indonesia has national law on MSMEs. The initial one was the Law on Small Enterprises Number 9 of 1995, which defines a small enterprise (SE) as a business unit with total initial assets of up to 200 million rupiah (Rp), not including land and buildings, or with an annual value of sales of a maximum of Rp 1 billion, and a medium enterprise (ME) as a business unit with an annual value of sales of more than Rp one billion but less than Rp 50 billion. The law does not explicitly define a microenterprise (MIE). In 2008, this law was replaced by the new Law on MSMEs Number 20. According to this new law, MSMEs are those annual sales/turnovers up to 50 billions rupiah and fixed investment (excluding land and building) less than 10 billions rupiah. Besides the Law on MSMEs, the National Agency of Statistics (BPS) define MSMEs based on total numberof workers, i.e. MIEs, SEs, and MEs as units with 1 to 4, 5-20, 20-50 workers, respectively.

In this country, MSMEs have historically been the main player in domestic economic activities, as they provide a large number of employment and hence, generating primary or secondary sources of income for many rural poor households. They generally account for more than 90 percent of all firms across sectors (Table IV.1) and they generate the biggest employment, providing livelihood for over 90 percent of the country's workforce, mostly women and the young. The majority of MSMEs, especially MIEs, which are dominated by self-employment enterprises without wage- paid workers, are scattered widely throughout the rural areas, and therefore, are likely to play an important role in developing the skills of villagers, particularly women, as entrepreneurs (Tambunan, 2006a, 2009b).

Table IV.2. Structure of Enterprises by Size Category and Sector, Indonesia, 2008 (units)

	MIEs	SEs	MEs	LEs	Total
Agriculture	26,398,113 (52.07)	1,079 (0.21)	1,677 (4.23)	242 (5.54)	26,401,111 (51.50)
Mining	258,974 (0.5)	2,107 (0.41)	260 (0.66)	80 (1.83)	261,421 (0.51)
Manufacture	3,176,471 (6.27)	53,458 (10.28)	8,182 (20.63)	1,309 (29.94)	3,239,420 (6.32)
Elect, gas & water supply	10,756 (0.02)	551 (0.11)	315 (0.79)	125 (2.86)	11,747 (0.02)
Construction	159,883 (0.32)	12,622 (2.43)	1,854 (4.68)	245 (5.60)	174,604 (0.34)
Trade, hotel & restaurant	14,387,690 (28.38)	382,084 (73.45)	20,176 (50.88)	1,256 (28.73)	14,791,206 (28.85)
Transport & communication	3,186,181 (6.29)	17,420 (3.35)	1,424 (3.59)	319 (7.30)	3,205,344 (6.25)
Finance, rent & service	970,163 (1.91)	23,375 (4.49)	3,973 (10.02)	599 (13.70)	998,110 (1.95)
Services	2,149,428 (4.24)	27,525 (5.29)	1,796 (4.53)	197 (4.51)	2,178,946 (4.25)
Total (percentage)	50,697,659 (100.00)	520,221 (100.00)	39,657 (100.00)	4,372 (100.00)	51,261,909

Source: Ministry of Cooperative and SMEs (www.depkop.go.id) and BPS (www.bps.go.id).

Table IV.3. Structure of Enterprises by Size Category and Sector, Indonesia, 2008 (workers)

	MIEs	SEs	MEs	LEs	Total
Agriculture	41,749,303	66,780	643,981	229,571	42,689,635
Mining	591,120	28,762	21,581	78,847	720,310
Manufacture	7,853,435	1,145,066	1,464,915	1,898,674	12,362,090
Elect, gas & water supply	51,583	19,917	31,036	54,233	156,769
Construction	576,783	137,555	51,757	31,016	797,111
Trade, hotel & restaurant	22,168,835	1,672,351	472,876	179,895	24,493,957
Transport & communic.	3,496,493	145,336	111,854	98,191	3,851,874
Finance, rent & service	2,063,747	313,921	279,877	156,064	2,813,609
Services	5,096,412	462,683	178,311	49,723	5,787,129
Total	83,647,711	3,992,371	3,256,188	2,776,214	93,672,484

Source: Ministry of Cooperative and SMEs (www.depkop.go.id) and BPS (www.bps.go.id).

Table IV.4. GDP of SME and LEs by Sector in Indonesia, 2006-2008 (Rp trillion)

Sector	Size of enter-prises	Current prices 2006	Current prices 2007	Current prices 2008	Constant prices (2000) 2006	Constant prices (2000) 2007	Constant prices (2000) 2008	GDP share (%) at constant prices (2000) 2006	GDP share (%) at constant prices (2000) 2007	GDP share (%) at constant prices (2000) 2008
Agriculture	MSME	414.66	524.06	679.45	251.28	260.38	272.76	13.60	13.26	13.65
	LE	18.56	23.17	33.84	11.13	11.21	11.58	0.60	0.57	0.58
Mining	MSME	40.48	51.79	69.16	18.91	20.39	21.69	1.02	1.04	1.09
	LE	326.03	389.04	474.21	149.12	150.98	150.61	8.07	7.69	7.54
Manufacture	MSME	219.68	255.47	435.33	129.20	133.73	172.18	6.99	6.81	8.62
	LE	699.86	813.34	945.41	384.90	404.35	385.58	20.84	20.59	19.30
Elect, gas & water supply	MSME	2.46	2.82	3.09	1.14	1.18	1.23	0.06	0.06	0.06
	LE	27.90	31.91	37.76	11.11	12.34	13.76	0.60	0.63	0.69
Construction	MSME	165.74	201.77	156.07	74.54	81.45	49.49	4.04	4.15	2.48
	LE	85.39	103.44	263.25	37.69	40.45	81.33	2.04	2.06	4.07
Trade, hotel & restaurant	MSME	483.57	569.99	666.81	300.53	326.07	348.52	16.27	16.60	17.44
	LE	17.98	20.83	25.31	11.99	12.88	14.80	0.65	0.66	0.74
Transport & communication.	MSME	126.74	135.90	152,16	61.31	64.66	68.45	3.32	3.29	3.43
	LE	105.07	129.35	160,29	63.67	78.28	97.63	3.45	3.99	4.89
Finance, rent & service	MSME	171.79	194.08	230.88	108.84	117.10	126.52	5.89	5.96	6.33
	LE	97.33	111.13	137.24	61.23	66.56	72.27	3.32	3.39	3.62
Other services	MSME	161.10	185.42	216,40	89.86	96.68	104.42	4.86	4.92	5.23
	LE	175.16	213.87	9,83	80.85	85.29	4.91	4.38	4.34	0.25
GDP	MSME	1 786.22	2 121.31	2604.69	1 035.61	1 101.64	1165.26	56.06	56.09	58.33
	LE	1 553.26	1 836.09	1564.14	811.68	862.34	832.47	43.94	43.91	41.67
GDP National (exl. oil & gas)		3 339.48	3 957.40	4168.83	1 847.29	1 963.97	1997.73	100.00	100.00	100.00

Source: Ministry of Cooperative and SMEs (www.depkop.go.id) and BPS (www.bps.go.id).

The structure of enterprises by size category indicates that the majority of enterprises in all sectors are from the MSME category, mainly MIEs whereas, the distribution of total MSMEs by sector shows that the majority of these enterprises in Indonesia are involved in agriculture (Tables IV.2 and IV.3). The second largest sector is trade, hotel and restaurants, while the third is manufacturing. In the latter sector, the enterprises are engaged mainly in simple, traditional activities such as the manufacturing of wood products, including furniture, textiles, garments, footwear, and food and beverages. Only a small number of MSMEs are involved in the production of machineries, production tools and automotive components. In the automotive industry, they operate through subcontracting systems with several multi-national car companies in Indonesia such as Toyota and Honda.

As shown in Tables IV.4 and IV.5, agriculture is the key sector for MSMEs, and within the group, agriculture is more important for MIEs and SEs than MEs. In the manufacturing industry, based on output contribution, MSMEs are traditionally weaker as compared to LEs. In this sector, MSMEs are engaged mainly in simple, traditional activities such as manufacturing of wood products, including furniture, textiles, garments, footwear, and food and beverages, and handicrafts. Only a small number of these enterprises, mostly SEs and MEs, are involved in the production of medium to high technology-based goods such as industrial machineries, production tools and automotive components. In these industries, they operate mainly as subcontractors producing certain components and spare parts for LEs (including foreign companies). This structure of MSMEs by sector is, however, not an

Indonesian unique; it is a key feature of this category of enterprises in developing countries, especially in countries where the level of industrialization is relatively low.

Table IV.5. Structure of GDP by Size of Enterprise and Economic Sector, Indonesia, 2008 (%; based on constant 2000 prices)

	MIE&SE	ME	LE	Total
Agriculture	87.37	8.57	4.06	100.00
Mining & quarrying	10.52	2.07	87.41	100.00
Manufacture	18.86	12.01	69.13	100.00
Elect., gas & water supply	1.36	6.87	91.77	100.00
Construction	16.37	21.47	62.16	100.00
Trade, hotel & restaurant	83.41	12.52	4.07	100.00
Transport & communication	25.40	15.81	58.79	100.00
Finance, rent & service	21.19	42.45	36.36	100.00
Services	83.50	12.00	4.50	100.00

Source: Ministry of Cooperative and SMEs (www.depkop.go.id) and BPS (www.bps.go.id).

With respect to the output growth, interestingly, the annual growth rates of MSMEs are always higher than those of LEs. However, this is not because the level of (labor or total factor) productivity in MSMEs is higher than that in LEs. It is mainly because the number of units of the MSME category is much larger than that of LEs. Within the MSMEs, the output growth of SEs and MIEs together is lower than that of MEs but the gap tends to become smaller by year during the period reviewed. (Figure IV.1).

MSMEs' contribution to the annual GDP growth is also higher than that of LEs (Figure IV.2). In 2005, the GDP growth rate was 5.69 percent, from which 3.33 percent originated from MSMEs, compared to 2.36 percent from LEs. In 2007, the MSMEs' share in GDP growth was 3.57 percent, and slightly declined to 3.54 percent in 2008. More interestingly, within the MSME group, the total contributions of MIEs and SEs to GDP growth have always been higher than that of MEs. In 2007, from the GDP growth rate at 6.32 percent, the total contribution from MIEs and SEs was about 2.42 percent, compared to 1.15 percent from MEs, and in 2008 the shares were 2.58 percent and 0.96 percent, respectively.

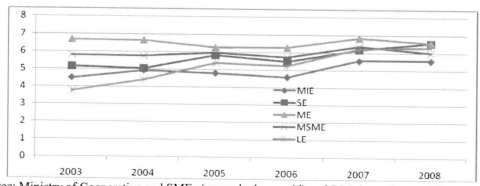

Source: Ministry of Cooperative and SMEs (www.depkop.go.id) and BPS (www.bps.go.id).

Figure IV.1. Output Growth by Size of Enterprise, Indonesia (%).

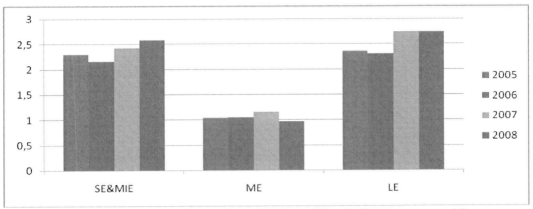

Source: Ministry of Cooperative and SMEs (www.depkop.go.id) and BPS (www.bps.go.id).

Figure IV.2. GDP Growth Contributions by Size of Enterprise, Indonesia (%).

As a comparison, Table IV.6 provides data on MSMEs in some other Asian countries. Although official data on MSMEs in these countries is very limited, some studies (e.g. Goh, 2007, ADB, 2009b, Tambunan, 2009b, and UN-ESCAP, 2009), which the table is based on, managed to make estimates of actual contributions of the enterprises in the particular countries' economy. As can be seen, in all countries where estimates are available, MSMEs reveal as the majority in number of units, employment creation and value added generation. With respect to value added contribution, MSMEs in Cambodia have the highest share, followed by those in Indonesia and China. In regard to employment creation, Cambodia and Indonesia are both in top position as their MSMEs contribute almost 100 percent of total employment creation.

With respect to export, as another important feature of MSMEs in developing countries, most of these enterprises are domestic market-oriented for a number of reasons. The most important one is their lack of four most crucial inputs, namely technology and skilled workers (so they cannot make highly competitive products with world standards), knowledge, especially about market potentials (including current market demand), and global business strategies, and capital to finance export activities, which for many, especially MIEs and Ses, is too costly, not only in dealing with export license but especially with logistic and promotion.

In Indonesia, for instance, in some groups of industries, many MSMEs are involved in export activities. Govenment data shows that MSMEs' exports continue to grow from year to year. In 2000, total exports of SMEs amounted to Rp75,448.6 billion and increased by more than 50 percent to Rp.122,311 billion (or 14,103 million US$) in 2006 and further to Rp 142,822 (or 16,697 million US$) in 2007. However, their share in the country's total export is always smaller than that of their larger counterparts. In 1990, the MSMEs' contribution to the total export (not including oil and gas) was around 11.1 percent, and increased to approximately 20 percent, compared to LEs at almost 80 percent, in 2006 or 2007. Within the group, MEs are much stronger than MIEs and SEs. In 1990, MEs' share in total non-oil and gas exports recorded at 8.9 per ent compared to 2.2 percent of MIEs and SEs together, and in 2007, the ratio was 15.04 percent (MEs) to 4.98 percent (MIEs and SEs) (Table IV.7).

Table IV.6. MSMEs' Contributions to Total Enterprises, Employment and Value Added in selected developing countries in Asia, 2000-2008

	China	India	Indonesia	Malaysia	Philippines	Thailand	Vietnam	Pakistan	Cambodia
Number of unit	99.7	95.0	99.9	94.4	99.6	98.0	96.8	Na	Na
Employment	74.0	80.0	99.0	40.4	69.1	55.8	96.8	90.0	99.0
Value added	60.0	40.0	63.1	26.0	32.0	47.0	39.0	40.0	76.7

Note: Na=data not available.
Sources: Goh (2007), ADB (2009b), UN-ESCAP (2009), Tambunan (2009b).

Table IV.7. Export of Indonesian SMEs in all sectors, 2006-2007

Year	Unit	Non-oil and gas Export				
		SEs	MEs	SMEs	LEs	Total
2006	Rp billion	30,365	91,946	122,311	484,775	607,086
	US$ million	3,501	10,602	14,103	55,896	69,998
	%	5.00	15.15	20.15	79.85	100.00
2007	Rp billion	35,508	107,314	142,822	570,594	713,416
	US$ million	4,129	12,479	16,607	66,349	82,957
	%	4.98	15.04	20.02	79.98	100.00

Source: BPS (Berita Resmi Statistik, No. 28/05/Th XI, 30 Mei 2008).

A majority of Indonesian MSMEs' exports came from the manufacturing industry, with the following key industries: wood, bamboo and rattan products, including furniture, leather products, including footwear, textile and garment, food and beverages, tobacco products, and handicrafts. However, their share in total exports of the sector is much smaller than that of LEs. As in other sectors, within the group, MEs always perform much better than their smaller counterparts in export. The share of MIEs and SEs together has never reached 10 percent. Based on official data issued by the Ministrty of Coperative and SME, in 2000, it was only 3.15 percent and then slightly decreased to around 3.0 percent in 2006. During the same period, the export share of MEs was 12.53 percent and later increased to 14.72 percent (Figure IV.3).

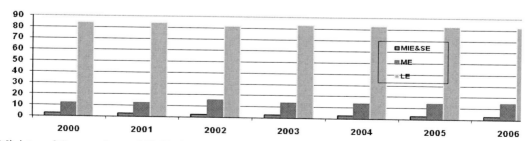

Ministry of Cooperative and SMEs (www.depkop.go.id).

Figure IV.3. Share of SMEs in Total Export Value in Manufacturing Industry in Indonesia (%)[*].

Data on MSMEs' exports in most other Asian developing countries is either not available or difficult to verify. So it is not easy (if not impossible) to assess the performance of Indonesian SMEs from a regional perspective, at least in Asia. However, some limited sources of information, mainly from research papers, may give some clue. For instance, based on Wattanapruttipaisan's (2005) study, direct contribution made by these enterprises to total export earnings in Southeast Asian countries is not more than 20 percent. This view is also supported by APEC's (2002) report on MSMEs in the region. According to this report, the enterprises contributed less than 30 percent of direct exports on average. From these sources, MSMEs in the region of Southeast Asia seem to be under-represented in the international trade relative to their role in the domestic economy. If indirect export is also taken into account, the report argues that their export contributions could be much larger than this 30 percent. In the manufacturing industry, MSMEs in the region often make up a significant part of the value or supply chain, and may thus not be included in the direct export data. Harvie (2004) also provides the same picture showing that MSMEs in East Asia generate about 30 percent of direct exports (or US 930 billion in 2000), much less than their contribution to employment (about 60 to 70 percent) or output (about 50 percent). The figures range from about 5 percent or less in Indonesia to about 40 percent of total exports in the Republic of Korea.

In Aris' (2006) study, using the baseline Census of Establishment and Enterprises, it is shown that Malaysian MSMEs in the manufacturing, agricultural and services sectors that could be qualified as exporting enterprises constituted only 0.4 percent of total MSMEs in all sectors in 2003, while they generated 8.5 per ent of total output, 6.4 percent of total value added and employed 2.7 percent of total employment in all sectors. In the manufacturing industry, the exporting MSMEs contributed 18.5, 21.5 and 11.1 percent, respectively, to total output, value added, and employment, although their number involved was only 3 percent of total MSMEs in the sector. In the agricultural and service sectors, exporting MSMEs were only about 0.2 percent of total MSMEs in the sectors. In his study, the establishment is assumed as an export-oriented unit if 50 percent and more of its total produced output are exported.

In Vietnam, Long's (2003) and Kokko's (2004) studies are probably the most comprehensive studies that give more detailed information about the involvement of MSMEs in export in the country. The Long's study is based on surveys in seven provinces (among the total of 61 provinces). It shows three important findings: (1) the average MSME only exported 16 percent of its output; (2) within the group, the importance of export differs between enterprises, with a relatively higher export ratio in modern enterprises (which are mainly from ME category), mainly located in the urban areas/cities, e.g. Hanoi, Haiphong, and Ho Chi Minh City; and (3) only about 3 percent of the exporting MSMEs were involved in direct exports, meaning that the majority of exporting MSMEs did export through intermediates such as trading companies or LEs via subcontracting arrangements. Overall, the study suggests that despite the high growth rate of Vietnamese export, which on average reached nearly 25 percent during 1996-2003, the ratio of MSMEs' export volume out of the country's total export was relatively low. Based on secondary data analysis covering the 1990s up to the early years of the 21st century and on own surveys, Kokko (2004) also found that the export intensity of his sampled SME is diminishing(at least with respect to direct export which in general is more easy to observe than indirect export). He gives a number of reasons for the low involvement of Vietnamese MSMEs in export activities, and one of them could be the rapid development of domestic market. With an average annual growth rate of the country's economy, over 7 percent in the period 1990-2003, it can be said that domestic market opportunities had expanded rapidly during that particular period. This may have encouraged many MSMEs in Vietnam to focus more on domestic rather than export markets. When domestic market opportunity is large, only very few MSMEs have been forced to search for export market opportunities because of weak domestic demand for their products. Another important reason is the high fixed cost of acquiring the necessary information about foreign markets in Vietnam, which, in fact, is a normal case in many developing countries where the information system is underdeveloped or inefficient. He argues that with the high cost of getting information about foreign markets, it is not surprising that only few MSMEs are export-oriented.

For the Philippines, the most recent study on MSMEs' export is from Aldaba (2008) who shows that MSMEs exports is never beyond 25 percent of the country's total exports, and in the manufacturing industry, the share is much smaller. However, across manufacturing sub-sectors there are major variations in this pattern. In many industries, exports from this category of enterprises are always larger than their larger counterparts. But, in other industries producing higher technology-based goods such as machinery, including electrical machinery, and transport equipments, LEs export much more than MSMEs do.

The most developed export-oriented MSMEs in the Philippines are found in Cebu, which is an international business center in the Central Visayas Islands of the Philippines. Its two Mactan Export Processing Zones (MEPZ I and II) have developed into clusters of export manufacturing (Beerepoot & Van Westen 2001). In addition to its foreign companies, Metro Cebu is also home to various, more traditional, home-grown manufacturing activities (i.e. MIEs and SEs) that produce and export a variety of simple goods such as furniture, fashion accessories, housewares and other handicrafts The urban economy is characterized by a large concentration of local manufacturers, mainly SEs and MEs, who have been able to take advantage of Cebu City's direct access to world markets, and its considerable supply of cheap but relatively skilled labor (Rodriguez, 1989). Helvoirt and van Westen (2008) found that the most important foreign market for MSMEs in Cebu is the US, as 59 percent of their 54 surveyed firms declaring their main buyers are from this country. Other important international markets are Europe and Asia (both 11 percent). In Europe, the Netherlands is an important trading partner, while Hong Kong serves as a large furniture buyer and Singapore as an important market for gifts, toys and housewares.

From various sources, including official data from the period 1990s-2006, Tambunan (2009b) managed to provide a picture about MSMEs contributions to total exports in a number of Asian developing countries as presented in Table IV.8. As can be seen, MSMEs in China play the leading role with their highest export contribution, between 40 and 60 percent of the country's total merchandizse exports, followed by Taiwan China (Chinese Taipei) with 56 percent. In South Asia, the export share of Indian MSMEs is close to 40 percent. Even, in the sports goods and garments sector, their contribution to exports is as high as 90 to 100 percent (Pandey, 2007). In Pakistan, for the past three decades, the fastest growing export industries have been dominated by SMEs. Important export contributions from the enterprise emanate from sub-sectors like cotton weaving and other textiles and, surgical equipment. In total, they generate 25 percent of manufacturing export earnings, or about 2.5 billion US dollar in 2005.

Table IV.8. Share of MSME exports in Total Exports in Selected Asian Developing Countries, 1990s and 2006

Country	Maximum Share (%)
PRC	60
India	40
Chinese Taipei	56
Vietnam	20
Singapore	16
Malaysia	15
Thailand	40
Philippines	25
Pakistan	25

Source: Tambunan (2009b).

MSMEs (especially MIEs and SEs) are often hampered by institutional constraints to grow in size and become viable/efficient larger enterprises. The constraints may differ from region to region, between rural and urban, between sectors, or between individual enterprises within a sector. However, there is a number of constraints common to all MSMEs, including the lack of capital, human resources, technology and information; difficulties in procuring raw materials, marketing and distribution; high transportation costs; problems caused by cumbersome and costly bureaucratic procedures, especially in getting the required licenses; and policies and regulations that generate market distortions. These are often referred to in the literature as external constraints to MSME growth.

Table IV.9. Four Most Important Constraints Facing MSMEs in Asian Developing Countries

Country	Raw materials	Marke-ting	Capital	Energy*	Infor-mation	Tech.& skill	Infra-structure	Tax	Inflation	Market Environ-ment**	Labour issues
Indonesia	√	√	√	√							
Philippines		√	√		√	√					
Vietnam			√			√	√			√	
Cambodia			√	√	√	√				√	
Lao PDR	√		√					√	√		
Thailand	√	√	√			√					
Malaysia	√		√		√	√					
Brunei		√	√		√	√					
China		√	√			√	√				
India		√	√				√			√	
Pakistan	√	√								√	√
Bangladesh		√	√	√		√				√	
Nepal	√	√	√			√				√	

* Includes electricity, ** Includes regulations, restrictions, legal framework, law and order, and discrimination policies in favor of LEs/MNC.

Source: Tambunan (2008).

Based on recent, though limited, information from government reports, national surveys and case studies, Tambunan (2008) managed to make a list of main constraints common to MSMEs in Asian developing (with sigh √), although the degree of importance of each constraint varies by country, depending on differences in many aspects including level of MSMEs development, nature and degree of economic development, public policies and facilities, and of course, nature and intensity of government interventions towards MSMEs. As presented in Table IV.9, the constraints include difficulties in getting raw materials with reasonable prices, difficulties in marketing, lack of capital and so on.

As can be seen, lack of capital experienced is among main constraints by MSMEs in all selected countries. The lack of capital is mainly due to lack of access to banks or other formal financial institutions. In many Asian developing countries, this problem is experienced mainly by MSMEs (and among the group, especially by MIEs and SEs) located in rural/backward areas. In Indonesia, the majority of rural MSMEs never received any credit from banks or other formal financial institutions. They depend fully on their own savings, money from relatives and credit from informal lenders for financing their daily business operations.

Other common constraints are lack of technology or skilled workers, and difficulties in marketing. The first one is the most important reason for the lacking of MSMEs behind their larger counterparts in GDP contribution or productivity and competitiveness. Lack of technology and skilled workers means lack of innovation which is required for quality improvement and higher productivity, and hence, output growth. This problem also affects their ability to market their products, since it makes them more difficult to compete in the domestic market with imported similar products or in export markets with suppliers from other countries whereas, in marketing, many MSMEs do not have the resources to explore their own markets. Instead, they depend heavily on their trading partners for the marketing of their products, either within the framework of local production networks and subcontracting relationships or orders from customers.

Most importantly, MSMEs face regulations and bureaucratic practices that solidify the dominance of LEs in the formally regulated economy and incentivized entrepreneurs in MSMEs to operate informally, meaning illegally and out of the government's regulatory reach. These prohibitive factors disproportionately affect MSMEs because of their limited human and financial resources. Data from the International Finance Corporation (IFC), as cited from Newberry (2006), show that the number of formalized MSMEs in a country increases with a more favorable investment climate, which includes a low cost of doing business and a short average time to start an enterprise.

A harsh regulatory environment also has a negative impact on MSMEs adhering to pollution standards. The International Organization for Standardization (ISO) 14001 is a set of voluntary environmental standards businesses may adhere to in order to prove their commitment to sustainable practices through a recognized authority. Most MSMEs, especially SEs and MIEs may refuse to utilize the organization's environmental standards because of inadequate support, time-consuming paperwork burdens and a general distrust of external intrusion. While, according to Newberry (2006), LEs can spread the fixed costs of compliance over a larger revenue base and MIEs generally operate below the purview of government agencies, SMEs are obliged to follow large-scale commercial enterprise norms for assessing and reporting their ecological impact. Government regulations that are designed for enforcement among LEs are not suited to MSMEs, which impairs the ability of the government to protect its natural resources.

Macroeconomic policies are also very important factors in affecting, directly or indirectly, the development of MSMEs. For instance, trade liberalization policies which have been adopted by many Asian countries, are sometimes very aggressive, such as in Indonesia after the economic crisis in 1997/98. It is generally expected that international trade liberalization that increases foreign competition in the domestic market will hurt some inefficient or uncompetitive MSMEs, while benefiting other efficient or competitive MSMEs. The efficiency effects of foreign trade liberalization may be observed in an increase in average plant size among MSMEs and (presumably) lower average costs. The international literature on the effect of foreign trade policy on MSMEs presents, however, some surprising and quite important findings. The seminal work of Tybout (2000), cited in Tambunan (2008), on the micro dynamic effects of international trade liberalization on manufacturing firms in developing countries, for instance, consistently shows just the opposite; that increases in import penetration as well as reductions in protection are associated with reductions, not increases, in plant size. Thus, rather than improve efficiency immediately, an important finding of that study is that liberalization may work against the scale efficiency of MSMEs in the short run (or if there are gains of efficiency, they are quite small). Tybout's findings are supported by Tewari's (2001) findings from the experience of Tamil Nadu in India over many years. After the government removed restrictions on many industries, including textile, allowing anyone to enter the industries, and simultaneously liberalized trade, there was a spate of entry by relatively small firms in those industries, notably textiles. Firms with four to five hundred spindles set up shop, in contrast to the 10 to 20 thousand spindle plants that larger firms operated. By the mid 1990s, the average plant size in the spinning industry had fallen significantly.

Valodia and Velia (2004) investigated the relationship between foreign trade liberalization at the macro level and its micro or firm- level adjustment effects in the South African manufacturing industry, and their findings suggest that there is a strong relationship between firm size and international trade. More than half of firms not engaged in international trade are small firms. At the opposite extreme, almost half of the firms that are involved in both importing and exporting are large firms employing more than two hundred workers. It seems that larger firms have been more successful at integrating their manufacturing activities into global chains of production.

Tewari and Goebel (2002) studied MSMEs competitiveness in Tamil Nadu (in Southern India). They found two interesting facts. First, these enterprises in some industries are doing better than those in others; just as some industries are doing better than others. Second, they tied to low-end market segments in large urban or metro areas appear to be the most vulnerable to cheap import competition from overseas. Ironically, MSMEs serving similar niches in the rural areas or in small towns do not face the same pressures. Their access to intricate, socially-embedded distribution networks linking them to rural markets appears to be a source of strength that non-local competitors will find too costly to replicate.

Based on official data (BPS), Table IV.10 provides information about the main constraints faced by MIEs and SEs in the manufacturng industry in Indonesia. It reveals that not all of the surveyed producers consider the lack of capital as their serious business constraints. For those who faced capital constraint were mainly MIEs located in rural/backward areas and they never received any credit from banks or from various existing government sponsored MSME credit schemes. They depend fully on their own savings, money from relatives and credit from informal lenders for financing their daily business operations.

Other problems include cumbersome and onerous business regulations and restrictions. Basically, these problems which hamper business activities in Indonesia reflect the poor governance in the country. One of the most egregious restrictive regulations which hampered bona fide business in Indonesia, including MSMEs, was the policy-generated barriers to domestic competition and trade. These policy-generated barriers included the barriers to inter-regional and inter-island trade and proliferation of several state and private monopolies which proliferated during the New Order era (1966-1998). The policy-generated barriers to domestic competition and trade included barriers to entry in certain economic activities, officially sanctioned cartels and monopolies, price controls, dominance of state-owned companies (SOCs) in certain sectors and preferential treatment for selected, favored LEs. However, shortly after the 1997/98 crisis, with the help of the International Monetary Fund (IMF), Indonesia started its large economic reforms in almost all sectors and dealing with almost all aspects of daily business, including reducing the dominance of SOCs in the economy.

Finally, from its assessment on MSMEs, especially their export performance in Indonesia, ADB (2002b), cited in Tambunan (2008), concludes that Indonesian enterprises have substantial growth potential. However, there are many obstacles that these enterprises have to face. On the supply side, the obstacles include (1) strengthening of the rupiah exchange rate, (2) instability of security and law enforcement, (3) high transaction costs due to corruption, (4) frequent labor activities demanding wage increases, and (5) lack of access to formal credit. With respect to the latter, the report argues that though there are several government departments and agencies involved in promoting MSME exports, including the National Agency for Export Development (NAFED), the Indonesian Export Training Centre (IETC) and the Export Promotion Board (all belonging to the Ministry of Industry and Trade), a majority of export-oriented MSMEs in Indonesia have no easy access to formal credits, and this situation makes them difficult to expand their production and hence, export or to improve the quality of their exported products. On the demand side, increasing competition from other countries, especially in footwear, fish and shrimp, chemical products, spices, coffee, tea, and jewelry, which involve mostly MSME suppliers. These Indonesian products are losing against similar competitive products from emerging economies such as People's Republic of China, India, Thailand, and Vietnam.

IV.3. IMPACT ON MSMEs: THEORETICAL DISCUSSION

Often stated in the literature that one comparative advantage of MSMEs relative to their larger counterparts is their flexibility and capacity to, shift from one product to another different product when market demand changes, and to expand easily when the economy is booming and to contract easily when there is an economic crisis. In Berry et al. (2001), these enterprises are construed as being especially important in industries or economies that face rapidly changing market or economic conditions, such as the sharp macroeconomic downturns. These enterprises work as a shock-absorber of business cycle. In Sandee et al (1998), it is stated that SMEs may therefore be expected to do relatively better under volatile macro conditions than LEs producing more standardized products, where reorganizations of the assembly line take time.

The conviction is based on some assumptions. First, MSMEs employ more relatives and friends than wage-paid employees, mostly to enable them to get some income and they would lay them off last, so the number of employees in these enterprises would not fall as fast as in LE during an economic crisis. Second, in countries like Indonesia where there is no unemployment benefit, the unemployed would try (or have) to start their own business to get any income and it will cause the rise of the number of MSMEs. Thus, the enterprises act as the last resort. One hypothesis from this assumption is that during an economic crisis, when many employees in the formal sector (LEs) are laid off, the number of MIEs and SEs will increase (thus, there is a negative relationship between GDP growth, or a positive relationship between the level of open unemployment, as an indicator of an economic crisis and the growth in units of MSMEs). Third, because they use less capital goods, most MIEs and SEs do not have special built factories, sunk costs are lower and labor-capital struggles are less frequent, another source of flexibility than in LEs. Fourth, MSMEs are much less reliant on formal markets and formal credit funds. The latter makes MSMEs less sensitive to a banking crisis (Poot, 1997; Berry et al, 2001).

Theoretically, any enterprises will be affected by a change in economic condition or an economic crisis such as the 1997/98 crisis or the 2008/09 global economic crisis, initially, either through their demand-side or supply-side, or both at the same time. The effect can be positive or negative. Thus, the impact of an economic crisis on enterprises in an industry or a sector must be analyzed through both the supply-side and demand-side approaches in order to capture the supply-side and demand-side effects of an economic crisis. As illustrated in Figure IV.4, the supply-side (SS) effects are the effects that occur via the markets for factors of production and other inputs; while, the demand-side (DS) effects occur via the output (final and intermediate) markets (Tambunan, 1998).

Table IV.10. Number of SEs and MIEs in the Manufacturing Industry by Main Problem

	SEs	MIEs	Total SEs & MIEs
Have no serious problem	46,485	627,650	674,135
Have serious problems	192,097	1,862,468	2,054,565
- lack or high prices of raw material	20,362	400,915	421,277
- marketing difficulties	77,175	552,231	629,406
– lack of capital	71,001	643,628	714,629
– transportation/distribution difficulties	5,027	49,918	54,945
– high price or short supply of energy	4,605	50,815	55,420
– high labor cost	2,335	14,315	16,650
– other problems	11,592	150,646	162,238
Total SEs & MIEs	238,582	2,490,118	2,728,700

Source: Tambunan (2008).

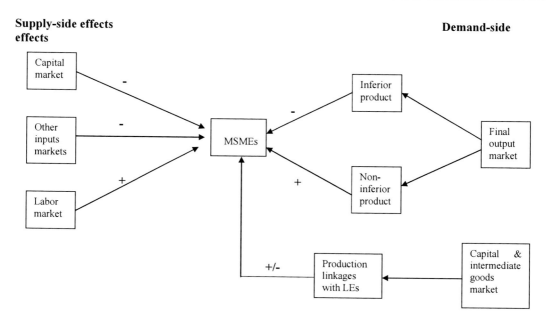

Figure IV.4. A Theoretical Framework of the Impact of an Economic Crisis on Individual MSMEs.

With respect to SS effects, as an example, an economic crisis causes a decline in real income per capita (like the one in 2008/09) leading to a decline in domestic market demand for many products produced by LEs. If this first stage of the crisis goes out of control, it may cause a huge capital flight and hence, a depreciation of national currency (or rupiah in the case of Indonesia). In this kind of economic crisis, the negative SS effects on MSMEs can occur mainly from two sources. First, financial/capital market effects: the monetary authority adopts a tight money policy (as a direct policy response to prevent capital flight or currency depreciation), or commercial banks reduce credit supply to the economy (as a response to non-performing loans of crisis-affected firms or due to lack of money reserve), causing a decline of money in circulation, increase in interest rates which makes higher money borrowing costs, and thus less credit demand from or less credit available for MSMEs. For many MSMEs, if informal sources of capital that they can borrow are not available, no credit supply from formal financial institutions will force them to reduce or even to stop their production. LEs which were used before the crisis to assist MSMEs financially (such as in Indonesia, where all state-owned companies are required to use a certain percentage of their profits to help MSMEs), may also reduce their supports to MSMEs because they also face financial difficulties.

Humphrey (2006) did an analysis on three most important types of international trade finance and potential impacts on each of them of an economic crisis, such as letter of credits (LCs), domestic bank credit, and trade credit (Table IV.11). LCs are specifically designed to facilitate international trade. The function of this mechanism is both to provide finance and provide assurances about payment to the exporting enterprises. If an irrevocable LC is issued, the exporter receives payment when it provides the specified documents to the advising/confirming bank. However, LCs require confidence and liquidity to be maintained at various points along the chain of payment from the importer, to the issuing bank, to the advising/confirming bank and to the exporter. In Indonesia, during the 1997/98 crisis, many national private banks were forced to close because they were financially unsound and many state-owned banks were merged in order to improve their financial conditions, reflecting the unhealthy condition of the national banking in the country at that time. As a result, foreign countries (exporters) did not accept the LCs issued by Indonesian banks. This situation is explained by Auboin and Meier-Ewert (2003), quoted by Humphrey (2006): *'Cross-border' international trade finance for imports became a particular problem at the peak of the crisis in Indonesia, where international banks reportedly refused to confirm or underwrite LCs opened by local banks because of a general loss of confidence in the local banking system. Given the high import content of exports (over 40 percent in the manufacturing sector), Indonesia's growth of exports was seriously affected by the difficulty of financing imported raw materials, spare parts and capital equipment used in its export sectors* (page 6).

Table IV.11. Trade Finance and Potential Impacts of an Economic Crisis

Type of trade finance	Potential impact of an Economic Crisis
LCs Importers use LCs issued by their banks (the issuing bank) as a means of assuring exporters that they will be paid. If the exporter submits the required documentation (invoices, bills of lading, etc.) to its bank (the advising or confirming bank), payment is made to the exporter.	The creditworthiness of the importer is undermined in the crisis and the issuing bank will not assume the risk. The issuing bank does not have sufficient funds to extend credit to the importer. The advising/confirming bank does not have confidence in the issuing bank. Trade finance institutions reduce their overall exposure or exposure to particular countries during a financial crisis, reducing trade credit across the board to firms and banks in those countries.
Domestic bank credit Domestic banks provide credit to exporters to cover pre-shipment or post-shipment costs. Such funding is similar to provisions of working capital in general, although it may be less risky to the extent that it is loaned against specific purchases and assets.	Financial outflows reduce liquidity in the domestic banking system. International banks operating in the domestic market reduce credit in order to cut the exposure of parent banks. Shortages of foreign currency prevent banks lending the foreign exchange needed for import of inputs or export freight charges.
Trade credit Companies extend credit to each other when buyers delay or advance payments to suppliers. This is called "trade credit", even within the domestic market. "Open account" trade involves importers paying invoices once goods are received. Equally, importers can extend credit to exporters if they pay for goods (all or in part) in advance.	General shortage of credit in domestic markets prevents impor-ters and/or exporters extending credit to each other. As credit become scarce, not only do banks reduce lending to their customers, but more creditworthy firms reduce lending to less creditworthy ones as their own access to finance is reduced. Firms reduce credit extended to suppliers or buyers because of the increased risk of non-repayment by these firms as more companies get into financial difficulties.

Source: Humphrey (2006, page 10).

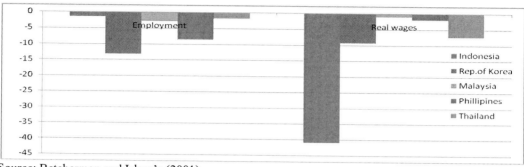

Source: Betcherman and Islam's (2001).

Figure IV.5. Percentage Changes in Employment in Industry (1996-1998) and Real Wages (1998) in the Most Severely Affected Countries by the 1997/98 Crisis.

Bank and trade credits are extensions of credit facilities that operate in many countries, including Indonesia. Firms may use bank lending to finance both working capital, capital investment, or to facilitate trade. This latter is especially important for import-dependent and export-oriented enterprises. Inter-firm (trade) credit is widely used in Indonesia. As explained in Humphrey (2006), when contracts specify, for example, that buyers have a period in which to pay invoices for goods received, typically, 30, 60 or 90 days, the supplier is, in effect, extending credit for that period. Firms that have well-developed trading relationships may adopt the same practice. To the extent that sophisticated global value chains linking together firms in different countries often involve repeat transactions and long-term relationships, it is not uncommon for trade to be conducted on these terms.

Second, inputs market effects: domestic prices of raw materials increase, and the increase can be caused by either the depreciation of national currency, e.g. against the US dollar, (for imported items), or by the decline in domestic production of such inputs because of higher production costs or lack of finance from banks, which creates excess demands in domestic market for the inputs.

An economic crisis also have positive SS effects via the labor market, i.e. the labor-market effects. During the 1997/98 crisis, many LEs, especially in the manufacturing industry in Indonesia, were stagnated or bankrupted, and, consequently, hundreds of people employed in those LEs were laid off and, thus, unemployment increased significantly. Based on Betcherman and Islam's (2001) study, Figure IV.5 shows percentage declines of employment in industry in the period 1996-1998 in the most severly affected countries. In Indonesia, the decline was the lowest at 1.5 percent. The figure also shows the decline in real wages in 1998 in these countries. Indonesia was the worst with -41.0 percent. The decline in real wages was mainly caused by hyper-inflation that occurred in that year (Figure IV.6) as a result of the rupiah depreciation. As explained before, because Indonesia does not have a social security system like in Western European countries which gives financial protection to the unemployed people with minimum income, therefore, those who lost their jobs in LEs were "pushed" to find work or to do any kind of income-generating activities, and this took place mainly in MIEs and SEs. Also, many employees in LEs as well as civil servants facing decline in their real wages during the crisis might had been forced to find or to conduct secondary jobs in MIEs and SEs. In other words, an increase in the unemployment rate in the formal sector accompanied with hyper-inflation (a significant increase in household expenditures on basic goods) during an economic crisis may encourage informal economic activities to expand, including MIEs and SEs.

From the demand-side, there are three major sources of demand for MSMEs' products: (1) community (individual consumers), (2) business, and (3) government (e.g. departments). The first source represents the final consumption demand in domestic and export markets; while the latter two sources comprise the intermediate demands. With respect to the second and third sources of demand, the stability of demand for domestic-made products during an economic crisis depends much on the survival capability of production linkages or inter-firm business linkages (i.e. private intermediate demand) and the government financial conditions which affect government expenditures (i.e. public intermediate demand), respectively. If many domestic LEs and government projects which had business links with MSMEs before the crisis reduce or stop their activities because of the crisis, their demand for MSMEs' products also decline.

But an economic crisis may also generate a larger opportunity (a positive effect) for MSMEs through production or demand linkages with LEs. In Indonesia, before the 1997/98 Asian financial crisis (before the depreciation of more than 100 percent of the rupiah against the US dollar), many domestic LEs were used to import all of their required inputs. Before the crisis or during the New Order era (1966-1998), the Indonesian currency (rupiah) was overvalued with the aim to support import substitution strategy in that time. With very cheap US dollar in rupiah, most companies in the country preferred import than domestic-made inputs. But, during the crisis period, many of these LEs turned back to domestic market for such inputs, either through a free market process or subcontracting arrangements. This generated a new demand for domestic MSMEs.

With respect to the final consumption demand, it is the primary source for the MSMEs' products, as they mostly produced simple consumption goods. The demand is primarily domestic (rural and urban); only a small fraction goes to foreign consumers, mainly tourists. In this respect, whether the impact of an economic crisis on MSMEs will be negative or positive, it will depend on the relationship between the types of goods produced by these enterprises and the level of consumers' incomes. According to the 'Engels' Law, if the goods produced by MSMEs are inferior (or non-inferior) or have negative (or positive and high) income elasticity, then the increase of income will lead to the decline (or increase) of demand for such goods.

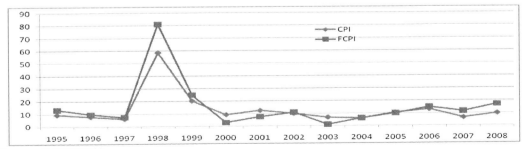

Source: IMF(2009b).

Figure IV.6. Growth Rates of Consumer Price Index (CPI) and Food Consumer Price Index (FCPI), 1995-2008 (%).

Now, given the fact that most goods/services produced by MSMEs in Indonesia, as in developing countries in general, are purchased by consumers from low-income groups or poor households, then the important question is: who will be affected most by an economic crisis, the very rich or the very poor people or the middle class? With an analytical framework (i.e. income elasticity approach) as given in Table IV.12, the hypothesis can be formulated as follows: if only the income of the rich declines as the result of an economic crisis, then, overall, the demand for MSMEs' products will increase, as many rich people who lost their incomes shift their demand to cheaper products made locally. On the contrary, if the poor is most affected by the crisis, the demand for MSMEs' products will be less. If the crisis affects all income groups though with different magnitudes, the net effect of the crisis can be negative, positive or even zero.

Finally, with respect to the export market, if it is a national currency crisis (depreciation), such as in 1997/98, then, theoretically, it will push up the price competitiveness of domestic-made goods, and hence, export will increase. Thus, it can be said that a national currency depreciation, at least theoretically, is positive for national export, including exports of MSME, *ceteris paribus*, other export determinants are constants. Unfortunately, during the 1997/98 Asian financial crisis, there was no strong national evidence to support this theory. This can be explained by the fact that most Indonesian MSMEs always face various constraints that make them difficult to do or to increase export. The constraints include lack of technology and skill which make the quality of their products always inferior.

If an economic crisis is as the one in 2008-09, it is negative for export. As explained earlier in Chapter II, the 2008/09 global economic crisis was initially a big financial crisis in the US and then spread to many other countries, including Japan and Europen countries. As these countries are traditionally the most important market destinations for many Indonesian goods, especially textiles, garments, wood/rattan made furniture, and leather products, the economic recessions in the US, Japan and Europe have led to a significant drop in many Indonesian export items to these countries.

To conclude, an economic crisis affects enterprises initially through their DD or/and SS sides. It depends on the main cause, the original and the type of the crisis. If it is a banking crisis, the initial effects will be mainly through a supply-side, i.e. a significant and sudden drop in credit supply to enterprises or a significant increase in lending interest rates. If it is a regional or global economic crisis leading to a decline in regional/world income, it will be primarily through a demand-side, i.e. less demand for export.

Table IV.12. Hypothesis on the Impact of the Income Decline due to an Economic Crisis on the Demand for MSME's Products by Different Income Groups and Natures of the Products

Income group	Nature of MSMEs' products	Measure of the income elasticity of demand	Change in demand as income declines
High	Very inferior	Negative & large	Increase
Middle	Inferior/less inferior	Negative/positive	Increase/decline
Low	Very non-inferior	Positive & large	Decline

IV.4. SOME EVIDENCE

IV.4.1. The 1997/98 Asian Financial Crisis

The Asian financial crisis in 1997/98 provides an opportunity to examine the resilience of MSMEs, not only in Indonesia but also in other ASEAN member countries. A study made by the World Bank in 2000, tried to investigate the relative impact of the crisis on enterprises from different sizes by examining the effects on their capacity utilization and employment. It was expected that in a sharp macroeconomic downturn, many enterprises would, if not die out, reduce their production volumes and hence, their employment, and thus the capacity utilization and employment rates in these enterprises would decline. Table IV.13 summarizes the findings in the four crisis-afflicted ASEAN member countries towards the end of 1998. It shows that in these countries, LEs tended to have higher rates of capacity utilization after the crisis than MSMEs, but the share of the latter category of enterprises with fewer workers, by and large, matched the share of LEs.[1] Unfortunately, the study does not look at the enterprises effected in different sectors, which, probably vary by sector.

Among Asian developing countries, and particularly in the ASEAN region, Thailand is among few countries which have some studies of MSMEs' condition during the crisis, probably because of the fact that the enterprises have been played an important role in the Thai economy before the crisis and the country was also seriously hit by the crisis. According to ILO estimations, about two million workers in the country had lost their jobs as a result of the crisis in 1998 only. Interestingly, the majority of them were laid off from MSMEs, i.e. 55 percent compared to 45 per ent from LEs. This may suggest that Thai MSMEs were more severely hit by the crisis than their larger counterparts. Unfortunately, no further information was given by ILO about the scale of the reduction, only the estimated number of firms that cut employment (ILO 1998). Also, the Thai government has not published comprehensive data on the death rate of MSMEs and different agencies provided different estimated figures on the dynamic of MSMEs during the crisis period, which make s it difficult to get the real picture based on government sources about the impact of the crisis on Thai MSMEs.

Perhaps, the most comprehensive literature which can give a better clue about the effects of the crisis on Thai MSMEs is from Chantrasawang (1999) and Régnier (2000, 2005). The first author states that its impact seems to be felt by most MSMEs. According to his paper, in that period, many of the enterprises were struggling with financial difficulties because of high interest rates and unavailability of other financial sources. He concludes that MSMEs have been particularly affected later on when the crisis has peaked and extended to many sectors, especially manufacturing industry. They have all been subjected to reduced output, consumption, employment and investment. The most pressing need, during the crisis, has been cash-flow to the firms as most commercial banks in the country have cut off credit to prevent further bank runs and loan losses.

---

[1] As a comparison, in South Korea, another crisis-afflicted non-ASEAN member country and also known for its well-developed MSMEs, capacity-utilization levels and shares of enterprises with less workers after the crisis in MSMEs and LEs were, respectively, 71 percent vs. 77 percent, and 61 percent vs. 80 percent (World Bank, 2000).

Table IV.13. Impact of the 1997/98 Asian financial crisis on firms by size in some ASEAN Countries

Country	Size of enterprises	Capacity-utilization level after the crisis (%)	Share of enterprises with fewer workers after the crisis (%)
Indonesia	MSME	51	54
	LE	63	45
Malaysia	MSME	64	29
	LE	73	40
Philippines	MSME	76	50
	LE	79	50
Thailand	MSME	57	56
	LE	67	45

Note: MSMEs are defined as enterprises with less than 150 workers.
Source: World Bank (2000).

Règnier reports that the Thai Ministry of Industry has only been able to document a slowdown in the establishment of new manufacturing MSMEs from 6093 in 1996 to 5022 in 1997 and 3130 in 1998. The number of MSMEs apparently continued to expand at an average rate of 6.1 percent per year for that period. Meanwhile, according to the Bank of Thailand (BOT), Southern Regional Branch Office (quoted by Règnier, in 1997 and 1998), there were 509 and 773 bankruptcies among MSMEs, compared to only 290 and 358 in 1995 and 1996, respectively. The number of new MSMEs also slowed down from 3019 in 1996 to 1689 in 1998. The Industrial Finance Corporation of Thailand (IFCT) (also cited by Règnier), on the other hand, has declared that there were 3391 and 2544 closed-down MSMEs, respectively, during the last quarter of 1998 and the first quarter of 1999.[2]

Règnier has not only analyzed secondary data from official sources but also conducted a survey on both export and domestic market-oriented MSMEs to assess their own views about the impact of the crisis on their businesses (or Thai MSMEs in general). According to his analysis, the crisis had three immediate implications for the Thai economy: (i) a sharp decline of domestic demand, combined with a credit crunch; (ii) a strong rise in input costs, mainly derived from the currency depreciation; and (iii) the surge of interest rates. In other words, Thai MSMEs were impacted by the crisis through demand, as well as supply-sides.

Règnier also provides the findings of the World Bank surveys of 1997 and 1998 on Thai MSMEs, aimed to get their perceived causes of their current output decline. These two surveys used eleven variables to measure the resilience of these enterprises during the crisis. An intensity rating scale (1: less important to 5: very important) has also been utilized to differentiate four types of enterprises: MSMEs vs. LEs, and domestic market-oriented vs. export-oriented enterprises. As can be seen in Table IV.14, the most important indicator is

---

[2] Tracing bankruptcies, especially among MSMEs in developing countries, is not an easy task. In Thailand, as well as in Indonesia, many or even most of MSMEs (especially SEs and MIEs) are not registered. As stated in Règnier (2000, 2005), new bankruptcy regulations have been recently adopted, but are hardly implemented, even in the case of LEs. Many MSME owners stop or change their business but they do not de-register their previous firms, while registration can remain on the books of the Ministry of Commerce for at least three consecutive years.

change in domestic demand, especially for domestic market-oriented producers from both categories of size.

Findings from an observation made by Berry, et al (2001) show that during the crisis, the overall share of MSMEs in Thai, total employment fell from around 60 percent in 1998 to 52 percent in 1999, but it later picked up to 65 percent in 2000. The share of the smallest firms (with fewer than 10 workers) which can be categorized as MIEs declined from 12 to 6 percent. It suggests that MSMEs in Thailand were also hit seriously by the crisis, but, differently than their larger counterparts, they managed to recover in a relatively short period.

Bakiewicz (2004) reviewed the findings of all studies available on the effects of the crisis on Thai MSMEs. He concludes that far-reaching conclusions on MSMEs behavior during the crisis in the country simply cannot be drawn. Only one thing is very clear: in export-oriented and strongly connected with foreign partners MSMEs suffered less and even gained thanks to devaluation and supports form foreign partners. The experiences of the crisis showed that its effects on MSMEs might be differentiated and depend on many factors. As he argued, there are only some premises that export orientation is important to face up to economic decline. But a success in export activity is usually a result of better management. The export-oriented firms are more proficient and it may influence their reactions to the crisis, not export as such. Hence, a large number of MSMEs in the economy do not have to add up automatically to a high level of shock-resistance.

Indonesia is probably the second country which has some evidence on the impact of the crisis on MSMEs. The evidence is mostly at a more disaggregated level from a large number of case studies. Most of these studies focus on MSMEs in the manufacturing industry, which generally indicates that although many MSMEs were also seriously hit by the crisis, they were overall relatively better off than LEs. For instance, Tambunan (1998) observed that many producers of traditional *batik* in Pekalongan in the province of Central Java and hundreds of MIEs and SEs producing footwear in several clusters, such as in Jakarta's industrial estate, known as PIK (*Perkampungan Industri Kecil*), Cibaduyut in Bandung district in the province of West Java province, and in Medan, the capital city of the province of North Sumatera, were forced to stop their production activities during the crisis period. What was often stated in newspapers in that time was that many MSMEs faced difficulties to continue their production not because the demand for their products declined but mainly because of the increase in prices of their necessary inputs in which some were imported. Many of them changed their professions and became traders or worked in transportation or construction in urban areas, or in agriculture as farmers or daily paid laborers. He concludes, however, that all of this evidence is still not enough to generalize that all or the majority of MSMEs in all industries or sectors were negatively affected by the crisis. In different industries or sectors, they may have had different experiences with the crisis, because individual entrepreneurs producing the same products or in different industries/sectors may face different internal and external conditions, e.g. constraints, challenges and opportunities, and different firms may have different capacities to cope with an economic crisis. Also, the nature of individual sectors also plays an important role: enterprises in 'closed' sectors, i.e. not linked to international markets via export and/or import are more protected from an economic shock like the 1997/98 crisis than their counterparts in 'open' oriented sectors, i.e. those with high dependence on export and imports.

Table IV.14. Perceived Causes of Current Output Decline in Thai MSMEs and LEs

No	Indicator	MSMEs and LEs by market orientation	
		Domestic market	Export market
1	Change in domestic demand	5	4
2	Change in exchange rate	4	4
3	Change in labor cost	3.5	3.5
4	Change in interest rate	3	3.5
5	Change in debt burden	3	3
6	Change in cash flow	3	3.5
7	Change in foreign demand	2.5	4.5
8	Change in credit from suppliers	3	3
9	Change in credit expansion	2.5	3
10	Change in cost of raw materials	3	3
11	Change in delivery of goods	3	3

Source: Régnier (2000, page 25).

Diermen et al. (1998) have some interesting evidence showing that some MSMEs in a number of manufacturing subsectors like furniture industries in Jepara in the province of Central Java and *batik* industries in some locations in the same province did well during the crisis period. The key reason was that when the rupiah became more expensive, these enterprises quickly took some important measures, including changing their behavior in buying inputs or production tools instead of depending on imported items to purchase locally made ones, in spite of the quality disadvantage vis-à-vis the imports. Before the crisis, they used to buy items such as nails, latches, and door bolts from abroad. This crisis-adjustment strategy had made it much easier to cope with the crisis financially while many other MSMEs which did not do the same strategy had very hard time. For instance, Diermen, et al (1998) also found the demise of *tahu* producers in some parts in the West Java province and small clove cigarette (*kretek*) producers in a number of villages in the Central Java province. In both cases, it was caused by a steep rise in the prices of inputs. Another example of import-dependent MSMEs in distress during the crisis shown in this study was a group of garment producers (often operating in subcontracting networks with LEs) who were strongly dependent on a steady flow of imported raw materials.

However, the positive side of this inputs-purchasing strategy may not always live forever. Sometimes, when local demand for local inputs or raw materials increase, the prices also go up (which then makes no difference in rupiah price between imported and locally-made inputs), and it does not always reflect the price/market law, that is, when there is an excess demand, the price automatically will increase. In many cases, as during the 1997/98 crisis period, traders or producers of highly demanded inputs often tried to make a big profit of the current situation by unecessarily pushing up their prices.

With respect to export, as explained before that, theoretically, the depreciation of the rupiah should have a positive effect on Indonesian exporters, including MSMEs. In some cases, however, Dierman et al (1998) found that some of the potential benefits of the fall of the rupiah to the Indonesian firms were negotiated away by foreign buyers. While the rupiah devalued by 60 percent in real terms (or around 80 percent in nominal terms), international buyers of Indonesian textile and garments have insisted on discounts of 20 to 40 percent, so the magnitude of the rise in domestic market prices in rupiah were less than expected. Also, foreign banks' unwillingness to accept LCs issued by Indonesian banks, as the direct consequence of the financially unsoundness of the Indonesian banking sector in that time, has reduced the benefits for Indonesian exporters from the fall of the rupiah. Many exporters enjoyed higher price competitiveness in the global market from the stronger US dollar against the rupiah, but they just could not expand their production and hence, export because of no capital.

In conclusion, Dierman et al's (1998) study does support the general theory that in this type of economic crisis, world trade-linked MSMEs are directly affected, while local markets-oriented ones (for inputs as well as output) are usually isolated from the negative effects since they do not have business transactions involving foreign currencies or exchange rates. The world trade-linked MSMEs can be distincted further into two categories, i.e. import-dependent and export-oriented MSMEs. This type of economic crisis will impact the first and the second categories, negatively and positively, respectively, since a national currency depreciation causes, on one hand, higher import costs and hence, more production costs, and on the other hand, higher price competitiveness and more foreign market opportunities, *ceteris paribus*.

Musa (1998) and Musa and Priatna's (1998) did a survey on credit access for MSMEs during the crisis, based on a sample of some 300 firms in eight provinces and in various sectors. They report that self-finance has remained the main source of funds for investment and working capital (this is also a key characteristic of MSMEs in Indonesia or in developing countries in general). More than 75 percent of the total sampled enterprises were fully reliant on their own funds to finance their business activities. Only fewer than 13 percent had access to formal finance, with the number dropping slightly since the outbreak of the crisis. The limited exposure of MSMEs to borrow funds from the formal sector was presumably one of the factors explaining the resilience of most of their sampled enterprises during the crisis. The main coping mechanisms undertaken by the sampled firms included the use of cheaper inputs to replace expensive (imported) materials and the reduction of the labor force. Of total respondents, 80 percent saw their business shrink (though only 21 percent of them reported laid-off workers); in 12 percent of cases, it stayed constant and 8 percent have achieved an increase, the latter occured mainly in export-oriented enterprises and those which have limited need for imported materials.

Wiradi (1998) reports that brick-making industries (dominated by MSMEs in terms of total number) in some villages in the West Java province have collapsed as a consequence of the substantial decline in urban building activities. The latter itself was mainly caused by a combination of three factors; lack of credit as the national banking sector collapsed, the substantial price increases of production materials as a result of the rupiah depreciation, and the shrinkage of urban demand for expensive houses/apartments and office buildings. Sandee (1998, 1999), however, found that tile and brick makers in many villages of the province could maintain pre-crisis production levels through a gradual replacement of urban markets by rural ones. This replacement was fueled by the relatively good condition of farmers in the area and the channeling of funds from the social safety net programs into rural building activities.

AKATIGA and the Asia Foundation (TAF)(1999) monitored the performance of 800 MSMEs in eighteen subsectors in a number of provinces in 1997 and 1998. The performance was measured with the volume of production and profits. It reports that during the period

1997-98, production volume in about 33 percent of the sampled firms and six subsectors (including one manufacturing subsector) continued to decline, 39 percent and six subsectors (four manufacturing subsectors) showed a decline but with the potential for improvement, and 28 percent and six subsectors (two manufacturing subsectors) showed improved performance.[3] Improved performance was observed more in other islands of the archipelago than in Java, and in rural areas than in urban areas. Its findings with relatively wide coverage show that as of 1998, when the crisis reached its climax, more than 70 percent of the surveyed units were negatively affected by the crisis in the broad sense. There could be many factors affecting the performance of MSMEs during the crisis and the impacts could vary, depending on individual enterprises. The survey found two crucial factors affecting many of the sampled enterprises; the sharp fall in final market demand and the rise in prices of imported materials; although the experience varied by individual enterprises, depending on types of goods they produced and location of production. In some districts or subdistricts, the increased inflation rates caused directly or indirectly by the crisis were higher than in other areas. In relatively remote areas, enterprises depending on imported inputs may have to pay higher prices for their purchased inputs due to transportaion costs than their counterparts located in cities close to harbors.

One interesting finding from this study is that while all export-oriented MSMEs in the sample showed improved performance, suggesting that they might have enjoyed higher price competitiveness due to the rupiah depreciation), that of domestic-market-oriented MSMEs varied partly because some benefited more than the others from increasing local demand for cheaper substitutes. Indeed, it was obvious in big cities such as Jakarta, Surabaya, Bandung and Medan, that many high-paid employees in the formal sector who were used to have daily lunch during working hours in expensive restaurants before the crisis moved to informal/cheap food stalls during the crisis period when inflation was high and the food prices in the formal restaurants increased much faster than those in the informal ones. The same happened with other households' routine consumption expenditures. Many households substituted imported T-shirts or shoes in luxury shopping complexes with locally-made ones in sidewalk informal shops. All of these changes in consumption behavior during the crisis period are good, at least theoretically, for MSMEs.

Table IV.15. Growth rates of SEs and MIEs in Indonesia, 1996-98

	1996	1998	Growth rates (%)
No of Units	2,867,241	2,196,899	-23.4
No of workers employed	6,613,848	5,303,204	-19.8
Male	3,669,881	2,946,175	-19.7
Female	2,943,967	2,357,029	-19.9

Source: Thee (2000).

---

[3] Six subsectors that continued to decline were the sugar refining, sidewalk food stalls in Java, floating-net fishing, *becak* (tricycle) transportation, urban/rural transportation, and the photo copy service industry; six declining subsectors with the potential for improvement were coffee refining, rattan manufacturing, shoe manufacturing, embroidery manufacturing, sidewalk food stalls outside of Java, and pushcart vendors; six improving subsectors were cacao plantations, paprika plantations, clove plantations, sidewalk vendors of imported second-hand clothes, pottery manufacturing, and furniture manufacturing.

Regarding input materials, especially the imported ones, according to the study, MSMEs had an obvious disadvantage compared with their larger counterparts due to their limited capacity to withstand price increases and their weaker position for accessing materials. Their limited capacity to cope with the increased prices of inputs were mainly because of their lack of capital and their weak bargaining power (especially those operated in the informal sector) vis-a-vis LE. With no strong bargaining position, it is normally difficult, if not impossible, for MSMEs to get price discounts or other ease facilities.

Hill (1999, 2001a,b) reports that the Indonesian manufacturing industry has contracted at about -15 percent during the crisis, though there are some differences between export-and local market-oriented activities. He concludes that every sector has shed labor, with the exception of agriculture, and that the biggest decline has occurred in the manufacturing industry. Hill also concludes that despite many MSMEsbeing hit by the crisis, in general, these enterprises were weathering the crisis better than LEs, because they were less reliant on formal markets and less reliant on formal credit which was far more costly during the crisis.

The resilience of MSMEs during the 1997/98 crisis is also highlighted by a Jellinek and Rustanto' (1999) paper, which argues that during that crisis, when many individuals or households shifted their consumption orientation from imported to locally-made or from expensive to cheap goods, there has been an unprecedented upsurge of especially MIEs and SEs, with new domestic market opportunities in blacksmith communities, such as furniture makers, fishing, agricultural tools, brick and tile making, and small-scale vending activities. They report, however, that many enterprises were finding it hard to keep up with the new orders. Again, as also evident in other studies, lack of capital was the main contributor to this problem. They judge that the crisis offered renewed opportunities to many MSMEs, particularly MIEs and SEs, that were gradually losing ground during the New Order era (1966-1998), the period when the adopted import substitution strategy to stimulate industrialization had given special treatments to Les; including multi-national companies at the cost of MSMEs. In their view, a policy correction, mainly through the depreciation of the rupiah, has created growth prospects for these enterprises.

The above findings are also supported by ADB's (2002) assessment, which found that Indonesian MSMEs (at least many of them) weathered the crisis well and grew at a faster pace than the rest of the economy, as a number of them turned to exports due to the favorable exchange rate of the rupiah. Based on official data, it shows that MSME exports grew by 3.6 percent in 1998 and slightly higher at 5.8 percent in 1999. In contrast, exports by large exporters declined by 0.8 percent in 1998 and by 7.5 percent in 1999. This may suggest that the weakness of the rupiah in that time did not give significant benefits to export-oriented LEs. One possible reason can be that many LEs were highly dependent on imported inputs, including the export-oriented ones. Thus, the weakness of the rupiah also meant higher production costs for these enterprises which reduced or even eliminated their potential price competitiveness raised from the rupiah depreciation. However, as shown in this assessment report, in comparison with their larger counterparts, MSMEs contribution to Indonesia's total non-oil and gas exports continues to be modest, from 2.8 percent in 1996 and up to 4.1 percent in 2000. The report concludes that while the recovery has been faster among MSMEs, it could have been higher if the constraints (especially access to credit, technology, market information, and skilled manpower) inhibiting their development had been addressed.

Rather different than the above findings, by using official estimates on SEs and MIEs, Thee (2000) shows that the crisis had an adverse impact on these enterprises (Table IV.15). In

1998, the number of SEs and MIEs and the number of both male as well as female workers they employed declined substantially, compared to 1996. Based on this figure, Thee argues that the reductions undoubtedly reflect the decline in their production volume brought upon by the crisis. According to him, the crisis affected these enterprises in two ways, by (1) sharply reduced domestic demand for their products, and (2) major disruptions in the banking sector, affecting the cost and availability of credit to these enterprises. Regarding the first channel, Thee's finding may suggest that substitution from imported to locally-made products (if it really took place at a large scale) may not have had a significant positive effect on MSMEs. This may happen for two main reasons. First, the larger part of the increasing demanded locally-made goods was towards those produced by LEs or foreign companies operated in Indonesia. Their capacity to organize mass productions gave them more price competitiveness than that of MSMEs, while their more technology superior than that owned by MSMEs secure the quality of their products in line with or not far below international standards. Second, as also evident by the previous study with the case of blacksmiths, many MSMEs might have faced difficulties to expand their production due to lack of capital.

In Berry et al's (2001) article, it is stated that scattered evidence from surveys undertaken by the Ministry of Cooperatives and SME during the crisis period taken together with annual data from the National Social and Economic Survey (SUSENAS), which provides useful data on employment trends, and with basic economic logic, leaves little doubt that the MSMEs have felt some negative impact from the crisis, and the enterprises have faired differently according to the sector The crisis creates pressure for firms to adopt adjustment strategies to cut production costs by substituting imported raw materials with locally-made or cheaper ones and improving efficiency in the production process, and to redirect output to new market opportunities whenever possible. The evidence from SUSENAS shows that during the crisis period, there have been no major changes in the structure of manufacturing employment, which suggests only modest job loss in MSMEs. Either most enterprises have been able to cope with the crisis without major reductions in their workforce or the creation of new firms has offset such reduction. As discussed much earlier, the crisis which led many employees out of work might have pushed them to open their own businesses or do any kind of income generating activities as a means to survive, giving MSMEs, especially MIEs and SE, a special role as the last income buffer for the poor.

Sandee et al. (1998) provide some evidence of the effect of the crisis on MSMEs in the furniture industry in two production centers in Jepara in the Central Java province and one in North Sulawesi. The industry was, and until now is, still among Indonesian key export-oriented industries. During the New Order era (before the 1997/98 crisis), the industry enjoyed rapid growth in output as well as employment, and MSMEs in the industry also experienced the booming. The fast output and export growth has produced greater standardization and a stricter division of labor and tasks among firms in the industry. This industry exemplifies an economic activity that uses domestic inputs and has plenty of export potential. Both LEs and MSMEs in the industry have been developing long-term linkages to overcome the present insecure environment. Prior to the crisis, the MSMEs in the industry had access to various regional and international trade networks, thanks to foreign actors who played an important role as intermediaries between domestic production networks and international buyers and at the time of the crisis, they also contributed significantly to easing the credit constraint caused by the collapse of the Indonesian banking system. Policy had also contributed positively to the transition through the development of the provincial harbor to accommodate container transport, the simplified procedures for foreign investors, and the improved facilities for clearing exports. As for the impact of the crisis on MSMEs in the industry, some of those already engaged in exporting (usually indirectly) were being pressured by contractors and LEs to sign long-term contracts; some became disguised wage labor.

Sato (2000) investigated how the crisis-affected MSMEs' performance and their responses to the crisis in the metal-working and machinery component industry. The enterprises produced components and metal products and they supplied these products to such customers as assemblers, user-factories, wholesalers, and retailers. The study is based on field surveys carried out periodically from the end of 1997 through early 1999 in five selected locations in Java: East Jakarta, Sukabumi (West Java), Surabaya and Malang (East Java), and Ceper (Central Java), covering 49 SMEs which included inactive ones but did not cover those that had totally closed down or had switched over to other business. The impact of the crisis on the performance of the surveyed MSMEs is graded into six levels: 'highly positive', 'positive', 'constant', 'negative', "highly negative" and "extremely negative," judging from the changes in profit and production volume between 1997 and 1998 while almost half (47 percent) of the enterprises suffered "negative" impact and 65 percent of the total fell into the broad negative range (levels 4 to 6). It is also a fact that 35 percent fell into the broad positive range in that the SMEs had positive growth or at least kept their production level constant. A notable point is that the sample distribution is bi-modal, having two peaks: one at the 'negative' and 'highly negative' samples and another at the 'highly positive' and 'positive' samples.

Another manufacturing subsector where MSMEs had suffered much from the crisis was copper handicrafts (Sandee 1998). Producers in a mountain village in the Central Java province are known for their modern designs that are popular throughout Java, especially in the urban areas. They occasionally export, but their trade networks remain embryonic. The industry is partially dependent on imported inputs and has suffered much from the substantial price increases during the crisis period. The shrinkage of urban demand had forced many firms to downsize. Unfortunately, the outbreak of the crisis, marked by the significant fall of the rupiah had not enabled producers to develop export networks. However, based on data from the Ministry of Industry, soon after 1999, production has recovered slightly owing to increased rural demand, leading to a production shift back to traditional products such as kitchen utensils that are popular in rural areas. These products have a much higher local content than do the modern designs.

The most recent study on the performance of Indonesian MSMEs during the 1997/98 crisis is from Wengel and Rodriguez (2006). Their interesting finding is that LEs and MSMEs responded differently to the crisis, although both exported their products. Where the former contracted and reduced their exports, the latter managed to maintain or even to expand their exports. Their finding supports what other previous discussed studies have found that generally, MSMEs weathered the crisis better than LEs, though many have also been hit hard. For their research, they used BPS survey data of 1996 and 2000 for more than 20,000 enterprises in a number of industries. The crisis caused a large turmoil in Indonesia's industrial structure, even though at the aggregate-level, the number of enterprises appeared to be almost unaffected. The surveys recorded 22,997 enterprises in operation in 1996 and 22,174 in 2000, thus, an apparently modest decline of 3.5 percent in the number of enterprises. The comparison of these two snapshots shows that 6,100 enterprises (26.5 percent of all enterprises in 1996) stopped their businesses between 1996 and 2000, and that 5,277 new enterprises started operations during the same period. Among the MSMEs, 35.7 percent were forced to close, and the 'out-of-business' percentage declined with industry size. Only 6.7 percent of the LEs closed between those two periods. While MSMEs recorded the most closures, they also showed the most vigorous response to the new opportunities presented in the five-year period. Despite the great upheaval in numbers of enterprises among the MSMEs, the number of jobs in enterprises with less than 50 workers remained about the same. Due to enterprise closures, about 121,000 jobs were lost; the expansion of the remaining enterprises with less than 50 employees led to 28,000 more jobs; and the new established enterprises created 91,000 jobs.

From all existing studies on the impact of the 1997/98 crisis on MSMEs in Indonesia and some other Asian developing countries where data/studies are available, the overall conclusion is that more LEs than MSMEs were severely affected by the crisis. With respect to MSMEs, through demand-side and labor market effects, it can even be said that the crisis had a positive effect on these enterprises. The 1997/98 crisis has enlightened some countries, like Malaysia, Thailand, Indonesia and the Philippines, on the importance of MSMEs to their economy, especially for the poor to survive.

Differently than Indonesia and Thailand, in Malaysia, official estimated figures, as well as case studies on effects of the crisis on MSMEs, are scarce. Only two publicly accessed works are available from Mustafa and Mansor (1999) and Abdullah (2002). As reported in Mustafa and Mansor (1999), the only estimated data was from the Ministry of International Trade and Industry which shows that at least 10 percent of existing MSMEs have disappeared during the crisis period. But, it is not clear whether the disappeared MSMEs had something to do with the crisis or just a normal business cycle phenomenon, especially since the fact that the Malaysian economy was much less affected by the crisis than Thailand, Indonesia and the Philippines.I In Abdullah (2002), it is stated that *during the economic crisis, the most affected businesses were SMEs, ... since they were largely reliant upon the domestic market. For SMEs that were unable to redirect their efforts to foreign market survival would become a priority, and cash flow became the immediate issue ... . SMEs found it very hard to secure loans from banks and other financial institutions. SMEs in the manufacturing sector that relied on imported goods faced substantial upward pressures on costs, and were reluctant to quote prices for their products as their costs were constantly increasing and eroding their competitiveness. SMEs that positioned themselves as major suppliers to multi-national corporations were substantially affected by resulting low order levels and even order cancellations* (page 185). In his work, Abdullah also reported briefly on a field study conducted by Moha Asri in 1999 on MSMEs in the Northern Region of Peninsular Malaysia in late 1999. The field study estimated that the profit margin of MSMEs fell by more than 89 percent, with more than 78 percent having declining orders and 76 percent of the surveyed MSMEs reducing their purchases of raw materials.

Evidence either from national sources or from individual case studies on the effects of the crisis on MSMEs in the Philippines is also relatively limited. Three often-mentioned studies on this subject are two works from Berry and Rodriguez and one from Tecson. In their first work in 2001, Berry and Rodriguez investigated the resilience of MSMEs exports, especially in the electronic and car parts manufacturing industries, to the crisis. They found that the crisis had reduced domestic sales, but the domestic market in electronics and car parts remained tiny, whereas export market for these products has remained buoyant. After the crisis, electronics (included machinery and transport equipment) have continued to dominate the export recovery in the country. The industry exported almost double its 1995 levels by the end of 1998, while all other industries reported export values similar to those of 1995. According to the study, only a small part of this export growth can be attributed to MSMEs owned by foreign investors in joint ventures. The crisis appeared to have had little effect on domestic market-oriented production of electronics (and to a less extent, car parts) because of limited linkages with the rest of the economy. Domestic production for the electronics industry is limited to indirect inputs such as carton packaging and some minor chemicals. As stated in their paper, probably the same is true for car parts as the country's third top export from the industry; input-output-peripheral units. The bulk of the domestic car parts production in the sector is destined to the electronic appliance industry that did show a sluggish trend during the crisis.

In their second work, Rodriguez and Berry (2002) report the findings of a 1998 World Bank survey of 287 MSMEs (under 150 workers in 1996, with an average of 67 workers) and 254 LEs in five groups of industry, i.e. food, textiles, clothing, chemical and rubber products. Most of the sampled MSMEs were more likely to have some foreign ownership than were LEs (54 percent compared to only one-fifth of LEs), and they were also more likely to export than their larger counterparts (74 percent compared to only one-third of LEs). The response to the crisis of these export-oriented, foreign owned MSMEs was, on average, better than that of LEs. First, according to capacity utilization estimates, LEs were hit the hardest. Their capacity utilization declined more (from 77 to 66 percent) between 1996 and 1998 than was the case for MSMEs (from 77 to 72 percent). Second, 42 percent of LEs reduced their activities on hours, while only 37 percent of MSMEs did the same. Also, LEs were more likely to use a compressed work week and forced vacation than MSMEs.

Tecson (1999) investigated the current status of supporting industries (including MSMEs) during the crisis and their prospects after the crisis in the Philippines. His analysis focuses especially on industries producing car parts for the domestic market. Although data on domestic production of car parts during his research was scarce, he concludes that it is likely that the economic downturn during the crisis period affected the domestic car market negatively, and many MSMEs, as well as LEs in the industries, were seriously affected.

IV.4.2. The 2008/09 Global Economic Crisis

From the Southeast Asia perspective, the 2008/09 crisis was very different than the 1997/98 crisis. Looking at the nature of the two crises, the 1997/98 crisis was an internal crisis within Asia (i.e. East and Southeast Asia), which hit the banking sectors, particularly in Indonesia and Thailand, and led further to the huge depreciations of their national currencies. As a direct result, national incomes per capita or economic growth rates in these countries declined and hence, domestic demand, especially for non-cheap products produced by LEs and imports, dropped significantly No evidence showed that during the 1997/98 crisis, external demand from such countries as the US, Japan and Europe for products from Indonesia and Thailand, including those made by MSMEs, declined.

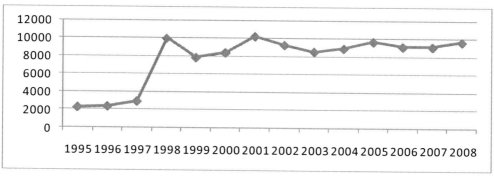

Source: IMF(2009b).

Figure IV.7. Official Exchange Rate of the Rupiah per US dollar, 1995-2008 (period average).

While the 1997/98 crisis was a regional economic crisis, the 2008/09 crisis, although it started first in 2007 as the US economic crisis, has ended as a global economic crisis through at least two main channels: financial and trade (export and import). With respect to the first channel, at least in many countries in Southeast Asia like Indonesia, Thailand, Malaysia, Philippines, Vietnam and Singapore, their national banking sectors were not affected significantly by the crisis. Thus, MSMEs in those countries depending on bank credits were not disturbed by the crisis. No evidence shows that many enterprises faced difficulties in getting bank credits in 2008 and 2009.

With respect to the import channel, since there were no capital flights from these Southeast Asian countries (at least not significant) as a response to the 2008/09 crisis, their national currencies did not depreciate and hence, no import reductions from domestic enterprises, including MSMEs, which dependent much on imported inputs. Whereas, during the 1997/98 crisis, many domestic companies in Indonesia closed their operations or reduced their production just because they could not pay imported inputs as the US dollar became very expensive in rupiah value. In the early months of the 2008/09 crisis, the Indonesian rupiah initially tended to respond to the crisis, not because of capital flight but was considered mainly as a psychological effect. Figure IV.7 shows that the depreciation of the rupiah was much larger in 1998 as compared to 2008.

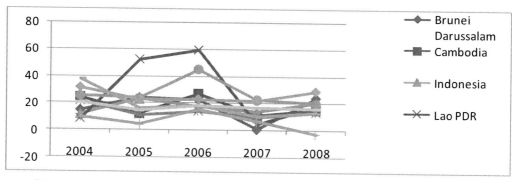

Source: IMF(2009b).

Figure IV.8. Growth Rates of Merchandise Exports in ASEAN, 2004-2008 (%, year-on-year).

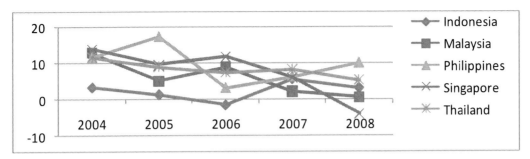

Source: IMF(2009b).

Figure IV.9. Growth Rates of Manufacturing Production Index in Selected ASEAN Member Countries, 2004-2008 (%, year-on-year).

With respect to the export channel, there is evidence showing that for most export-oriented Asian developing countries, the contraction in international trade, especially demands from the US, Japan, and other crisis-affected developed countries for goods such as textiles, garments, leather products, and furniture, has been the most important, driving a severe contraction of demand for their exports that began in the last quarter of 2008 and through the whole year. This has led to a corresponding decline in industrial production in many member countries (ADB, 2009b). With respect to ASEAN, however, only two member countries had experienced the decline in growth rates of merchandise exports in that period, namely Thailand from 16.5 percent in 2007 to 15,7 percent in 2008, and from 6.4 percent in 2007, down significantly to -2.8 percent in 2008 in the Philippines. Indonesia was among the member countries experiencing increased growth rates of merchandise exports during the same period, rising up by slightly more than 50 percent from around 13.3 percent in 2007 to 20.1 percent in 2008 (Figure III.8). However, the growth rate of Indonesian manufacturing production index declined in the same period from approximately 5.6 percent in 2007 (much higher than in the previous years) to around 3.1 percent in 2008 (Figure III.9). Others like Malaysia, Thailand and Singapore also experienced the same, even the last country had a negative growth in 2008. Only the Philippines shown the increase from 6.3 percent to slightly above 10 percent between the same years

Also stated in many newspapers and reports that some Japanese multi-national companies (MNCs) were also affected by the world economic recession, this would also impact many MSMEs in the Southeast Asian region (including Indonesia), since many of them have been heavily dependent on the Japanese global production chain network through subcontracting arrangements, directly or indirectly with Japanese MNCs.[4] This view is also supported by ADB (2009b, page 16) stating that *SMEs can also be an important part of the production value chain. Thus, even if they do not export, their products feed into the production of goods that do. This is certainly the case in the automobile industry where SMEs producing a variety of components are linked to large automobile manufacturers through subcontracting*

---

[4] In Indonesia, many Japanese companies, especially in the automotive and electronic industries, have strong production linkages with local MSMEs. The structure of subcontracting production linkages in the Indonesian automotive industry ranges from only one tier level to two or more tier levels which forms a pyramid production system: car assemblers subcontract some parts of their production process to one or more local LEs. The LEs then subcontract further some parts of the received orders to some MEs, and the latter do the same with some SEs or MIEs.

relationships ... . Moreover, backward links in production mean that not only exporting sectors, but also those that produce inputs in other sectors will be affected.[5] Thus, theoretically, the decline in the world demand for goods manufactured by Japanese MNCs with regional/global production systems would have adverse affects on many MSMEs in the region as their intermediate demands for components and spare parts produced by ther subcontractors would also decline.

Besides export-oriented manufacturers, the economic contraction in the industrialized world can also be expected to hurt local enterprises engaged in travel and tourism. As shown in Table IV.16, there is some indication that the number of foreign tourists visiting Indonesia declined in the early months of 2009. Of course, it is hard to conclude whether the decline was caused mainly by the crisis or there were other explanations. However, theoretically, if the crisis had caused a significant decline in the number of foreign tourists from say, the US, Japan or Eurozone countries to regions in Indonesia which have large tourism sectors such as Bali and D.I. Yogyakarta, it would have negative effects on local MSMEs through two channels: direct and indirect. The direct one: less demand from foreign tourists for handicrafts produced by or services (e.g. local transportation, cheap accomodations, small food stall) provided by local MSMEs. The indirect one: through regional income multiplier effects, less productions/revenues in the local tourism sector would cause regional income and demand for local MSMEs' goods and services to decline.

Table IV.16. Number of Foreign Tourist Arrivals Through 5 Main Airports, 2008-2009

Year/Month	5 Main Airports				
	Sukarno-Hatta	Ngurah Rai	Polonia	Batam	Juanda
2008	1,464,717	2,081,786	130,211	1,061,390	156,989
-April	105,338	154,777	9,180	78,838	10,597
-May	122,627	`167,342	11,655	87,079	12,646
-June	120,270	178,258	9,698	98,404	12,416
-July	145,635	190,662	11,898	85,560	14,006
-August	149,635	195,758	14,890	94,257	18,171
-September	97,764	189,247	8,021	74,690	17,363
-October	120,683	189,142	10,477	82,630	11,011
-November	117,008	172,813	11,134	90,102	13,858
-December	150,209	176,901	16,512	112,794	15,727
2009					
-January	92,136	173,919	11,248	81,601	10,665
-February	97,985	146,192	9,133	68,964	9,916
-March	121,699	168,036	13,617	87,154	13,061
-April	96,709	188,189	11,481	77,788	11,582

Source: BPS (2009).

---

[5] The extent of the backward production links can be illustrated by data from input-output tables. ADB (2009b) gives some empirical evidence. For instance, in the wearing apparel industry, a large chunk of final value added comes from intermediate goods and services. Thus a US$1 drop in apparel exports implies a drop in intermediate manufacturing inputs of 53.6 cents in China, 43.6 cents in India, and 46.9 cents in Indonesia.

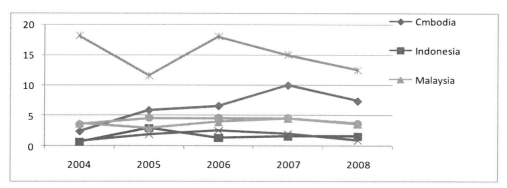

Source: IMF(2009b) and World Development Indicators online (World Bank, www.worldbank.org/world development/ indicators).

Figure IV.10. FDI Net Inflows to Selected ASEAN Member Countries, 2004-2008 (% of GDP).

In addition to the above transmission channels, ADB (2009b) found another channel; the availability of finance from banks and other formal financial institutions through which Asian enterprises have been affected by the 2008/09 crisis. It states the following: *while Asia's financial institutions and systems have so far been relatively stable and largely unscathed—thanks to their limited exposure to subprime assets and related financial products and the relative strength of Asia's banking systems —access to external finance has remained tight as investors from industrial countries have pulled back from developing countries to bolster balance sheets at home, and plans for direct investment have been postponed or shelved* (page 5). As shown before in Chapter II, foreign capital inflows to Asian developing countries have fallen, especially portfolio investments, since peaking in 2008. In contrast to portfolio investment, however, foreign direct investment (FDI) inflows to some Asian developing countries kept increasing in 2008. Within ASEAN, in that year, only Indonesia experienced a positive growth rate in FDI net inflows, i.e. from 6,928.2 million US dollar in 2007 to 8,340.3 million US dollar in 2008; while in the remaining member countries, FDI net inflows declined. In terms of percentage of GDP, the ratio in Indonesia in 2008 is more or less the same as in 2007 at 1.6 percent, while dropping in other member countries. Singapore, which has always had the highest FDI net inflows as percentage of GDP in the region, recorded 15.0 percent in 2007, and declined to 12.5 in 2008 (Figure IV.10).

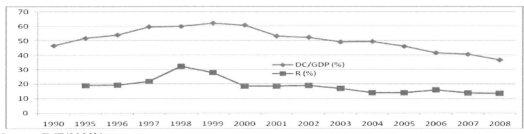

Source: IMF(2009b).

Figure IV.11. Domestic Credit (DC) Provided by Banking Sector and Lending Interest Rate (R) in Indonesia, 1990-2008.

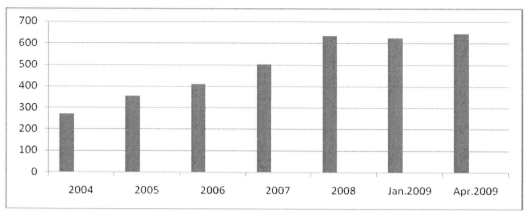

Sumber: Bank Indonesia (www.bi.go.id/creditdata).

Figure IV.12.Development of Credit for MSMEs, 2004-Januari 2009 (Rp billion).

As discussed before, an economic crisis can also affect firms through tightening bank credit to finance external trade (export and import) activities. ADB (2009b) also found that trade financing has shrunk because of the crisis. The evidence is based on a survey conducted by IMF of 40 banks in many countries, including in Asia, in early 2009 which suggests a worldwide decline in the value of trade finance in between January and October 2008, while syndicated loans for trade finance in Asia contracted the most since the 1997/98 Asian financial crisis. In addition, this IMF survey evidence suggests that lending to MSMEs fell more sharply than lending to LEs. Also, as reported further by ADB, there is growing evidence in the region that banks have constrained lending to riskier borrowers, which tend to be MSMEs (especially MIEs and SEs). In Indonesia, official data indicates that domestic credits (DC) provided by banking sectors in terms of percentage of GDP declined but not in 2008; instead it begun to decrease in 1999, after peaking in that year at 62.1 percent (increased from 46.7 percent in 1990), and continued annually and reached almost 37 percent in 2008 (Figure IV.11). Thus, with this decreasing trend of credit development, it is hard to say that the decline in 2008 as compared to 2007 was particularly related to the crisis. Another interesting fact is that the long-term development of lending interest rates (R) also shows a decreasing trend since 1998. This may suggest that although the DC/GDP ratio continued to decrease in 2008, limited credit in the domestic economy in that particular year was not so significant.

Even data from Bank Indonesia suggests that despite the crisis, bank credit flows to MSMEs continued to increase. In 2007, total credit received by these enterprises was around Rp 502 billion, and increased to almost Rp 634 billion in 2008. In January 2009 alone, total credit given to MSMEs was almost Rp 625 billion and in April 2009, recorded approximately Rp 645 billion (Figure IV.12). Indeed, the resilience shown by MSMEs and their crucial role as the last resort for laid off employees in the formal sector during the the 1997/98 crisis was the main reason for the Indonesian government to open more access to credit for these enterprises especially when they had a hard time in 2008/09.[6]

---

[6] Nevertheless, as another key characteristic of MSMEs in developing countries, the enterprises typically face considerable difficulty accessing formal finance, such as from banks. ADB (2009b) shows that in Asian developing countries, with the exception of Malaysia, MSMEs, especially MIEs and SEs, are less likely than LEs

Among all of the above discussed economic crisis transmission channels, information from various sources including public media, official data, estimates, and governments statements suggests that the export market was the main important one (demand-side channel) through which the 2008/09 crisis affected the Indonesian economy, including MSMEs. This view is also supported by Griffith-Jones and Ocampo's (2009) assessment of impacts of the crisis on developing countries. They argue that the main channel of transmission of the crisis to exporters of manufactured goods and services in these countries was through the decline in world trade volumes.[7] Based on their analysis, the growth of world trade volume experienced a strong slowdown since mid-2007, to a rate of around 2 percent by September 2008. This rate turned negative in November and December 2008 as China, the most dynamic world exporter, also experienced negative export growth and even sharper negative import growth during the crisis period.

So, as the 2008/09 global economic crisis was primarily a world income/demand crisis, and so export was the main transmission channel of the effect, at least from the point of view of exporting developing countries, including Indonesia.I It can be said that the most (if not the only) affected MSMEs in these countries would be the export-oriented MSMEs. In Indonesia, as in many other Asian developing countries, looking at the ways they are involved in the export activities, four types of exporting MSMEs can be found: (1) export directly without using middlemen or intermediaries; (2) export indirectly through subcontracting production linkages with export-oriented LEs or via business arrangements with traders/trading companies; (3) export indirectly through selling to visited foreign tourists; and (4) export indirectly by producing certain components or semi-final goods for domestic market-oriented LEs also bought by visited foreign tourists. The first two categories can be considered as primary export-oriented MSMEs (though the first one is more directly), while the last two categories as primarily domestic market-oriented MSMEs. Due to their many limitations, the majority of export-oriented MSMEs in the Southeast Asian region do exports indirectly (Wattanapruttipaisan, 2005; Tambunan, 2009b).

With the above distinction of export-oriented MSMEs, Figure IV.13 illustrates theoretically, how the 2008/09 crisis may affect these MSMEs in Asian developing countries. Two main crisis transmission channels were (1) less world demand for MSMEs' products, i.e. final goods and intermediate goods, components, and spareparts produced for both domestic- and export-oriented LEs, and (2) less visited tourists which caused less demands in local markets for MSMEs products.

Although empirical evidence on the effect of the crisis on MSMEs' export in Asian developing countries is scarce, some authors have managed to figure it out. For instance, Nguanbanchong (2009) finds that in some of these countries, export-oriented MSMEs in labor-incentive manufacturing (e.g. textile, garment, footwear, seafood processing, electronic) and also those producing items for tourism were most affected by the demand slump caused by the crisis. Many workers in these enterprises, especially women, have been affected in a number of ways such as layoffs of fixed as well as contract workers; reduction of work days or hours; and freezes on the minimum wage.

---

enterprises to use bank finance. In most of the countries, the share of bank finance in working capital is often at least 10 percentage points less for MIEs and SEs than larger enterprises.

[7] According to them, the crisis was driven by the reversal of the three positive 'shocks' that developing countries experienced during the boom period in several years before the crisis: rapid growth of remittances, capital flows and trade. For more discussion, see Griffith-Jones and Ocampo (2009).

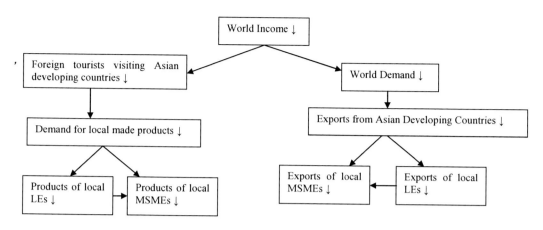

Figure IV.13. Transmition Channels of the Effects of the 2008/09 Crisis on Exports of MSMEs in Asian Developing Countries.

In China, Liu (2009) finds that enterprises producing daily goods such as toys, clothing, textile products, shoes, furniture, sports gears, and stationeries were most affected, with the east coastal region being hit most severely. Most of the enterprises that were forced to shut down were export-oriented MSMEs. In January 2009, the number of new orders mainly from the US and European markets received by the MSMEs dropped by a minimum of 20 per ent to a maximum of 50 percent. There were also many suspensions and cancellations of contractual export orders. From January 2009 to February 2009, the cumulative realized values of goods exported and shipped by industrial MSMEs with annual sales of over CNY5 million in Zhejiang province was CNY82.8 billion, a decrease of about 17 percent year on year. The ratio of export value to the sales production value of industrial MSMEs with annual sales of over CNY5 million also declined to the low level of 22.8 percent. In January 2009, about 52.5 percent of total MSMEs surveyed by the Bureau of Trade and Economy in Shenzhen incurred a reduction in orders from abroad. In January and February of the same year, the number of orders received by MSMEs in Sichuan and Shanxi provinces dropped greatly, and shutdown was imminent for many. Many of export-oriented MSMEs chose to limit or cease production and narrow their product lines, or they began to turn to domestic market development.

According to a report from the Economist Intelligence Unit (EIU, 2010), by the end of 2008, more than 100,000 directly and indirectly export-oriented MSMEs had ceased production. In Wenzhou in Zhejiang province and Dongguan in Guangdong, where some of the country's biggest concentrations of export-oriented MSMEs are found, about 30,000 of them were affected by the crisis and many of them shut down in late 2008 and early 2009. Even the Chinese government stated that, partly because of their greater dependence on foreign markets, Chinese MSMEs were in worse trouble during the global economic crisis than during the 1997/78 Asian financial crisis. In addition, in a survey of 500 Hong Kong MSMEs on mainland China in the second quarter of 2009, 69 percent replied that weak export demand was a "serious" or "very serious" difficulty facing their operations. Many of the respondents work for export-oriented enterprises in neighboring Guangdong. Their most important markets are the US and Eurozone countries.

Table IV.17. Most Affected Exports by the Crisis in Selected Asian Developing Countries

Country	Commodities
China	Non-electrical and electrical machinery and apparatuses, wearing apparel (including footwear), textile, professional and scientific equipments
Hong Kong, China	Non-electrical and electrical machinery, wearing apparel (including footwear), iron, steel and non ferrous metal, plastic products,
India	Textiles and garment, jewelry and related articles, basic iron and steel, grain mill products, textile yarns, fabrics and made-up articles, casting of iron, steel and non-ferrous metal
Indonesia	Textiles and garment, basic precious and non-ferrous metals, produced, processed and preserved meat, fish, fruit, vegetables, oils and fats, basic chemicals, rubber and plastics products, electrical machinery and apparatus.
Malaysia	Industrial equipments, processed and preserved meat, fish, fruit, vegetables, oils and fats, basic chemicals, rubber and plastics products, metal manufactures and general industrial non-electrical machinery, yelecom, sound recording and reproducing apparatus, office accounting and computing machinery
Philippines	Electrical machinery and apparatus, office accounting and computing machinery, road vehicles and components, clothing, leather products and footwear, processed and preserved meat, fish, fruit, vegetables, oils/fats, beverages
Singapore	Basic chemicals, rubber and plastic products, food products, tobacco products, electrical machinery and apparatus, office accounting and computing machinery, metal manufactures, general industrial non-electrical machinery and equipment
Vietnam	Food and beverages, leather, leather products and footwear, textiles, rubber and plastics products, wood products (excl. furniture)

Source: Khor and Sebastian (2009), ADB (2009), recent database from the ASEAN Secretariat, and national data on trade from some individual countries.

Given the fact that the majority of export-oriented MSMEs do exports indirectly through subcontracting with export-oriented LEs, the actual number of export-oriented MSMEs affected by the crisis is likely to be much larger than what could be identified so far. However, since no data is available on how many of these enterprises subcontract with the export-oriented LEs in the region, evidence on the most affected exports by commodity and country may give some clue, at least in what commodities export-oriented (directly and indirectly) MSMEs were most affected. Based on various sources, including Khor and Sebastian's study (2009), ADB (2009), and recent database from the ASEAN Secretariat, Table IV.17 shows the most affected exports during the period quarter 1, 2008 and quarter 1, 2009 in selected Asian developing Countries. Some of these, such as textile, clothing, leather, food and beverages, are important products of MSMEs, either as subcontractors or final producers for both domestic and export markets.

SMERU Research Institute (2009b) provides some local evidence on the impact of the crisis on MSMEs in the textile and garment (TG) industry in Indonesia. The province of West Java is the center of Indonesian TG industries, and the affected TG industries are located in Bandung and Cimahi. According to the Indonesian Textile Producers Association (API), in 2009, the livelihoods of 50,000 TG producers in approximately 150 enterprises in the district (*Kabupaten*) of Bandung were threatened with bankruptcy as a result of the increase in the price of imported raw materials, which had caused production costs to rise by about 20 percent. In one industrial area in the district (Dayeuhkolot Industrial Bonded Area (KBI)), there were 12 MSMEs in the industry that were likely to temporarily lay off thousands of contract workers.

Handicraft industries connected with tourism, which are dominated by MSMEs, have also been affected by the crisis. According toSMERU's (2009b,c) report, in the second half of 2008 there were several handicraft industries in Bali which have started asking their workers to stay at home. The most important handicraft in this province is silversmith. In 2008, Bali had around 300 registered silversmiths who employed more than 20,000 people. In many villages, almost all people are involved in this industry. In Desa Celuk, for example, as reported by SMERU (2009b), more than 50 percent of the people were silversmiths, and it was found that 30 of them have been temporarily laid off. Because of the crisis, the production of silver handicraft has dropped by 50 percent from an average of around 100 kg to 50 kg per month per worker. A similar problem has haunted many craftsmen who make wooden masks in Desa Tegallalang, Ubud, Bali. Many of them were found to have stopped their production. Handicraft industries in some other provinces also faced similar problems. For instance, many *songket* cloth weavers in Palembang and Ogan Ilir in the province of South Sumatera have stopped production because some of their overseas buyers, especially from Singapore and the US, have not been purchasing their products since October 2008. In the province of East Java, by the mid-2008, production in the brass-casting handicraft industry has dropped by up to 50 percent because of a decline in demand from markets in many countries, including the US, US$120 million to US$60 million per month, while it was estimated that the number of workers who have lost their jobs has risen by 50 percent.

IV.5. CASE STUDY OF MSMES IN THE INDONESIAN FURNITURE INDUSTRY

IV.5.1. General Picture about the Impact

One of the various Indonesian key export commodities affected by the crisis was furniture, and the industry is traditionally dominated by MSMEs. The Indonesian Rattan Furniture and Craft Producers Association (AMKRI) announced in 2009 that due to the decline in foreign demand for Indonesian furniture, the industry may have to lay off nearly 35,000 workers in the early part of that year. In May 2009, as announced by the Chairman of the Indonesian Furniture Producers (ASMINDO), Mr. Ambar P. Tjahyono (reported in Kompas newpaper on Tuesday, 11 August 2009), the export value of Indonesian furniture to a number of countries was found to have declined by 30 percent in the second quarter 2009. In the first quarter of 2009 the realized Indonesian export value of furniture already dropped by

35 per ent compared to the same period last year. According to ASMINDO, there was also some decline for furniture in the domestic market.

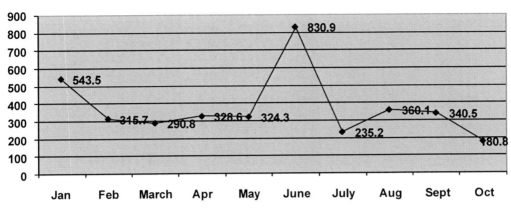

Source: ASMINDO Secretariat, 2009.

Figure IV.14. Indonesian Export Volume of Rattan Furniture, 2008 (1000 kg).

The Indonesian National Statistics Agency (BPS) also reported a decline of 28 percent in timber exports for the first quarter of 2009 in comparison with the same quarter in 2008. The Agency reported timber products were exports worth US$559.7 million for the first quarter of 2009 while the Jakarta Globe reported a sharp decline of 23.2 percent in the export volume of wooden furniture, doors and window frames. Similarly, the value of exports declined by 15.8 percent when compared to the export value of the first quarter of 2008 (US$ 375.8 million). BPS data processed by the Secretariat of ASMINDO shows that Indonesian export of furniture products from other non-wood materials (i.e. rattan, bamboo, iron, plastic, etc.) also declined in 2008, and in the first quarter of 2009, the value of total exports of furniture from all materials was around US$ 434.5 million. Specifically for rattan furniture, since June 2008, the export volume has declined significantly (Figure IV.14).

ASMINDO examined the impact of the crisis on the furniture industry. For the study, it conducted a survey in May 2009 in a number of key clusters of furniture industries in Indonesia such as Trangsan, Luwang, Gatak, and Sukoharjo (all are cited in Java Island). The findings show that since 2008: (i) total output container declined from more or less 360 to 100 container on average per month; (ii) total producers/exporters dropped from 50 units to 30 units (small and large); (iii) total MIEs (or home industries) also declined from 510 units to 250 units; (iv) total employment went down from around 7,600 workers to 3,000 workers; and (v) total sales of raw materials and intermediate inputs to the clusters also dropped significantly. According to the surveyed producers, the decline was mainly caused by the fall in demands from countries of their destination such as the US and some countries in Europe. Without strong evidence, this may have a strong relation with the 2008/09 crisis.

It was also found that, of producers surveyed who were still in operation during the survey period, many have to reduce their production volume. This negative impact of the crisis was expected since furniture, especially from wood and rattan, is generally considered a durable and non-essential product, which is sold on a perceived rather than actual value. Consequently, demand for this kind of final (consumption) product is strongly affected by economic fluctuations: an economic downturn will substantially influence demand and purchases will be delayed (Andadari, 2008).

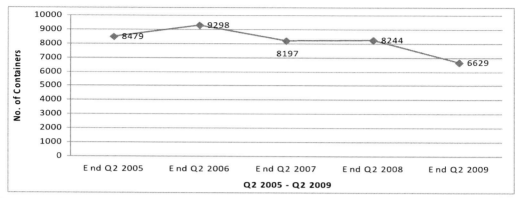

Source: Regional Office, Department of Industry, Cirebon, 2009.

Figure IV.15. Export of Furniture from Cirebon, based on number of container, 2005-2009.

In Cirebon, in another key cluster of furniture industries in Indonesia, the picture was similar though the decline started earlier. There used to be approximately 426b ratten businesses, which employed about 80,000 workers. According to Mr. Sumarca, the chairman of the Cirebon office of ASMINDO, the export of wood and rattan furniture declined since 2005. Regional government data on export of furniture from Cirebon shows that before 2005, the average export was around 2,500 containers/month and in 2005, in total, it went down to 14,611 containers or 1,218 units/month and in June 2009, the total containers were 824 units (Figure IV.15). Based on volume, in 2005, the total export was 49,614,791 kg., or on average 4,134,566 kg./month, and in 2008, it was slightly higher at 50,548,560 kg or 4,212,380 kg/month. In June 2009, the volume reached at 2,926,142 kg, much lower than the average at 4,038,197 kg./month (Figure IV.16). Based on value in US dollar, in 2005, the value was US$ 122,090,576, or slightly above US$ 10 million, and in 2008, it was US$140,566,161, or US$11.7 millions on average per month. In June 2009, the value reached US$8.2 millions, down from approximately US$10 millions the month before (Figure IV.17).

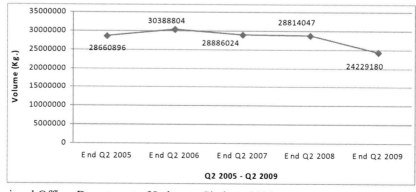

Source: Regional Office, Department of Industry, Cirebon, 2009.

Figure IV.16. Export of Furniture from Cirebon, based on Volume (kg.), 2005-2009.

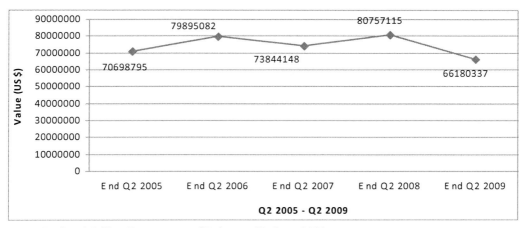

Source: Regional Office, Department of Industry, Cirebon, 2009.

Figure IV.17. Export of Furniture from Cirebon, based on Value (US$), 2005-2009.

Based on the information from the Cirebon office of ASMINDO, from 2005 to 2009, demand for Cirebon furniture declined by around 50 percent. If one container on average needs 60 to 70 workers, then the 50 percent decline would certainly cause a significant negative employment effect in the region. Until July/August 2009, as a result of the drop in export of furniture, many workers in the furniture industry, especially women, were without work. Probably because female workers usually do simple or final parts of the production process in the furniture industry (which is generally a male job) such as packaging, they were the first victims of the crisis. Yet according to his knowledge, as a further consequence, in 2009, Cirebon has, for the first time, sent many women abroad looking for work (known in Indonesia as *tenaga kerja Indonesia*/TKI). Also, many former female workers in the industry ended as domestic servants,[8] while laid off furniture's male workers moved to other sectors like construction, services, trade and local transport activities.

As stated by Mr Sumarca, the decline of furniture exports from Cirebon was caused by three subsequent factors, thus not only by the crisis. First, a new regulation issued in 2005 by the Ministry of Industry and the Ministry of Trade, allowing free export for unprocessed wood and rattan, which also go to highly competitive countries in wood and rattan furniture such as China and Vietnam. This decision did not only cause scarcity problem of raw materials in local markets for domestic furniture producers, but also caused more difficulties for domestic producers to compete with China's and Vietnam's own made furniture, particularly rattan furniture since rattan is only available in Indonesia. Second, the oil ((BBM)

---

[8] There are two scenarios regarding further implication of this development. First scenario, as average incomes of domestic servants are usually lower than incomes of unskilled workers in the furniture industry, depending on types of occupations (e.g. temporary vs. permanent), the changed occupation from industrial workers to domestic servants would increase poverty. Second scenario, as average incomes for unskilled workers working abroad (e.g. Malaysia and in the Middle East countries) are higher than in the furniture industry, the particular female workers and their families would be better off, and even poverty in their villages would decline. Thus, it depends on what those unemployed women, temporary workers and unskilled workers from the surveyed enterprises did. If they could not find other better jobs, this would have a serious consequence on poverty in the region. During the Suharto era from 1966 up to 1997, the poverty rate declined substantially as annual economic growth increased significantly. But during the 1997/98 crisis, the poverty rate increased significantly, mainly because many unskilled workers and female employees in large companies were out of work, and many of them (not all as assumed) could not find jobs with the same or higher level of wage as they had before.

prices increased in 2006 which pushed up production costs, especially prices of processed woods and rattan and other supporting materials. Third, the 2008/09 crisis. All of these three factors subsequently affected the export volume of wood and rattan furniture from Cirebon in the last 4 years. In addition, Mr Sumarca expected in that time that the implementation of international certification (regarding good forestry management and to prevent illegal logging) for wood products from Indonesia in April 2010 would further affect negatively the export of wood furniture from Indonesia, including Cirebon.

In Solo, one of the key clusters of furniture manufacturers in Indonesia, data from the Solo branch office of ASMINDO also shows a similar picture that exports of furniture in value and volume from this region dropped since the second quarter (Q2) of 2007 (Figures IV.18 and IV.19). Of its total members of 200 furniture producers, during 2008-2009, about 30 to 40 percent of them closed their activities, 20 percent stagnated and 10 percent have become suppliers to big furniture exporting companies.

In other parts of the Central Java province, many wood processing industries, especially those producing wooden handicrafts decorated with batik patterns and furniture from rattan, wood, and bamboo also faced a similar problem. SMERU (2009a), from its media-monitoring and various interviews, shows that these industries experienced a decline in export demands. In Purbalingga, virtually all industries involving wood and bambo products have obtained no overseas buyers since the crisis began, and as a result, their production fell by 30 percent.

In the province of East Java, according to SMERU (2009a), by mid-2008, the wood processing industry had undergone a fall in demand of between 30 and 50 percent. However, there were also some positive stories from the furniture industry in this province. As quoted from the Jakarta Post newspaper (Friday, 27 February 2009), despite a general downturn in spending due to the crisis, furniture producers in East Java experienced an export rise of 15 percent in 2009 due to a flurry of closures in the furniture industry in China. According to the newspaper, furniture producers in East Java, especially Surabaya, lobbied former buyers of Chinese goods to commit to importing Indonesian products. According to the report, 40 percent of the country's furniture exports, worth US$2 million per year, came from East Java, and 35 percent of the products were exported to Europe, 29 percent to the United States, 9 percent to Japan and 37 percent to Africa and the Middle East.

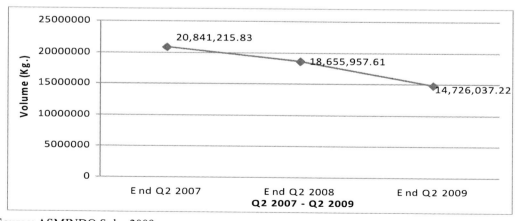

Source: ASMINDO Solo, 2009.

Figure IV.18. Export of Furniture from Solo based on Volume (Kg.) Q2 2007 - Q2 2009.

IV.5.2. Field Survey: Findings and Discussion

Differently than during the 1997/98 Asian financial crisis, with respect to the 2008/09 global economic crisis, studies on the impact on MSMEs in Indonesia are rather limited, which have been discussed briefly before. Besides evidence from these studies, along the year 2009, several newspapers announced that many firms (including MSMEs) in some export-oriented manufacturing subsectors experienced difficulties, mainly because world demand for their exports declined. As reported in the newspapers, for many owners of the affected firms, stops or cuts in orders from their buyers from abroad came as unexpected, which did not give them enough time to prepare. Some affected producers said that they had no idea how to sell their already produced goods to other unexplored countries or to domestic markets.

Probably the only comprehensive research in examining the impact of the world economic recession in 2008/09 on Indonesian MSMEs so far is from Tambunan and Sugarda (2009) on MSMEs in the furniture industry. In order to observe the impact of the crisis on these enterprises more closely, they have conducted two types of surveys during the period July-August 2009 using a structured questionnaire form: (a) the enterprise survey covering 39 enterprises (manufacturers and suppliers); and (b) the worker survey on a total of 79 workers, including 18 workers who have been laid off and 20 workers still working but were vulnerable to be laid off in that time. These two surveys were conducted in the same geographical locations, namely furniture estates and vicinities in the West Java and Central Java provinces, namely in Cirebon, Jepara and Solo. In addition, in these locations, unstructured interviews were also carried out with some key local government officials and other key stakeholders including chairmen of local offices of ASMINDO. For the purpose of the analysis, the impact of the crisis referred to the impact that has taken place since the end of the second quarter (Q2) of 2008 (30 June 2008). The main aim of the survey was not only to assess the crisis' impact on their revenues or incomes, but also to explore their crisis-coping mechanisms, especially with respect to employees.

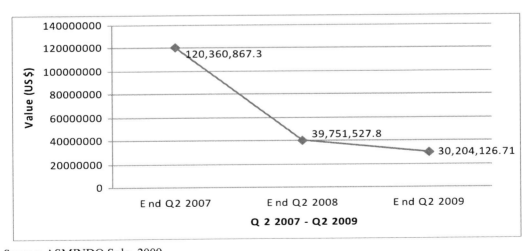

Source: ASMINDO Solo, 2009.

Figure IV.19. Export of Furniture from Solo based on Value (US$.) Q2 2007 - Q2 2009.

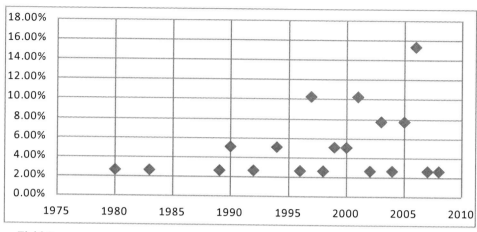

Source: Field Survey.

Figure IV.20. Start-up Year of the Sampled Enterprises by Year (% of total sampled enterprises) (N=39).

With respect to the enterprise survey, the 39 respondents were selected randomly (10 units in Jepara, 10 units in Cirebon and 19 units in Solo).[9] Based on the number of workers, the majority of the sampled firms were MIEs or SEs with total employees ranging from 5 to 20 workers. They were in the informal sector in the sense that they were not registered and thus their labor recruitment or wage payment systems did not follow the existing formal rules (e.g. labor laws, government regulations on working conditions, safety, etc.). Many were established in years before the 1997/98 crisis, suggesting that they managed to survive during that big crisis. Only eleven enterprises in the sample were found to have been started during the period 2005-2008 (Figure IV.20). Only one enterprise, a medium sized firm, located in Cirebon, was foreign-owned with an approximate share of 99 percent from Taiwan.

Regarding the respondents' market orientation, most of them were found to have been involved in export activities, directly (manufacturers) or indirectly (suppliers to other exporting companies), for many years, or even since they started their businesses. However, the degree of export orientation varies by individual enterprises. For instance, by the second quarter of 2008 (Q2 2008), with 10 percent of their total revenues from export, there is only one enterprise; with 30 percent there is also only one enterprise; and with 100 percent there are 17 enterprises in the sample whereas, by Q2 2009, there are six enterprises with 100 percent of their total revenues from domestic market. Three of them used to export in 2008, but during the survey period, they focused on domestic market, because, as they said, they saw more domestic market opportunities. In that period, there are 17 enterprises that were 100 percent export-oriented (Table IV.18). The most important export market destinations for the majority of the surveyed enterprises were the US, Australia and some West European countries like Spain, France, Italy, Germany and the Netherlands (Figure IV.21). These

---

[9] With respect to the category of the sampled enterprises, the majority of them were manufacturers making final goods (25 units), and the other respondents were 1st suppliers (11 units) and 2nd and 3rd suppliers (3 units). Many of the suppliers have been involved in subcontracting systems with the companies for many years; even some of them started since the first year of their establishment.

countries have been the most important traditional markets for the Indonesian exports of furniture and other wood products.

Table IV.18. Export orientation (based on % of Their Total Production) of the Sampled Enterprises, Q2 2008 – Q2 2009 (N=39)

Percentage of total production for export	Q2 2008		Q2 2009	
	Number of respondents	% of total respondents	Number of respondents	% of total respondents
0	3	7.7	6	15.4
10	1	2.6	-	-
15	-	-	-	-
20	-	-	2	5.1
25	-	-	1	2.6
30	1	2.6	-	-
35	-	-	-	-
40	1	2.6	1	2.6
45	-	-	-	-
50	1	2.6	1	2.6
55	-	-	-	-
60	3	7.7	1	2.6
65	1	2.6	1	2.6
70	2	5.1	3	7.7
75	1	2.6	-	-
80	3	7.7	3	7.7
85	-	-	-	-
90	4	10.3	2	5.1
95	1	2.6	1	2.6
100	17	43.6	17	43.6

Source: Field Survey.

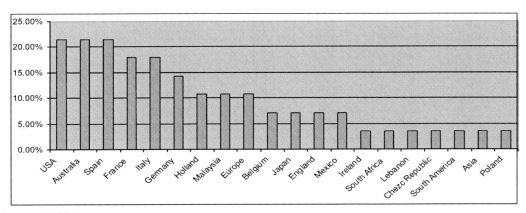

Source: Field Survey.

Figure IV.21. Most Important Export Destinations Based on the Sampled Enterprises' Export Revenues per 30 June (Q2) 2008 (% of total sampled enterprises) (N=39).

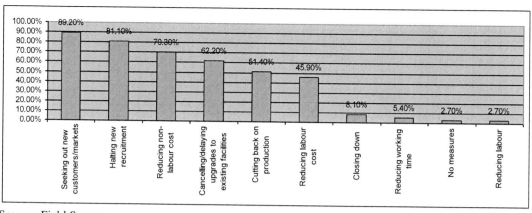

Source: Field Survey.

Figure IV.22. Crisis-Adjustment Measures Taken by the Sampled Enterprises to Cope with the Impact of the Crisis (% of total sampled enterprises) (N=37).

In order to assess the impact of the crisis on the sampled enterprises, first they were asked whether their production has changed since the end of the second quarter (Q2) 2008 (30 June 2008). Two enterprises answered 'no'. Thus, the sample was reduced to 37 enterprises, i.e. only those who experienced production change. Production change can be positive (increase) or negative (negative). Most of them experienced, however, production decline. According to them, the decline of their production during that period was due to the drop in demand, mainly from abroad. However, the percentage of decline was found to vary by individual respondents. Among them were Mr. Tugiyono, Mr. Suparno, Mr. Sunarto and Mr. Sigit. The first respondent used to export 4 containers, 40 feet (ft) per month before the crisis. During the survey, he was found not to export directly anymore but he became a supplier for an exporting company in D.I. Yogyakarta, with about 4 trucks per month. Mr. Suparno had to reduce his employees from 25 workers to only 8 workers because he got fewer orders. Mr. Sunarto who used to export one container per month before the crisis, was found to have no more orders. Mr. Sigit, who has a company named PT. Pradan Sirat in Solo, was also among many furniture producers in the region who have experienced a significant decline in orders from abroad since the end of 2008. He used to export about 8 to 10 containers /month before 2008 and during the survey he was found to send only 4 to 5 containers /month.

None of the respondents said that other factors, such as price increases of inputs or lack of access to credit from banks or other formal financial institutions also contributed to the decline in their production. This was one important difference with the 1997/98 crisis, when very expensive inputs and lack of credits were the main factors which forced many companies including MSMEs to close down or to reduce production. This evidence may thus confirm the general view discussed earlier that the 2008/09 crisis was significantly different than the 1997/98 crisis, not only in nature of the crisis but also in the way it had affected MSMEs or the Indonesian economy in general.

It can be said as a normal business practice or strategy that when an enterprise facing an unanticipated decline in demand market for its products, especially when the decline is not expected as a short-term phenomenon, it will take some adjustment measures to mitigate the pressure on its profit. The measures can be in a variety of forms such as less production volume, less working hours, lay-off workers, etc., depending on the real impact of the decline on the production or financial condition of the enterprise, and, probably more importantly, the expectation of the owner/manager of the enterprise about the short-term prospect of the decline. To explore if this normal business strategy is also valid in MSMEs, the respondents were also asked whether they have undertaken some measures to cope with the impact of the crisis and if they did, they were then requested to identify and to rank the crisis-adjustment measures they have undertaken since the end of Q2 2008. They were given two questions; what measures they have undertaken (they were requested to rank the measures they took), and how have they adjusted their existing workforce due to the impact of the crisis on their business. With respect to the first question, the respondents were given a number of business-adjustment measures which include such as cancelled/delayed upgrading of existing facilities; reduced production, employees and labour costs, sought out new customers/markets, and halted new recruitment.

As can be seen in Figure IV.22, the highest ranked measure is sought out new customers or markets. Indeed, the Indonesian government tried to encourage exporters who have experienced a decline in foreign demand for their goods, especially those who have been traditionally concentrated their export in the US, Japan and European countries to diversify their foreign market or to shift their focus away from these countries towards other unexplored and least crisis-affected regions such as Africa and Middle East, or to explore the domestic market oportunities during the crisis period. Export market diversification or domestic market exploration indeed should be considered as a right decision in facing this crisis, since it was a demand-side crisis, which has affected the Indonesian economy mainly through export channel, not a supply-side crisis, through inputs market channel. In fact, in order to stimulate domestic demand, the Indonesian government has launched a fiscal stimulus package in 2009. However, not enough evidence is yet available on the effectiveness of this fiscal policy.

From the sample, there were some producers who did not take any special measures to cope with the impact of the crisis, mainly because they thought that the crisis would not last for long. The survey also found that three respondents have closed down their business. But as they said, their decision to stop production was only temporary, and in the meantime, they did something else like opening up a small shop selling cigarettes, candies, and other simple basic goods, or working as a daily-paid worker in the construction sector, or as suppliers of certain materials for other furniture firms still in operation. They did such activities while waiting for the market situation to become normal again, so they could start again as furniture producers/exporters.[10]

With respect to the second question, first, the employment situation in the surveyed enterprises is presented here briefly. On average, the enterprises surveyed employed 5 to 10 workers, mainly skilled production employees. Only some employees have been found to have top positions as managers. Not all had permanent jobs. Even in the majority of the enterprises surveyed, most of their workers were temporary workers whose employment was based primarily on the number of orders. Almost all of the enterprises surveyed have female workers. More interestingly, it was found that most of the surveyed enterprises have no written contract with their employees but this is normal for especially MIEs or SEs or

---

[10] In fact, during the survey, the respondents were also requested to give their own opinion on the short-term prospect of the crisis, specifically their expectation over the next six months about the demand (domestic as well as external) for their products. Although most of them suffered from a severe revenue decrease, the majority of the surveyed producers are optimistic in which they expect the demand will increase.

enterprises in the informal sector in developing countries. Some workers have been found to have a written contract but only for 1 year or less. It was also found that in some enterprises surveyed, their employees were not paid regular monthly wages, but based on orders.

Back to the second question, the respondents were given a list of options of possible labor-adjustment measures, including: developed alternative work arrangements (i.e. job sharing, etc.); provided training to workers during low production times; reduced working time/hour, wages, bonuses, and benefits, offered unpaid leave, and laid-off workers. The findings, as shown in Figure IV.23, indicate that the most important forms of labor adjustments made by the majority of the respondents were reduced working time (37.80 percent), followed by developed alternative work arrangements (32.40 percent) and layed off workers (21.60 percent). With respect to working time, the reduction, however, varies by enterprises, since the impact of the crisis on enterprise's financial condition also varies. For many respondents, the main reason for not to chosing to laying off workers, but, instead, less working time was that they expected the crisis would be temporary, and to find/recruit new employees was not easy because, first, they must compete with other producers in their clusters in finding new workers, and, second, they must train them, and all of these cost them money, energy and time. The survey also found that some respondents did not take special measures on their existing employees. The main reason was similar, that they expected the crisis was only a short-term phenomenon, and if they laid-off their workers, to find new workers later on would be difficult. Or, the producers could not, for instance, reduce wages of their workers because the workers have been working for long time, they were considered as family.

The respondents were also requested to tell how many of their employees, especially women and low-educated workers, have been affected by the types of measures they chose. In many surveyed firms, female workers were mostly affected by the labor adjustment measures, but the percentage of the affected female workers varies by the type of measure. For instance, the survey found that from 14 enterprises which have chosen less working hours of their employees as their primary labor adjustment measure, only one enterprise (7.1 percent of 14 units) where female workers were not affected by the measure; one enterprise with 2 percent of its female workers were affected; one enterprise with 5 percent; 3 enterprises with 15 per ent; and two enterprises where all female workers were affected (Figure IV.24).

Variation of affected female workers by enterprise was also found in the case of employees benefit reduction. Of the 6 enterprises which have chosen this type as their primary labor adjustment measure, there was only one enterprise (17 percent) where no female workers were affected, and so on, as presented in Figure IV.25, while, with respect to unpaid leave as the main labor-adjustment measure, of the 5 enterprises which chose this measure, only two enterprises where 35 and 50 percent, respectively, of female workers were affected (Figure IV.26).

Finally, 7 enterprises laid-off some of their workers. From these enterprises, only one enterprise (14.3 percent) had none of its female workers affected, while in other two enterprises (29 percent), all female workers have been laid off (Figure IV.27). Some respondents considered female workers as not so important as production workers since they usually do simple works such as packaging. One respondent said that furniture industry is traditionally a male job. They hired female workers usually not as a necessity, but mainly as helpers paid lower than production male workers. It is different than in, for example, garments, textile and tobacco industries, where female workers are predominant.

The survey also provides evidence on the impact of the crisis on the average working times and the average earnings (wages and bonuses). It shows that of the 37 sampled enterprises, the majority (68 percent) said there was no change in average working time of their permanent employees. The remaining 12 enterprises (32 percent) experienced a decrease in average working time. The rate of decrease, however, varies by enterprise. One enterprise (8.3 percent) experienced a decline at 99 percent; one enterprise at 80 percent, and so on (Figure IV.28). Out of 37 enterprises, 22 (59.50 percent) said no any change in average incomes of their permanent employees; 14 (37.80 percent) experienced a decrease; and only one (2.70 percent) experienced a positive change. From those 14 enterprises, the rate of decline varies by enterprise; two enterprises (14.3 percent) experienced 99 percent of decline, and the lowest decline at 10 percent experienced by one enterprise (Figure IV.29).

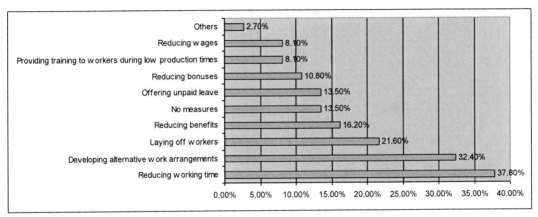

Source: Field Survey.

Figure IV.23. Affected existing workers in the Sampled Enterprises by form of adjustment (% of total sampled enterprises) (N=37).

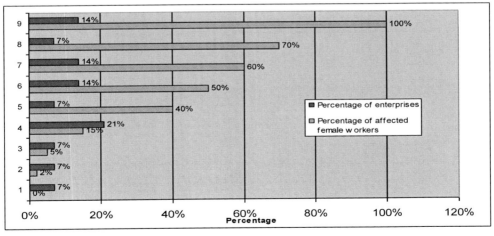

Source: Field Survey.

Figure IV.24. Affected Female Workers (% of total female workers) by Reduced Working Time in the Sampled Enterprises (N=14).

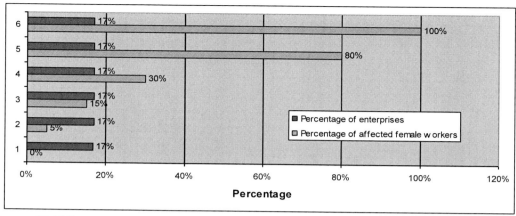

Source: Field Survey.

Figure IV.25. Affected Female Workers (% of total female workers) by Reduced Benefits in the Sampled Enterprises (N=6).

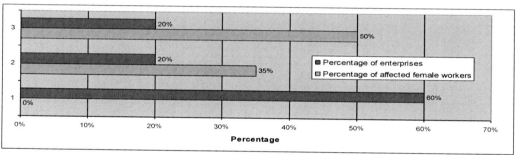

Source: Field Survey.

Figure IV.26. Affected Female Workers (% of total female workers) by Offered Unpaid Leave in the Sampled Enterprises (N=5).

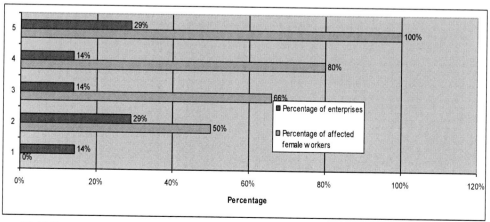

Source: Field Survey.

Figure IV.27. Affected Female Workers (% of total female workers) by Laid –off Workers in the Sampled Enterprises (N=7).

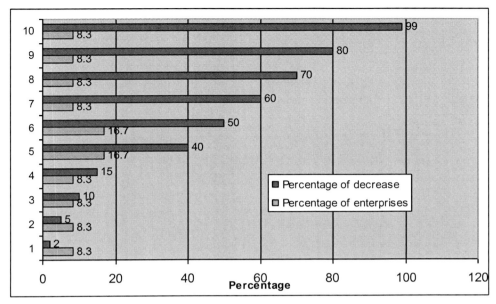

Source: Field Survey.

Figure IV.28. Percentage of Avg. Working Time Decrease of Permanent Employees in the Sampled Enterprises (N=12).

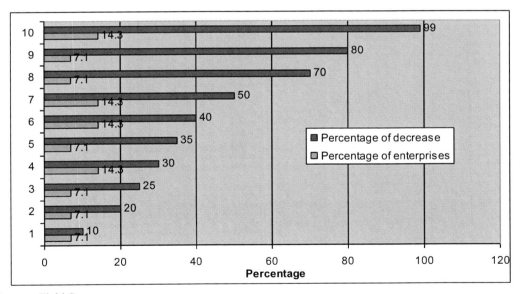

Source: Field Survey.

Figure IV.29. Percentage of Avg. Incomes Decrease of Permanent Employees in the Sampled Enterprises (N=14).

With respect to temporary employees experienced lower working hours and lower income during the crisis, it was found that in the first case, 17 respondents did not experience any change in average working time of their temporary employees, while in the remaining enterprises, it declined. The decline also varies by enterprise: in two enterprises the rate of decrease reached 99 percent, while one enterprise has the lowest rate at 5 percent (Figure IV.30). In the second case, 15 enterprises did not experience any change in average incomes of of their temporary employees, 3 enterprises experienced a positive change by 5, 15, and 20 percent, respectively. Negative changes happened in the remaining 19 enterprises, though the rate varies by enterprise: three enterprises (or 15.8 percent of them) have the highest rate at 99 percent and the lowest 10 percent experienced by the other three enterprises (Figure IV.31).

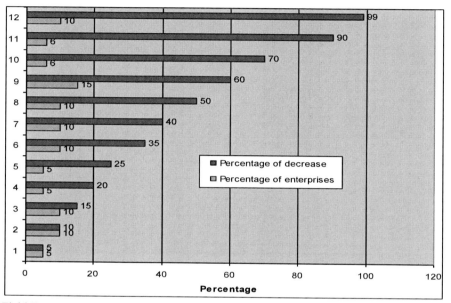

Source: Field Survey.

Figure IV.30. Impacted Avg. Working Time of Temporary Employees in the Sampled Enterprises (N=20).

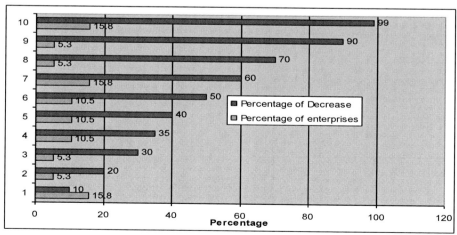

Source: Field Survey.

Figure IV.31. Percentage Avg. Earnings Decrease of Temporary Employees Decrease in the Sampled Enterprises (N=19).

Impact on Micro, Small and Medium Enterprises

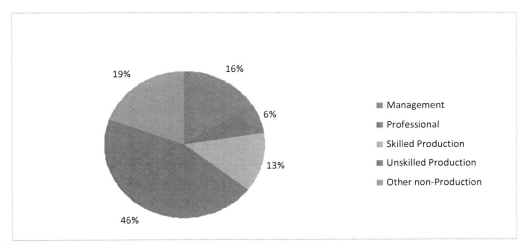

Source: Field Survey.

Figure IV.32. Types of Affected Workers by Income Reduction in the Sampled Enterprises (% of total sampled enterprises) (N=37).

Another important issue that the survey focused on was the type of workers according to skill/education most affected by reduction in income (wages and bonuses) and working hours. The findings show, which may be generally expected, that unskilled production workers, mainly female, were the most affected type of employees by these labor-adjustment measures: around 46 percent of the total sample with respect to income reduction (Figure IV. 32), and 53 percent with respect to working hour reduction (Figure IV.33). The percentages of decrease in income and working hours experienced by unskilled production workers, however, varies, by enterprise. For instance, in the case of income reduction, the highest drop was 90 percent, and lowest rate was 2 percent.

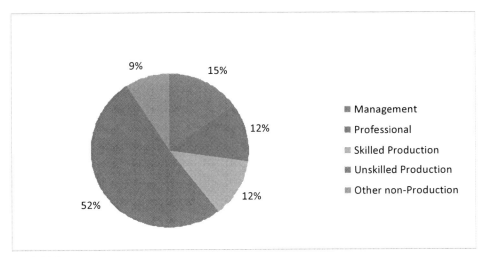

Source: Field Survey.

Figure IV.33. Types of Affected Workers by Working Hour Reduction in the Sampled Enterprises (% of total sampled enterprises) (N=37).

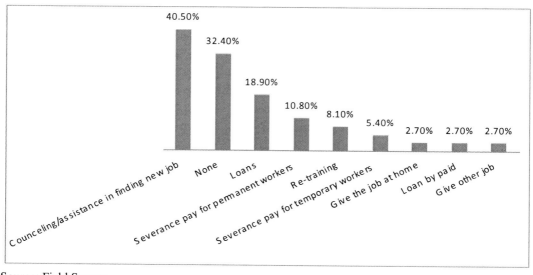

Source: Field Survey.

Figure IV.34. Type of Support Prvided by the Sampled Enterprises to Their Workers in case of layoffs (% of total sampled enterprises) (N=37).

Finally, the respondents were asked about the types of supports they provide to their workers in case of layoffs such as severance pay, re-training, counseling/assistance finding new jobs, loans and so on. The findings show that many of the surveyed enterprises did not provide any support, and from those who provided supports, the largest percentage was the form of counseling/assistance in finding new jobs, followed by loans and severance pay but only for permanent workers (Figure IV.34).

With respect to the worker survey, the majority (72 percent) of the total sample of 79 workers were male. From the education point of view, the majority of the respondents (63 percent) have only secondary education. About 46 percent of the total sample were skill production staffs; only few in the sample have top positions as managers. About 60 percent of the respondents were temporary workers, which was mainly based on orders. More interestingly, it was found that 81 percent of the sampled workers have no written contract. This is, however, a normal phenomenon for workers in MIEs and SEs in the informal sector. Of the remaining respondents, 15 percent have a written contract only for 1 year or less. Also, not all respondents were paid a regular monthly wage.

As in the case of the enterprise survey, the 79 respondents were given the following question: have you recently been laid off, and if not, if you are currently still working, has your employer reduced your working hours or your wages and/or bonuses? For those who answered with no to both questions, they were then excluded for further analysis. So, the final sample covers only 73 workers, and from them it was found that they have experienced a variety of labor adjustment measures, from less weekly-work hours, less paid benefits, less bonus, and reduction in average monthly income. The reduction of these items vary by respondent. For instance, it was found that few respondents experienced only a small decline in their monthly income, while others in other enterprises experienced higher percentages of reduction. This is probably because different enterprises in the industry may have faced different marketing or financial problems due to the crisis.

Finally, the respondents who experienced the decline in their income were then asked two questions: (1) about their coping mechanisms with respect to their daily expenditures, and (2) any supports that they may have received to cope with their reduced incomes. The findings with respect to the first question are shown in Table IV.19. The respondents who have reduced their expenditures were given two options; complete or partial reduction. The findings regarding the second question are shown in Figure IV.35, which indicate that severance pay has been the most important support that they counted on.

Table IV.19. Impacts on Labor Adjustment on Expenditures of the Sampled Workers (Number of Respondents) (N=73)

		All regions	JEPARA	CIREBON	SOLO
Reduce expenditures on housing	No	22	15	2	5
	Yes Complete	17	4	8	5
	Yes Partial	34	8	10	16
Reduce expenditures on food/nutrition	No	18	2	8	8
	Yes Complete	14	10	2	2
	Yes Partial	41	15	10	16
Reduce expenditures on education	No	56	19	14	23
	Yes Complete	4		4	
	Yes Partial	13	8	2	3
Reduce expenditures on health	No	32	3	11	18
	Yes Complete	5		3	2
	Yes Partial	35	23	6	6
Reduce expenditures on utilities/ transport/ communications	No	9	4		5
	Yes Complete	16	2	11	3
	Yes Partial	48	21	9	18
Reduce expenditures on durable goods	No	9	6	1	2
	Yes Complete	28	3	11	14
	Yes Partial	36	18	8	10
Reduce expenditures on entertainment	No	5	3	1	1
	Yes Complete	40	16	11	13
	Yes Partial	28	8	8	12

Source: Field Survey.

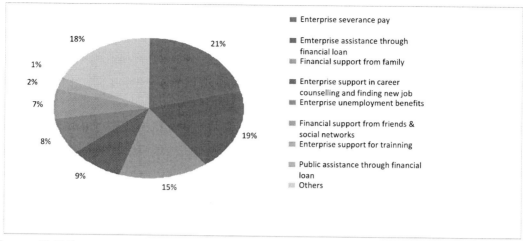

Source: Field Survey.

Figure IV.35. Supports the Sampled Workers Received to Cope with Their Reduced Incomes and Expenditures (% of total sampled workers)(N=73).

IV.6. OVERALL FINDINGS

In the past 20 years, Indonesia has been hit by two economic crises. The first and the biggest one was in 1997-1998, known as the Asian financial crisis and the recent one was in 2008/09, known as the global economic crisis caused by a large scale financial crisis in the US. This chapter aims to assess the impact of the 2008/09 crisis on MSMEs in Indonesia. The simple question of this chapter is whether these enterprises, which generally are more domestic-oriented or even more isolated from the world economy compared to their larger counterparts, were also negatively affected by the crisis. Based on a review of key literature on the impact of the 1997/98 crisis on MSMEs in some ASEAN member countries, including Indonesia, this chapter has shown that many enterprises of this size group were also hit. The transmission channels were mainly from the supply side. However, as compared to LEs, the affected MSMEs were few. Thus, the 1997/98 crisis experience may suggest that MSMEs in general are more resilient to an economic crisis than their larger counterparts. At least four factors may explain this performance: (a) most MSMEs employ more relatives and friends and use local inputs. This made them less sensitive to the increase in domestic prices of imported inputs when national currencies depreciated; (b) many unemployed, laid-off employees from LEs, started their own business to get any income and this had caused the number of MSMEs to rise; (c) sunken costs in MSMEs are usually lower and labor-capital struggles are less frequent (d) MSMEs are much less reliant on formal markets and formal credit funds, and thus they were less impacted by the collapse of domestic financial sector during the crisis

With respect to the 2008/09 global economic crisis, although the empirical evidence is scarce, some studies show that there were also many affected MSMEs and the main channel was the demand-side, especially export demand. Different than the 1997/98 crisis, most MSMEs affected by the 2008/09 crisis were mainly export-oriented firms. In addition to these studies, this chapter has discussed the findings of a study conducted by Tambunan and Sugarda (2009) on MSMEs in the furniture industry. Although their findings cannot be used to represent the condition of Indonesian MSMEs during the crisis period, they may give some important facts, especially about how a group of MSMEs in an industry cope with the crisis. As shown before, the most important types of labor adjustment taken by the majority of the sampled firms were reducing working time, followed by developing alternative work arrangements and laying off workers. Female workers, temporary workers and unskilled production employees were the most affected by their adoped adjustment measures. However, this finding does not come as a surprise (in fact, this also usually occurs in LEs) for a number of reasons. First, the types of work performed by women in the furniture industry are usually simple parts of the production process such as packaging or preparing raw materials. This kind of task can also be performed by the core workers if necessary. Moreover, male workers are predominant in the furniture industry, differently than in such as textile and garment, and food and beverages industries where the core employees are women. In other words, if the survey had been focused on the garment industry instead, a different picture would have revealed. Second, temporary workers are usually employed for certain periods when order volume is high. Most female workers are included in this category, though the percentage varies by enterprise, ranging from 10 to 70 percent; and some enterprises have only male temporary workers. Thus, when production slows down, they are no longer needed. Third, since skilled workers are not easy to find, especially in regions where there are many furniture producers but not many skilled workers available, many of the affected enterprises hold onto their workers with the hope that the crisis would be temporary.

For the laid off workers, of the enterprises surveyed which provided supports, the most used forms were counseling/assistance in finding new jobs, followed by loans and severance pay but only for permanent workers. It is also not really suprising, as employers and employees relationships in MSMEs are like family relationships. The owners or employers can feel how hard it is for their employees to be without jobs , so they try with what ever they can to mitigate the hardship.

Chapter 5

REGIONAL VULNERABILITY TO ECONOMIC CRISIS: AN ANALYSIS WITH INDONESIA DATA

V.1. BACKGROUND

In the past 12 years, many countries in Southeast Asia have been hit by two big economic crises; the 1997/98 Asian financial crisis and the 2008/2009 global economic crisis. The experiences indicate that those countries are very vulnerable to almost any type of economic shocks, either from internal sources (e.g. the 1997/98 crisis) or external sources (e.g. the 2008/09 crisis), for the following main reasons:

(1) The countries have become more open to the world economy as compared to, say, 3 decades ago; although the degree of openness varies by country, depending on internal factors such as institution, economic policy orientation, political regime, and constraints. Indonesia's economy, for instance, has become more integrated with the global economy since the introduction of economic reform packages in the 1980s and accelerated after the 1997/98 crisis toward more trade liberalization in goods as well as services, and banking and investment (direct as well as portfolio) liberalization. Consequently, the country now is more vulnerable than ever before to any economic crises such as the recent one in 2008-2009. As discussed previously, the crisis has led to world demand for some Indonesian exports to decline. Many countries in the region, especially Indonesia, Thailand, Malaysia and certainly Singapore now are also very vulnerable to a regional or global banking crisis as financial transactions between those countries and foreign capital markets have been accelerating in the past 3 decades. For Indonesia, its economy started to become vulnerable since its government begun to liberalize the country's current and capital accounts in the 1970s. As these countries have been among key destinations in Southeast Asia for short-term foreign investments, known as 'hot money', they are also vulnerable to capital flights, which happened during the 1997/98 Asian financial crisis which led to huge depreciations of the national currencies, especially Indonesian rupiah and Thai bath, and ended up as the worst national economic crisis these countries ever experienced;

(2) though at a decreasing rate, countries such as Indonesia, Malaysia and Thailand are still dependent on exports of many primary commodities such as mining and agriculture (including plantation crops such as palm oil). Consequently, any world-price/demand instability for those commodities, particularly palm oil, rubber, and coffee, will become a serious shock for their economy. For Indonesia, if the world demand or world price for their exported agricultural commodities decline, the effects on their economy will be greater than in the case of mining, since the majority of the countries' populations are still living in rural areas and most of them are working in the agricultural sector; much more than those working in the mining sector. Moreover, the majority of the poor in Indonesia and Thailand are found in agriculture and in the informal non-farm economic activities related to agriculture;

(3) since the past two decades, Indonesia has been increasingly depending on imports of a number of food items such as rice, food grains, cereals, wheat, corn, meat, dairy, vegetables and fruits, or even oil. Consequently, increases or instabilities of world prices or world production failures of these commodities will have particular effects on domestic consumption and food security in the country;

(4) in countries like Indonesia and the Philippines, more working populations, including women, went abroad as migrant workers, and hence, livelihoods in many villages in these countries have been increasingly depending on remittances from abroad. Consequently, any economic crises that hit the host countries (such as what happened in Dubai, United Arab Emirate (UAE) during its financial crisis in 2009) will hit the countries' economy too; particularly the livelihoods in villages;

(5) Indonesia is a huge populated country which means that there is always high domestic for food consumption so acceleration in domestic agricultural production growth is a must, but this depends on various factors, including climate, which is an exogenous factor. As it is located between the Pacific ocean and the Indian ocean in the line of equator, Indonesia is very vulnerable to the El Nino phenomenon which may cause failures in rice harvest (and other agricultural productions) and hyperinflation.

According to a report of a pilot study in Indonesia and other several developing countries conducted by the Institute of Development Studies,UK (IDS, 2009), Indonesia is considered the most vulnerable country to food, fuel and trade shocks, but less vulnerable to capital shock. As can be seen in Table V.1, with respect to the first two types of shocks, the study made a distinction between demand-side and supply-side. From the demand-side, the level of Indonesian vulnerability to the shocks is high, as most domestic consumed foods and fuel are imported. For the food shock, it is because food demand in Indonesia is high or it keeps accelerating (due to its large and continued increase in population), especially of the proportion of the population is near the poverty line. For the fuel shock, it is because there are many people, especially in the category of poor and near poor, with fuel shortages; thus sustained adequate domestic supply of fuel with reasonable prices is very crucial. From the supply-side, the level of vulnerability is low for food but high for fuel. It is low for food because, as said before, the country has been depending much on imported food, and imported food may play as the last resort for Indonesian food security when a harvest failure happens in the country. It is high for fuel because the world price of fuel tends to increase while Indonesian import of fuel tends to increase annually due to sustained increase in domestic demand.

With respect to trade shock, Indonesia's vulnerability is high due to the country's high dependence on few commodities for export earnings. This means that when world demand for those commodities decline, it will have a serious impact on Indonesian trade balance (i.e. trade balance deficit will increase and foreign currencies stock will decline) and hence, the rate of economic growth will diminish. Regarding capital shock, it is relatively low because Indonesia is not yet fully linked to international markets via private capital inflows, although currently, the share of foreign, private, short-term investments in Indonesia's total (non-loan) capital inflows is much higher than 3 decades ago.

From experiences with many economic crises in many parts of the world since the end of the second WorldWar, there are two categories of economic crises ever occurred, based on the nature of the process. Some crises were sudden events, and the 1997/98 Asian financial crisis was among this category: no any signs of something wrong, but suddenly capital flight happened, which started first in Thailand and followed soon in Indonesia, Philippines and South Korea. Just before the capital flight occured, the economy of these countries was booming, exports expanded annually, and foreign investments kept coming. Even Indonesia, together with Thailand and Malaysia, were regarded as the new "Asian tigers" (in that time, Asian developing countries which were already regarded as Asian tigers were Hong Kong China, Taipei China, Singapore and South Korea).

Other crises did not come suddenly, but gradually. This category may include the 2008/2009 global economic crisis which was initially a domestic financial/economic crisis in the US and after several months, it then gradually became a global economic crisis in 2008. Thus, the world may have anticipated the global effect of that crisis. Therefore, this crisis cannot be considered as a shock (not like the 1997/98 Asian financial crisis which was really a shock- based on reasons already explained). Another example was the first oil crisis in 1973/74. In fact, the Organization of Petroleum Exporting Countries (OPEC), sponsored by Saudi Arabia, has issued first a warning that they will stop oil supply immediately to the West if the US and its ally keep supporting Israel during the Arab-Israel war. Thus, the OPEC's decision in that time which led the world oil supply to decline and hence, the to world economy to fall into a big recession was anticipated by the world.

Table V.1. Indonesia's Vulnerability to Food, Fuel, Trade and Capital Shocks

Type of Shock	Level of Vulnerability
Food shock	
-demand	high
-supply	low
Fuel shock	
-demand	high
-supply	high
Trade shock	high
Capital flow shock	low

Source: IDS (2009).

Economic crises are also often multi-faced or intercede with each other. The 1997/98 crisis can be considered as this type of crisis. In Indonesia, it started first as a currency crisis caused by a sudden huge capital flight, and followed by a banking crisis. The real sector also collapsed as many firms, especially conglomerates, stopped production since they could not pay back their debts any more to domestic or foreign banks, or because they could not import inputs any more as the import costs increased significantly. In 1998, the crisis reached its climax when the Soeharto regime collapsed, marking the beginning of a political crisis, shortly after a huge social unrest erupted.

With the above background, it is then highly reasonable to state that countries like Indonesia, Philipines, Thailand, Malaysia and Singapore which have experienced many economic crises in the past many years and will so in the future, should have an economic vulnerability monitoring system. By monitoring regularly the vulnerability level of provinces, districts, sub-districts, sectors, and households/communities to economic crises, governments in those countries have enough time to react and so they can make the right targeting of sectors, regions or households to be supported when an economic crisis really occurs.

V.2. DEFINITION

Identifying vulnerability or exposure of countries, regions, communities, sectors, households or individuals to exogenous economic shocks has become an important issue lately. Before identifying vulnerability, first, vulnerability itself should be defined. As mentioned in many academic papers, e.g. Adger, et al. (2004) and Briguglio, et al. (2008), vulnerability is not a straightforward concept; it is different than the concept of poverty. Until the present day, there is still no general consensus as to the precise meaning of vulnerability. But, generally speaking, vulnerability refers to potential for loss or damage from exogenous shocks. In the economic area, economic vulnerability refers to risks caused by exogenous shocks (can be from internal or external sources) to three key systems in the economy, i.e. production, distribution (of output and inputs) and consumption.

In Adger, et al.(2004), it is stated that the vulnerability of an industry, a region or a community, to a shock relates to its capacity to be harmed by that shock. In Briguglio et al.'s (2008), it is ascribed to inherent conditions affecting a country's or a region's or an household's exposure to exogenous shocks. Guillaumon (2007) defines the economic vulnerability of a country to an exogenous shock by the risk for the country to see its ecomomic development or growth hampered by the shock the country faces. According to him, there are two main kinds of exogenous shocks, or two main sources of vulnerability: *1) environmental or "natural" shocks, namely natural disasters, such as earthquakes or volcanic eruptions, and the more frequent climatic shocks, such as typhoons and hurricanes, droughts, floods, etc. ; 2) external (trade and exchange related) shocks, such as slumps in external demand, world commodity prices instability (and correlated instability of terms of trade), international fluctuations of interest rates, etc. "* (page 6).

Hoddinott and Quisumbing (2003) define vulnerability as the likelihood that at a given time in the future, the welfare of an individual or household will drop to a level below some norm or benchmark. More concretely, it is the likelihood of someone being poor next year, in ten years time, or in old age. From the economic point of view, the welfare is generally measured by level of consumption expenditure or nominal income, and the norm or benchmark as the poverty line. Now, the problem of this definition is how to determine the norm or benchmark which may vary not only by different individuals, households, communities or regions, but also over time, as other things such as price and taste never stay constant.

The concept of vulnerability is often used as a synonym for poverty, although, it is different than the concept of poverty. As in their own words, Hoddinott and Quisumbing (2003) say that the concepts of vulnerability and poverty are linked but they are not identical. Poverty measures are generally fixed in time, thus poverty is essentially a static concept. For instance, based on official data for March 2008, the proportion of population living under the current poverty line (the poverty rate) in Indonesia was around 15.42 percent; declined slightly from 16.58 percent in one year before. By contrast, as explained in Lipton and Maxwell (1992), vulnerability is a dynamic process: it captures changes and processes of people/individuals who move in and out of poverty. In Moser (1998), it is stated that, *although poor people are usually among the most vulnerable, not all vulnerable people are poor, a distinction which facilitates differentiation among low-income populations* (page 3). Thus, vulnerable people are not always poor, and non-poor people are vulnerable to become poor if there is a shock.

In Chaudhuri et al. (2002) it is writen: *vulnerability is an ex ante (forward-looking) rather than an ex post concept. Poverty status can be observed at a specific time period, given the welfare measure and the poverty threshold. By contrast, household vulnerability is not directly observed, rather it can only be predicted...* (page 12). As an example, suppose that the financial condition of a household has deteriorated in the past few years. If this financial condition can be used as an indicator for identifying vulnerability, then it can be said that the level of vulnerability of the household has increased in the past few years. This experience with the sustained decline in the past few years may give tendency to expect that the financial condition of the household will deteriorate further, with the assumption that other financial determinant factors will not change. So the household is expected to become more vulnerable to shocks. This example suggests that time-series data is required in order to capture the long-term process of changes in levels or indicators of vulnerability.

Given the definition and the link between vulnerability and poverty as discussed above, vulnerability can be assessed through different approaches. Hoddinott and Quisumbing (2003) mentioned three principal approaches: (1) vulnerability as expected poverty (VEP), (2) vulnerability as low-expected utility (VEU), and (3) vulnerability as uninsured exposure to risk (VER). Those approaches are explained mathematically in Gaiha and Imai (2008). VEP is an ex ante vulnerability measure, proposed by Chaudhuri, et al (2002) who applied it to the Indonesian household data. It was also applied to the Indian household data by Gaiha and Imai (2004). In their research, vulnerability of a household is defined as the probability that the household will fall into poverty in the future:

$$V_t = P_r(C_{t+1} \leq Y) \tag{V.1}$$

where vulnerability of household at time t, V_t, is the probability that the household's level of consumption (representing income) at time t+1, (C_{t+1}), will be below the poverty line, Y.

In the measure of VEU, vulnerability is defined as the difference between the utility (U) derived from some level of certainty-equivalent consumption, Y_{ce}, at and above which the household is not considered vulnerable and the expected utility of consumption (EU). In other words, this Y_{ce} is akin to a poverty line. Consumption of a household, C, has a distribution in different states of the world, so this measure takes the form:

$$V = U(Y_{ce}) - EU(C) \tag{V.2}$$

where U is a concave, strictly increasing function. Following Gaiha and Imai (2008), equation (V.2) can be rewritten as:

$$V = [U(Y_{ce}) - U(E_c)] + [U(E_c) - EU(C)] \tag{V.3}$$

The first bracketed term on the right is a measure of poverty in terms of the difference in utility between Y_{ce} and C. The second term measures the risk that a household faces. The latter can be decomposed into aggregate or covariate and idiosyncratic risks, as shown below in the equation (V.4):

$$\begin{aligned} V = &[U(Y_{ce}) - U(E_c)] \text{ (poverty)} \\ &+ \{U(E_c) - EU[E(C\,X)]\} \text{ (covariate or aggregate risk)} \\ &+ \{EU[E(C\,X)] - EU(C)\} \text{ (idiosyncratic risk)} \end{aligned} \tag{V.4}$$

where $E(C\,|\,X)$ is an expected value of consumption conditional on a vector of covariant variables, X.

VER is designed to assess ex post welfare loss from a shock (e.g., crop failure), as opposed to an ex ante assessment of future poverty in VEP. Based on Gaiha and Imai (2008), this measure can be explained with the following example. Consider a household, h, living in a village, v, at time t. Let $\Delta \ln C_{htv}$ denotes change in log consumption or the growth rate of consumption per capita of the household between two periods, t and t-1, and AS and IS are aggregate/covariate and idiosyncratic shocks, respectively. With a set of binary variables identifying each village separately, Vd and a vector of household characteristics, HC, then VER could be estimated through the following equation:

$$\Delta \ln C_{htv} = \sum_h \lambda_h AS + \sum_h \beta_h IS + \sum_{tv} \delta_v(Vd) + \eta HC_{htv} + \Delta \xi_{itv} \tag{V.5}$$

The coefficients λ and β seek to capture the effects of covariate, AS and IS, respectively. These effects are net of coping strategies and public responses (Gaiha and Imai, 2008).

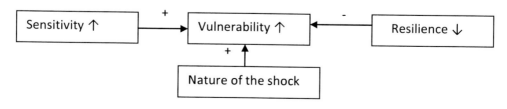

Figure V.1. Main Factors Affecting the Level of Vulnerability.

All of those three approaches share a common characteristic; they predict a measure of welfare, which can be consumption, income, or other alternative welfare indicators could also be used instead. Among the three approaches, the first one seems to be easiest to be used since it is not only relatively straight forward to calculate, but it can also be estimated with a single cross-section using national data.[1] If the welfare is defined in terms of the level of consumption expenditure (for Indonesia, using SUSENAS data), then in a simple way, it can be said that vulnerability of an household in 2010, for instance, is the probability that the household's level of consumption in 2011 will be below the consumption poverty line. In this case, the consumption poverty line is taken as a threshold.

Furthermore, vulnerability has several dimensions which should be taken into account in the process of identification of determinants (or indicators) of vulnerability. According to many, such as Blaike and Brookfield (1987), Bayliss-Smith (1991), and Moser (1998), there are two dimensions of vulnerability: (1) its sensitivity, i.e. the magnitude of individuals', households', or communities' response to a shock, and (2) its resilience, i.e. the ease and rapidity of individuals', households', or communities' recovery from a shock. As stated in Moser (1998), *analyzing vulnerability involves identifying not only the threat but also the "resilience", or responsiveness in exploiting opportunities, and in resisting or recovering from negative effects of a changing environment* (page 3). He sees vulnerability as insecurity and sensitivity in the well-being or welfare (which is generally measured by total income or value of total tangible assets owned) of individuals, households or communities in the face of a negative changing environment (which can be ecological, economic, social or political), and implicit in this, their responsiveness and resilience to risks that they face during such a negative change. Whereas, for Briguglio et al. (2008) economic resilience is associated *with actions undertaken by policymakers and private economic agents which enable a country to withstand or recover from negative impacts* (e.g. production declines, poverty increases) *of shocks* (page 2). In Allen (2003), vulnerability is viewed as representing the set of socio-economic factors that determine people's ability to cope with stress or change.

Guillaumon (2007) also agreed with those two dimensions, but he added another dimension; the nature of the shocks. Precisely, he argues that vulnerability can be seen as the result of three components: *(a) the size and frequency of the exogenous shocks, either observed (ex post vulnerability) or anticipated (ex ante vulnerability); (b) the exposure to the shocks ; (c) the capacity to react to the shocks, or "resilience"* (pages 6&7). In Hoddinott and Quisumbing (2003), vulnerability is stated to be dependent on four main factors: (1) the nature of the shock (e.g large-scale disasters such as droughts, earthquakes, floods or landslides; world market instability, social or political unrest), (2) the availability of additional sources of income, (3) the functioning of labor, credit and insurance markets, and (4) the extent of public assistance. The second, third and fourth factors are related to incomes or money available and thus they are related to the level of resilience.

Based on the above explanation, in a simple way, it can thus be concluded that the level of vulnerability of a household or a region, depends on the function of three factors (Figure V.1): the degree of sensitivity, the degree of resilience and the nature of the shock. At least, theoretically, it can be hypothesized that the function has a positive relationship with the first

---

[1] The first approach has other advantages: (1) it produces a "headline" vulnerability figure, (2) it can identify vulnerable but not poor households. See Hoddinott and Quisumbing (2003) for more discussions on models regarding their proposed approaches.

factor (i.e. more sensitive, more vulnerable), a negative relationship with the second factor (more resilience or more capacity/capability to recover, less vulnerable), and a positive relationship with the third factor (larger shocks, more vulnerable). Each of the three factors has a number of indicators.

V.3. INDICATORS

Vulnerability indicators are the most common methodology in vulnerability assessment. The standard practice is to compile a list of indicators using criteria such as suitability, following a conceptual framework or definitions; availability of data; and sensitivity to shocks. Briguglio, et al. (2008) state that the choice of indicators is somewhat subjective. However, to minimize the subjectivity, they emphasize that the choice must be based on a set of desirable criteria related to appropriate coverage, simplicity and ease of comprehension, affordability, suitability for comparisons and transparency. This section proposes a list of indicators that can be used to assess the economic vulnerability.

As discussed earlier, the level of vulnerability depends on three main factors, i.e. degree of sensitivity, degree of resilience (capacity/capability to recover), and the nature of the shock. In the literature on vulnerability, among the three factors, the attention has been given more on the capability of individuals or households or regions/countries to recover from a shock/crisis. The main reason is that sensitivity is, to a certain extent, a natural given. For instance, Singapore is very vulnerable to any external economic crises, simply because it is a very small country which makes it fully dependent on international economy (trade, investment, finance) as well as foreign countries for its energy and clean water needs. Whereas, resilience is about the capacity that people or regions have to take required actions in coping with a shock. Thus, it has to do with what he/she or a community or a region can do to escape/recover as soon as possible from negative effects of an exogenous shock. For policy makers on poverty alleviation, knowing individuals'/ households'/regions'recovery capabilities to recover is very important since it determines the right choice of forms or types of interventions required to help effectively and efficiently the poor in the case of an economic crisis.

Now the question is, what are the suitable indicators to reflect the crisis-coping capability of regions or individuals or households? According to many, such as Streeten et al. (1981), the capabilities of individuals or households to recover from a shock are influenced by many factors ranging from prospects of earning a living, to the social and psychological effects of deprivation and exclusion. These include individuals' basic needs, employment at reasonable wages and health and education facilities. Swift (1989) analyzes vulnerability and security as a function of assets. In his model, he classifies assets into three categories: (1) investments (i.e. human investments in education and health, and physical investments in housing,equipment and land); (2) stock (e.g. food, money or valuables such as jewelry); and (3) claims on others for assistance (e.g. friendship, kinship, networks and patrons in the community (including international) and government). In Moser (1998), it is stated that the capability of an individual to recover from the negative effects of an economic shock depends much on the means he/she owned, namely the assets and entitlements (e.g. labor, cattle, building, land) that he/she can mobilize and manage in the face of hardship caused by the shock. Vulnerability is therefore, according to Moser (1998), closely linked to asset ownership: the more assets a person has, the less vulnerable he/she is, and the greater the erosion/reduction[2] of his/her assets, the greater his/her insecurity.

If the economic vulnerability is defined, in a general sense, as the welfare loss (caused by a shock) associated with poverty, then, from the above discussion, in identifying vulnerability indicators, determinants (directly and indirectly) of welfare or income should be identified first. For example, if employment is considered as an important source/determinant of welfare, then employment should be also included as an economic vulnerability indicator.

By level of aggregation, economic vulnerability can be assessed at macro-level: country, region or community, and micro-level: an individual or an household. The following two sub-sections propose important indicators of vulnerability at macro-and micro-levels, respectively.

V.3.1. Macro-Level Indicators

Table V.2 shows a number of indicators to assess an economic vulnerability at the macro-level.[3] The indicators represent various dimensions of an economic vulnerability (e.g. trade, economic structure, economic size, and human resource). Some of the indicators are considered as sensitivity indicators, while others as resilience indicators, or both. Sensitivity indicators refer to inherent and permanent characteristics (which may not be subject to policy or government) which render regions/countries prone to exogenous shocks. Resilience indicators refer to a crisis-coping capability. Furthermore, among these indicators, Table V.3 shows the key macro-level indicators by types of economic crisis.

As explained in the previous chapter, the effects of an economic crisis on a country can vary among regions within the country. Some provinces or districts can be hit very hard, while others may not feel the effects. Therefore, this section focuses on the provincial level, and for the empirical illustrations within the discussions of each of the indicators, this section uses Indonesian data.

In reality, however, not all of these indicators can be or need to be used for two main reasons. First, too many indicators complicate the procedure and data for many of these indicators may not be available across regions, especially in developing countries. Second, many of these indicators are interrelated with each other and thus some indicators can be used to represent some others. As an example, by using data from more than 50 countries, Briguglio et al (2008) have found that all components of their so-called economic resilience index are positively related to each other, though the correlation is not so strong as shown in Table V.4.

---

[2] Swift (1989) argues that in the case of need (e.g. during a changing economic environment), assets can be transformed into production inputs or directly into consumption. Reducing assets increases vulnerability although this may not be visible.

[3] See many studies discussing economic vulnerability indicators, which include, among others, Briguglio (1992, 1995, 1997), Pantin (1997), UNCTAD (1997), Crowards and Coulter (1998), Atkins et al. (1998), and Briguglio et al. (2008).

Table V.2. Concept and Measurable Indicators of Economic Vulnerability at Macro-level (e.g. Province)

No	Indicator	Nature	
		Resilience	Sensitivity
1	Size -Total population (number of people/inhabitants) -Total income/gross regional products (Gross Regional Product/GRP) -Total trade (export + import) as % of GRP -Total government expenditure as % of GRP	X	
2	Population density & structure -Total population/km square (number of people/km square) -Total population by gender (number or %) -Total population by age (number or % by age groups)	X	
3	Geographical location -Distance to nearest city (economic center/administrative area) (km) -Distance to nearest national/provincial road or railway (km) -Proportion of region by geographical location and topographical areas (e.g. mountain side, coastal, valley/river basin areas, slope of a hill/hilly, plain) to total administrative area (rural and urban) (%) -Proportion of village by location (hinterland rural, forest area, non-forest area) to total administrative area (rural and urban) (%) -Regions having inter-city railway station or bus station (yes/no) -Total households in a region having fixed telephone lines (%) -Total subscribers of mobile phone in a region (%) -Total households in a region having satelite/cable television (%). -Total households in a region having access to internet (%).	X	X
4	Structure of Household Consumption -Ratio of food to non-food consumption/expenditure -Percentage of food consumption in total consumption (food and non-food) -stock or production of food versus demand for food or food requirement		X
5	Economic openness -Total trade (export + import) as % of GRP -Total external investment as % of GRP or total gross regional capital formation		X
6	Export dependence and diversity -Total export as % of GRP -Total export by sector (%)		X

No	Indicator	Nature	
		Resilience	Sensitivity
7	Import dependence and diversity -Total import as %of GRP -Total import by sector (%)		X
8	Economic Diversification -Distribution of total GRP by sector (%) -Distribution of total employment by sector (%)		X
9	Real income per capita -Total income/GRP in real value (inflation correction)/total population	X	
10	Households by income quintile -Distribution of total households by income groups	X	
11	Poverty -Percentage of total population living under the current poverty line (poverty rate) -The average distance between the current expenditure of the poor and the current poverty line, as % of poverty line (poverty gap index) -The percentage distribution of expenditure among the poor (poverty depth index)	X	
12	Adult literacy rate and school enrollment ratios -Number of adults who can read and write as % of total adults -Number of children who are currently having primary, secondary and tertiary education as % of total children from a particular school age group (level of education)	X	
13	Health condition -Number of malaria cases per 100.000 population -Number of tuberculosis cases per 100.000 population -Number of HIV/AIDS cases per 100.000 population -Reports of health problem (sickness or accident) -Number of underweight children as % of total children in particular age group. -Number of infant/child mortality as % of total children in particular age group -Maternal mortality ratio (% of total population in particular group (per 100,000 live births) -morbidity rate (% of patients with a particular disease during a given year per given unit of population) -malnutrition rate (% of population who are undernourished (minimum level of dietary energy consumption)) -Average duration of illness (days) -Live expectancy at birth (average age) -Number of population having access to good healthcare faciities/can afford good health treatment	X	

Table V.2. Continued

No	Indicator	Nature	
		Resilience	Sensitivity
14	Technology capability -Number of engineers as % of total population -Number of scientists and researcher as % of total population -Number of population with university degree as % of total population -Number of universities/technical schools -Number of R&D institutes -Number of population with access to communication and information as % of total population	X	
15	Social and economic infrastructure -Number of school by type/level of education -Number of hospital and other health service providers/health facilities -Number of public utilities by type -Number of road by km., type and condition -Number of banks and other financial institutions -Number of transportation facilties by type and condition -Number of other facilities, e.g. telecommunication, sanitation, clean water supply, electricity, etc. -Number of population having access to all those facilities	X	
16	Social capital -Number of cooperatives, producers, business association, trade unions, etc. -Number of social organization activites, e.g. non-government organizations/NGOs, foundation, bonds, sport clubs, youth associations, etc. per 100.000 people. -Number of people as members of those social groups (as % of total population)	X	
17	Women participation in employment/economic activities -Total female workers as % of total workers -Total female entrepreneurs as % of total entrepreneurs	X	
18	Macroeconomic stability -Percentage of general price increases (inflation rate) -Percentage of total population in the working population age currently having no jobs as % of total working population (unemployment rate) -Total government budget as % of GRP -Total public debt as % of GRP -Annual rate of GRP growth (%) -Total general allocation funds (GAF) to regional/local	X	

	government from central government, as % of GRP -Ratio of GAF to regional government incomes from local sources)		
19	Microeconomic market efficiency -Number of workers in private sector as % of total employment -Total micro, small and medium enterprises as % of total enterprises -Total ouput of state-owned companies as % of GRP	X	

Table V.3. Key Macro-level Indicators by Types of Economic Crisis

Type of crisis	Key Vulnerability Indicators
Production crisis -e.g. food crisis	Size (total population) Population density Import dependence Economic diversification Infrastructure Tech. Capability
Banking crisis	Economic openess Macroeconomic stability Microeconomic market efficiency
Currency crisis	Economic openess Import dependence Macroeconomic stability Microeconomic market efficiency
Export crisis e.g. world demand/income crisis	Export dependence Export diversity
Energy crisis	Import dependence (on energy) Tech. capability Size (total population)

For many indicators presented in Table V.2, their inter-relationships are mainly through GDP, population and poverty, as illustrated in Figure V.2. For instance, indicators 14 and 15 are among indicators which have positive relationships with GDP: higher technology capability and better infrastructure induce higher GDP, and GDP growth with change in poverty is negatively related: higher GDP leads to less poverty (represented by indicators 10 and 11). With respect to geographical location (indicator 3), remoteness is negatively related to GDP growth, while close to centers of economic and administrative activities (which are regions with good infrastructure, technology capability, human resource, etc.), is positively related to GDP growth. Thus, GDP can be used instead to represent indicators 14,15,10,11 and 3 (the latter can also be represented by economic openness (indicator 5)). The patterns of such relationships, however, are based on the assumption that other determinant factors are constant.

Table V.4. Correlation Matrix of Some Indicators

Indicator	MS ME GG SD
MS	1.00
ME	0.17 1.00
GG	0.29 0.68 1.00
SD	0.22 0.40 0.67 1.00

Source: Briguglio et al (2008).

Small size of a region limits the region's ability to reap the benefits of economies of scale and constrains production possibilities. Therefore, the size should be considered as a resilience indicator to exogenous shocks (Guillaumont, 2007). There is generally no agreed definition as to which variable should be used to measure the size of a region or a country and as to what should be the cut-off point between a small and a large region. But, population is generally used as an indicator of the size of a region or a country. Guillaumont (2007) also states that, among several ways by which the size of a region can be measured, the most meaningful is the number of its inhabitants. Especially to assess the main economic consequences of the size of a region, independently from its income per capita, the most usual measure is the number of its population.

1) Size

Alternatively, total output or gross domestic product (GDP), or gross regional product (GRP) at the provincial level, in real value (after inflation correction) can also be used. However, this indicator may not give a real picture about the economic size of a region since the economic size is not always in proportion with the physical size of a region, while total population tends to be more proportional with the physical size of a region. In other words, small regions reflected by small popualtions may have larger GDP than larger regions. For instance, Singapore is just a small island in physical term, but its economic size based on total GDP in real value is much larger than that of many countries in e.g. Africa which are much bigger in land area than Singapore. Guillaumont (2007) argues that when investigating the channels by which size matters for economic development, links with economic vulnerability appear very clearly. According to him, there are at least three main channels (or intermediate variables) through which small size influences the exposure components of economic vulnerability: trade (export and import) intensity, government size and social cohesion. Thus, as one hypothesis, the smaller the (population) size of a country, the higher is its international trade to GDP ratio (and the more 'dependent' is its economy to international trade/economy), *ceteris paribus*.[4]

---

[4] However, many small countries have managed to generate or to maintain a relatively high GDP per capita or economic stability in comparison with many larger countries in spite of their high exposure to external economic shocks. One good example is Singapore. Although this country is highly sensitive to regional economic crisis such as the 1997/98 Asia financial crisis or the global economic recession occurred in 2008/09, as it is fully linked to the world economy through trade, finance and investment, the country has managed to generate high rates of economic growth and macroeconomic stability. Briguglio (2003) terms this phenomenon as the 'Singapore paradox'. See also Briguglio (1995) and most recent works of e.g. Alesina and Spolaore (2004) and Winters and Martins (2004) on the links between the level of economic vulnerability and the consequences of the size of countries.

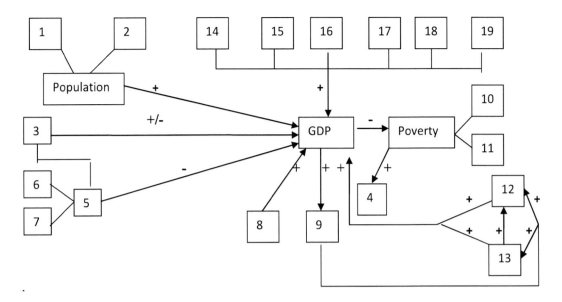

Figure V.2. Relationships among the Indicators.

For an empirical illustration, Table V.5 presents official data on total population and GRP at constant prices of 2000 in Indonesia by province. As can be seen, total population is concentrated in Java, consisting of four provinces, i.e. West Java, Banten, Central Java ,and East-Java, and two special administration regions, namely D.I. Yogyakarta, and DKI Jakarta, the capital city of Indonesia. With GRP and total population at only around 9 million people, DKI Jakarta has the highest economic size. By using data from this table, Tambunan and Asmanto (2010) produced the economic size index of provinces in Indonesia. And, then, based on this index, provinces can be classified into three categories according to their level of vulnerability, as shown in Figure V.3.

Source: Tambunan and Asmanto (2010).

Figure V.3. Economic Size Index in Indonesia by Province.

Table V.5. Economic Size of Indonesia by Province, 2007-2009

Province	Population (000 persons) 2007	Population (000 persons) 2009	Real GRP (bill Rp) 2008
Nangroe Aceh Darussalam	4,223.8	4,363.5	34,080
North Sumatera	12,834.4	13,248.4	106,172
West Sumatera	4,697.8	4,828.0	35,007
Riau	5,071.0	5,306.5	91, 085
Jambi	2,742.2	2,834.2	15,297
South Sumatera	7,020.0	7,222.6	58,080
Bengkulu	1,616.7	1,666.9	7,354
Lampung	7,289.8	7,491.9	34,415
Bangka Belitung	1,106.7	1,138.1	9,885
Riau islands	1,392.9	1,515.3	37,021
DKI Jakarta	9,064.6	9,223.0	353,539
West. Java	40,329.1	41,501.6	290,171
Central Java	32,380.3	32,864.6	167,790
D. I. Yogyakarta	3,434.5	3,501.9	19,209
East Java	36,895.6	37,286.2	204,799
Banten	9,423.4	9,782.8	68,831
Bali	3,479.8	3,551.0	24,901
West Nusa Tenggara	4,292.5	4,434.0	16,800
East Nusa Tenggara	4,448.9	4,619.7	11,426
West Kalimantan	4,178.5	4,319.1	27,684
Central Kalimantan	2,028.3	2,085.8	16,726
South Kalimantan	3,396.7	3,496.1	27,538
East Kalimantan	3,024.8	3,164.8	103,168
North Sulawesi	2,186.8	2,228.9	15,428
Central Sulawesi	2,396.2	2,480.3	14,770
South Sulawesi	7,700.3	7,908.5	44,550
Southeast Sulawesi	2,031.5	2,118.3	10,011
Gorontalo	960.3	984.0	2,521
West Sulawesi	1,016.7	1,047.7	3,873
Maluku	1,302.0	1,339.5	3,787
North Maluku	944.3	975.0	2,651
West Papua	716.0	743.9	6,369

Source: BPS (www.bps.go.id).

2) Population Density and Structure

As explained in point 1), total population is positive for the economy regarding economies of scale and production possibilities. More population means more manpower is available for production activities. However, the positive side of having a large population is not without limit. Beyond a certain limit considered as an economic efficient limit (which is difficult to determine, however), it is then regarded as an over-population which may have negative effects on production and hence, welfare. The related hypothesis is that, beyond that limit, population density and production capability or income per capita tend to be negatively related: too much population for a given land means less space for production, *ceteris paribus*. Another hypothesis derived from the first hypothesis is that, beyond that limit, population density and vulnerability tend to be positively related. Moreover, according to such as Cova and Church (1997), Mitchell (1999), and Cutter, et al. (2000), high-density areas complicate evacuation out of harm's way; although this is more relevant for natural disasters.

Table V.6. Non-Productive Age and Female Population (% of Total Population) and Population Density in Indonesia by Province, 2007-2009

Province	Non-productive population 2007	Female population 2007	Population density (persons /km^2) 2008	Population density (persons /km^2) 2009
Nangroe Aceh Darussalam	34.76	51.04	76	77
North Sumatera	39.07	50.22	180	182
West Sumatera	37.80	51.15	113	114
Riau	35.79	49.0	59	60
Jambi	33.95	49.66	61	62
South Sumatera	33.77	50.02	118	120
Bengkulu	34.92	49.57	83	84
Lampung	35.42	49.23	196	199
Bangka Belitung	32.67	49.24	68	69
Riau islands	32.60	50.38	180	187
DKI Jakarta	27.35	48.35	12,355	12,459
West. Java	33.98	49.87	1,108	1,124
Central Java	33.56	50.3	995	1,002
D. I. Yogyakarta	31.21	50.58	1,107	1,118
East Java	32.14	50.97	794	798
Banten	34.27	49.6	1,065	1,085
Bali	32.46	50.07	645	652
West Nusa Tenggara	36.35	51.13	221	225
East Nusa Tenggara	42.39	50.68	98	100
West Kalimantan	35.51	49.36	35	36
Central Kalimantan	34.65	48.81	13	14
South Kalimantan	32.94	49.88	89	90
East Kalimantan	33.38	47.42	16	16
North Sulawesi	33.73	49.45	158	160
Central Sulawesi	37.22	49.24	36	36
South Sulawesi	36.58	51.29	169	171
Southeast Sulawesi	39.38	50.05	56	63
Gorontalo	36.05	50.15	80	81
West Sulawesi	40.23	49.96	61	58
Maluku	41.13	50.42	28	29
North Maluku	39.29	49.13	24	25
West Papua	39.62	48.34	6	6
Papua	38.20	47.82	7	7

Source: BPS (www.bps.go.id).

Population structure by gender and age is also important in determining the level of vulnerability of a region. Regions or countries where women are marginalized are more vulnerable to economic shocks than those where there are is no gender discrimination. Also, regions where the proportion of unproductive population (people not within the working population age, and sick/physical unable persons) is high are more vulnerable to economic shocks than those where the number of productive age as a percentage of total population is high. In many studies, it is shown that extremes of the age spectrum affect the movement out of harm's way. For instance, parents lose time and money caring for children when daycare facilities are affected, and elderly may have mobility constraints and this may increase the burden of care and thus reduce resilience capability.[5]

As an empirical illustration, Table V.6 presents data on population structure, i.e. population under 15 and above 65 years old (non-productive age), female population, and population density, in Indonesia by province for 2007. From the above explanation, it can be expected that provinces with a high percentage of non-productive population will have more difficulties in coping with an economic crisis than those having more working population. With respect to women as a percentage of total population, in Indonesia (as for many other developing countries), women in general are still 'underdeveloped' in many respects (especially in rural/backward areas) as compared to developed nations. Thus, one hypothesis is that provinces with a higher ratio of female to male are less resilient than provinces with more male than female during an economic crisis.

3) *Geographical Location*

Location isolation, i.e. insularity, peripherality and remoteness leads to high transport costs and marginalization in all aspect of life, economically, socially as well as politically. The degree of economic openness of a region also determines its geographical location. According to many studies, remoteness from world markets (for output as well as inputs) is a structural handicap not only because it is a factor of vulnerability: even if transport costs have decreased (as a result of improvement in existing transportation systems and means driven by technological progress), distance remains an important obstacle to trade and investment.[6] Thus, based on those studies, one hypothesisis is that: the more remote a region the higher its sensitivity to exogenous shocks, *ceteris paribus*. However, remoteness of a region may also act as a saver or buffer for the region from external economic shocks, but only if the shocks are from outside the region. In other words, remote areas may not be impacted by economic crises from external sources as they are not opened to or not integrated with the international economy/markets. In this case, remote areas are less sensitive to shocks from outside. But, when a crisis originated within the region, then its remoteness becomes a serious obstacle for the region in coping with the crisis. For example, if the region experiences a harvest failure, it may face a serious food crisis since the region cannot get rice from outside due to its remoteness. Therefore, geographical condition can be considered as a resilience or a sensitivity indicator, depending on sources of the crisis.

---

[5] See Hewitt (1997), Ngo (2001), and Cutter, et al. (2000).
[6] See e.g. Brun et al.(2005), Carrère and Schiff (2005), and Guillaumont (2007).

Table V.7. Condition and Location by Province in Indonesia, 2007

Province	Condition (%)	Location (%)
Nangroe Aceh Darussalam	20.1	18.92
North Sumatera	14.98	10.74
West Sumatera	33.31	32.06
Riau	12.97	21.56
Jambi	30.02	13.81
South Sumatera	20.84	12.65
Bengkulu	28.56	21.35
Lampung	12.9	11.69
Bangka Belitung	1.57	36.11
Riau islands	6.79	29.17
DKI Jakarta	0.0	0.0
West. Java	23.2	12.3
Central Java	22.41	18.6
D. I. Yogyakarta	15.24	8.91
East Java	15.82	18.45
Banten	11.75	7.61
Bali	10.65	10.65
West Nusa Tenggara	11.2	20.7
East Nusa Tenggara	46.7	28.48
West Kalimantan	37.66	30.46
Central Kalimantan	57.36	49.32
South Kalimantan	15.96	10.32
East Kalimantan	27.14	25.99
North Sulawesi	23.82	16.78
Central Sulawesi	12.89	30.07
South Sulawesi	20.47	11.83
Southeast Sulawesi	14.73	34.83
Gorontalo	21.12	26.92
West Sulawesi	31.37	33.29
Maluku	7.76	33.48
North Maluku	5.25	30.75
West Papua	25.8	48.57
Papua	43.39	47.49

Source: BPS (www.bps.go.id).

As an example, Table V.7 presents two indicators of geography in Indonesia which data is available at the provincial level, namely, condition: proportion of regions by geographical locations to total administrative area (rural and urban), and location: proportion of villages by location (hinterland rural, forest area, non-forest area) to total administrative area (rural and urban).

Table V.8. Structure of Household Consumption in Indonesia by Province, 2007 and 2008 (000 Rp)

Province	2007 Total	2007 Food	2008 Total	2008 Food
Nangroe Aceh Darussalam	336.9	204.2	382.1	230.1
North Sumatera	351.6	188.0	391.8	211.7
West Sumatera	378.3	212.7	402.0	229.9
Riau	492.2	242.1	520.3	261.7
Jambi	367.6	194.2	381.0	203.4
South Sumatera	329.7	177.5	361.3	198.0
Bengkulu	313.5	167.7	363.6	190.5
Lampung	329.5	163.6	334.1	173.3
Bangka Belitung	472.2	255.6	521.1	280.4
Riau islands	516.6	243.2	560.2	274.2
DKI Jakarta	773.4	272.8	863.7	313.9
West. Java	367.3	180.5	396.9	199.4
Central Java	281.4	140.6	306.3	157.8
D. I. Yogyakarta	390.6	163.3	416.9	178.7
East Java	295.3	143.5	332.0	164.7
Banten	431.1	196.9	454.5	213.3
Bali	440.5	193.0	429.0	195.6
West Nusa Tenggara	256.4	141.2	300.4	167.5
East Nusa Tenggara	214.7	128.2	237.3	141.6
West Kalimantan	297.4	172.9	349.2	201.4
Central Kalimantan	355.7	205.6	418.2	251.7
South Kalimantan	414.3	222.5	443.5	235.6
East Kalimantan	516.1	227.4	585.3	253.9
North Sulawesi	350.8	184.6	341.5	183.2
Central Sulawesi	275.3	150.2	319.6	174.3
South Sulawesi	291.9	151.9	321.0	168.1
Southeast Sulawesi	260.5	141.9	274.6	148.3
Gorontalo	264.7	137.1	275.9	150.0
West Sulawesi	255.3	148.0	275.9	164.3
Maluku	287.0	163.7	286.6	175.5
North Maluku	367.3	204.3	305.4	216.1
West Papua	293.1	169.3	409.4	205.3
Papua	351.4	208.9	346.9	219.5
Indonesia	353.4	174.0	386.3	193.8

Source: BPS (www.bps.go.id).

4) Structure of Households Consumption

This indicator is particularly relevant for food crisis. Provinces or districts with higher rice consumption to non-rice consumption ratio (on average per household/person or in total) or higher percentage of rice consumption in total food and non-food consumption are more vulnerable than those with lower ratio or percentage to this kind of crisis. Food crisis occurs in a region when local stock or production of food is lower than local food consumption. Thus, food crisis has to do with local adequacy of food, and this can be monitored on the basis of total supply relative to total requirement (i.e net supply). In order to get information on whether the food supply is adequate, stock position over time should be monitored. This can be done by using (as indicator) monthly estimates of food stocks held by households, commercial trades and public sector, or in Indonesia, it is the task of BULOG (a special government agency dealing with, among others, rice distribution) at the regional/district level.[7] Since local stock, by definition, is the sum of local production and import, the level of food import also determines the local adequacy of food. In its turn, the level of food imports in a region is determined by its commercial import capacity, i.e volume of foods that the region can afford to import without harming local economic efficiency in distribution of productive resources.

Table V.8 shows households' expenditure in food and total consumption in Indonesia by provinces for 2007 and 2008. By using the national percentage of food in total households expenditures as a threshold, it can be hypothesized that provinces with the food percentages higher than the national level are more exposed to a food crisis than those with lower than it, *ceteris paribus*.

5) Economic Openness

A province with a high degree of economic openness means that the province does intensively export and import, which can be measured by the ratio of international trade (export plus import) on GRP. According to Briguglio et al. (2008), economic openness is, to a significant extent, an inherent feature of an economy, conditioned mainly by two factors: (1) the size of the domestic market which affects the export-to-GDP ratio (i.e. smaller domestic market leads to more export, *ceteris paribus*), and (2) domestic availability of resources and its ability to efficiently produce the range of goods and services to meet domestic market demand. This will affect the imports-to-GDP ratio (i.e. poorer in resources and less capacity to produce efficiently leads to more import, *ceteris paribus*).

Besides trade, the degree of economic openness can also be reflected by the ratio of foreign (external) capital or investment (net capital inflow) to GDP. No doubt that trade (especially export) and investment have a positive effect on economic growth. But, a region with high degree of economic openness is particularly sensitive to outside economic conditions. As stated in Briguglio et al. (2008), *economic vulnerability is defined as the exposure of an economy to exogenous shocks, arising out of economic openness*...(page i).
[8]Thus, the hypothesis related to this indicator is that regions with an open economy face more vulnerable to exogenous shocks than those with a protected economy, *ceteris paribus*.

---

[7] An alternative approach of measuring national/regional adequacy of food, as suggested by the Food and Agriculture Organization (FAO), is focusing on price differences across markets. In Indonesia, as a huge country in terms of land size and scattered in many islands, it is not surprise that price levels for food, e.g. rice, are different in different locations/markets. The differences in price levels reflect real costs of transporting food from one market to another, which consist not only of transportation cost but also 'local' costs (e.g. illegal as well as legal retributions). According to FAO, under this approach, price information for a selected normal period can be used as a benchmark against which to assess changes in price differences in subsequent periods. The result is an index based on spatial price differentials (www.fao.org).

[8] Empirical works on the construction of an economic vulnerability index is often based on the premise that a country's vulnerability to exogenous shocks stems from a number of inherent economic features, including high degrees of economic openness, export concentration and dependency on strategic imports. See Briguglio (1995), Briguglio and Galea (2003), Farrugia (2004), and Briguglio et al. (2008).

Table V.9. Exports and Imports as Percentages of GRP in Indonesia by Province, 2007

Province	Exports	Imports
Nangroe Aceh Darussalam	0.78	0.15
North Sumatera	19.96	5.35
West Sumatera	10.74	1.04
Riau	33.18	24.02
Jambi	11.49	2.87
South Sumatera	11.54	0.74
Bengkulu	7.09	-
Lampung	12.82	3.77
Bangka Belitung	22.07	-
Riau islands	-	-
DKI Jakarta	5.97	23.17
West Java	16.58	7.0
Central Java	5.22	3.2
D. I. Yogyakarta	2.29	0.45
East Java	9.84	7.82
Banten	27.69	45.58
Bali	5.92	1.36
West Nusa Tenggara	19.52	3.42
East Nusa Tenggara	0.29	0.24
West Kalimantan	8.28	0.86
Central Kalimantan	9.24	0.88
South Kalimantan	36.27	1.96
East Kalimantan	10.99	2.68
North Sulawesi	12.9	2.07
Central Sulawesi	5,0	0.02
South Sulawesi	19.66	2.31
Southeast Sulawesi	5.08	0.08
Gorontalo	0.78	-
West Sulawesi	-	-
Maluku	11.56	1.45
North Maluku	57.51	0.74
West Papua	0.11	8.18
Papua	99.85	-

Source: BPS (www.bps.go.id).

As an empirical illustration, Table V.9 presents exports and imports in Indonesia by province for 2007. With respect to export as a percentage of GRP, Papua, located in the eastern part of the country, reveals as the most open economy. Its highest export to GRP ratio among provinces in Indonesia is mainly because, on one hand, the province's economy is heavily relied on exports of a small number of agricultural and mining commodities and, on the other hand, local market is small (due to small population and low real income per capita; though not the lowest in Indonesia) and industrialization is very low (Papua is among the least developed provinces in Indonesia). Thus, the vast majority of all agricultural and mining commodities are for export without being further processed locally to generate value added to the province's economy. Therefore, Papua is most likely to be hit seriously if world prices for their exported commodities decline significantly and suddenly.

With respect to import, DKI Jakarta, Riau and Banten reveal as high importing provinces. Different import to GRP ratios by province reflects differences between provinces such as real income per capita and degree of industrialization. DKI Jakarta has the highest income per capita in Indonesia and it, together with Banten, is among the most industrialized regions in the country. Most of key manufacturing industries in Indonesia are located in this capital city and its surrounding areas (called Greater Jakarta) including Banten, besides in the Central and East Java provinces. Therefore, Greater Jakarta import consumption, capital and intermediate goods more than other less developed and less rich provinces do. It can thus be expected that when there is a world stock crisis for a commodity which DKI Jakarta imports most of, it will hit hard the city's economy via price channel: inflation raises.

6) Export Dependence and Diversity

Regions with a strong export dependence, measured by the export-to-GRP ratio, has a greater exposure to exogenous shocks compared to regions with less exports. In Asian Development Bank's report on the impact of the 2008/09 crisis on Asian developing countries, it is stated that Indonesia was less dependent on external demand over time (and much better than many other Asian countries) which was one reason that made Indonesia more resilient during the crisis as compared to many other crisis-affected countries, as well as in comparison with the Indonesian experience of the 1997/98 crisis. A sizable domestic demand (due to huge population and high income per capita) can serve as an effective shock absorber while small or weak domestic demand cannot compensate for loss in external demand (ADB, 2010b).[9] The hypothesis is that the higher the degree of export dependence of a region, the higher the region's economy dependence on world market/economy, and thus the greater is the exposure of the region to exogenous shocks (e.g. world market instability), *ceteris paribus*.

For an empirical illustration, Figure V.4 (derived from Table V.9) shows export dependence in provinces in Indonesia. Again, Papua is the most vulnerable province to any world economic instabilities since it has the highest export-GDP ratio, almost 100 percent. The above hypothesis is more valid for exports of primary commodities (especially agriculture and, to a lesser extent, mining with oil and gas in particular), since the world prices for such commodities are often unstable; while that of manufactured goods are stable, or have sustained increasing or decreasing trends.

The risks of being negatively impacted by export instability is exacerbated when high export dependence is only on a narrow range of exports (for instance, Indonesia on exports of oil during the Soeharto era). According to Briguglio et al.'s (2008), *dependence on a narrow range of exports gives rise to risks associated with a lack of diversification, and therefore, exacerbates vulnerability associated with economic openness* (page 5). In other words, within the open economies, those with low export market diversification (higher export

---

[9] The reports shows that total domestic consumption/demand (to measure demand diversity), i.e. private consumption + gross domestic fixed investment formation, and government consumption, as percentage of GDP in Indonesia increased from around 88.0 percent in 2000 to 97.0 percent in 2008. As a comparison, it declined in the Philippines from 103.9 percent to 94.8 percent, and in Thailand, it increased from 89.4 percent to 94.1 percent (ADB, 2010b).

concentration) are more vulnerable than those with the reverse situation to external shocks.[10] In the same ADB's report, more diversified export is also considered as an important reason why Indonesia was more resilient during the 2008/09 crisis as compared to other affected countries. Although somewhat less diversified than in 2000, Indonesian's score is much better than most other Asian countries (ADB, 2010b).[11] Thus, it can be hypothesized that the more diversified export base of a country is, the more resilient is the country's economy. In applying this hypothesis to the provincial level, it can be said that, given the export-to-GRP ratio, there is a positive (negative) relationship between the level of export concentration (the level of export diversity) and the level of vulnerability, *ceteris paribus*. Again, this hypothesis is more valid for exports of primary commodities.

A shock can be caused by significant declines in world prices or drops in world demand for key commodities. As a theoretical illustration, let the world prices or demand for Indonesian key exports of agricultural commodities decline. As the first (direct) result: farm/agricultural incomes decrease. This process, however, will not stop here. There is a multiplier effect: declined farm incomes reduce consumption as well as intermediate demands within the rural areas, and as the final/overall result: rural poverty increases. In this case, the transmission indicators are export revenues, consumption and intermediate demands, and employment. The most vulnerable groups are farmers and exporting companies, including their employees. In a report from the World Bank and the ASEAN Secretariat in 2009, it is stated that in some countries in Southeast Asia, the 2008/09 crisis is most likely to be felt among a few regions that produce commodities such as estate crops, for which world prices have dropped significantly.[12] In Indonesia, regions where export-oriented factories, such as garment factories, are located (e.g. Bandung/West Java, and Greater Jakarta) are also more likely to feel the impacts (World Bank and ASEAN, 2009).

In export of services, it is a crisis for exporting countries when, for instance, the number of foreign tourists declines sharply or a significant drop in remittance receipts from overseas migrants. According to the same report from the World Bank and the ASEAN Secretariat (World Bank and ASEAN, 2009), the 2008/09 crisis has been transmitted to ASEAN

---

[10] The effect of export declines or export instability, as a main source of economic vulnerability in especially primary commodities-export-depending countries, have been discussed for many years in the literature using economic growth regressions. From those discussions/studies, there is a general consensus to conclude that export instability (or in some studies, terms of trade instability) has a negative effect on economic growth (see, Bleany and Greenaway, 2001; Fosu, 1992, 2002; Guillaumont et al. 1999, Combes and Guillaumont, 2002, and Mendoza 2000). More significant effects are found in some studies which tested simultaneously the positive effects of export growth and the negative effects of export declines and when the export instability (seen as the size of the shock) is weighted by the average export to GDP ratio during the crisis period. See Combes and Guillaumont (2002).

[11] To measure export diversity, ADB uses the average coefficient of variation for top 10 exports and destinations. It shows that in Indonesia, it declined from 0.7 in 2000 to 0.6 in 2008. As a comparison, in the Philippines: 1.5 and 1.4 and in Thailand: 0.8 and 0.5 (ADB, 2010b).

[12] According to the report, the average prices of crude petroleum, copper, palm oil, coffee, and rice have fallen by 25-50 percent since the start of the crisis and through the first quarter of 2009, although prices of major commodities have started to rebound since then. ASEAN countries exporting primary commodities have experienced delines in their export values for such commodities. For example, Myanmar has experienced a decline in the value of exports of natural gas due to decreasing global demand and falling commodity prices. The value of natural gas exports to Thailand, its biggest trade partner, was expected to drop by 50 percent year-on-year because of the crisis (World Bank and ASEAN, 2009).

economies through several transmission channels, and among the most important ones were fewer tourist arrivals[13] and reduced remittance receipts from overseas migrants.[14]

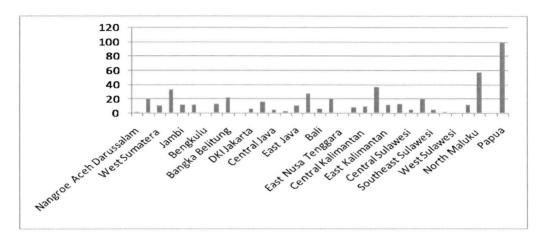

Source: BPS (www.bps.go.id).

Figure V.4. Export Dependence in Indonesia by Province, 2007 (%).

7) *Import Dependence and Diversity*

Regions with a high degree of import dependence, especially strategic imports such as energy (i.e. fuel),[15] food, other crucial natural resources, and industrial supplies, exacerbated by limited import substitution possibilities are very sensitive to instabilities in world supplies (availability) or world prices (costs of import) on that particular imports. Thus, on one hand, as one hypothesis, at the provincial level, the ratio of imports to GRP and the level of sensitivity to external shocks are positively related, *ceteris paribus*. On the other hand, as another hypothesis, given the ratio, the lower the import market diversity (higher import concentration), the higher the sensitivity to external shocks, *ceteris paribus*. As an empirical illustration, Figure V.5 presents the import dependence in Indonesia by province based on data from 2007.

The world has experienced many times which prove that a significant and less anticipated increase in world prices or sudden and huge drops in the world stocks for worldwide tradable commodities can become a big crisis for importing countries if those items are crucial commodities for them like food (e.g. rice) and oil or gas. For instance, in 1974, the decision made by the organization of petroleum exporting countries (OPEC) to reduce their oil supply

---

[13] Official data from the ASEAN Secretariat shows that during the first seven months of 2009, foreign tourist arrivals fell by 14 pe cent in Indonesia and 20 percent in Vietnam, compared with the same period in 2008. In Cambodia, the number of tourists declined by 2.2 percent in the first two months of 2009 compared to a year earlier (World Bank and ASEAN, 2009).

[14] According to a World Bank estimation, during the crisis period, international remittances have fallen by 7-10 percent (World Bank, 2009). In Indonesia, Koser (2009) estimates that remittances have declined to US$3 billion in 2009, from US$6 billion in 2007. A qualitative assessment of migrant workers from the Philippines made by the Philippines Central Bank suggests that the frequency and size of remittances sent home also declined, though overall remittance growth in the Philippines was estimated to remain low but positive in the first half of 2009 (BSP, 2009).

[15] Import dependency on energy can also be used as an indicator (e.g. imported energy as percentage of total energy consumed) showing the degree of energy dependence.

as a response to the Arab-Israel conflict was a big crisis for oil importing countries as the world price for oil increased significantly. With no change in total oil import, this 'first oil crisis' had increased energy costs and hence, domestic production costs in the oil importing countries to increase and resulted in hyper-inflation in the world. In this kind of crisis, the impact can be relatively moderate if the oil importing countries make an adjustment by subsidizing imported oil with alternative energies or by improving efficiency in the use of oil as energy for their domestic production. This was indeed what happened since then. The developed countries, especially the US, European countries and Japan took some measures to, on one hand, reduce their dependence on oil from the Middle East, and, on the other hand, to increase their efficiency in using energy. As the result, the worldwide impact of the second oil crisis by the end of 1970s/early 1980s was much smaller than that of the first one. In this case, the transmission indicators are import (the cost of imported oil), inflation and employment and their families. The most vulnerable group are, first, the importing companies and their employees, and, second, through domestic production linkages, other related companies or sectors, including their employees and their families.

In its report on the impact of the 2008/09 global economic crisis on some Asian developing countries, ADB states that countries are more resilient if they are net producers of energy. With respect to Indonesia, based on the average production excess of energy as percentage of GDP, the country in the past 10 years has deteriorated hugely on this indicator as its net oil exports have turned negative from 4.5 in 2000 to -0.3 in 2008 (ADB, 2010b).

8) Economic Diversification

The higher the percentage share of output from manufacturing industries or agriculture in the formation of GDP, the higher the economic concentration or the lower the economic diversification. Furthermore, given the level of domestic market demand (determined by population size and real income per capita), high levels of economic concentration also means high import dependence for other goods and services which have small (or no) domestic production (reflected by their small GDP contributions). Thus, the related hypothesis is that the higher the economic concentration (or the lower the economic diversification) of a region, the more vulnerable the region is to external shocks, *ceteris paribus*. But, of course, it depends on which sectors are mostly hit by a shock. If non-key sectors (those with low GDP shares) are mostly hit, the overall impact may be smaller than if the key sectors (those with high GDP contributions) are mostly affected.

Economic diversification can also be measured by distribution of total employment by sector. This ratio also tells the same story that a singular reliance on one economic sector for income generation creates a form of economic vulnerability. As explained in Cutter, et al. (2003), *the boom and bust economies of oil development, fishing, or tourism-based coastal areas are good examples—in the heyday of prosperity, income levels are high, but when the industry sees hard times or is affected by a natural hazard, the recovery may take longer. The agricultural sector is no exception and is, perhaps, even more vulnerable given its dependence on climate. Any change in weather conditions or increases in hydrometeorological hazards, such as flooding, drought, or hail, can affect the annual and decadal incomes and the sustainability of the resource base* (page 253).

The next two tables give empirical illustrations in Indonesia. Table V.10 shows the share of manufacturing industry in total employment in the province of Nangroe Aceh Darussalam by district. As can be seen, there are no districts where the employment is concentrated in the manufacturing industry, whereas Table V.11 shows an alternative indicator, namely the number of villages by main income sources of the majority of population and by province in

Indonesia. It reveals that in almost all provinces, agriculture is still the main important source of income.

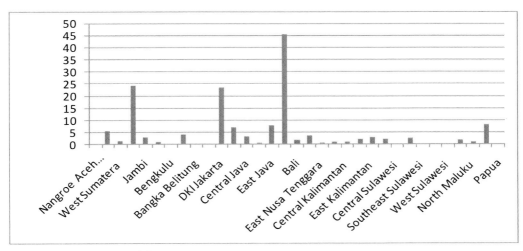

Source: BPS (www.bps.go.id).

Figure V.5. Import Dependence in Indonesia by Province, 2007 (%).

Table V.10. Share of Manufacturing in Total Employment in Nangroe Aceh Darussalam Province by District, 2007

District	%
Kab. Simeulue	15.63
Kab. Aceh Singkil	17.62
Kab. Aceh Selatan	14.42
Kab. Aceh Tenggara	8.47
Kab. Aceh Timur	16.95
Kab. Aceh Tengah	10.50
Kab. Aceh Barat	15.01
Kab. Aceh Besar	12.52
Kab. Pidie	14,.35
Kab. Bireuen	13.14
Kab. Aceh Utara	13.70
Kab. Aceh Barat Daya	15.20
Kab. Gayo Lues	9.40
Kab. Aceh Tamiang	11.98
Kab. Nagan Raya	13.00
Kab. Aceh Jaya	14.27
Kab. Bener Meriah	6.84
Kab. Pidie Jaya	14.35
Kota Banda Aceh	25.51
Kota Sabang	13.25
Kota Langsa	24.15
Kota Lhokseumawe	23.83
Kota Subulussalam	13.11

Source: BPS (www.bps.go.id).

Table V.11. Distribution of Villages by Key Sector and Province in Indonesia, 2008 (unit)

Province	Agriculture	Mining	Manufacturing	Total villages
Nangroe Aceh Darussalam	5972	14	25	6424
North Sumatera	5128	6	76	5767
West Sumatera	723	5	10	924
Riau	1432	8	13	1604
Jambi	1204	1	3	1303
South Sumatera	2787	9	23	3079
Bengkulu	1253	3	4	1351
Lampung	2189	-	19	2339
Bangka Belitung	193	87	2	334
Riau islands	238	3	18	326
DKI Jakarta	7	-	25	267
West. Java	4503	12	288	5871
Central Java	7341	9	457	8574
D. I. Yogyakarta	345	-	11	438
East Java	7307	13	402	8505
Banten	1122	-	183	1504
Bali	562	1	29	712
West Nusa Tenggara	812	3	8	913
East Nusa Tenggara	2676	2	4	2803
West Kalimantan	1687	3	6	1791
Central Kalimantan	1372	27	1	1448
South Kalimantan	1756	7	18	1974
East Kalimantan	1218	24	18	1417
North Sulawesi	1316	6	7	1494
Central Sulawesi	1592	4	4	1686
South Sulawesi	2639	10	12	2946
Southeast Sulawesi	1870	8	14	2028
Gorontalo	531	1	4	584
West Sulawesi	524	-	1	536
Maluku	853	1	7	906
North Maluku	965	9	2	1036
West Papua	1159	5	1	1205
Papua	3239	5	4	3311

Source: BPS (www.bps.go.id).

By using provincial data on output shares of manufacturing and agriculture in 2007 and employmet shares of the same sectors in 2009, Tambunan and Asmanto (2010) produce the economic structure index of provinces in Indonesia. With this index, provinces can be classified into three categories as shown in Figure V.6, i.e. low, medium and high shares. As can be seen, on average, the GRP and employment contributions of the two sectors are higher in the western than in the eastern parts of the country.

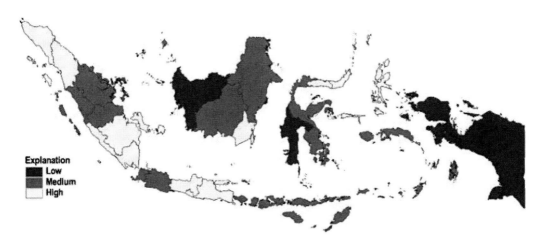

Source: Tambunan and Asmanto (2010).

Figure V.6. Economic Structure Index in Indonesia by Province.

Thus, as an hypothesis, it can be expected that regions where the majority of workforce work in one sector are less resilient to shocks than those with relatively equal distribution of employment by sector, *ceteris paribus*. Here too, it depends on which sectors are mostly impacted by a shock. For instance, back to Table V.10, if an external shock hits the industry more than other sectors, like what happened during the 2008/09 crisis, unemployment in districts like Kota Banda Aceh, Kota Langsa and Kota Lhokseumawe is most likely to increase faster than those in other districts, since the three distrcits have the highest employment shares of manufacturing. In Table V.11, the economy of Java provinces is more likely to face a recession than that of the rest of the country.

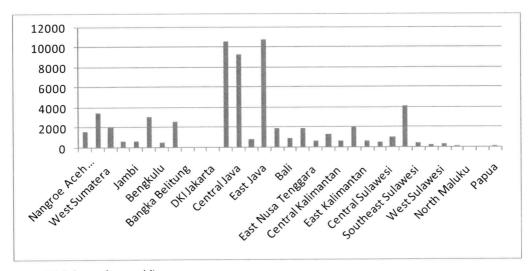

Source: BPS (www.bps.go.id).

Figure V.7. Paddy Production in Indonesia by Province, 2009 (000 tons).

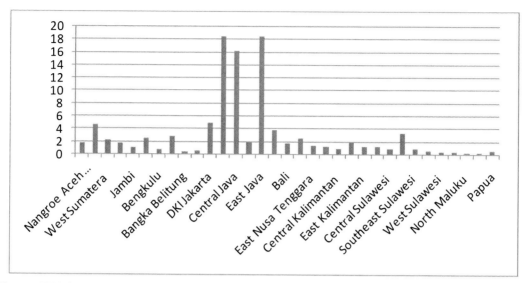

Source: BPS (www.bps.go.id).

Figure V.8. Number of Non-Agricultural Establishment as Percentage to National in Indonesia by Province, 2006.

For countries which have no data on GDP and employment distributions by sector at lower aggregate levels such as province, district or village, data on total production of agricultural commodities can also be used as a proxy. For instance, Indonesia has data on total production of paddy at the provincial level, as shown in Figure V.7. It can be assumed that the economy of provinces with higher annual production volumes of paddy is more likely to be dominated by agriculture than provinces with low paddy productions. In other words, the level of economic diversification (or economic concentration) in the first group of provinces is most likely to be lower (higher) than that in the second one.

Data on the number of establishments or enterprises in non-agricultural sector can also be used as an alternative indicator to measure the level of economic diversification. The basic assumption is that the economy of provinces with more establishments outside agriculture is less concentrated in agriculture or is likely to be more diversified than those where there are only few non-agricultural firms. Figure V.8 presents data on the number of non-agricultural establishments as percentage to national in Indonesia by province.

Of course, these two alternative indicators are far from perfect. For provinces with less or zero rice productions or with less numbers of non-agricultural enterprises, it does not automatically mean that their economy is more diversified. The economy of the provinces may concentrate in other few sectors. For instance, as can be seen in Figure V.7, Riau islands has no paddy production, but it is also not an industrialized province either. Its economy is dominated by ground and palm oils. Jakarta, on the other hand, with very low paddy production, is an industrialized region and it has strong financial and services sectors.

9) Real Income per Capita

Real income per capita is often used as a welfare indicator, which indicates the purchasing power of an economy. However, it does not show the total welfare since national data on income only captures actual incomes earned from employment and commercializing own tangible assets (excluding human resource), e,g, own unused house for rent. It does not include potential incomes that own used tangible assets can generate based on current market values/prices. Actual earned incomes of a person may be lower than his/her potential incomes, meaning that his/her total welfare is higher than his/her actual earned incomes. Therefore, total welfare is more appropriate than total income to indicate the ability of a person or a household to absorb losses and enhance resilience to negative impacts of shocks. It can be that a person has no income because he/she is unemployed, but he/she is potentialy rich because he/she owns many lands and has many houses that he/she (can) rent/sell, or many livestocks that he/she can sell. Of course, the main problem here is lack of data on current market values of total tangible assets owned by individuals or households, though it is not impossible to estimate them. The related hypothesis is that communities in wealthy regions (not only measured by their observed actual earned incomes but also their own tangible assets) are able to absorb and recover from losses more quickly than those in poor regions[16]

As an empirical illustration, Table V.12 presents data on income per capita in Indonesia by province for 2007. It shows that the country's capital city, DKI Jakarta, is the most wealthy region in the country. It is not rich in natural resources but in highly skilled manpower and financial capital, as normally all capital cities are, especially in developing countries, the concentration of these two crucial inputs for economic growth. The second most rich region in Indonesia based on income per capita indicator is the East Kalimantan province which is rich not in human capital but in oil while the most poor region is Nusa Tenggara which lacks any crucial production inputs.

10) Household by Income Quintile

However, high real income or wealth per capita will be meaningless when the achieved total income/wealth is not equally distributed among the population. This will say that even when real income per capita is high, poverty rates can also be high at the same time if income disparity is high. The income inequality in a region is often measured by the so-called gini coefficient, or by categorizing total households in the region by income quintile. Thus, the related hypothesis is that regions where most households are from the lowest income group are more vulnerable to an economic shock than regions where most households are from the highest income group, *ceteris paribus*.

Since data on household incomes in many developing countries is often scarce, household consumption expenditures can be used instead as a proxy. Although, consumption expenditure of an household may not reflect the real picture of the household's income level, since there are savings (income is higher than consumption) and loan (income is lower than consumption). As an example, Table V.13 presents data on the share of poorest quintile in national consumption by income quintile in the province of Nangroe Aceh Darussalam by district in Indonesia.

---

[16] In Downing et al. (2001), GDP per capita and Gini ratio are used as indicators of economic coping capacity (resilience). See also, e.g. Puente (1999), Platt (1999), Cutter, et al. (2000), and Peacock, et al. (2000).

Table V.12. Income per Capita in Indonesia by Province, 2007

Province	Income per capita (mill. Rp)
Nangroe Aceh Darussalam	8.58
North Sumatera	8.64
West Sumatera	7.03
Riau	18.20
Jambi	5.13
South Sumatera	7.83
Bengkulu	4.26
Lampung	4.45
Bangka Belitung	9.09
Riau islands	27.23
DKI Jakarta	42.64
West Java	7.24
Central Java	4.78
D. I. Yogyakarta	5.33
East Java	7.97
Banten	7.21
Bali	7.11
West Nusa Tenggara	3.80
East Nusa Tenggara	2.49
West Kalimantan	6.35
Central Kalimantan	8.06
South Kalimantan	7.89
East Kalimantan	32.80
North Sulawesi	6.50
Central Sulawesi	5.67
South Sulawesi	5.46
Southeast Sulawesi	4.58
Gorontalo	2.54
West Sulawesi	3.51
Maluku	2.65
North Maluku	2.75
West Papua	10.04
Papua	9.97

Source: BPS (www.bps.go.id).

11) Poverty

The rate of poverty in a region is generally measured by the proportion of total population in the region living under the current poverty line. The poverty rate is one indication for the level of sensitivity as well as the level of resilience of a region to external/exogenous shocks, as it is generally believed that only individuals or households who are not poor (i.e. who have money or assets) are more able to face a crisis than the poor. Thus, one hypothesis is that poor regions (i.e. regions where the majority of total population are poor) are more vulnerable to an economic crisis, or they will face more difficulties to cope with shocks (either from internal or external sources), than wealthy regions (i.e. regions where most poeple are living above current poverty line), *ceteris paribus*.

For an empirical example, Table V.14 presents data on the poverty rate in Indonesia by province for the period 2006-2008. As can be seen, the most poor provinces based on this indicator are Papua and West Papua. DKI Jakarta as the center for government administration, financial sector, and highly skilled human capital, has the lowest poverty rate. Thus, it can be expected that the provinces of Papua and West Papua are the most vulnerable regions in Indonesia. However, again, it depends on the type of crisis. As explained before, these are heavily primary commodities-dependent provinces so they are more vulnerable to any shocks that reduce world demand or prices for their exported primary commodities, than, say, to a financial crisis caused by capital flights as occurred during the 1997/98 crisis.

Table V.13. Share of Poorest Quintile in National Consumption by Income Quintile in Nangroe Aceh Darussalam Province by District, 2007

District	Income Quintile				
	Q1	Q2	Q3	Q4	Q5
Kab. Simeulue	5.51	15.36	26.57	31.21	21.35
Kab. Aceh Singkil	6.06	16.62	24.00	27.13	26.19
Kab. Aceh Selatan	7.50	17.10	23,.15	28.56	23.68
Kab. Aceh Tenggara	19.36	18.59	17.39	20.45	24.21
Kab. Aceh Timur	7.76	14.53	20.08	32.27	25.35
Kab. Aceh Tengah	1.73	9.47	24.35	41.79	22.66
Kab. Aceh Barat	1.68	5.69	12.95	27.76	51.91
Kab. Aceh Besar	4.27	9.03	11.85	26.15	48.70
Kab. Pidie	1.61	9.87	20.97	33.23	34.33
Kab. Bireuen	7.47	13.58	26.08	31.83	21.04
Kab. Aceh Utara	11.89	17.11	23.67	27.48	19.85
Kab. Aceh Barat Daya	8.79	23.10	27.33	26.13	14.65
Kab. Gayo Lues	13.37	21.74	18,.04	19.06	27.79
Kab. Aceh Tamiang	5.85	17.86	24.34	31.60	20.35
Kab. Nagan Raya	6.85	11.76	18.69	29.17	33.53
Kab. Aceh Jaya	3.75	10.35	14.88	21.52	49.50
Kab. Bener Meriah	3.53	14.63	25.08	36.72	20.04
Kab. Pidie Jaya	2.26	16.36	26.61	28.70	26.06
Kota Banda Aceh	0.00	0.12	0.66	6.19	93.03
Kota Sabang	0.41	2.86	7.76	20.38	68.59
Kota Langsa	4.34	9.48	13.84	22.27	50.07
Kota Lhokseumawe	4.56	8.92	11.21	19.40	55.92
Kota Subulussalam	13.87	18.71	19.86	19.16	28.40

Source: BPS (www.bps.go.id).

Table V.14. Poverty Rate in Indonesia by Province, 2006-2008 (%)

Province	2006	2007	2008
Nangroe Aceh Darussalam	28.3	26.7	23.5
North Sumatera	15.0	13.9	12.6
West Sumatera	12.5	11.9	10.7
Riau	11.9	11.2	10.6
Jambi	11.4	10.3	9.3
South Sumatera	21.0	19.2	17.7
Bengkulu	23.0	22.1	20.6
Lampung	22.8	22.2	21.0
Bangka Belitung	10.9	9.5	8.6
Riau islands	12.2	10.3	9.2
DKI Jakarta	4.6	4.6	4.3
West Java	14.5	13.6	13.0
Central Java	22.2	20.4	19.2
D. I. Yogyakarta	19.2	19.0	18.3
East Java	21.1	20.0	18.5
Banten	9.8	9.1	8.2
Bali	7.1	6.6	6.2
West Nusa Tenggara	27.2	25.0	23.8
East Nusa Tenggara	29.3	27.5	25.7
West Kalimantan	15.2	12.9	11.1
Central Kalimantan	11.0	9.4	8.7
South Kalimantan	8.3	7.0	6.5
East Kalimantan	11.4	11.0	9.5
North Sulawesi	11.5	11.4	10.1
Central Sulawesi	23.6	22.4	20.8
South Sulawesi	14.6	14.1	13.3
Southeast Sulawesi	23.4	21.3	19.5
Gorontalo	29.1	27.4	24.9
West Sulawesi	20.7	19.0	16.7
Maluku	33.0	31.1	29.7
North Maluku	12.7	12.0	11.3
West Papua	41.3	39.3	35.1
Papua	41.5	40.8	37.1
Indonesia	17.8	16.6	15.4

Source: BPS (www.bps.go.id).

It is often thought that the poverty rate and the rate of employment (or unemployment) are negatively (positively) related: higher unemployment (or lower employment) leads to higher poverty rate, *ceteris paribus*. But, this theoretical hypothesis is more valid in the case of formal employment or open unemployment, not for informal employment. The latter is officially regarded as hidden/disguised unemployment, since most of formally unemployed people in developing countries including Indonesia, where no government sponsored unemployment benefit schemes are found in the informal sector (not captured by official data on employment/unemployment). They are considered as hidden/disguised unemployment because, while looking for better employment opportunities (which are mostly available in the formal sector), they (are pushed to) do any kind of income-generating activities as a means to survive. Given the fact that incomes generated in the informal sector are generally low, therefore, most of them while working in the sector are poor. Probably because of this fact, the informal sector is often seen as a place for the poor, not as source for poverty reduction.[17]

Table V.15. Open Unemployment Rate in Indonesia by Province, 2007-2009 (%)

Province	2007 Aug.	2008 Aug	2009 Feb.
Nangroe Aceh Darussalam	9.8	9.6	9.3
North Sumatera	10.1	9.1	8.3
West Sumatera	10.3	8.0	7.9
Riau	9.8	8.2	9.0
Jambi	6.2	5.1	5.2
South Sumatera	9.3	8.1	8.4
Bengkulu	4.7	4.9	5.3
Lampung	7.6	7.2	6.2
Bangka Belitung	6.5	6.0	4.8
Riau islands	9.0	8.0	7.8
DKI Jakarta	12.6	12.2	12.0
West. Java	13.1	12.1	11.9
Central Java	7.7	7.4	7.3
D. I. Yogyakarta	6.1	5.4	6.0
East Java	6.8	6.4	5.9
Banten	15.8	15.2	14.9
Bali	3.8	3.3	2.9
West Nusa Tenggara	6.5	6.1	6.1
East Nusa Tenggara	3.7	3.7	2.8
West Kalimantan	6.5	5.4	5.6
Central Kalimantan	5.1	4.6	4.5
South Kalimantan	7.6	6.2	6.8
East Kalimantan	12.1	11.1	11.1
North Sulawesi	12.4	10.7	10.6
Central Sulawesi	8.4	5.5	5.1
South Sulawesi	11.3	9.0	8.7
Southeast Sulawesi	6.4	5.7	5.4
Gorontalo	7.2	5.6	5.1
West Sulawesi	5.5	4.6	4.9
Maluku	12.2	10.7	10.4
North Maluku	6.1	6.5	6.6
West Papua	9.5	7.7	7.7
Papua	5.0	4.4	4.1
Indonesia	9.1	8.4	8.1

Source: BPS (www.bps.go.id).

---

[17] Many economic activities, such as petty traders, self-employment and micro enterprises, in the informal sector are (or initially) supply-side or known as 'supply-push' activites: people are 'pushed' to conduct their own businesses because they could not find better employment opportunities or their current incomes as employees in

This implies that the rate of poverty can be assumed to have a positive relationship with the percentage of labor force being unemployed officially (so called open unemployment). Despite the fact that the coefficient (or elasticity) of the poverty-unemployment relationship may be low due to the present of the informal sector. data on officially registered, open unemployment or employment are still useful as an alternative indicator or a proxy for poverty, and hence, vulnerability or resilience. According to Mileti (1999) and Cutter et al.(2003), the potential loss of formal employment following a shock not only exacerbates the number of unemployed workers in a community or region, but it also contributes to a slower recovery (i.e. less resilience to) from the shock.

As an empirical example, Table V.15 shows the level of open unemployment in Indonesia by province for the period 2007-2009. The variety of open unemployment rate among provinces may, partly, reflect the variety in the importance of informal sector in generating under-or hidden unemployment among provinces. There are two possibilities for provinces with low open unemployment rates regarding the present of the informal sector. First, low open unemployment rates reflect the true situation that unemployment is indeed low. In this case, there is no or very few hidden/disguised unemployment and so the informal sector is small. Second, it may not reflect the true picture that in reality, actual unemployment is higher than the reported open unemployment. In this case, the rate of hidden/disguised unemployment is high and automatically, the informal sector is largely present.

12) Educational Advancement

Educational advancement is generally measured by two human capital indicators; adult literacy rate and school enrollment ratios. Alternatively, it can also be measured by an index known as the human development index (HDI) from the United Nations Development Program (UNDP).[18] It is also appropriate to make a distiction between male and female literacy rate, or female literacy as a ratio to total literate population. Educational advancement is generally considered an important determinant of regions/communities' crisis coping capability. Briguglio, et al. (2008) argue that social development is another essential component of economic resilience, and educational advancement is considered a good indicator of social development. However, higher-educated people are not only likely to be more resilient but they are also equally or even more prone to shocks than low-educated people, since the former category of population tend to be more open to the global community or involved in international related jobs whereas, the uneducated persons tend to isolate themselves from outside or they do mostly international, unrelated local activities.

Thus, from the above theoretical framework, given that more or less vulnerability will depend on a combination of sensitivity, resilience and nature of shock (see Figure V.1), one hypothesis is that regions with a highlyeducated population are less vulnerable to shocks than those of the majority of the population that has only primary school, *ceteris paribus*.

---

the formal sector (e.g. supermarket security) are not enough to meet their daily needs, not because there was an initial demand for their products.

[18] HDI is probably the most well-known national-level aggregate index relating to human welfare. The HDI is based on the earlier Physical Quality of Life Index and related to the Human Poverty Index, and is an aggregate measure of well-being based on education and health status, as well as income and inequality so the HDI can also be used not only as an alternative indicator for education, but also for health and poverty . See Downing et al (2001), and Adger, et al. (2004) for further discussion on HDI. Downing et al (2001) propose the HDI as a reasonable measure of "present criticality", which is equivalent to vulnerability.

Table V.16. Education Advancement in Indonesia by Province, 2007 and 2008

Province	Adult literacy (2007)	School enrollment (2007)	HDI (2008)
Nangroe Aceh Darussalam	95.9	8.6	70.8
North Sumatera	97.0	8.6	73.3
West Sumatera	96.6	8.3	72.0
Riau	97.8	8.6	75.1
Jambi	95.3	7.7	72.0
South Sumatera	97.0	7.7	72.1
Bengkulu	94.5	8.1	72.1
Lampung	93.5	7.3	70.3
Bangka Belitung	95.3	7.5	72.2
Riau islands	94.8	8.2	74.2
DKI Jakarta	98.7	10.7	77.0
West. Java	95.5	7.5	71.1
Central Java	89.1	7.0	71.6
D. I. Yogyakarta	89.5	8.9	74.9
East Java	87.5	7.1	70.4
Banten	95.2	8.2	69.7
Bali	87.1	7.9	71.0
West Nusa Tenggara	79.4	6.8	64.1
East Nusa Tenggara	87.3	6.6	66.2
West Kalimantan	88.3	6.8	68.2
Central Kalimantan	97.2	8.0	73.9
South Kalimantan	95.0	7.5	68.7
East Kalimantan	96.2	8.9	74.5
North Sulawesi	99.1	9.0	75.2
Central Sulawesi	95.3	8.0	70.1
South Sulawesi	86.0	7.2	70.2
Southeast Sulawesi	90.9	7.9	69.0
Gorontalo	95.2	7.1	69.3
West Sulawesi	87.0	7.1	68.6
Maluku	97.3	8.6	70.4
North Maluku	95.5	8.6	68.2
West Papua	90.8	7.9	68.0
Papua	73.0	6.4	65.0
Indonesia	92.1	7.6	71.2

Source: BPS (www.bps.go.id), BAPPENAS (www.bappenas.go.id).

As an empirical illustration, Table V.16 shows information on adult literacy, school enrollment and HDI (in which adult literacy is included) in Indonesia at the regional level. There are two ways to assess the level of regional vulnerability using those items as indicators. First, by comparing among provinces, and those with lowest values for the items are considered the most vulnerable provinces. Second, by using a pre-determined threshold, which can be the national level. For instance, in the case of HDI, the national level in 2008 is 71.5 so it can be assumed that provinces with the values of HDI higher than 71.5 are more resilient than provinces with lower than that level to an economic shock, by keeping other resilience determinants constant. Furthermore, from Figure V.9, it is more clear that based on HDI, the less educated and hence, the most vulnerable provinces, are mainly found in the eastern part of the country.

13) Health Condition

As in the case of educational advancement, health condition is also another crucial human capital indicator, since high educational advancement can never be achieved in a unhealthy society. In other words, education and health go together, or they are complementary to each other. Briguglio, et al. (2008) also consider advancements in health standards to be conducive to economic resilience. The related hypothesis is that healthy communities are more able to face a crisis with minimum damage/loss compared to unhealthy communities, *ceteris paribus*.

Two indicators often used to measure health condition are life expectancy at birth (LE) and infant mortality rate (IMR). As an empirical assessment, Table V.17 shows these two indicators for Indonesia by province. As can be seen, many provinces have higher LE than the average national level, as a threshold. It can be expected that those provinces are more resilience than others to economic shocks, *ceteris paribus*. With respect to IMR, many provinces performed badly as compared to the national level. If the national level is taken as a threshold, than these provinces can be expected to be more vulnerable than others to an economic shock, *ceteris paribus*. In addition, based on few indicators which data is available, Figure V.10 shows that provinces with the most healthy population, and thus less vulnerable, are found mainly in the western part of the country.

Source: Tambunan and Asmanto (2010).

Figure V.9. Human Development Index Indonesia by Province, 2007.

Table V.17. LE and IMR in Indonesia by Province, 2007 and 2008

Province	IMR(%) 2007	IMR(%) 2008	LE(age) 2007	LE(age) 2008
Nangroe Aceh Darussalam	32.6	32.1	69.0	69.1
North Sumatera	22.3	22.7	71.6	71.7
West Sumatera	27.1	26.3	70.5	70.7
Riau	22.3	21.8	71.9	72.0
Jambi	27.5	26.9	70.3	70.5
South Sumatera	25.6	25.0	70.9	71.1
Bengkulu	29.4	28.6	69.9	70.1
Lampung	25.8	24.8	70.9	71.1
Bangka Belitung	26.4	26.0	70.7	70.8
Riau islands	20.6	20.3	72.3	72.4
DKI Jakarta	8.4	8.2	75.8	75.9
West. Java	27.9	27.1	70.3	70.5
Central Java	21.4	20.7	72.1	72.3
D. I. Yogyakarta	8.7	8.5	75.5	75.7
East Java	25.4	24,5	71.0	71.2
Banten	32.0	31.3	69.2	69.3
Bali	12.9	12.7	74.1	74.1
West Nusa Tenggara	44.6	43.2	66.0	66.3
East Nusa Tenggara	32.3	31.2	69.1	69.4
West Kalimantan	28.0	27.4	70.2	70.4
Central Kalimantan	22.8	22.4	71.7	71.8
South Kalimantan	34.9	33.9	68.4	68.7
East Kalimantan	20.2	19.0	72.5	72.7
North Sulawesi	12.1	11.5	74.4	74.6
Central Sulawesi	35.9	34.9	68.2	68.4
South Sulawesi	28.2	27.4	70.2	70.4
Southeast Sulawesi	32.6	31.8	69.0	69.2
Gorontalo	32.0	30.8	69.2	69.5
West Sulawesi	28.2	27.4	70.2	70.4
Maluku	32.6	31.8	69.0	69.2
North Maluku	35.5	34.3	68.3	68.6
West Papua	32.7	31.6	69.0	69.3
Papua	31.7	30.7	69.3	69.5

Source: BPS (www.bps.go.id).

Table V.18. Number of Universities and Technical High Schools (THS) in Indonesia by Province, 2008

Province	University Private	University State	THS
Nangroe Aceh Darussalam	7	2	2
North Sumatera	26	2	6
West Sumatera	7	2	2
Riau	3	2	4
Jambi	2	1	3
South Sumatera	10	1	4
Bengkulu	4	1	1
Lampung	7	1	2
Bangka Belitung	1	1	1
Riau islands	3	2	3
DKI Jakarta	51	4	14
West. Java	32	9	33
Central Java	33	4	-
D. I. Yogyakarta	21	3	8
East Java	71	8	26
Banten	7	2	11
Bali	9	2	2
West Nusa Tenggara	8	1	-
East Nusa Tenggara	8	1	2
West Kalimantan	4	1	1
Central Kalimantan	3	1	1
South Kalimantan	2	1	1
East Kalimantan	10	1	5
North Sulawesi	8	2	1
Central Sulawesi	7	1	2
South Sulawesi	13	2	8
Southeast Sulawesi	7	1	3
Gorontalo	2	1	-
West Sulawesi	1	-	1
Maluku	3	1	1
North Maluku	2	1	-
West Papua	2	1	-
Papua	6	1	1

Source: Department of Education and Culture (www.kemdiknas.go.id).

It is generally recognized that in addition to human capital, technology is also a crucial determinant of economic development or economic well-being. Technology capability of a region is determined by many factors, including people's access to advanced technologies, either through education, vocational training, workshops, or self-learning with full access to information (e.g. internet, newspapers, television, etc.). Thus, one hypothesis is that regions with higher technology capability are more resilient than those with low technology capability to exogenous shocks, *ceteris paribus*.

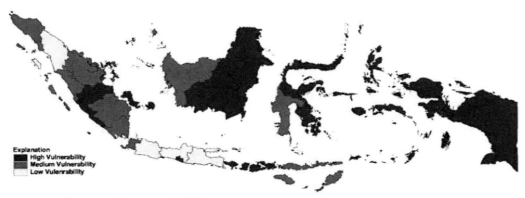

Source: Tambunan and Asmanto (2010).

Figure V.10. Health Condition Index in Indonesia by Province, 2008.

14) Technology Capability

At the national level, the most used indicators are such as R&D investment/expenditure as percentage of GDP, number of scientists and engineers as percentage of total population or per one million persons, and tertiary enrollment. At the regional/provincial level, besides those items, such as the number of R&D institutions, the number of people with technical university certificates as a percentage of total population, and the number of universities and/or high technical schools can be used as alternative indicators. Table V.18 shows the latter indicators with Indonesia by province.

15) Social and Economic Infrastructure

Social and economic infrastructure, e.g. school, hospital, public utilities, roads, bridges, harbors, telecommunication facilities, transportation facilities, sanitation, clean water supply, industrial estates, electricity, irrigated areas (for agricultural-based regions), financial institutions, etc. are very important determinants of vulnerability or resilience of a region. In this respect, one hypothesis is that regions with well-developed social and economic infrastructures face lower vulnerability or have higher coping capability to shocks compared to regions with underdeveloped infrastructures.

As an example, Table V.19 presents two indicators of social and economic infrastructure conditions in provinces in Indonesia, such as education facilities (e.g. university/academy, primary school, and senior and junior high schools, muslim boarding school) and health facilities (including general and maternity hospitals, policlinics/medical centers, public health centers (*puskesmas*) and their subsidiaries, village health and maternily posts (*poskesdes* and *polindes*, respectively), integrated health posts (*posyandu*). Each facility is weighted by a minimum standard of services per 100,000 people.

The number of villages by the availability of education and health facilities can also be used as an alternative indicator. As an example, Table V.20 shows the number of villages in Indonesia having primary school and junior and senior high schools (these schools are generally considered very important facilities for the formation of society's basic and general education), and Table V.21 shows the number of villages by key health facilities. As can be seen, the proportion of villages having these facilities varies by provinces, and DKI Jakarta and other provinces in Java are among the top rank.

Table V.19. Education and Health Facilities in Indonesia by Province, 2007

Province	Education	Health
Nangroe Aceh Darussalam	13.67	17.38
North Sumatera	11.15	16.72
West Sumatera	13.42	16.35
Riau	19.02	27.56
Jambi	23.08	25.44
South Sumatera	20.93	28.7
Bengkulu	18.81	23.14
Lampung	14.02	17.26
Bangka Belitung	18.5	22.2
Riau islands	25.02	33.16
DKI Jakarta	12.34	8.67
West. Java	7.31	10.16
Central Java	4.79	6.52
D. I. Yogyakarta	3.67	7.02
East Java	6.03	7.66
Banten	8.39	14.18
Bali	9.63	11.71
West Nusa Tenggara	17.05	16.42
East Nusa Tenggara	20.71	30.7
West Kalimantan	30.69	37.1
Central Kalimantan	38.15	51.33
South Kalimantan	21.96	23.89
East Kalimantan	35.7	48.56
North Sulawesi	15.95	25.74
Central Sulawesi	31.63	37.92
South Sulawesi	17.37	20.68
Southeast Sulawesi	30.99	33.95
Gorontalo	20.18	19.79
West Sulawesi	29.99	37.43
Maluku	39.59	55.57
North Maluku	33.26	48.25
West Papua	48.08	66.43
Papua	40.62	59.22

Source: BPS (www.bps.go.id).

If education and health facilities reflect social infrastructures, current development of roads by kilometer (km), type and condition of electricity and public access to it are then among good indicators of economic infrastructures. Mustajab's (2009) PhD dissertaion on infrastructure investment in Indonesia is probably the most recent study on infrastructure development in the country. The study shows that the distribution of road development in the country is not balanced among regions (islands, provinces, districts, subdistricts; rural and urban). Within Indonesia, Java and Bali are still the most developed regions with respect to roads. Within Java, however, many villages are still not supported by paved roads. By using official data, it shows that only 52 percent of total villages in Indonesia have paved roads in

2003. In terms of accessibility to four-wheel motor vehicles, only 85 percent of total villages can be reached by car. Looking at asphalt road, the eastern part of the country reveals as the least developed area than the western part (Figure V.11).

Table V.20. Distribution of Villages by Basic and General Education Facilities and Province in Indonesia, 2008 (unit)

Province	Primary	Junior high school	Senior high school	Total villages
Nangroe Aceh Darussalam	3216	882	469	6424
North Sumatera	4625	1790	912	5767
West Sumatera	878	518	271	924
Riau	1553	866	384	1604
Jambi	1261	555	257	1303
South Sumatera	2792	1023	475	3079
Bengkulu	1107	358	124	1351
Lampung	2256	1135	491	2339
Bangka Belitung	340	150	61	334
Riau islands	312	175	81	326
DKI Jakarta	266	253	228	267
West. Java	5859	3471	1448	5871
Central Java	8463	3147	1104	8574
D. I. Yogyakarta	437	305	140	438
East Java	8443	3964	1728	8505
Banten	1498	991	469	1504
Bali	707	295	131	712
West Nusa Tenggara	906	619	339	913
East Nusa Tenggara	2701	841	247	2803
West Kalimantan	1757	716	268	1791
Central Kalimantan	1431	481	171	1448
South Kalimantan	1828	646	246	1974
East Kalimantan	1193	522	232	1417
North Sulawesi	1370	574	190	1494
Central Sulawesi	1625	577	214	1686
South Sulawesi	2838	1224	547	2946
Southeast Sulawesi	1687	533	247	2028
Gorontalo	533	257	73	584
West Sulawesi	511	220	76	536
Maluku	856	405	184	906
North Maluku	949	356	155	1036
West Papua	746	142	58	1205
Papua	1683	319	127	3311

Source: BPS (www.bps.go.id).

Table V.21. Distribution of Villages by Key Health Facilities and Province in Indonesia, 2008 (unit)

Province	General hospital	Maternity hospital	Policlinic	*Puskesmas*	Total villages
Nangroe Aceh Darussalam	40	40	172	305	6424
North Sumatera	152	354	859	513	5767
West Sumatera	39	117	83	241	924
Riau	41	96	220	187	1604
Jambi	23	40	50	158	1303
South Sumatera	38	78	138	282	3079
Bengkulu	15	10	33	156	1351
Lampung	31	162	253	259	2339
Bangka Belitung	10	10	24	56	334
Riau islands	18	40	50	55	326
DKI Jakarta	92	183	240	241	267
West. Java	177	392	1449	1010	5871
Central Java	205	659	1289	861	8574
D. I. Yogyakarta	41	97	119	120	438
East Java	219	486	715	951	8505
Banten	39	164	427	192	1504
Bali	30	42	36	114	712
West Nusa Tenggara	17	20	26	137	913
East Nusa Tenggara	30	19	102	281	2803
West Kalimantan	25	29	68	220	1791
Central Kalimantan	17	16	53	176	1448
South Kalimantan	23	17	75	209	1974
East Kalimantan	33	26	86	209	1417
North Sulawesi	27	37	58	148	1494
Central Sulawesi	19	13	24	160	1686
South Sulawesi	49	74	118	406	2946
Southeast Sulawesi	21	7	16	187	2028
Gorontalo	8	9	28	78	584
West Sulawesi	7	2	12	75	536
Maluku	20	5	30	150	906
North Maluku	13	1	9	91	1036
West Papua	11	7	35	97	1205
Papua	26	12	248	245	3311

Source: BPS (www.bps.go.id).

During the New Order regime (1966-1998), the development of basic infrastructure, including road, was given high priority. The end of the 1970s was the beginning of toll-road development. The process was disturbed by the 1997/98 Asian financial crisis. Then, after the crisis, the improvement of existing and the construction of new roads have again become a high development priority. Many new toll-roads have been planned for 2009 and onwards. However, as shown in Figures V.12 and V.13, most of new planned toll roads are in Java.

Source: Mustajab (2009) (from BPS, 2005).

Figure V.11. Percentage of Villages with Asphalt Road in Indonesia, 2005.

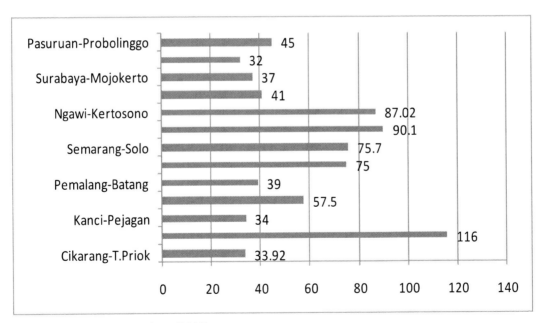

Source: Diredja and Damardono (2009).

Figure V.12. Development Priority of Trans-Java Toll Roads by Location, 2009 (km).

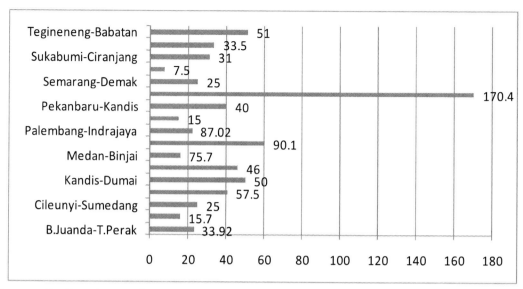

Source: Diredja and Damardono (2009).

Figure V.13. Development Plan for New Toll Roads in Indonesia by Location, 2009 (km).

With respect to electricity, based on Village Potential Statistics 2005, Mustajab (2009) finds that villages in Java and Bali have better access to electricity from PLN (stated own electricity company) compared to other regions in the country. While about 99 percent of the villages in DKI Jakarta and 82 percent in D.I.Yogyakarta are connected to electrical grids, only around 30 percent of the villages in the province East Nusa Tenggara have access (Figures V.14). [19]

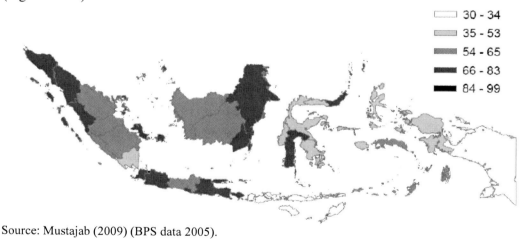

Source: Mustajab (2009) (BPS data 2005).

Figure V.14. Percentage of Villages with PLN Electricity in Indonesia, 2005.

---

[19] Even in many provincial cities or big cities in provinces outside Java, access to or electricity capacity is limited. For instance, as stated in Kompas newspaper (Infrastruktur Daerah, 24 April 2009), in Palangkaraya, the capital of Central Kalimantan, the need for electricity reached 26.4 megawatt (MW) but during the peak hours, i.e. 17.00-22.00 p.m., the city has a deficit of 2 MW.

Source: Tambunan and Asmanto (2010).

Figure V.15. Socio-Economic Infrastructure Index.

Based on some indicators on social-economic infrastructure, e.g. education, health, financial and economic facilities coverage per 100,000 people, transportation represented by lengths of road and road condition (including whether it is accessible for cars), and proprotion of population having access to electricity, and by using secondary data from various sources (e.g. BPS (Podes), Ministry of Education, Ministry of Health, Bank Indonesia, Ministry of Transformation, and Ministry of Energy, Mining and Mineral Resources), Tambunan and Asmanto (2010) produce the social-economic infrastructure index of provinces in Indonesia. With this index, provinces can be classified into three categories as shown in Figure V.15. As can be seen, it comes as a surprise that Java (including the west-part where the Indonesian capital is sited), which in fact is more developed than the rest of the country, is among regions with less accessibility. However, it can happen, because Java is more populated thanother provinces. In other words, a region with well-developed roads may still emerge as a less accessible region than a least-developed region because the former is more populated leading to higher population density not only with respect to land but also to existing roads than in the latter region.

16) Social Capital

The importance of social capital is generally acknowledged as critical in building and maintaining the trust necessary for social cohesion and progress. In the economic area, social capital is important as a determinant factor of the feasibility and productivity of economic activities (Putman, 1993). This suggests a positive link between the nature of the economic development process and social capital. In regions where social capital is strongly present, the economic development goes smoothly. In general, social capital can be defined at reciprocity within communities, between individuals, and among households based on trust deriving from social ties. Social ties and trust go together. Putnam (1993) defines the "stocks" of social capital as the informal (unorganized) and formal (organized) reciprocal networks of trust and norms embedded in the social organization of communities, with social institutions both hierarchical and horizontal in structure. In Adger, et al. (2004), social capital is seen as the ability to act collectively while for Hoddinott and Quisumbing (2003), social capital includes networks, norms and social trust that facilitates cordination and cooperation. In relation to the issue of vulnerability, Adger, et al. (2004) emphasize that the way in which society at large acts collectively to confront hazards and reduce risk is a complex, yet extremely important, factor in determining the level of vulnerability. [20] Thus, one hypothesis from this is that a community with well-developed social capital (reflected in strong community level trust and collaboration), faces low vulnerability (or high resilience) to a shock, *ceteris paribus*.

At the micro-or household-level, social capital or social cohesion is embedded in household and intra-household-level relationships. According to Moser (1998), the capacity of a region or community to respond to a shock depends not only on community-level trust and collaboration, but also on households' social cohesion. Thus, social capital (at the macro-/community-level) and social cohesion (at the micro-/household-level) are two important invisible intangible assets which determine the response capacity of a region to a crisis. It can be said that a strong social cohesion is the necessity condition that a region must have to be more resilient to a crisis. A strong social cohesion is the base for a strong social capital. Household and intra-household relations are especially important in an economic crisis because they are an effective and efficient mechanism for pooling income and consumption sharing. For instance, in response to an economic crisis, household strategies may include increase reliance on extended family support networks or increase labor migration and remittances (Morse, 1998).

The importance of social capital at the time of an economic crisis may be reflected in many forms, and the most important ones as evident in many developing countries are the increased reliance of poor households on informal credit sources (e.g. through rural cooperatives or from relatives and friends instead of banks or other formal financial institutions, including government sponsored credit schemes), the increased informal support networks among households or farmers through farmers association, or increased community-level activities supported by existing non-government organizations (NGOs) (Morse, 1998).

In Indonesia, during the Soekarno era (the first president after the independence in 1945) in the period 1945-1966, social capital was even regarded more important than the strength of the military force to keep the unity of the new born country in its struggle against the colonialization. The social capital was promoted with the slogan *gotong-royong*: i.e. helping each other among individuals in all aspects of life. These days, social capital in Indonesia is still obviously present in the time of natural disasters and during economic hardships. Many villages that experienced economic hardships because of various reasons, such as harvest failure, show that the impact could be minimized not by government supports but because of this *gotong-royong* culture.

Table V.22 provides information on a number of cooperative units and cooperative members in Indonesia by province, based on data from the State Ministry of Cooperative and SME (Menegkop & UKM). These can be included as among key indicators of social capital, since the presence of cooperatives may indicate the willingness of people to work together. It can be assumed that in regions where there are many established cooperatives (for example, cooperatives of producers, farmers, micro enterprises, or factory workers) and a high

---

[20] For more discussion on the importance of social capital, see, among many others, Lochner, et al (1999), Paldam and Svendsen (2000),and Adger, et al (2003).

proportion of the population are members of cooperatives, the social capital in those regions is stronger than in regions where there are no kinds of cooperation among people, producers, or farmers.

Table V.22. Cooperative in Indonesia by Province, 2007 and 2008

Province	Number of unit 2007	Number of unit 2008	Number of members (people) 2007	Number of members (people) 2008
Nangroe Aceh Darussalam	5,800	6,570	485,254	494,564
North Sumatera	9,232	9,540	1,212,832	1,222,187
West Sumatera	3,388	3,424	560,845	540,418
Riau	4,103	4,421	583,092	578,355
Jambi	2,845	2,972	319,956	291,025
South Sumatera	4,041	4,164	726,984	746,920
Bengkulu	1,305	1,415	131,947	144,394
Lampung	3,084	3,219	730,420	631,332
Bangka Belitung	705	794	73,367	73,494
Riau islands	1,419	1,576	362,184	131,284
DKI Jakarta	6,847	7,203	971,040	979,860
West Java	22,522	21,272	6,222,006	4,251,889
Central Java	17,090	17,617	4,387,110	4,576,355
D. I. Yogyakarta	2,095	2,195	610,550	639,533
East Java	17,918	18,656	5,002,532	5,057,750
Banten	5,338	5,572	872,203	926,059
Bali	3,232	3,504	788,774	849,781
West Nusa Tenggara	2,695	2,898	540,386	585,933
East Nusa Tenggara	1,486	1,614	388,660	401,367
West Kalimantan	3,102	3,456	425,626	578,655
Central Kalimantan	2,061	2,315	194,659	212,875
South Kalimantan	2,074	2,137	294,644	294,644
East Kalimantan	3,649	3,828	386,594	405,260
North Sulawesi	5,377	5,460	508,780	488,319
Central Sulawesi	1,539	1,686	237,531	243,650
South Sulawesi	6,774	7,017	1,117,959	1,196,668
Southeast Sulawesi	2,560	2,568	192,678	194,761
Gorontalo	827	865	109,608	120,555
West Sulawesi	583	645	67,970	72,322
Maluku	2,026	2,260	107,524	115,237
North Maluku	977	955	59,028	63,113
West Papua	1,046	1,057	69,883	52,512
Papua	2,053	2,089	145,441	157,547

Source: Menegkop & UKM (www.depkop.go.id).

Table V.23. Distribution of Villages by Selected Social Organizations and Provinces in Indonesia, 2008 (unit)

Province	Muslimion srvices	Christian services	Death management institutions	Non-government organiszation	Total villages
Nangroe Aceh Darussalam	5763	101	3479	516	6424
North Sumatera	3899	3236	4277	1080	5767
West Sumatera	864	58	491	254	924
Riau	1562	356	1263	403	1604
Jambi	1280	147	687	235	1303
South Sumatera	2921	385	2209	559	3079
Bengkulu	1189	114	648	204	1351
Lampung	2306	771	1587	506	2339
Bangka Belitung	319	84	275	69	334
Riau islands	306	97	230	114	326
DKI Jakarta	266	188	156	183	267
West. Java	5845	385	1769	1199	5871
Central Java	8481	2068	3509	931	8574
D. I. Yogyakarta	434	292	158	100	438
East Java	8350	1512	5237	1401	8505
Banten	1497	124	513	344	1504
Bali	197	92	671	102	712
West Nusa Tenggara	796	37	472	322	913
East Nusa Tenggara	417	1742	764	378	2803
West Kalimantan	1050	1018	748	324	1791
Central Kalimantan	841	902	764	249	1448
South Kalimantan	1759	160	1749	239	1974
East Kalimantan	836	846	673	319	1417
North Sulawesi	597	1265	1165	315	1494
Central Sulawesi	1274	832	614	203	1686
South Sulawesi	2196	751	691	546	2946
Southeast Sulawesi	1839	230	459	186	2028
Gorontalo	542	96	463	138	584
West Sulawesi	333	264	83	63	536
Maluku	386	615	228	94	906
North Maluku	535	424	469	128	1036
West Papua	251	1009	91	117	1205
Papua	267	2501	376	208	3311

Source: BPS.

However, cooperative is more economic rather than social-oriented, aiming at the enhancement of members' welfare. For instance, cooperatives of milk producers aim to improve the incomes of the producers through working together in production, marketing and inputs purchasing. If data is available, the number of social organization activities (or percentage of population involved in such activites), other than cooperatives, would be much better for measuring the current strength of social capital. Indonesia has some data for this as shown in Table V. 23.

17) Women's Participation in Employment/Economic Activities

Gender issue is probably more relevant for developing rather than developed countries or countries with highly empowered female or high women emancipation rates. Due to many constraints facing them (e.g. culture, religious, norm, customs, male-biased practices), the level of marginalization of women in the first group of countries are relatively high[21] while, women empowerment or more opportunities for women to get good educations and employment and to do economic activities will reduce poverty. Consequently, when there is a crisis, as argued in the literature, women in developing countries have a more difficult time during recovery compared to men (or women in developed countries), often due to sector-specific employment, lower wages, family care responsibilities, and cultural constraints that limit their flexibility.[22] It can be hypothesized that regions with low marginalized women are less vulnerable to external shocks than those with low level of women emancipation, *ceteris paribus*.

Based on data from the National Labor Survey (SAKERNAS), Table V.24 presents two often used indicators; labor force participation rate by gender and number of employed women, to measure the level of women's participation in employment in the Province of Nangroe Aceh Darussalam by district. The labor force participation of women is measured by the proportion of women employed to total women population aged 15-65 years old.[23] As can be seen, in all districts, the labor participation rates of males are higher than that of females; although the ratio of male to female employment varies by district. The second indicator, measured as a percentage of total labor force, also varies by district, although the average percentage of all districts is between 50 and 60. The variations may reflect differences among districts in many women employment determinant factors such as employment opportunities, education of women (percentage of educated women in total women population), financial condition of women's families/households, ratio of married women to total women population, etc.

18) Macroeconomic Stability

Following the work of Briguglio et al. (2008) in the construction of a resilience index, macroeconomic stability is considered an important variable that captures the effect of shock absorption or shock counteraction policies. Macroeconomic stability relates to an internal economic equilibrium (i.e. aggregate demand equals aggregate supply), which is manifested in a sustainable fiscal or government financial/budget position (government expenditures relative to tax and other goverment incomes), higher GRP growth rate, low inflation rate, and unemployment/employment rate close to its natural rate. It also relates to external balance, which is reflected in the balance of payment (international current account plus capital balance), or trade balance (total export minus total import in goods and services) or international current account position (i.e. trade balance plus balance in international

---

[21] See Tambunan (2009b) for his research on women entrepreneurship in Asian developing countries and his review on literature on the issue.
[22] See, among others, Enarson and Scanlon (1999), Morrow and Phillips (1999), Peacock, et al. (2000), and Cutter, et al. (2003).
[23] According to Indonesian official definition (SAKERNAS), those between 15 and 65 years old and have jobs during at least the past week, either working or temporarily not working for some reasons such as waiting for harvest or time off, are considered employed.

payments not included in the capital balance), or the level of external debt (e.g. external debt-to-GRP ratio).

With respect to fiscal position, one hypothesis is that higher fiscal deficit (more expenditure than incomes), higher public/foreign debt, lower sustainability of government budget, more constraint on the use of fiscal tools, less resilience, and thus, higher vulnerability, *ceteris paribus*. According to ADB (2010b), lower public debt from 40.9 percent in 2000 to 31.2 percent of GDP in 2008 was also contributed to Indonesia's resilience during the crisis period. Since the end of the 1997/98 crisis, Indonesia's position has improved, though it remains behind many of its Asian peers such as Thailand and Malaysia. From the government income side, the average of change in tax revenue in comparison to the average of change in GDP during the period 2000-2008 has also increased from 3.0 to 3.4 percent, and now, according to the report, among the better indicators in Asia. This indicates that tax revenue in Indonesia does provide a natural automatic stabilizer or shock absorber in the economy, as it automatically adjusts as economy accelerates or decelerates as during the crisis period (ADB, 2010b).

Table V.24. Female Employment in the Province of Nangroe Aceh Darussalam by District, 2007

District	Labor force participation rate (%)		Number of employed women (%)	
	Male	Female	Male	Female
Kab. Simeulue	67.15	25.32	52.82	53.88
Kab. Aceh Singkil	65.44	27.80	56.57	58.13
Kab. Aceh Selatan	69.35	34.45	67.97	57.66
Kab. Aceh Tenggara	60.00	31.96	53.08	54.64
Kab. Aceh Timur	72.23	34.60	58.73	63.84
Kab. Aceh Tengah	77.76	61.49	71.49	80.56
Kab. Aceh Barat	69.07	29.50	52.03	57.89
Kab. Aceh Besar	62.99	30,.66	45.91	58.47
Kab. Pidie	64,.27	41.05	62.64	59.32
Kab. Bireuen	68.16	37.94	61.90	59.49
Kab. Aceh Utara	62.31	27.76	48.89	54.67
Kab. Aceh Barat Daya	67.33	32.17	58.49	59.39
Kab. Gayo Lues	71.90	42.75	58.25	67.44
Kab. Aceh Tamiang	71.07	34.42	64.10	61.23
Kab. Nagan Raya	70.51	46.28	63.49	67.03
Kab. Aceh Jaya	70.64	30.26	62.92	58.69
Kab. Bener Meriah	73.77	54.67	65.50	75.18
Kab. Pidie Jaya	67.16	45.74	48.24	67.17
Kota Banda Aceh	68.14	34.32	55.50	64.17
Kota Sabang	70.82	35.24	59.78	62.73
Kota Langsa	68.90	28.05	55.53	57.41
Kota Lhokseumawe	65.97	26.27	53.39	48.32
Kota Subulussalam	68.88	29.83	59.14	60.53

Source: BPS (www.bps.go.id).

Table IV.25. Actual Expenditure of Provincial Governments in Indonesia, 2008 (billion Rp)

Province	Revenue	Expenditure
Nangroe Aceh Darussalam	6,644.8	8,518.7
North Sumatera	2,957.3	3,289.3
West Sumatera	1,317.0	1,485.9
Riau	3,463.1	4,358.5
Jambi	1,136.1	1,429.2
South Sumatera	2,472.8	2,743.4
Bengkulu	872.3	1,155.2
Lampung	1,505.3	1,730.3
Bangka Belitung	722.0	864.0
Riau islands	1,178.5	1,382.5
DKI Jakarta	18,791.5	20,523.3
West. Java	5,696.3	6,050.0
Central Java	4,845.2	5,394.3
D. I. Yogyakarta	1,162.0	1,629.1
East Java	5,358.4	6,111.3
Banten	2,028.9	2,154.4
Bali	1,289.0	1,502.3
West Nusa Tenggara	1,034.8	1,093.8
East Nusa Tenggara	938.9	1,139.4
West Kalimantan	1,289.2	1,301.8
Central Kalimantan	1,187.7	1,371.2
South Kalimantan	1,508.4	1,705.9
East Kalimantan	4,085.9	6,166.3
North Sulawesi	847.3	1,099.8
Central Sulawesi	929.2	974.0
South Sulawesi	2,026.1	2,118.3
Southeast Sulawesi	885.3	883.7
Gorontalo	471.9	567.5
West Sulawesi	549.9	575.9
Maluku	778.8	806.3
North Maluku	663.9	690.2
West Papua	780.1	999.1
Papua	5,558.8	5,448.8

Source: BPS (www.bps.go.id).

At the provincial level, since local/provincial governments are not allowed to make public debt, provincial government's actual revenue and expenditure-to-GRP ratio or provincial government expenditure as percentage to provincial government receipt can be used instead as indicators of regional fiscal sustainability. Table IV.25 presents 2008 data on actual governemnt expenditure of provincial governments in Indonesia.

With regard to inflation, aggregate output (GRP) and unemployment, the related hypothesis is that higher inflation, lower GRP growth rate and higher unemployment rates (higher government expenditures or fiscal deficit), higher welfare costs caused by a shock, lower resilience, *ceteris paribus*. Therefore, output growth, unemployment and inflation are often associated with resilience of a shock-absorbing nature (Briguglio et al., 2008).[24]

As an empirical illustration, Table V.26 presents monthly inflation rates in selected important cities in Indonesia for the period July-August 2007, and Figure V.16 shows real GRP (at constant market prices 2000) growth rates in Indonesia by province. The variety in the inflation rates reflect differences among the cities in cost-push and demand-pull factors of inflation. The cost-push factors include the level of efficiency in production process, government determined minimum wage, distribution system, transportation costs and the availability of inputs. The demand-pull factors are total population and its structure and income per capita.

Table V.26. Inflation rates in Selected Important Cities in Indonesia, July-August 2007

Provincial City	July	August
Banda Aceh	0.80	1.45
Medan	1.20	0.91
Padang	0.75	0.45
Pekanbaru	0.31	0.57
Jambi	1.06	0.35
Palembang	0.41	-0,14
Bengkulu	1.61	0.54
Bandar Lampung	0.79	1.33
Batam	0.15	0.33
Jakarta	0.36	0.45
Bandung	0.29	0.50
Surakarta	0.16	0.42
Semarang	0.46	0.32
Yogyakarta	0.32	0.77
Malang	0.31	0.04
Surabaya	0.25	-0.20
Tangerang	0.03	0.60
Denpasar	0.38	0.50
Pontianak	1.29	0.76
Banjarmasin	0.26	0.54
Balikpapan	1.17	0.66
Samarinda	-0.18	0.78
Menado	0.46	0.65
Makassar	0.41	1.21
Ambon	1.10	1.27
Jayapura	-0.56	0.81
National	0.45	0.56

Source: BPS.

---

[24] In their proposed resilience index, Briguglio et al. (2008) include the sum of these two variables, also known as the economic discomfort index (or often said as economic misery index).

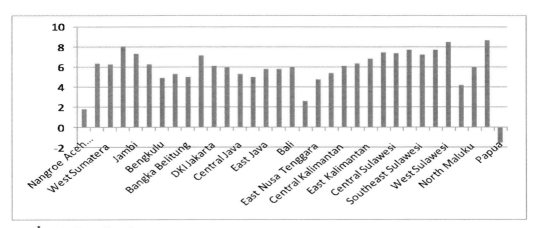

Note: * excluding oil and gas.
Source: BPS (www.bps.go.id).

Figure V.16. Real GRP growth rates in provinces in Indonesia, 2008 (%)*.

Inflation is also an indicator of the credibility of central bank. The more central bank is able to control inflation, the greater is the central bank's credibility, and the more latitude it has to ease monetary conditions in an economic slowdown. According to ADB (2010b), in this particular area, Indonesia has improved significantly since the end of the 1997/98 crisis,[25] though it is severely laggard compared to other Asian countries. This statement is, however, not relevant for the context of province, since in Indonesia, the monetary policy is still the monopoly of the central government.

With respect to external debt, following Adger, et al. (2004), a country's ability to pay for emergency planning or to finance recovery programs such as social safety nets or fiscal stimulus during a crisis will be affected by its indebtedness, i.e. the extent to which the national wealth or more specifically, government incomes are diverted for paying back loans and their interest. Moreover, economic policy in highly indebted countries is very often determined by the international financial institutions, which impose structural readjustment and trade liberalisation programs, which gives less flexibility for the countries to pursue their own policies. Indonesia has experienced this during the 1997/98 Asian financial crisis with the International Monetary Fund (IMF), which reduced the capacity of the government to pursue policies to reduce the impact of the crisis on the poor. Ndikumana and Boyce (2003) also find that debt can encourage capital flight, further exacerbating national economic well-being of highly indebted countries and hence, it reduces their capability to cope with a shock.

Thus, the related hypothesis is that higher external debt (measured by debt as percentage of GDP), more difficult to mobilize resources in order to offset the negative effects of external shocks, and thus less resilience. To apply this hypothesis at the regional/provincial level in Indonesia, loans or funds from central government, so-called general allocation funds (GAF), as a percentage of GRP or as a ratio to local government revenue (LGR), can be used as an alternative indicator. As an example, Table V.27 presents 2008 data on LGR and GAF in provinces in Indonesia.

Table V.27. LGR and GAF (billion Rp)

Province	LGR	GAF
Nangroe Aceh Darussalam	6,644.8	557.3
North Sumatera	2,957.3	727.9
West Sumatera	1,317.0	631.7
Riau	3,463.1	198.4
Jambi	1,136.1	468.8
South Sumatera	2,472.8	545.8
Bengkulu	872.3	482.5
Lampung	1,505.3	570.5
Bangka Belitung	722.0	391.1
Riau islands	1,178.5	5.8
DKI Jakarta	18,791.5	0
West. Java	5,696.3	0
Central Java	4,845.2	0
D. I. Yogyakarta	1,162.0	19.5
East Java	5,358.4	0
Banten	2,028.9	18.1
Bali	1,289.0	21.6
West Nusa Tenggara	1,034.8	37.2
East Nusa Tenggara	938.9	42.6
West Kalimantan	1,289.2	31.1
Central Kalimantan	1,187.7	40.2
South Kalimantan	1,508.4	36.0
East Kalimantan	4,085.9	0
North Sulawesi	847.3	28.1
Central Sulawesi	929.2	35.2
South Sulawesi	2,026.1	35.1
Southeast Sulawesi	885.3	29.9
Gorontalo	471.9	25.4
West Sulawesi	549.9	85.7
Maluku	778.8	36.6
North Maluku	663.9	36.5
West Papua	780.1	22.0
Papua	5,558.8	750.0

Source: BPS (www.bps.go.id).

19) Micro-economic Market Efficiency

Micro-economic market efficiency is also considered as an important component of the resilience index proposed by Briguglio et al. (2008). The theoretical justification of using this component is the following: an economy will gain more benefits if all existing productive resources are efficiently allocated through the undistorted price mechanism. Following an external shock, the more efficient an economy is, the more rapidly is the market adjustment

---

[25] According to the report, the difference between Indonesian inflation rate (%, y-o-y) and inflation rates in other countries in the G7 Country group in 2000 was -15.1 and declined to -6.7 in 2008 (ADB, 2010b).

process to achieve a new equilibrium, the less are the costs of the crisis recovery. To apply this component at the regional level in Indonesia, since not many indicators of market efficiency are available at that particular level, the percentage of private companies (or regional state-owned companies) in total enterprises; the percentage of micro, small and medium enterprises (MSMEs) as percentage of total enterprises; total private employment as percentage of total employment; percentage of credits from private banks (or from state-owned banks) in total credits; and total non-tax retributions (or as percentage of total tax incomes), can be used instead as alternative indicators. The basic idea here is that bureaucratic control of business activities (reflected by high percentage of state-owned companies in total enterprises or high GDP contributon of state-owned companies) is also thought to inhibit market efficiency. It can be hypothesized that in regions where government interventions/controls in daily social life, private initiatives and own capability to cope with an economic crisis are much weakers than in regions with the reverse situation, *ceteris paribus*.

As an example, Table V.28 shows total number of micro and small enterprises, which are private entities, in Indonesia by regions. The concentration of this group of enterprises in Java and Sumatera reflect the uneven distribution of economic activities in the country, especially non-mining economic activities are concentrated in the western part of the country.

V.3.2. Micro-Level Indicators

Previously, Section V.3.1 has referred to the vulnerability at the macro-level, which can be a country or a province or a district. But what really matters is, in fact, the vulnerability of people or households, especially of the poor. It is clear that the vulnerability of a country to an economic shock is closely associated with the vulnerability at the micro level, depending on how the shock is transmitted within the economy and on the people's or households' life, so this Section V.3.2 focuses on the vulnerability at the micro-level, namely households. In analyzing the vulnerability of households, the key questions are (WFP, 2005): who are the most vulnerable households? How many are they? Where do they live? Why they are vulnerable? What is the magnitude of the problem of vulnerability? What are the main characteristics of vulnerable households?

Table V.28. Number of Micro and Small Enterprises in Indonesia by Region, 2003-2005

Region	Number (000) 2003	Number (000) 2005	% 2003	% 2005
Western regions	2136	2034.4	80.9	79.7
-Sumatera	312	228.6	11.8	8.95
-Java and Bali	1824	1805.8	69.1	70.7
Eastern regions	506	519.6	19.2	20.3
-Nusa Tenggara	169	181.1	6.4	7.1
-Kalimantan	121	125.1	4.6	4.9
-Sulawesi	199	190.6	7.5	7.5
-Maluku and Papua	16	22.8	0.6	0.9
Indonesia	2642	2554	100.0	100.0

Source: Tambunan (2009c).

Vulnerability of an household has three main components: (1) the shock on the household incomes, which depends on the shock itself, and exposure and resilience at the macro level; (2) the exposure of the household to the shock, and (3) the household's capacity to react, i.e. the household's own resilience. Conversely, if all households appear to be vulnerable, it will be reflected by a low resilience at the macro level. In other words, there is a postive relationship between the resilience (or the level of vulnerability) at the macro level and that at the micro level (Guillaumont, 2001).

Let us take Indonesia as among coffee exporting countries in the world as an example to understand this relationship. Suppose there is an unforeseen fall in the world price of coffee. Theoretically, all coffee producing/exporting regions in Indonesia will be affected but the actual impact will depend on the following conditions: (1) the size of the fall, (2) the share of the coffee exports in the country's total exports as well as in its GDP, and (3) Indonesia's capacity to manage this shock relative to its total exports and GDP. The latter reflects the resilience of the affected regions within the country, i.e. coffee producing provinces or districts. The vulnerability at the micro level, i.e. the farmer level, depends on three key factors, namely (1) on the size of the producer/farmer price fall, which will be the result from a combination of the world price fall, domestic processing of the product, distribution or trading system (which determines the actual price received by the farmers), and from taxation; (2) on the number of farmers concerned and the revenues share in their total incomes from producing/exporting coffee (exposure); and (3) on their capacity to insure, to borrow or to draw on their own assets, in order to compensate the loss of income and to maintain their level of basic needs fulfillment (resilience). Within coffee producing provinces, provinces where most coffee farmers can cope well with the crisis are, in fact, less vulnerable than those where their coffee farmers are much less resilient. The capacity of coffee farmers to cope with the crisis, in turn, depends on many factors, considered as household characteristics, such as farmer's education, size of his family, and education level and employment status of members of his family.

Table V.29 proposes key household characteristics, covering 9 aspects (employment, education, consumption, gender, sources of income, size and structure, health, assets, and location) to be used in order to measure the household vulnerability. These household characteristics have been proved empirically as the most important determinants of household poverty by many studies. For instance, Chaudhuri et al. (2002)[26] provide a conceptual framework of household-level vulnerability and they purpose a simple method to estimate it empirically with cross-sectional data (since time series data is not available). [27]They have applied the method in their case study in Indonesia by using household-level data from the December 1998 and August 1999 mini-social-economic surveys (SUSENAS). In their

---

[26] See Christiaensen and Boisvert (2000) on measuring household food vulnerability using Mali data, Cunningham and Maloney (2000) using Mexican data, and Glewwe and Hall (1998) with Peru as the case study.

[27] Their purposed framework is simple because its empirical implementation entails a very modest extension of the standard approach to poverty assessment, since poverty and vulnerability (to poverty) are linked (conceptually), though they are not identical (Hoddinott and Quisumbing, 2003). Household poverty assessment deals with the observed poverty status of an household (defined simply by whether or not the household's observed level of consumption expenditure are above or below a pre-determined poverty line). It is an ex-post measure of a household's well-being. Household vulnerability assessment, on the other hand, deals with the future, thus it is ex-ante measure of an household's well being. So, if poverty probabilities of households with different sets of characteristics (some, if not all, are given in Table V.28) can be predicted, then in effect, the vulnerability of these households can be estimated (Chaudhuri et al.,2002).

conceptual framework, by using consumption expenditure to measure poverty status, the vulnerability level of a household in period t is defined as the probability that the household will find itself consumption-poor in period t +1 (see again equation V.1). The level of vulnerability in period t is defined in terms of the household's consumption prospects in period t +1. Their assessment of an household's vulnerability was based on their inferences about its future consumption prospects. And in order to do that, they used an analytical framework about both the inter-temporal aspects and cross-sectional determinants of consumption patterns at the household level. Their analytical framework has the following reduced form of expression for consumption (C_t), showing that household's consumption is determined by observable household characteristics:

$$C_t = c(X_h, A_t, B_h, D_{ht}) \tag{V.6}$$

Table V.29. Concept and Measurable Indicators of Economic Vulnerability at Household (Micro-)-level

No	Indicator	Nature Resilience	Nature Sensitivity
1	Employment condition and status of the head of the household -household with unemployed/employed heads -household by type of employment status of the head	X	X
2	Education of the head of household -household by level of education of the head	X	X
3	Structure of household consumption -ratio food to non-food consumption	X	X
4	Gender and age status of the head of household -household by gender of the head -household by age of the head	X	X
5	Sources of household income -household by sources (sector) of income	X	X
6	Household size and structure by employment and education -household by size (number of members) -household by number of dependent members	X	X
7	Health condition -household by number of "permanent" sick members	X	X
8	Assets ownership -household by number, type or market values of own assets	X	
9	Location -household living in remote/isolated areas -hoseuhold living in areas linked to centers of economic activities/ administration/public services -household living urban areas/cities		X

where Xh represents household characteristics such as household size, location, educational attainment of the household head, etc. (which are also presented in Table V.28); A_t is a vector of parameters describing the state of the economy at time t; and B_h and D_{ht} represent, respectively, an unobserved time-invariant household-level effect, and any idiosyncratic factors (shocks) that contribute to differential welfare outcomes for households that are otherwise observationally equivalent. To estimate coefficients, they relied on regression methods.

1) Employment Condition and Status of the Head of the Household

It is generally expected that households with unemployed heads, *ceteris paribus*, are more vulnerable than those with heads having permanent jobs. Furthermore, there is a strong relationship between the status of employment (e.g. part/full time, contract workers, seasonal workers) and the level of wage/income, *ceteris paribus*. In this respect, one hypothesis is that the better the employment status (i.e. permanent/full job) of the head, *ceteris paribus*, the higher the degree of resilience, the lower the household's vulnerability.

2) Education of the Head of the Household

Theoretically, the level of formal education is positively related with employment condition and status or with wage/income (as the level of education is positively related with the level of productivity), *ceteris paribus*. From their study on vulnerability in Bulgaria using a panel dataset 1994, Ligon and Schechter (2003) found that households with employed and educated heads are less vulnerable to shocks than other households are. An hypothesis derived from this theoretical thought is that the higher the level of formal education of the household head, the higher the degree of resilience and the lower the vulnerability of the household, *ceteris paribus*.

3) Structure of Household Consumption

This indicator is particularly relevant for a food crisis. As an example, stock or local production of rice declines, while demand for rice keeps constant or increases. Consequently, local prices of rice goes up leading to higher household expenditure on rice. Households with higher rice consumption to non-rice consumption ratio or higher percentage of rice consumption in their total consumptions are more vulnerable than those with lower ratio or percentage to this kind of crisis. The vulnerable households are affected through two channels, i.e. production effect (less rice is available) and price effect (higher price).[28]

4) Gender and Age Status of the Head of the Household

As explained before in discussing vulnerability indicators at the macro-level, gender issue of the head of household is more relevant for developing countries than in more developed countries or countries with higher empowered female or societies with no gender discriminations. Given many constraints facing women in developing countries (e.g. culture,

---

[28] Food crisis from the household point of view is not only because of lower stock or production or higher price, but also because of lack of access. According to FAO, household food security is about access to food supplies for households. It is insecure when households have inadequate access to food. FAO sees that in order for people to be food secured, they need to have both physical and economic access to the basic food they need. These accesses, however, need to be sustainable. Thus, essential components of household food security are: (1) physical access; (2) economic access ; and (3) sustainability of access (www.fao.org).

religious, norm, male-biased practices), it is generally expected that household with female head, *ceteris paribus*, are more vulnerable or have more difficulties to cope with external shocks compared to those with male heads (see the discussion on macro-level indicators related to this issue).

With respect to age, as age is negatively related to the level of productivity, beyond a certain age which is considered as the optimal productive age, it can be hypothesized that there is a positive link between age of the household head and household's vulnerability; with the assumption that other factors keep constant.

5) *Sources of Household Incomes*

Sources of incomes of households also determine their level of vulnerability, depending on the type of crisis. Let the world price for crude palm oil (CPO) decline significantly due to over-supply. At the macro-level, regions within Indonesia producing CPO will be directly affected. At the micro-level, within the regions, households with CPO production or trading as their main sources of income are the first victim of the crisis. The second victim are households working (either as producers or employees) in other CPO-related sectors (e.g. transportation and industries producing inputs for CPO production). Thus, the hypothesis here is that, depending on the type of crisis, households with a higher degree of income diversification are less vulnerable than those with a lower degree of income diversification.

6) *Household Size and Structure by Employment and Education*

As in the case of country or province, size is also relevant at the household level: a large sized household has more economies of scale than a smaller sized household. But a large sized household may be more vulnerable to a crisis than a smaller sized household, if the former household has many dependent members (higher dependency ratio), or unproductive/unemployment members (lower productive age proportion), or low-educated members. In Cutter,et al. (2003), it is explained that households with large numbers of dependents (or single-parent households) often have limited finances to outsource care for dependents, and thus must combine work responsibilities and care for dependent household members. All these affect the resilience or the recovery capacity from shocks. In other words, diverse livelihood activities by a range of household members is a good hedge against the failure of one or another of these income streams due to shocks. For example, because of the 2008/09 crisis, one member of a household has lost his/her job. But the household still can survive the crisis because it has other members who still work despite the crisis. While a household with only one member has a job before the crisis, even if he/she gets a new job after the crisis, his/her income and hence, his/her household income may be lower than in the pre-crisis period. [29]

Thus, family structure by productive/working members or dependent/unemployed members (or educated members as an alternative indicator) also plays an important role in determinng the level of resilience/vulnerability of a household. One hypothesis related to this is that the smaller the size, given the household structure, or the better the structure (low

---

[29] In Downing et al. (2001), dependency ratio, together with fertility, literacy, and life expectancy are used as main indicators of human resources coping capacity. See also, e.g. Morrow (1999), Puente (1999), and Heinz Center for Science, Economics, and the Environment (2000).

dependency ratio; low illiteracy rate), given the size, the higher the level of resilience and the lower the vulnerability, *ceteris paribus*.

7) Health Condition

Human capital consists of education/skill and health. As education, health conditions of household members are also very important determinants of the household's capability to respond to a crisis. The related hypothesis is that the better the health condition of a household, *ceteris paribus*, the higher and the lower, respectively, the household's resilience and vulnerability.

8) Assets Ownership

The capability of a household to respond to an economic crisis is not only determined by income but by its total welfare, which is employment income plus income which can be generated from its total assets,[30] such as. natural capital (land and livestock), physical capital (house, transportation means, agricultural tools); financial capital (e.g. bank account/saving, net loans outstanding), and other non-labor assets/human capital. According to Hoddinott and Quisumbing (2003), all those assets (including social capital) through their allocation across a number of activities such as food production, cash crop production, and other income-generating activities/assets determine the capability of households to respond to shocks. Cutter, et al. (2003) constructed an index of social vulnerability to environmental hazards (called the Social Vulnerability Index) for the US, based on 1990 county-level socioeconomic and demographic data. In their model, personal wealth is measured by employment income and also by median house values and median rents. By using a factor analytic approach, their analysis shows that the wealth factor explains 12.4 percent of the variance. Based on this finding, it can be concluded that wealth enables households to quickly absorb and recover from losses. On the other hand, lack of wealth is a primary contributor to social vulnerability as fewer individual and community resources for recovery are available, thereby making the community less resilient to shocks. Thus, the related hypothesis is that the more assets owned by a household, the higher the household's resilience, and the lower its vulnerability, *ceteris paribus*.

9) Location

According to Cova and Church (1997), Mitchell (1999), and Cutter, et al. (2000), rural residents may be more vulnerable than urban residents to shocks due to lower incomes and more dependent on locally-based resource extraction economies (e.g., farming, fishing). The related hypothesis is that, given the above household characteristics, households located in remoted areas (e.g. mountain, hill, rural) are more vulnerable, as they are less resilient (they face many contraints to recover) than households in open/fully accessible locations/urban, to shocks, *ceteris paribus*. However, as already discussed in the previous section on vulnerability indicators at the macro-level regarding the geographical location, remoteness can also act as an isolator from crises from outside. Thus, it depends on the type of the crisis.

---

[30] If there is data on employment income and total value (or total expected incomes) of all assets (not including human capital/labor), both datas should be used as total family incomes.

V.4. PRACTICAL USE: SOME EXAMPLES

As explained before, the meaning of those vulnerability indicators is that they can be used to monitor changes in the level of vulnerability of countries or provinces or districts (macro-level indicators) and households (micro-level indicators). Of course, those indicators are useful if data for the indicators is available, both cross-section and time series data (or panel data). With cross-section data, by comparing regions, or households within a region, the most vulnerable region or group of households can be identified at one time (static) when there is an imminent crisis. Thus, policymakers can make the right choice regarding which region or group of households should get the first priority for emergency help.

With time-series data with sufficient length, changes in the level of vulnerability of regions or households within regions can be monitored, and since (as explained before) vulnerability is a dynamic process, regions or households which tend to have a higher potential for loss or damage when there is a crisis that can be identified. With this information, policymakers can take the right actions in order to prevent or at least to mitigate the impact if a crisis hit the identified regions or households. Thus, a region may look "healthy" now, shown by its low vulnerability level based on a certain indicators or a combination of some indicators (depending on type of the crisis), but in some years from now it may become the most vulnerable region based on the same indicators.

Although all of the proposed indicators are considered important to be monitored, the selection of 'key' indicators among them should get the first priority to be monitored, and the selection should depend on the type of crisis that actually occurred or is expected to happen. Moreover, as discussed earlier, some indicators are related to some others, so some indicators may represent other indicators. Two examples are given below.

V.4.1. A Fall in the World Price of CPO

A significant decline of the world price of crude palm oil (CPO) is imminent due to a current over-supply of the commodity in the world market (Figure V.17). Over-supply means that the amount of CPO actually traded in the world market is above the 'equilibrium' amount (i.e. demand equals supply in a given equilibrium price), which will automatically push down its world market price. How much the price will decline, will depend on the size of net supply. The larger the positive deviation between the actual supply and the "equilibrium" supply, the larger the price decline, with the assumption that the world demand for CPO does not change. The amount of over-supply and the actual price (i.e. the difference between the actual price and the equilibirum price) in the world market act as the early warning indicators. The decline of world price of CPO will have a negative impact on CPO producing regions within Indonesia, Thailand and Malaysia (the three key CPO producing countries in Southeast Asia). To identify the most vulnerable regions to this crisis within the CPO producing regions, the GRP share of CPO, total employment created by CPO sector and its backward and forward related sectors as percentage of regional total employment, and export of CPO as percentage of regional total export are the key indicators to be monitored.

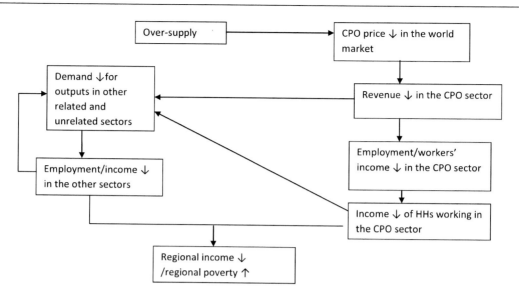

Figure V.17. Vulnerable regions, sectors and households to a CPO Price Declines in the World Market.[31]

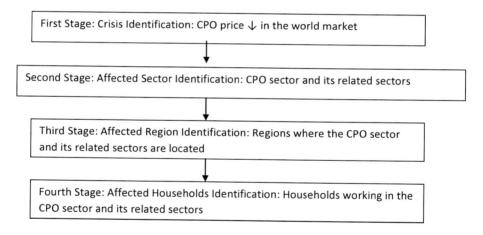

Figure V.18. Stages of the Mapping Process of the Impact of the CPO Price Crisis.

At the micro-level, within the CPO producing regions, households (HH) with CPO production or trading as their main sources of income are the first victim of the crisis. The second victims are households working (either as producers or employees) in other CPO-related sectors (e.g. transportation and industries producing inputs for CPO production). Thus, one hypothesis here is that, depending on the type of crisis, households with a higher degree of income diversification are less vulnerable than those with a lower degree of income diversification.

---

[31] The overall impact in the corresponding region (income multiplier effects of the crisis) can be measured easily if social accounting matrix (SAM) data is available. While with the input-output (I-O) table, the measured impact does not include changes in incomes of the corresponding households (working in the CPO sector and its linked sectors).

Next, the mapping process of the impact of the CPO crisis should go through four subsequent stages (Figure V.18). First, crisis identification, i.e. the decline in the world price of CPO. The identification is based on the signal sent by early warning indicators, i.e. over-supply of CPO in the world market followed soon by the decline of its world price. To consider the movement of these indicators as an early warning signal, first, a threshold for over-supply or CPO price decline must be determined by calculating the standard deviation of the difference between the "normal" trend and the actual revealed trend of the price or supply change. Thus, if the price change of CPO is taken as the early warning indicator, and the current world price of CPO falls below the determined threshold, it sends a signal.

Second, identification of impacted domestic sectors: one sector directly hit, namely the CPO/palm oil sector and other sectors indirectly affected because they are related to the CPO sector, i.e. sectors supplying inputs and providing services to the CPO/palm oil sector. The CPO related (backward) sectors can be distinguished into thee categories by the degree of the impact, i.e. 'heavily', 'moderately' and 'slightly' affected, or with the scale from 1 (almost unaffected) to 5 (fully affected). Suppose the CPO sector has two related sectors: A and B. Sector A is said to be heavily affected if it supplies 70 percent of its output as input to the CPO sector, and sector B is slightly affected if only 10 percent of its total output as inputs for the CPO sector.

Third, identification of affected regions within Indonesia, i.e. not only regions where the CPO sector is located but also regions where its related sectors are located. If the CPO sector and its related sector are sited in the same regions, the analysis is not so difficult. In this case, the affected regions can be grouped into various categories by the degree of the impact (and hence, by the degree of vulnerability). A region where the CPO sector contributes to, say, 70 percent of the region's total income (GRP), or generates 70 percent of the region's total employment would certainly be the most affected region, compared to a region where the GRP or employment share of the CPO sector is only 20 percent. However, a region where CPO is not the key sector may still be significantly impacted by the CPO crisis, if the CPO sector together with its related sectors in total generate 70 percent of the region's GRP.

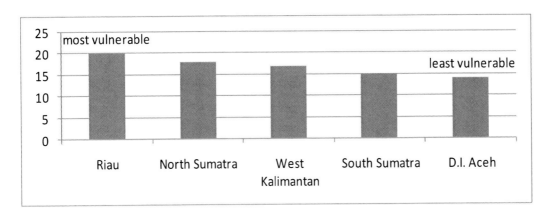

Figure V.19. Vulnerability of CPO Producing Provinces to CPO Crisis: Regional Comparison Approach (dummy data).

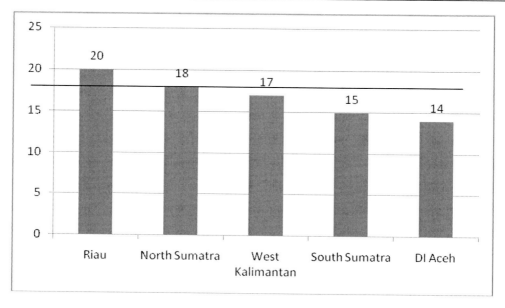

Figure V.20. Vulnerability of CPO producing provinces to CPO Crisis: Threshold Approach (dummy data).

If the related sectors are not located in the same provinces as the CPO sector is located, but instead they are scattered in other non-CPO producing provinces, the analysis will be more complex. Because by using GRP and employment shares of CPO sector as vulnerable indicators, these other provinces may not identified as vulnerable regions to the CPO crisis because they do not have CPO sector. If these CPO related sectors have the largest contributions to their respective regions' GRP or employment, the impact of the crisis on these regions can also be significant.

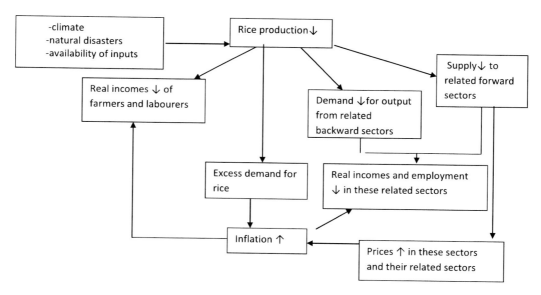

Figure V.21. Vulnerable Regions, Sectors and Households to a Rice Production Failure.

Finally, identification of affected households in the identified crisis-affected regions. Also here, the affected households can be grouped into various categories by the degree of the impact. Households working in the CPO sector will experience the highest degree of the impact than those working in the related sectors (except if the related sectors supply all of their outputs to the CPO sector). Households depending only on CPO production/export as their income will feel the impact more seriously than those having more sources of income (more true if income from the CPO sector only forms a small fraction of their total incomes).

Thus, for this case, data on export commodities, regions of production (for instance, Riau in Sumatera, Indonesia, in the case of CPO), shares of the individual commodities in total output (or GRP) and total employment in the individual regions, and other key variables of the individual regions, such as percentage of population living under the current poverty line (poverty rate), households by income quintile, etc. must be regularly available.

Suppose that data on CPO production by province is available, and within the country, there are more than one provinces identified as CPO-producing regions, though the degree may vary between the regions based on GRP or employment share of the sector. In Indonesia, there are 5 main important CPO-producing provinces in Indonesia: Riau, North Sumatera, West Kalimantan, South Sumatera and D.I. Aceh. Now the question is: which one of them is the most vulnerable to a CPO crisis? There are two approaches for identifying the most vulnerable province; regional comparison approach and threshold approach. If GRP share of CPO is used as an indicator, then the first approach will obviously show that Riau with the highest CPO's GRP share (20 percent) is most vulnerable, and D.I. Aceh with the lowest share (14 percent) is the least vulnerable (Figure V.19). This approach does not need a threshold, just look at the maximum and minimum levels.

But, is Riau really the most vulnerable region to the crisis, or can North Sumatera (despite its share is only two percentage points below Riau) be considered as more of a save? If the government has only a limited funds for supporting CPO-producing regions in the case of CPO crisis, should North Sumatera be excluded from the support? To solve this issue, the second approach is more appropriate. In this approach, the GDP share of CPO at the national level can used as a threshold. Let it be 18 percent (the horizontal line in Figure V.20). Based on this, Riau still reveals as the most vulnerable CPO-producing region as it is the only region which has a positive deviation from the threshold but North Sumatera cannot be ignored either since it is just above the threshold line. As in the case of poverty alleviation, programs should not only help those living under the poverty line but also those just above the line.

V.4.2. Crop (Rice) Failure

The failure of rice production will immediately push up its price in a domestic market, if there is no rice import. At the same time, incomes of rice farmers and laborers will decline. Regarding the backward linkages of the rice sector, the rice production failure will automatically reduce farmers' demand for inputs from other (upward) sectors while with respect to its forward linkages, since less rice stock is available, productions in other (downward) sectors which use rice as their inputs, such as restaurants and food processing industries, as well as sectors providing services to the rice sector such as transportation and distributor, will also drop. Consequently, total output and hence, income or employment in rice-related (backward and forward) sectors will also decline. But the final impact of the rice production failure does not stop here. The less incomes received by the rice farmers and laborers will also reduce their demands for consumption goods and services produced by other sectors. Thus, a significant multiplier effect (initial effect in the rice sector + total production linkages effects + total consumption linkages effects) from the rice production failure will occur, and the size of the multiplier effect will depend on the size or intensity of the production and consumption linkages between the rice sector and the rest of the local/regional economy (Figure V.21).

The mapping process of the impact of the rice production failure is the same as in the case of CPO price decline discussed before, which consists of four subsequent stages. The first stage is the most crucial one because making a wrong identification of a coming crisis will result in a wrong identification of sectors, regions and households most likely to be affected.

Rice production failure in a region, however, will not result in a crisis if the region imports rice to fill the current excess demand. Thus, stock of rice should be monitored instead of local production only. Rice stock is the sum of local rice production plus the import of rice. If local rice production declines, stock will keep constant, as long as import of rice increases in the same amount as the rice production decline. Furthermore, to see whether a region has adequate stock of rice, total rice consumption in the region should also be monitored. Total rice consumption is total population x average minimum rice consumption per capita. If in a region its current stock of rice is larger (lower) than its rice requirement, then the region is said to have surplus (deficit) in rice.

Based on the above explanation, there are at least two propositions. Proposition I: the more the rice surplus in a region, the lower the vulnerability of the region to a food (rice) crisis. Thus, the key indicator to be monitored is the level of rice surplus (Figure V.22). Proposition II: given the volume of local rice production and the average rice consumption per capita, the larger the total population in a region, the higher the vulnerablity of the region to a food (rice) crisis. Here, at least three indicators should be monitored: volume of rice production, rice consumption, and number of population, with the latter being the key indicator (Figure V.23).

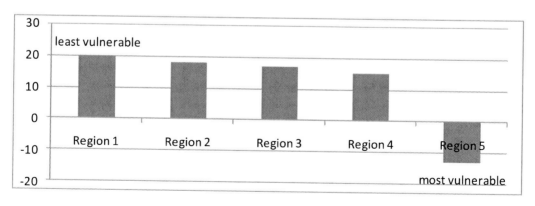

Figure V.22. Vulnerability of Regions to Rice Crisis: Surplus Approach.

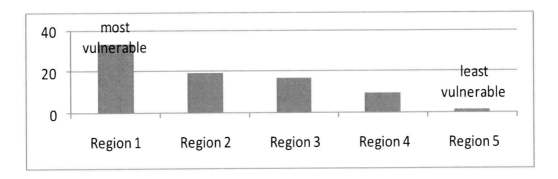

Figure V.23. Vulnerability of Regions to Rice Crisis: Total Population Approach.

V.5. CONSTRUCTION OF AN ECONOMIC VULNERABILITY COMPOSITE INDEX

If economic vulnerability indicators are only few and all are measured in the same unit (e.g. monetary), they are easy to use in measuring the economic vulnerability levels of different regions. But, when the indicators are many and they are measured in different units (e.g. monetary, unit, percentage, ratio, etc.) a composite index, called economic vulnerability index (EVI), is required. There are three basic methods for computing EVI: (1) normalization procedure; (2) mapping on a categorical scale; and (3) regression method.

Normalization procedure is the most commonly used to obtain data for the components (or indicators) of an composite index, with each component representing a facet of economic vulnerability.[32] For instance, in Table V.2 there are more than 50 components for measuring the economic vulnerability levels of different provinces in Indonesia, and they are measured in different units, ranging from Rp value; km; percentage; ratio; and number of people, household, school, hospital, etc. Therefore, in order to facilitate aggregation and comparison of data from different sources, the original data must be 'standardized' or 'normalized' to permit averaging, with the average being called a composite index, by transforming the original data into indices ranging from 0 to 100 based on minimum and maximum values in a set of reference provinces (or countries in the case of international comparison) using the following formula:[33]

$$V_{ij} = (X_{ij} - minX_i)/(maxX_i - minX_i) \times 100 \ (V.5) \ [34]$$

where, in the case of province, V_{ij} is the standardized observation associated with the ith component for province j; X_{ij} is the value (original data) of the ith component for province j;

---

[32] See, among many others, Briguglio (1992, 1995; 1997, 2003), Briguglio and Galea (2003), Briguglio, et al. (2008), Crowards and Coulter (1998) and Crowards, (1999), UNCTAD (1997), and Wells (1996, 1997).

[33] In other words, normalization is needed in order not only to avoid the unit of measurement of the individual indicators, but also help in avoiding undue influence of a specific indicator of the composite index because of its value (WEP, 2005). The UNDP also uses this methodology for its HDI.

[34] In its study on community-level characteristics of food insecutiry and vulnerability in Timor Leste, World Food Program (WFP) used the following formula for mapping food insecurity: index (for each indicator) = (value of the indicator)/(arithmetic mean of the indicators across districts/regions) (WFP, 2005).

maxX$_i$ and minX$_i$ stands for the maximum and minimum value of the ith component for all provinces in the sample.[35]

Some adjustments in the formula are required, however, in the case of certain components. For instance, with respect to distribution population by education. Provinces with a high ratio of educated populations (a proxy for human resource capital) would yield a high value of V and a high EVI (indicating high economic vulnerability), which is not the case, as provinces with a highly-educated population usually have relatively greater resilience to shocks. In such cases, the following variant of the standarization procedure is used:

$$AV_{ij} = 100 - V_{ij} \qquad (V.6)$$

where AV$_{ij}$ is the rescaled index number representation with values ranging from 0 to 100 related to the ith component for province j

But, there are at least two important shortcomings of this method. First, the weights for averaging the components, which can be based on equal or varying weights assigned to each component, are arbitrarily chosen. Second, the distribution of the normalized variables are heavily influenced by outlier observations, or the distribution is skewed or has long tails. In this case, the ranking of regions/provinces could be unduly bunched and would obscure the extent of the differences among the majority of provinces. For example, with respect to import dependency indicators as shown in Figure V.3, the outlier is the province of Banten, and followed by the province of Riau and DKI Jakarta. Certainly, the result would be much different if the percentages of these three regions are much lower than they are now. Therefore, to minimize this kind of problem, bounds should be imposed on the extreme outliers to allow for a better comparison of values in the distribution. The bounds are numbers used to define the low and high end of the distribution of the index number series before the application of the normalization procedure. Accordingly, the bounds replace the actual provincial data in the calculation of the index concerned. For instance, in the case of Figure V.3, a minimum bound of 'X' percent and a maximum bound of 'Y' percent should be imposed on provinces with import (M)-GDP ratios below or above those levels, respectively. Thus, provinces with M/GDP ratios smaller than X percent are replaced by X percent, while Y percent is used for those provinces with M/GDP ratios above Y percent.

With respect to mapping on a categorical scale, it is much more suitable for qualitative. For instance, the quality of land with qualifications: good and bad condition. This method involves mapping the scores on a categorical scale ranging from the lowest possible incidence, say, 1 to the highest, 5. To make a composite index, the scores for each component of the index can be averaged. For instance, in their construction of environment vulnerability index for three countries in the Pacific, i.e. Australia, Fiji and Tuvalu, Kaly et al. (1998) used the scale of 1 to 7. As with the case of a normalization method discussed before, this method also has a degree of arbitrariness and subjectivity in assigning scores and in weighing the components of the index.

---

[35] In order to reduce the undue impact of outliers on the distribution of the observations, value of 1 can be assigned to the top decile of values in the observations. See. Crowards, (1999), Crowards and Coulter (1998), and UN (2000). From Guillaumont (2001), Crowards (1999) and UN (2000), it reveals that the choice of indicators measuring procedure is still debated. Some say that the indicators should be measured on the same scale, depending on the maximum and minimu values; while others purpose that the scale should be limited at the highest and the lowest decile value.

The third method was used first by Wells (1997) and then by Atkins et al. (1998). In this method, GDP volatility (Δ GDP) was considered as a manifestation of economic vulnerability and therefore, was taken as a proxy of economic vulnerability. Then they regressed GDP volatility on a number of explanatory variables (X) which represented causes of vulnerability:

$$\Delta GDP = c + \sum_{n=1}^{\infty} a_n \Delta X_n \quad (V.6)$$

where c is a constant. The coefficients (a) on the explanatory variables were then taken as weights for averaging the vulnerability components. Thus, this method does not require the 'normalization' of the observations.

Differently than the other two methods, this method does not have arbitrariness and outlier problems in weighing the components or in assigning scores for the components of the index. However, the construction of EVI using the regression method has a serious problem, the assumption of GDP as a proxy of economic vulnerability. The issue here is whether it is the right approach instead of going through a cumbersome regression procedure to compete the EVI. This issue is important because it will determine the level of predictive ability of the model.

Based on the explanation of the three basic methods, the normalization method seems to be the best one. Using this method, the whole process consists of four subsequent steps. The first step is to define indices (V) for all indicators used in the corresponding dimension. The indices are defined in such a way that the higher the value of the indicators, the higher the EVI which indicates the presence of a higher level of vulnerability (and vice versa). The second step is to determine weights (w) for all indices to construct a composite index (CI) of the corresponding dimension. The third step is the determine weights for all CIs of all dimensions. The final step is to construct an EVI. Suppose there are two dimensions of economic vulnerability, each with three indicators/indices, then the process is as illustrated in Figure V.24. After the EVI is built up, the index can then be translated into a map by province.

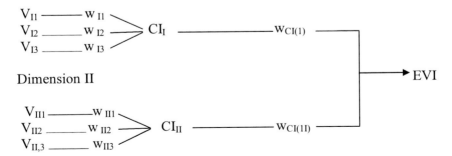

Figure V.24. Process of Constructing an EVI.

Back to Table V.2 regarding indicators of economic vulnerability at macro level (e.g. province or district). As explained before, some of the indicators are related to some others (see Figure V.2). In other words, some indicators can be used to represent some other indicators. so by eliminating other non-necessary indicators, EVIs for each provinces in Indonesia can be constructed from, say, 5 components (indices) representing four dimensions of economic crisis, such as human resource (education and health), trade (export and import), economic diversification (GRP shares of primary sectors) and household food consumption (share in total consumption):

$$EVI = w_a A + w_b B + w_c C + w_d D + w_e E \qquad (V.7)$$

where
- A = education, e.g. number of uneducated people as percentage of total population, or number of children who cannot read as percentage of total children;
- B = health, e.g. number of HIV/AIDS cases per 100.000 population, or number of underweight children as percentage of total children in a particular age group, or number of infant/child mortality as percentage of total children in a particular age group;
- C = trade dependency, i.e. sum of export and import as a percentage of GRP;
- D = economic diversification/concentration, e.g. total output shares of primary sectors (i.e. agriculture and mining) in GRP;
- E = household food consumption, i.e. total food consumption as a percentage of total consumption.
- w = weight.

Then, the final step in constructing an EVI is to weigh its components. As with the selection of indicators, selecting the weighing procedure may also involve subjective decisions. Guillaumont (2001) discusses two ways to aggregate the components in a composite index, i.e. equal and revealed weight. The first one is the simple way, that is, after measuring each component, to calculate an an unweighted (or an arithmetic) average of the components. In this way, the actual weight is not chosen a priori but given by the number of components: more components mean lower weight of the component. In the second way, the weights are drawn from an econometric model, in which all components are regressed on GDP so that they reflect the estimated impacts of the different components on GDP growth. This approach is consistent with the definition of economic vulnerability as discussed before suggesting a negative relationship between economic vulnerability and economic growth.

The following selected works on the construction of an EVI using different weighting may give some idea about the weighting procedure:

Guillaumont and Chauvet (1999), quoted from Guillaumont (2001), used a set of component indicators to build a composite indicator of vulnerability, with the weights drawn from an econometric exercise. The components retained are the respective instabilities of real exports (goods and services) and of agricultural production, of population size and also the trend in the terms of trade. These four factors appear to be significant, besides some common control variables, in a growth regression, pooling two eleven-year periods and covering 95 observations.

World Food Program (WFP): in its 2005 study on food insecurity and vulnerability in Timo Leste, its composite index for each dimension of food security (availability, access and utilization) is based on the average of the value of indices for all indicators used in the corresponding dimension. The composite index for food (in)security is based on a combined rank of each region going in the order from the lowest rank to the worst index for any region.

The United Nations Committee for Development Policy built up an EVI and applied it since 2000 as a criterion of identification of the Least-Developed Countries. Revisions have been made several times. The present EVI is calculated from 7 component indices (originated from 5 component indices), of which three shock indices (instability of exports, instability of agricultural production and a homelessness (due to natural disaster) index) and four exposure indices (smallness of population size, remoteness of area, export concentration, output share of agriculture, forestry and fisheries in the formation of GDP). An arithmetic averaging is used for the sake of simplicity and transparency, which gives the following weights to each component: the exposure sub-index (0.5) composed of smallness of population size (0.25), remoteness (0.125), export concentration (0.0625), share of agriculture, forestry and fisheries (0.0625), and the shocks sub-index (0.5) composed of instability of exports of goods and services (0.25), instability of agricultural production (0.125), homelessness (due to natural disaster) index (0.125)(Guillaumont, 2009a,b; UN, 2000).

To sum up, from the above discussion, although there is a kind of 'normal' procedure to follow such as literature survey, interviews, forum discussion, time series data analysis and regression method, subjectivity in selecting indicators and weighing the components of a composite index does play an important role. In the case of weighing, if a composite index has only two indicators, should they have, each, 0.5 weight, or, say, 0.75 and 0.25, an so on? It is a subjective decision. The same problem is also valid for the selection of indicators or components of a composite index. The question is: should the index include only 5 or should it have less or more variables? Although the decision may involve a long trial and error process, at the end, it is a subjective choice. It is a choice between: a simple process with less variables or more variables but more complex procedure. For instance, back to equation V.7, for their EVI for provinces in Indonesia, Tambunan and Asmanto (2010) used four indicators; population, GRP, economic structure and trade share. With this calculated EVI, provinces can be classified into three categories as shown in Figure V.25.

Source: Tambunan and Asmanto (2010).

Figure V.25. EVI in Indonesia by Province.

REFERENCES

Abdullah, Moh. Asri (2002), "An Overview of the Macroeconomic Contribution of Small and medium Enterprises in Malaysia," in Charles Harvie and Boon-Chye Lee (eds.), *The Role of SMEs in National Economies in East Asia*. Cheltenham: Edward Elgar.

ADB (2002), "Report and Recommendation of the President to the Boards of Directors on a Proposed Loan and Technical Assistance Grant to the Republic of Indonesia for the Small and Medium\ Enterprise Export Development Project", ADB RRP: INO 34331, November, Jakarta: Asian Development Bank.

ADB (2008), *Asian Development Outlook 2008*, Manila: Asian Development Bank.

ADB (2009a), *Asian Development Outlook 2009 Update*, Manila: Asian Development Bank

ADB (2009b), *Key Indicators for Asia and the Pacific 2009*, Manila: Asian Development Bank.

ADB (2009c), "Global Economic Crisis and ADB's Response: An Update", December, Manila: Asian Development Bank.

ADB (2010a), *Asian Development Outlook 2010*, Manila: Asian Development Bank.

ADB (2010b), "Impact and Policy Responses: Indonesia, Philippines and Thailand", Report 6, ADB Regional Forum on the Impact of Global Economic and Financial Crisis, 14-15 January, Manila: Asian Development Bank.

Adger, W. N., Khan, S. R. and Brooks, N. (2003), "Measuring and enhancing adaptive capacity", in UNDP, *Adaptation Policy Framework: A Guide for Policies to Facilitate Adaptation to Climate Change*, UNDP, Vienna.

Adger,W.N.,N. Brooks, M. Kelly, G. Bentham, M.Agnew,and S. Eriksen (2004), "New Indicators of Vulnerability and Adaptive Capacity", Final Project Report, January, Oslo: Tyndall Center for Climate Change Research

AKATIGA and the Asia Foundation (1999), "The Impact of Economic Crisis on Indonesian Small and Medium Enterprises," study for the United States Agency for International Development, Jakarta.

AKATIGA (2009), "Laporan Studi Penghidupan Masyarakat Pedesaan NTT dan NTB: Krisis dan Perubahan. Studi Kasus: Desa Ajoabaki, Kecamatan Mollo Utara, Kabupaten Timor Tengah Selatan, Desa Pengadangan, Kecamatan Pringgasela, Kabupaten Lombok Timur. Ringkasan Eksekutif", Desember, Bandung: AKATIGA Pusat Penelitian Sosial.

AKATIGA and Oxfam Australia (2010), "Global Crisis and Migration in NTT and NTB. Diskusi Dampak Krisis Global pada Pekerja Migran", paper presented at the workshop

"Impacts of Global Financial Crisis", 2 February, SMERU Research Institute and AusAid, Jakarta.

Aldaba, Rafaelita M. (2008), 'SMEs in the Philippine Manufacturing Industry and Globalization', in Hank Lim (ed.), 'Asian SMEs and Globalization', ERIA Research Project Report 2007 No. 5, March, Bangkok/Tokyo: IDE-JETRO.

Alesina, A., and E. Spolaore (2004), *The Size of Nations*. Cambridge, MA: MIT Press.

Allen, K. (2003), "Vulnerability reduction and the community-based approach", in Pelling (ed.), *Natural Disasters and Development in a Globalizing World*. Routledge, London.

Andadari, Roos Kities (2008), "Local Clusters in Global Value Chains. A case study of wood furniture clusters in Central Java (Indonesia)", the Tinbergen Institute Research Series no. 421, Amsterdam: Tinbergen Institute & Vrije Universiteit

APEC (2002), *Profile of SMEs and SME Issues in APEC 1990-2000*, Singapore: APEC Secretariat.

Aris, Normah Mohd. (2006), "SMEs: Building Blocks for Economic Growth", paper presented at the National Statistics Conference, 4-5 September, Department of Statistics, Kuala Lumpur.

ASEAN-World Bank (2009), "ASEAN Assessment o the Social Impacts of the Global Financial Crisis", A Snap-shot Report for notation at the 15th ASEAN Summit, 23 October, Cha-am Hua Hin, Thailand.

ASMINDO (2007), "Tinjauan tentang Industri Permebelan dan Kerajinan Indonesia", Kadin Roadmap Industri, 27 Juni, Kadin Indonesia.

AusAid (1999), "Impact of the Asia crisis on children: issues for social safety nets", First Report, May, Canberra: Australian Agency for International Development.

Atje, Raymond and Pratiwi Kartika (2009), "A Bumpy Road toward ASEAN Economic Community 2015", paper presented at the ASEAN Roundtable Discussion on Financial Crisis, 18 June, Bangkok.

Atkins, J., Mazzi, S. and Ramlogan, C. (1998), *A Study on the Vulnerability of Developing and Island States: A Composite Index*, August, the Commonwealth Secretariat, London.

Bailey, Peter (2008) "Cambodian Small and Medium sized Enterprises Constraints, Policies and Proposals for their Development", in Hank Lim (ed.), 'Asian SMEs and Globalization', ERIA Research Project Report 2007 No. 5, March, Bangkok/Tokyo: IDE-JETRO.

Bakiewicz, Anna (2004), "Small and Medium Enterprises in Thailand. Following the Leader", *Asia & Pacific Studies*, 2: 131-151

BAPPENAS, BPS and World Bank (2009), "Analysis of CMR Round 1: August 2009", presented at the Bappenas Meeting on the Monitoring of the Impact of the Global Economic Crisis, 10 December, Jakarta: Bappenas.

BPS (2009), *Trends of the Selected Socio-Economic Indicators of Indonesia*, October, Jakarta: Badan Pusat Statistik.

Bayliss-Smith, T. (1991), "Food security and agricultural sustainability in the New Guinea Highlands: Vulnerable people, vulnerable places", *IDS Bulletin*, 22(3): 5-11.

Betcherman, G. and R. Islam (eds.) (2001), *East Asian Labor Markets and the Economic Crisis: Impacts, Responses, and Lessons*. Washington, DC: The World Bank and the International Labor Organization.

Beerepoot, Niels & Guus van Westen (2001), "The Mactan Export Processing Zone in Comparative Perspective", *Philippine Quarterly of Culture & Society*, 29: 226-251

Berg, Andrew and Catherine Pattillo (1999a), "Predicting currency crises: the indicators approach and an alternative," *Journal of International Money and Finance*, August, 18(4): 561 - 586.

Berg, Andrew and Catherine Pattillo (1999b), "Are currency crises predictable? A test, " *IMF Staff Papers*, June, 46(2): 107 - 138.

Berg, Andrew and Catherine Pattillo (1999c), "What caused the Asian crises: An early warning system approach," unpublished manuscript, Washington D.C., International Monetary Fund.

Berg, Andrew, Eduardo Borensztein, and Catherine Pattillo (2004), "Assessing Early Warning Systems: How Have They Worked in Practice?", IMF Working Paper, March, Research Department, Washington, D.C.: International Monetary Fund.

Berry, Albert dan Brian Levy (1994), "Indonesia's Small and Medium-Size Exporters and Their Support Systems", Policy Research Working Paper 1402, December, Policy Research Department, Finance and Private Sector Development Division, World Bank, Washington, D.C.

Berry, Albert and Edgard Rodriguez (2001), "Dynamics of Small and Medium Enterprises in a Slow-Growth Economy: The Philippines in the 1990s", paper, June (Stock No. 37181), The International Bank for Reconstruction and Development/The World Bank, Washington, D.C.

Berry, Albert, Edgard Rodriguez and Henry Sandee (2001), "Small and Medium Enterprise Dynamics in Indonesia", *Bulletin of Indonesian Economic Studies*, 37(3): 363-84

Berry, Albert., Edgard Rodriguez and Henry Sandee (2002), "Firm and Group Dynamics in the Small and Medium Enterprise Sector in Indonesia", *Small Business Economics,* 18(1–3):141–161.

Bilson, John F.O. (1979), "Leading Indicators of Currency Devaluations", *Columbia Journal of World Business*, 14 (Winter).

Blaike, P. and Brookfield, H.C. (1987), *Land Degradation and Society*, London: Methuen.

Bleaney, M., and D. Greenaway (2001), "The Impact of Terms of Trade and Real Exchangen Rate Volatility on Investment and Growth in Sub-Saharan Africa", *Journal of Development Economics*, 65 (2): 491-500.

BPS (2009a), "Survei Monitoring Krisis Global 2009-2010", power point presentation, Jakarta: Deputi Bidang Statistik Sosial, Badan Pusat Statistik.

BPS (2009b), *Statistik Indonesia*, Jakarta: Badan Pusat Statistik.

BPS (2009c), *Data Strategis BPS*, Jakarta: Badan Pusat Statistik

BPS (2009d), "Berita Resmi Statistik", No.69/11/Th.XII, 10 November, Jakarta: Badan Pusat Statistik.

Briguglio, L. (1992), *Preliminary Study on the Construction of an Index for Ranking Countries According to their Economic Vulnerability,* UNCTAD/LDC/Misc., 4, Geneva.

Briguglio, L. (1995), "Small Island States and their Economic Vulnerabilities", *World Development* Vol. 23, 1615-1632.

Briguglio, L (1997), "Alternative Economic Vulnerability Indices for Developing Countries", report prepared for the Expert Group on Vulnerability Index, 17-19 December 1997, UN(DESA), New York.

Briguglio, L. (2003), "The Vulnerability Index and Small Island Developing States: A Review of Conceptual and Methodological Issues", paper prepared for the AIMS

Regional Preparatory Meeting on the Ten Year Review of the Barbados Program of Action, September, Praia, Cape Verde.

Briguglio, L. and W. Galea (2003), "Updating the Economic Vulnerability Index", Occasional Chapters on Islands and Small States,2003-2004, April, Malta: Islands and Small States Institute, University of Malta.

Briguglio, L., G. Cordina, N. Farrugia, and S. Vella (2008), "Economic Vulnerability and Resilience. Concept and Measurements", Research Paper No.2008/55, May, Helsinki: UNU-WIDER.

Brun, J-F., C. Carrere, P. Guillaumont, and J. de Melo (2005), "Has Distance Died? Evidence from a Panel Gravity Model", *World Bank Economic Review*, 19 (1): 99-101.

BSP (2009), "Overseas Filipino Remittances", Manila: Central Bank of Philippines (http://www.bsp.gov.ph/statistics/keystat/ofw.htm.

Calvo, Guillermo A. (1995), "Varieties of Capital-Market Crises", Center for International Economics, Working Paper No.15 (November), College Park: University of Maryland.

Carrère, C., and M. Schiff (2004), "On the Geography of Trade". WB Policy Research Working Paper 3206. Washington, DC: World Bank.

Chantrasawang, Nathavit (1999), "Current Issues of SMEs in Thailand: Its Linkages with FDI and the Impact of the Financial Crisis", paper presented at the International Conference on Small and Medium Enterprises At New Crossroads: Challenges and Prospects", 28-3-September, Universiti Sains Malaysia, Penang, Malaysia.

Chaudhuri, S. and L. Christiaensen (2002), "Assessing household vulnerability to poverty: Illustrative examples and methodologies issues", paper presented at the IFPRI-World Bank Conference on Risk and Vulnerability, 23-24 September, Washington, D.C.

Chaudhuri, S., J. Jalan, and A. Suryahadi (2002), "Assessing household vulnerability to poverty: a methodology and estimates for Indonesia", Department of Economics Discussion Paper No.0102-52, New York: Columbia University.

Chhibber, Ajay, Jayati Ghosh and Thangavel Palanivel (2009), "The Global Financial Crisis and the Asia-Pacific region. A Synthesis Study Incorporating Evidence from Country Case Studies", UNDP Regional Centre in Asia and the Pacific, November, Bangkok.

Christiaensen, Luc J. and Richard N. Boisvert (2000), "On measuring household food vulnerability: case evidence from northern Mali", Cornell University Department of Agricultural and Resource Economics Working Paper no. 2000-05, March, Ithaca.

Collins, Susan M. (1995), "The Timing of Exchange Rate Adjustment in Developing Countries", seminar paper, Washington, D.C.: Georgetown University.

Combes, J.-L., and P. Guillaumont (2002), "Commodity Price Volatility, Vulnerability and Development", *Development Policy Review*, 20 (1): 25-39.

Cova, T. J., and R. L. Church (1997), ''Modeling Community Evacuation Vulnerability Using GIS.'' *International Journal of Geographical Information Science*,11:763–84.

Crowards, T. (1999), "An Economic Vulnerability Index for Developing Countries, with Special Reference to the Caribbean: Alternative Methodologies and Provisional Results", March, Caribbean Development Bank, St. Michael, Barbados, W.I.

Crowards, T and Coulter, W. (1998), "Economic Vulnerability in the Developing World with Special Reference to the Caribbean", Caribbean Development Bank. St. Michael, Barbados, W.I.

Cunningham, W. and W.F. Maloney (2000), "Measuring Vulnerability: Who Suffered in the 1995 Mexican Crisis?", mimeo, The World Bank, Washington, D.C.

Cutter, S. L., J. T. Mitchell, and M. S. Scott (2000), ''Revealing the Vulnerability of People and Places: A Case Study of Georgetown County, South Carolina'', *Annals of the Association of American Geographers*, 90(4):713–37.

Cutter, Susan L., Bryan J. Boruff, and W. Lynn Shirley (2003), "Social Vulnerability to Environmental Hazards", *Social Science Quarterly*, 84(2): 242-261.

Darmawan, Danang and Chikako Yamauchi (2010), "The Global Financial Crisis and Changes in Labor Market Activities of Rural-urban Migrants in Indonesia", paper presented at the workshop "Impacts of Global Financial Crisis", 2 February, SMERU Research Institute and AusAid, Jakarta.

Demirguc-Kunt, Asli and Enrica Detragiache (1997), "The Determinants of Banking Crises: Evidence from Developing and Developed Countries", September, IMF Working Paper 97/106, Washington, D.C., International Monetary Fund.

Dierman, Peter van, Tulus Tambunan, Mangara Tambunan and Thee Kian Wie (1998), "The IMF 50-point Program: Evaluating the Likely Impact on SMEs," draft report for the Asia Foundation, Jakarta.

Djaja, Komara (2009), "Impact of the Global Financial and Economic Crisis on Indonesia. A Rapid Assessment", paper prepared for the ILO, Secretary Coordinating Ministry for Economic Affairs, Indonesia

Downing, T. E., Butterfield, R., Cohen, S., Huq, S., Moss, R., Rahman, A., Sokona, Y. and Stephen, L. (2001), *Vulnerability Indices: Climate Change Impacts and Adaptation*, UNEP Policy Series, UNEP, Nairobi.

Eddy Gunawan, Eddy (2006), "Industry Furniture Knock Down", Kadin Roadmap Industri, 27 Juni, Kadin Indonesia.

Edin, Per-Anders, and Anders Vredin (1993), "Devaluation Risk in Target Zones: Evidence from the Nordic Countries", *The Economic Journal*, 103 (January).

Edison, Hali J. (2000), "Do Indicators of Financial Crises Work? An Evaluation of An Early Warning System", International Finance Discussion Papers, No 675, July, New York: Board of Governors of the Federal Reserve System.

Edwards, Sabastian and Julio Santaella (1993), "Devaluation Controversies in the Developing Countries: Lessons from the Bretton Wood Era", in Michael D. Bordo and Barry Eichengreen (ed.), *A Retrospective on the Bretton Woods System: Lessons for International Monetary Reform*, Chicago: University of Chicago Press.

Eichengreen, Barry, Andrew Rose, and Charles Wyplosz (1995), "Exchange Market Mayhem: The Antecedents and Aftermath of Speculative Attacks", *Economic Policy*, 21 (October).

Eichengreen, Barry, Andrew Rose, and Charles Wyplosz (1996), "Contagious currency crises: first tests"", *Scandinavian Journal of Economics*, 98, 4.

EIU (2010), "Towards the recovery Challenges and opportunities facing Asia's SMEs", A report from the Economist Intelligence Unit, Hong Kong

Enarson, E., and J. Scanlon (1999), ''Gender Patterns in Flood Evacuation: A Case Study in Canada's Red River Valley'', *Applied Behavioral Science Review*, 7(2):103–24.

ESCAP (2010), *Economic and Social Survey of Asia and the Pacific 2010*, Bangkok: UN-ESCAP

Feridhanusetyawan, Tubagus, Haryo Aswicahyono and Titik Anas (2000), "The Economic Crisis and the Manufacturing Industry: The Role of Industrial Networks", CSIS Working Paper Series WPE 053, January, Jakarta: CSIS.

Fillaili, Rizki (2010), "Impact and Coping Strategies of Community during Global Financial Crisis", paper presented at the workshop "Impacts of Global Financial Crisis", 2 February, SMERU Research Institute and AusAid, Jakarta.

Fillaili, Rizki; Widjajanti I. Suharyo; Bambang Sulaksono; Hastuti; Sri Budiyanti and Syaikhu Usman (2009), "Pilot Qualitative Study on Crisis Impact and Response: Indonesia", Research Report (draft), April, Jakarta: SMERU Research Institute.

Fosu, A. K. (1992), "Effect of Export Instability on Economic Growth in Africa", *The Journal of Developing Areas*, 26 (3): 323-32.

Fosu, A. K. (2002), "Economic Fluctuations and Growth in Sub-Saharan Africa: The Importance of Import Instability", *The Journal of Development Studies*, 37 (3): 71-84.

Fu, Xiaolan and V.N. Balasubramanyam (2004), "Exports, FDI, Growth of Small Rural Enterprises and Employment in China", Working Paper No.278, ESRC Center for Business Research

Gaiha, R., and K. Imai (2004). 'Vulnerability, Persistence of Poverty, and Shocks-Estimates for Semi-Arid Rural India'. *Oxford Development Studies*, 32 (2): 261-81.

Gaiha, Raghav and Katsushi Imai (2008), "Measuring Vulnerability and Poverty. Estimates for Rural India", Research Paper No,2008/40, April, World Institute for Development Economic Research, UNU-WIDER, United Nations University, Helsinki.

Ghosh, J. (2007) "Informalization, migration and women: recent trends in Asia", in Debdas Banerjee and Michael Goldfield (eds.), *Labor, Globalization and the State*, Routledge 2007

Glewwe, P. and G. Hall (1998), "Are some groups more vulnerable to macroeconomic shocks than others? Hypothesis tests based on panel data from Peru", *Journal of Development Economics*, 56: 181-206.

Goh, Mark (2007), "High-growth, Innovative Asian SMEs for International Trade and Competitiveness: Challenges and Solutions for APO Member Countries", Tokyo: Asian Productivity Organization.

Goldstein, Morris (1996), "Presumptive Indicators/Early Warning Signals of Vulnerability to Financial Crises in Emerging Market Economies", Washington, D.C.: Institute for International Economics.

Griffith-Jones, Stephany and José Antonio Ocampo (2009), "The Financial Crisis and Its Impacts on Developing countries", Working Paper No. 53, April, International Policy Center for Inclusive Growth, Brazil.

Guillaumont, Patrick (2001), "On the Economic Vulnerability of Low Income Countries", Etudes et Documents E 2001.02, February, CERDI-CNRS, Université d'Auvergne.

Guillaumont, Patrick (2007), "Design of an Economic Vulnerability Index and its Use for International Development Policy", CERDI-CNRS, Université d'Auvergne, paper presented at the WIDER Conference on Fragile States-Fragile groups, 15-16 June, Helsinki.

Guillaumont, Patrick (2009a), "A retrospective Economic Vulnerability Index", note brève/3, November, fondation pour les études et recherches surle développement international, Clermont-Ferrand, France.

Guillaumont P. (2009b), "An Economic Vulnerability Index: Its Design and Use for International Development Policy", *Oxford Development Studies*, 37(3): 193-228.

Guillaumont, P., S. Guillaumont Jeanneney, and J. F. Brun (1999), "How Instability Lowers African Growth", *Journal of African Economies,* 8 (1): 87-107.

Hardy, Daniel C., and Ceyla Pazarbasioglu (1998), "Leading Indicators of Banking Crises: Was Asia Different?", IMF Working Paper No.98/91, Washington, D.C.: International Monetary Fund.

Harvie, C. (2004), "East Asian SME capacity-building, competitiveness and market opportunities in a global economy", Economics Working Paper Series, WP 04-15, University of Wollongong.

Heinz Center for Science, Economics, and the Environment (2000), *The Hidden Costs of Coastal Hazards: Implications for Risk Assessment and Mitigation*, Covello, Cal.: Island Press.

Helvoirt, Bram van and Guus van Westen (2008), "Inter-firm Relations and Regional Development: Experiences from the Central Visayas, Philippines", paper presented at the 12th EADI General Conference Global Governance for Sustainable Development, July, Geneva.

Herrera, Santiago and Conrado Garcia (1999), User's Guide to an Early Warning System for Macroeconomic Vulnerability in Latin American Countries, Paper presented in the XVII Latin American Meeting of the Econometric Society, August, Cancun.

Hewitt, K. (1997), *Regions of Risk: A Geographical Introduction to Disasters*, Essex, Longman, UK.

Hill, H. (1999), "Indonesia in Crisis", unpublished draft postscript for the second edition of *The Indonesian Economy since 1966.* Cambridge: Cambridge University Press.

Hill, Hall (2001a), "Small and Medium Enterprises", *Indonesia Asian Survey,* 41(2): 248-270.

Hill, Hal (2001b), "Small and Medium Enterprises in Indonesia: Old Policy Challenges for a New Administration", *Asian Survey* 41(2): 248-70.

Hoddinott, John and Agnes Quisumbing (2003), "Methods for Microeconometric Risk and Vulnerability Assessments", Social Protection Discussion Paper Series No.0324, December, Social Protection Unit, Human Development Network, The World Bank, Washington, D.C.

Humphrey, John (2009), "Are Exporters in Africa Facing Reduced Availability of Trade Finance", research paper, March, Institute of Development Studies Brighton, UK

IDS (2009), "Accounts of Crisis: Poor People's Experiences of the Food, Fuel and Financial Crisis in Five Countries", Report on a pilot study in Bangladesh, Indonesia, Jamaica, Kenya and Zambia, January-March 2009,31March,Instituteof Development Studies, Sussex University (UK).

ILO (1998), *The Social Impact of the Asian Financial Crisis.* Bangkok: ILO Regional Office.

ILO (2009), *Labour and Social Trends in Indonesia 2009. Recovery and beyond through decent work*, Jakarta: ILO Office for Indonesia.

IMF (1998), *World Economic Outlook 1998*, Washington, D.C.: The International Monetary Fund.

IMF (2009a), *World Economic Outlook: Crisis and Recovery*, April, Washington, D.C.: The International Monetary Fund.

IMF (2009b), *International Financial Statistics* (CD-ROM), Washington, D.C.: The International Monetary Fund.

Jellinek, L. and B. Rustanto (1999), "Survival Strategies of the Javanese during the economic crisis", Consultancy Report to the World Bank, Jakarta.

JICA-RI & ICASEPS (2009), "Financial Crisis Monitoring Survey-June 2009. Final Report", Jakarta: Japan International Cooperation Agency Indonesian Office and The Indonesian Center for Agriculture Socio Economic and Policy Studies, Ministry of Agriculture.

Kaly, U., Briguglio, L., McLeod, H., Schmall, A., Pratt C. and Pal, R. (1998). *Environmental Vulnerability Index (EVI) to Summarize National Environmental Vulnerability Profiles*. SOPAC, Fiji.

Kaminsky, Graciela (1998), "Currency and Banking Crises: The Early Warnings of Distress", International Finance Discussion Po.629, October, Washington, D.C.: Board of Governors of the Federal Reserve System,

Kaminsky, Graciela and Carmen M, Reinhart (1996), "The twin crises: the causes of banking and balance-of-payments problems", International Finance Discussion Paper No.544 (March), Washington, D.C.: Board of Governors of the Federal Reserve System.

Kaminsky, Graciela, and Carmen Reinhart (1999), "The twin crises: The causes of banking and balance of payments problems," *American Economic Review*, 89:3: 473 - 500.

Kaminsky, Graciela, Saul Lizondo, and Carmen M. Reinhart (1997), "Leading Indicators of Currency Crises", July, IMF Working Paper 97/79, Washington, D.C., International Monetary Fund.

Kaminsky, Graciela, Saul Lizondo and Carmen Reinhart (1998), "Leading indicators of currency crises," *International Monetary Fund Staff Papers*, 45: 1-48.

Khor, Niny and Iva Sebastian (2009), "Exports and the Global Crisis: Still Alive, though Not Quite Kicking Yet", ADB Economics Working Paper Series No. 190, December, Manila: Asian Development Bank.

Klein, Michael W., and Nancy Marion (1994), "Explaining the Duration of Exchange-Rate Pegs", NBER Working Paper No.4651, February, Cambridge, Mass.: National Bureau of Economic Research.

Kokko, Ari and Fredrik Sjöholm (2004), "The Internationalization of Vietnamese SMEs," Working Paper No 193, June, Stockholm School of Economics

Kokko, Ari and Fredrik Sjöholm (2005), "The Globalization of Vietnamese SMEs", *Asian Economic Papers*, 4(1): 152-177.

Koser, Khalid (2009), "The Global Financial Crisis and International Migration: Policy Implications for Australia," July 2009, Lowy Institute for International Policy, Canberra.

Krugman, Paul (1979), "A Model of Balance of Payments Crises", *Journal of Money, Credit, and Banking*, 11 (August).

Lauridsen, Laurids S. (2004), "Foreign Direct Investment, Linkage Formation and Supplier Development in Thailand during the 1990s: The Role of State Governance", The European Journal of Development Research, 16(3):.561–586

Levy, Brian, Albert Berry and Jeffrey Nugent (eds.) (1999), *Fulfilling the Export Potential of Small and Medium Firms*, Boston: Kluwer Academic Publishers.

Ligon, Ethan and Laura Schechter (2003), "Measuring Vulnerability", *The Economic Journal*, 113: C95-C102.

Lipton, M. and Maxwell, S. (1992), "The new poverty agenda: An overview", Discussion Paper No.306, Institute of Development Studies (IDS), Sussex University, Brighton (UK).

Liu, Xiangfeng (2009), "Impacts of the Global Financial Crisis on Small and Medium Enterprises in the People's Republic of China", ADBI Working Paper Series No. 180, December, Tokyo: Asian Development Bank Institute

Lochner, K., Kawachi, I. and Kennedy, B. P. (1999), "Social capital: a guide to its measurement", *Health and Place*, 5: 259-270.

Long,Nguyen Thang (2007), "Current situation and orientation for development of SMEs in industry", *Industrial Magazine*, September.

Long, Nguyen Viet (2003), "Performance and obstacles of SMEs in Vietnam Policy implications in near future", paper, International IT Policy Program (ITPP) Seoul National University, Seoul.

Masson, Paul, Eduardo Borensztein, Andrew Berg, Gian Maria Milesi-Ferretti and Catherine Pattillo (1999), "Anticipating balance of payments crises: The role of early warning systems," unpublished manuscript, Washington D.C., International Monetary Fund.

McCulloch, Neil and Amit Grover (2010), "Estimating the National Impact of the Financial Crisis in Indonesia by Combining a Rapid Qualitative Study with Nationally Representative Surveys", 16 March, Institute of Development Studies, Sussex University.

Mendoza, E. G. (1997), "Terms-of-Trade Uncertainty and Economic Growth", *Journal of Development Economics*, 54 (2): 323-56.

Milesi-Ferretti, Gian Maria, and Assaf Razin (1995)," Current Account Sustainability", research paper, Washington, D.C.: International Monetary Fund.

Mileti, D. (1999), Disasters *by Design: A Reassessment of Natural Hazards in the United States*, Washington, D.C.: Joseph Henry Press.

Mishra, Satish (2000), "Systematic Transition in Indonesia. Implications for Investor Confidence and Sustained Economic Recovery", Working Paper: 06/00/03, March, Jakarta: UNSFIR.

Mitchell, J. K., (ed) (1999), *Crucibles of Hazard: Mega-Cities and Disasters in Transition*, Tokyo: United Nations University Press.

Montiel, P. and C. Reinhart (1997), "The Dynamics of Capital Movements to Emerging Economies During the 1990s", mimeo, July, University of Maryland.

Morrow, B. H. (1999), ''Identifying and Mapping Community Vulnerability'', *Disasters*, 23(1):11–18.

Morrow, B. H., and B. Phillips (1999), ''What's Gender 'Got to Do With It'?'', *International Journal of Mass Emergencies and Disasters*, 17(1):5–11.

Moser, Caroline O.N. (1998), "The Asset Vulnerability Framework: Reassessing Urban Poverty Reduction Strategies", *World Development*, 26(1): 1-19.

McCulloch, Neil and Amit Grover (2010), "Estimating the national impact of the financial crisis in Indonesia by combining a rapid qualitative study with nationally representative surveys", Draft, January, Institute of Development Studies, University of Sussex. Brighton (UK).

Murniningtyas, Endah (2009), "Global Financial Crisis: Impact Channels in Indonesia", ADB edit, November, Manila: Asian Development Bank.

Mustajab, Mohammad (2009), *Infrastructure Investment in Indonesia: Process and Impact*", dissertation, January, Rijksuniversiteit Groiningan, the Netherlands.

Musa, Agustina (1998), "A Study on Access to Credit for Small and Medium Enterprises (SMEs) in Indonesia before and during the Economic Crisis (1997–1998)," study for the Asia Foundation and the United States Agency for International Development, Jakarta.

Musa, Agustina, and Ple Priatna (1998), "The Policy Reform for Capital of SME (Small-Medium Enterprises) in Indonesia: Impact Analysis of Financial Crisis: Study Report," report for the Asia Foundation, Jakarta.

Mustafa, R. and Mansor, S.A. (1999), "Malaysia's Financial Crisis and Contraction of Human Resource: Policies and Lessons for SMIs", paper presented at the APEC Human Resource Management Symposium on SMEs, 30-31 October, Kaoshiung.

Muto, Megumi and Shinobu Shimokoshi (2009a), "How Education and Experience Impact Job Opportunities of Migrant Workers (Very Preliminary Results)", Working Paper for Conference on the "Impact of the Global Economic Slowdown on Poverty and Sustainable Development in Asia and the Pacific", 28-30 September, Hanoi.

Muto, Megumi and Shinobu Shimokoshi (2009b), "Urban-Rural Transmission Mechanisms in Indonesia in the Context of the Crisis (Very Preliminary Results)", Working Paper for Conference on the "Impact of the Global Economic Slowdown on Poverty and Sustainable Development in Asia and the Pacific", 28-30 September, Hanoi.

Narain, Sailendar (2003), "Institutional Capacity-Building for Small and Medium-Sized Enterprise Promotion and Development", *Investment Promotion and Enterprise Development Bulletin for Asia and the Pacific*, 2, New York: United Nations and Bangkok: UNESCAP.

Ndikumana, L. and Boyce, J. K. (2003), "Public debts and private assets: Explaining capital flight from sub-Saharan African Countries", *World Development*, 31 (1):107-130.

Newberry, Derek (2006), "The Role of Small- and Medium-Sized Enterprises in the Futures of Emerging Economies", December, The New Venture Programs, the World Resources Institutes.

Ngo, E. B. (2001), "When Disasters and Age Collide: Reviewing Vulnerability of the Elderly", *Natural Hazards Review*, 2(2):80–89.

Nguanbanchong, Aphitchaya (2009), "Feminized Recession Impact of Global Economic Crisis on Women in Southeast Asia", paper presented at the seminar on Gender and the Economic Crisis: Impact and Responses, Oxford, 15-16 September.

Obstfeld, Maurice (1996), "Rational and Self-Fulfilling Balance-of-Payments Crises", *The American Economic Review*, 76 (March).

Paldam, M. and Svendsen, G. T. (2000), "An essay on social capital: looking for the fire behind the smoke", *European Journal of Political Economy*, 16: 339-366.

Pandey A P (2007), 'Indian SME's and their uniqueness in the country'. MPRA Paper No. 6086, http://mpra.ub.uni-muenchen.de/6086/.

Pantin, D. (1997), *Alternative Ecological Vulnerability Indicators for Developing Countries with Special Reference to SIDS*, Report prepared for the Expert Group on Vulnerability Index. UN(DESA), 17-19 December 1997.

Peacock, W., B. H. Morrow, and H. Gladwin (eds.) (2000), *Hurricane Andrew and the Reshaping of Miami: Ethnicity, Gender, and the Socio-Political Ecology of Disasters*, Miami, Fla.: Florida International University, International Hurricane Center.

Platt, R. (1999), *Disasters and Democracy: The Politics of Extreme Natural Events*, Washington, D.C.: Island Press.

Poot, H. (1997), :"Indonesia, SMEs, Finance and BPDs," Rotterdam: Netherlands Economic Institute.

Puente, S. (1999), "Social Vulnerability to Disaster in Mexico City", in J. K. Mitchell (ed.), *Crucibles of Hazard: Mega-Cities and Disasters in Transition*, Tokyo: United Nations University Press.

Punyasavatsut, Chaiyuth (2008), "SMEs in Thailand Manufacturing Industry and Globalization", in in Hank Lim (ed.), 'Asian SMEs and Globalization', ERIA Research Project Report 2007 No. 5, March, Bangkok/Tokyo: IDE-JETRO.

Purnomo, Herry, Ramadhani Achdiawan, Nunung Parlinah, Rika Harini Irawati and Melati (2009), „Value Chain Analysis of Furniture: Action research to improve power balance and enhance livelihoods of small-scale producers", paper submitted to XIII World Forestry Congress 2009, Buenos Aires.

Putnam, R. (1993), *Making Democracy Work: Civic Traditions in Modern Italy*, Princeton, NJ.: Princeton University Press.

Ratha, D., S. Mohapatra, and A. Silwal (2009a), "Outlook for Remittance Flows 2009–2011: Remittances Expected to Fall by 7 to 10 Percent in 2009," *Migration and Development Brief*, 10, Development Prospects Group, World Bank (http://siteresources.worldbank.org/INTPROSPECTS/Resources/334934-1110315015165/MigrationandDevelopmentBrief10.pdf.)

Ratha, Dilip, Sanket Mohapatra, and Ani Silwal (2009b), "Migration and Remittance Trends 2009}. *Migration and Development Brief* 11, 3 November, Development Prospects Group, World Bank, Washington, DC. (http://siteresources.worldbank.org/INTPROSPECTS/Resources/334934-1110315015165/MigrationandDevelopmentBrief10.pdf.)

Régnier, Philippe (2000), *Small and Medium Enterprises in Distress – Thailand, the East Asian Crisis and Beyond*, Aldershot: Gower Publishing Limited.

Régnier, Philippe (2005), "The East Asian financial crisis in Thailand: distress and resilience of local SMEs", in Charles Harvie and Boon-Chye Lee (eds.), *Sustaining Growth and Performance in East Asia*, Cheltenham and Northampton, MA: Edward Elgar.

Riyadi, Dedi M. Masykur and Endah Murniningtyas (2010), "Global Financial Crisis: Monitoring and Response in Indonesia", paper presented at the International Conference on Impact of the Global Financial Crisis, 4-5 February, Beijing.

Roda, Jean-Marc, Philippe Cadène, Philippe Guizol, Levania Santoso and Achmad Uzair Fauzan (2007), *Atlas of Wooden Furniture Industry in Jepara, Indonesia*, France: French Agricultural Research Centre for International Development

Rodriguez, Edgard A. (1989), "The Economic Boom in Metro Cebu: Its Indicators and Implications", NEDA Region VII, Cebu City

Rodriguez, Edgard and Albert Berry (2002), "SMEs and the New Economy: Philippine Manufacturing in the 1990s," in Charles Harvie and Boon-Chye Lee (eds.), *The Role of SMEs in National Economies in East Asia*,Cheltenham: Edward Elgar.

Sadewa, Purbaya Yudhi (2010), "Perekonomian Indonesia Sedang "Bubble"?", *Kompas*, Bisnis & Keuangan, Senin, 19 April: 21.

Sandee, Henry (1998), "The Impact of the Crisis on Small-Scale Industries in Indonesia: Some Preliminary Findings From Central Java," discussion paper., Vrije Universiteit, Amsterdam.

Sandee, Henry (1999), "The Impact of the Crisis on Village Development in Java. Workshop Report", *Bulletin of Indonesian Economic Studies* 35(1):141–43

Sandee, Henry, R. K. Andadari, and S. Sulandjari (1998), "The Impact of Indonesia's Financial Crisis on Clustered Enterprise: A Case Study on the Jepara Furniture Cluster." Discussion paper. Vrije Universiteit, Amsterdam.

Sandee, Henry, Roos Kities Andadari and Sri Sulandjari (2000), "Small Firm Development during Good Times and Bad: The Jepara Furniture Industry", in C. Manning and P. van Dierman (eds.), *Indonesia in Transition: Social Aspects of Reformasi and Crisis*, Indonesia Assessment Series, Research School of Pacific and Asian Studies, Australian National University, Canberra, and Institute of Southeast Asian Studies, Singapore.

Sandee, Henry, B. Isdijoso, and Sri Sulandjari (2002), *SME clusters in Indonesia: An analysis of growth dynamics and employment conditions*, Jakarta: International Labor Office (ILO).

Sato, Yuri (2000), "How did the Crisis Affect Small and Medium-Sized Enterprises? From a Field Study of the Metal Working Industry in Java", *The Developing Economies*, XXXVIII(4): 572–95

Schiller, J. (2000), "Inside Jepara (a tale of two cities—part 2)", *Inside Indonesia*, 63(Jul.-Sept.): 2.

SMERU (2009a), "Monitoring the Socioeconomic Impact of the 2008/2009 Global Financial Crisis in Indonesia", Monitoring Upfate, July-October, Jakarta: SMERU Research Institute

SMERU (2009b), "Monitoring the Socioeconomic Impact of the 2008/2009 Global Financial Crisis in Indonesia", Media Monitoring No.04/FS/2009, November, Jakarta: SMERU Research Institute

SMERU (2009c), "Pemantauan Dampak Sosial-Ekonomi Krisis Keuangan Global 2008/09 di Indonesia", presented presented at the Bappenas Meeting on the Monitoring of the Impact of the Global Economic Crisis, 10 December, Jakarta: Bappenas.

Streeten,P.; Burki, S.; ul Hag, M.; Hicks, N. And Stewart, F. (1981), *First Things First: Meeting Basic Needs in Developing Countries*, Oxford: Oxford University Press.

Subandoro, Ali and Futoshi Yamauchi (2009), "Note: Impacts of Global Financial Crisis on Rural Households-Snap Shot Findings from Central Java and South Sulawesi", paper, November 4, International Food Policy Research Institute.

Sugiyama, Etsuko, Heni Kartikawati, Hiroshi Saito, Jaka Aminata, Takuya Miyajima, Roosiana, and Tamako Watanabe (2000), "Situation Analysis of Small and Medium Enterprises in Laguna", Working Group 1, Overseas Fieldwork 2000, Laguna.

Swift, J. (1989), "Why are rural people vulnerable to famine?", *IDS Bulletin*, 27(2): 49-57.

UN (2000), "Poverty Amidst Riches: the Need for Change", Report of the Committee for Development Policy on the 2nd Session, Department of Economic and Social Affairs, April, New York: United Nations.

UNCTAD (1997), *The Vulnerability of Small Island Developing States in the Context of Globalization: Common Issues and Remedies*, Report prepared for the Expert Group on Vulnerability Index, UN(DESA), 17-19 December 1997.

UN-ESCAP (2009), *Globalization of Production and the Competitiveness of Small and Medium-sized Enterprises in Asia and the Pacific:Trends and Prospects*, Studies in Trade and Investment 65, Bangkok: United Nations.

Tambunan, Tulus T.H. (1998), "Impact of East Asia Currency Crisis and Economic Development on Indonesia's SMEs and Priorities for Adjustment", paper presented at the SME Resourcing Conference, March 20-21, ASEAN CCI, Jakarta

Tambunan, Tulus T.H. (2000), *Development of Small-Scale Industries During the New Order Government in Indonesia*, Aldershot, et.al.: Ashgate.

Tambunan, Tulus T.H. (2002), "Building "An Early Warning System" For Indonesia with the Signal Approach", EADN RP2-4, September, EADN Regional Project on Indicators and Analyses of Vulnerabilities to Economic Crises, Bangkok: East Asian Development Network.

Tambunan, Tulus T.H. (2006), *Development of Small & Medium Enterprises in Indonesia from the Asia-Pacific Perspective*, LPFE-Usakti, Jakarta.

Tambunan, Tulus T.H. (2008), *Development of SMEs in ASEAN*, Readworthy Publications, Ltd, New Delhi.

Tambunan, Tulus T.H. (2009a), "The Rise in Non-Tariff Protectionism and Recovery From the 2008/009 Global Economic Crisis: The Indonesian Story", paper presented at the Research Workshop on Rising Non-tariff Protectionism and Crisis Recovery, 14-15 December, Macao, UN-ESCAP.

Tambunan, Tulus T.H. (2009b), *Small and Medium Enterprises in Asian Developing Countries*, London: Macmillan Palgrave.

Tambunan, Tulus T.H. (2009c), *UMKM di Indonesia*, Jakarta: Ghalia Indonesia.

Tambunan, Tulus T.H. (2009d), *Development of Small & Medium Enterprises in ASEAN Countries*, New Delhi: Readworthy.

Tambunan, Tulus T.H. and Ardha Prapanca Sugarda (2009), "The Impacts of the Global Economic Crisis on the Indonesian Furniture Industry", (with), Policy Discussion Paper Series, No. 11/08/09, Center for Industry, SME & Business Competition Studies, University of Trisakti, Jakarta.

Tambunan, Tulus T.H. and Priadi Asmanto (2010), "Conceptual Framework on Economic Vulnerability", Materials Preparation for Advisory Meeting with BAPPENAS, February, Jakarta: UNDP.

Tecson, Gwendolyn (1999), "Present Status and Prospects of Supporting Industries in the Philippines," in *Present Status and Prospects of Supporting Industries in ASEAN (I): Philippines—Indonesia*. Tokyo: Institute of Developing Economies, Japan External Trade Organization.

Tewari, Meenu (2001), "The challenge of reform: How Tamil Nadu's textile and apparel industry is facing the pressures of liberalization," paper prepared for the Center for International Development, Harvard University, Cambridge, MA (http://www.soc.duke.edu/sloan_2004/Papers/Tewari%20paper_Indian% 20 apparel_18June2004.pdf)

Tewari, Meenu and Jeffery Goebel (2002), "Small Firm Competitiveness in a Trade Liberalized World Lessons for Tamil Nadu", April, Research Paper (http://www.cid.harvard.edu/archive/india/pdfs/ tewari_small firms_ 042102. pdf).

Thee Kian Wie (2000), "The Impact of the Economic Crisis on Indonesia's Manufacturing Sector", *The Developing Economies*, XXXVIII (4): 420–53

Titiheruw, Ira S; Hadi Soesastro; and Raymond Atje (2009), "Global Financial Crisis", Discussion Series Paper 6: Indonesia, May, London: Overseas Development Institute (ODI) and Jakarta: Center for Strategy and International Studies (CSIS).

Valodia, Imraan and Myriam Velia (2004), " Macro-Micro Linkages in Trade: How are Firms Adjusting to Trade Liberalization, and does Trade Liberalization lead to improved Productivity in South African Manufacturing Firms?, paper presented to the African Development and Poverty Reduction: The Macro-Micro Linkage Conference, Development Policy Research Unit (DPRU) and Trade and Industrial Policy Secretariat (TIPS), 13-15 October.

Wattanapruttipaisan, Thitapha (2003a), " Promoting SME Development: Some Issues and Suggestions for Policy Consideration", *Bulletin on Asia-Pacific Perspectives*, pp. 57-67

Wattanapruttipaisan,Thitapha (2003b), "Four Proposals for Improved Financing of SME Development", *Asian Development Review*, 20(2), December.

Wattanapruttipaisan, Thitapha (2005), "SME Development and Internationalization in the Knowledge-Based and Innovation-Driven Global Economy: Mapping the Agenda Ahead", paper presented at the International Expert Seminar on "Mapping Policy Experience for SMEs" Phuket, 19-20 May.

Wells, J. (1996), Composite Vulnerability Index: A Preliminary Report", London: Commonwealth Secretariat.

Wells, J. (1997), Composite Vulnerability Index: A Revised Report", London: Commonwealth Secretariat.

Wengel, Jan ter and Edgard Rodriguez (2006), "SME Export Performance in Indonesia After the Crisis", *Small Business Economics*,26: 25–37

WFP (2005), "Food Insecurity and Vulnerability Analysis Timor Leste", April, VAM Tim, The United Nations World Food Program, Dili.

WFP & UNICEF (2008), "Pilot Monitoring of High Food Price Impact at Household Level in Selected Vulnerable Areas. August-November 2008. Report", Jakarta: United Nations World Food Program and UNICEF.

Winters, L. A., and P. M. G. Martins (2004), "When Comparative Advantage is not Enough: Business Costs in Small Remote Economies", *World Trade Review*, 3 (3): 347-83.

Wiradi, G. (1998), "Rural Java in a Time of Crisis: With Special Reference to Curug Village, Cirebon, West Java," paper presented at The Economic Crisis and Social Security in Indonesia, Berg-en-Dal, The Netherlands.

World Bank (2000), *Asian Corporate Recovery*, Washington, D.C.

World Bank. (2004), "SME", World Bank Group Review of Small Business Activities, Washington, DC: World Bank.

World Bank (2008a), "Battening Down the Hatches". Indonesia Quarterly Economic Update, 10 December. Washington, DC: World Bank.

World Bank, (2008b), *World Development Indicators 2008*, Washington, DC.

World Bank (2009a), "Crisis Monitoring and Response. Using Lot Quality Assurance Sampling (LQAS)", power point presentation, 11 May, World Bank Poverty Team, Jakarta.

World Bank (2009b), "Developing Indonesia's Crisis Monitoring and Response System", power point presentation, 6 June, World Bank Poverty Team, Jakarta.

World Bank (2009c), "Indonesia Quarterly Update, June 2009", Jakarta: World Bank Office.

World Bank (2009d), "Migration and Development Brief 10," July 13, Washington, D.C.

World Bank (2009e),"Indonesia Economic Quarterly. Back on Track", 52200, December, Jakarta.

World Bank (2009f), "Battling the forces of global recession", a World Bank economic update for the East Asia and Pacific Region," April 2009, Bangkok.

World Bank (2010a), *Global Economic Prospect. Crisis, Finance and Growth 2010*, Washington, D.C.

World Bank (2010b), "Indonesia's Crisis Monitoring and Response System (CMRS). Analysis and Presentation of CMRS Data. First Round Summary Report, 25 January, Jakarta.

World Bank (2010c), "Indonesian Economic Quarterly. Building momentum", March, Jakarta.

World Bank and ASEAN (2009), "ASEAN Assessment on the Social Impacts of the Global Financial Crisis", A Snap-shot Report for notation at the 15th ASEAN Summit, Cha-am Hua Hin, Thailand, 23 October.

Yudo, Teguh, Ira S. Titiheruw and Hadi Soesastro (2009), "The Impact of the Global Financial Crisis on Indonesia's Economy", Study Report submitted to The United Nations Development Program (UNDP), September, Jakarta: Centre for Strategic and International Studies (CSIS).

Zavadjil, Milan (2009), "Indonesia's strong balance sheets—key to weathering the global financial crisis", 19, November, East Asia Forum.

INDEX

A

access, 78, 102, 104, 105, 106, 109, 117, 119, 120, 127, 128, 140, 162, 163, 164, 192, 194, 198, 199, 212, 225
accessibility, 65, 195, 199
accounting, 23, 34, 40, 53, 131, 216
acquisitions, 23
adjustment, 11, 63, 75, 82, 83, 90, 105, 116, 120, 140, 142, 143, 147, 148, 151, 178, 208
adult literacy, 188, 189
adults, 17, 163
advancement, 188, 190
advancements, 190
adverse conditions, 36
Africa, 23, 136, 141, 166, 229, 232, 233
age, 78, 159, 162, 163, 164, 170, 191, 211, 213, 224
agencies, 49, 79, 95, 104, 106, 113
aggregation, 161, 221
agricultural sector, 9, 12, 69, 83, 154, 178, 182
agriculture, 33, 47, 50, 56, 69, 70, 81, 83, 97, 115, 119, 154, 175, 178, 179, 180, 182, 224, 225
aluminium, 50, 77
analytical framework, viii, 63, 82, 83, 112, 211
animal husbandry, 83
annual rate, 36
apparel industry, 239
arithmetic, 221, 224, 225
ASEAN, 10, 12, 21, 23, 24, 26, 27, 28, 30, 31, 36, 38, 39, 44, 51, 113, 114, 124, 125, 127, 131, 150, 176, 177, 228, 238, 239, 241
assessment, 4, 11, 28, 64, 72, 94, 106, 119, 129, 158, 160, 177, 190, 210, 211
assets, 16, 23, 53, 59, 66, 77, 89, 95, 109, 127, 159, 160, 161, 183, 184, 200, 210, 211, 214, 236
authority, 14, 104, 108
average costs, 105

average earnings, 143

B

bail, 53
balance of payments, 33, 234, 235
balance sheet, 60, 127, 241
Bangladesh, 23, 33, 36, 72, 103, 233
bank failure, vii, 1, 18
bank financing, 9
banking, vii, 2, 3, 8, 14, 16, 20, 59, 60, 81, 107, 109, 112, 117, 120, 123, 124, 127, 128, 153, 156, 234
bankruptcy, 114, 132
banks, 2, 9, 14, 16, 24, 53, 59, 62, 75, 81, 104, 105, 109, 110, 117, 122, 127, 128, 140, 164, 200
Barbados, 230
bargaining, 119
barriers, 18, 56, 106
base, 68, 83, 93, 104, 176, 178, 200
basic education, 75
basic needs, 53, 84, 160, 210
Beijing, 237
benefits, 37, 48, 74, 117, 119, 142, 148, 166, 208
beverages, 4, 28, 29, 30, 39, 44, 55, 86, 97, 100, 131, 151
births, 163
bonds, 20, 53, 59, 164
bonuses, 74, 89, 142, 143, 147, 148
borrowers, 128
bounds, 222
brass, 132
Brazil, 232
Bulgaria, 212
business cycle, 14, 37, 106, 122
business strategy, 141
businesses, vii, 1, 8, 17, 24, 34, 56, 62, 63, 69, 70, 78, 81, 83, 95, 104, 114, 120, 122, 134, 138, 187

buyer, 5, 59, 87, 102, 109, 110, 116, 120, 132, 136, 137

C

cable television, 162
cacao, 50, 68, 77, 118
Cambodia, 10, 12, 24, 26, 31, 33, 36, 38, 39, 51, 52, 99, 100, 103, 177
Caribbean, 23, 230
cash, 22, 54, 113, 116, 122, 214
cash flow, 116, 122
casting, 131, 132
category a, 95
cattle, 160
Central Asia, 23, 34
central bank, 3, 33, 51, 53, 207
certificate, 53
certification, 136
challenges, 4, 115
changing environment, 159
chemical, 106, 123
chemicals, 123, 131
Chicago, 231
child labor, 82
child mortality, 163, 224
children, 3, 4, 17, 65, 72, 73, 75, 79, 88, 89, 90, 163, 170, 224, 228
China, vii, 1, 4, 18, 19, 22, 25, 27, 28, 31, 33, 34, 38, 39, 42, 51, 52, 53, 71, 83, 94, 99, 100, 102, 103, 106, 126, 129, 130, 131, 135, 136, 155, 232, 234
Chinese government, 130
circulation, 108
civil servants, 22, 54, 89, 110
civil society, 72
classes, 9, 82
climate, 69, 80, 104, 154, 178
closed economy, 59
closure, 41
clothing, 94, 123, 130, 131
clustering, 43
clusters, 48, 57, 87, 102, 115, 133, 136, 142, 228, 238
coal, 48, 50, 56, 72, 73, 74, 77
coastal region, 130
coefficient of variation, 32, 39, 176
coffee, 10, 50, 68, 106, 118, 154, 176, 210
collaboration, 68, 76, 200
commercial, 16, 24, 104, 108, 113, 173
commodity, 7, 8, 10, 11, 28, 30, 60, 69, 131, 156, 175, 176, 215
communication, vii, 15, 61, 85, 90, 96, 97, 98, 164

communities, 72, 75, 77, 79, 119, 156, 157, 159, 183, 188, 190, 199
community, 17, 24, 57, 72, 73, 74, 75, 76, 79, 85, 87, 111, 156, 160, 161, 188, 200, 214, 221, 228
community support, 72
comparative advantage, 14, 106
compensation, 78
competition, 30, 78, 105, 106
competitiveness, 9, 16, 18, 53, 55, 56, 104, 105, 112, 117, 118, 119, 120, 122, 233
competitors, 105
compliance, 104
composition, 3, 68, 85, 86, 88
comprehension, 160
computing, 131, 221
conflict, 11, 178
consensus, 156, 176
constant prices, 97, 167
construction, vii, viii, 12, 15, 26, 30, 34, 37, 40, 56, 79, 115, 135, 141, 173, 196, 203, 222, 223, 224
consumer goods, 48, 50, 74, 94
consumers, 59, 94, 111, 112
consumption, 3, 4, 9, 10, 12, 14, 22, 32, 33, 47, 54, 57, 59, 60, 61, 62, 63, 64, 65, 66, 68, 72, 75, 78, 81, 90, 111, 113, 118, 119, 133, 154, 156, 157, 158, 159, 161, 162, 172, 173, 175, 176, 183, 200, 210, 211, 212, 220, 224
containers, 18, 134, 140
conviction, 107
cooking, 65
cooperation, 200, 201
coping strategies, 64, 73, 78, 158
copper, 10, 121, 176
correlation, 82, 161
corruption, 57, 106
cost, 9, 10, 65, 66, 102, 104, 107, 116, 119, 120, 142, 173, 178, 206
cotton, 102
counseling, 148, 151
covering, 3, 85, 101, 121, 137, 210, 224
credit market, 8
credit squeeze, 20
creditworthiness, 109
creep, 18
criminal activity, 78
criminality, 76
crises, vii, viii, 1, 2, 4, 5, 7, 10, 13, 25, 38, 39, 81, 85, 94, 123, 150, 153, 154, 155, 156, 160, 170, 214, 229, 231, 234, 235
cultivation, 56
culture, 86, 200, 203, 212

currency, vii, viii, 1, 2, 9, 10, 12, 14, 16, 20, 30, 32, 81, 108, 109, 110, 111, 112, 114, 117, 156, 229, 231, 234
customers, 104, 109, 121, 141

D

data analysis, 225
data collection, 64, 82, 84
database, 21, 23, 24, 26, 27, 29, 31, 32, 38, 43, 52, 131
death rate, 113
debts, 9, 16, 30, 33, 156, 236
deficit, 59, 155, 198, 220
democratization, 57, 81
demographic data, 214
demographic structure, 80
dependency ratio, 213, 214
deposits, 59
depreciation, 1, 9, 10, 12, 13, 14, 16, 41, 108, 110, 111, 112, 114, 116, 117, 118, 119, 124
deprivation, 160
depth, 73, 85, 163
devaluation, 4, 115
deviation, 215, 219
direct investment, 127
direct observation, 41, 50, 73, 85
disaster, 225
disbursement, 22
discomfort, 206
discretionary policy, 54
discrimination, 83, 103, 170
distortions, 69, 80, 103
distress, 116, 237
distribution, 45, 61, 80, 83, 97, 103, 105, 107, 121, 156, 158, 163, 173, 178, 181, 194, 206, 209, 210, 222
diversification, 141, 165, 175, 178, 182, 213, 216, 224
diversity, 162, 163, 165, 175, 176, 177
division of labor, 120
domestic credit, 128
domestic demand, 14, 32, 44, 55, 56, 57, 102, 114, 115, 116, 120, 123, 141, 155, 175
domestic economy, 1, 4, 7, 8, 22, 46, 81, 101, 128
domestic labor, 12
domestic markets, 25, 109, 137
domestic violence, 76
dominance, 104, 106
draft, 231, 232, 233
drought, 178

E

early warning, viii, 7, 215, 217, 229, 235
earnings, 37, 101, 102, 155
earthquakes, 156, 159
elasticity of demand, 112
election, 22, 59
electricity, 11, 54, 73, 103, 164, 193, 194, 198, 199
elementary school, 80
emergency, 207, 215
emergency planning, 207
empowerment, 53, 57, 203
energy, 11, 12, 56, 65, 107, 142, 160, 163, 165, 177, 178
energy consumption, 163
enforcement, 76, 105
enrollment, 17, 189, 193
entrepreneurs, 4, 78, 93, 96, 104, 115, 164
environment, 54, 73, 104, 120, 159, 161, 222
equilibrium, 203, 209, 215
equipment, 23, 55, 102, 109, 123, 131, 160
equities, vii, 1, 18
equity, 32, 38
erosion, 161
ethnicity, 78
EU, 1, 18, 20, 158
Europe, 23, 34, 87, 102, 112, 123, 133, 136
European market, 130
evacuation, 169
evidence, viii, 4, 17, 19, 36, 47, 48, 64, 66, 69, 70, 71, 81, 83, 84, 85, 92, 112, 115, 116, 120, 123, 124, 125, 126, 128, 129, 131, 132, 133, 137, 140, 141, 143, 150, 230
excess demand, 8, 110, 116, 220
excess supply, 69
exchange rate, 12, 14, 53, 106, 116, 117, 119
exclusion, 160
exercise, 224
expenditures, 3, 64, 66, 74, 90, 91, 111, 118, 149, 173, 183
exposure, 16, 109, 117, 127, 156, 157, 159, 166, 173, 175, 210, 225
external constraints, 103
external financing, 59
external shocks, 30, 60, 176, 177, 178, 203, 207, 213
extraction, 56, 214

F

factor analysis, 47
factories, 10, 40, 48, 74, 78, 80, 83, 107, 121, 176
families, 8, 10, 12, 18, 70, 77, 79, 85, 135, 178, 203

family firms, 95
family income, 89, 214
family relationships, 151
family support, 200
famine, 238
farmers, 8, 10, 48, 68, 69, 72, 73, 83, 115, 117, 176, 200, 210, 219
farms, 80
FDI, 2, 12, 18, 20, 30, 32, 38, 39, 127, 230, 232
fertility, 213
fertilizers, 11, 75
Fiji, 222, 234
Filipino, 230
firm size, 105
fiscal deficit, 204, 205
fiscal policy, 54, 141
fish, 50, 57, 65, 76, 77, 83, 106, 118, 119, 131, 178, 214, 225
fixed costs, 104
flexibility, 14, 18, 53, 106, 107, 203, 207
flight, 12, 108, 124, 155
flooding, 178
floods, 156, 159
fluctuations, 23, 133, 156
footwear, 4, 18, 29, 40, 56, 94, 97, 100, 106, 115, 129, 131
force, 3, 30, 63, 108, 200, 203, 204
formal education, 212
formal sector, 14, 40, 46, 57, 70, 76, 78, 81, 88, 107, 110, 117, 118, 128, 186, 188
formation, 8, 23, 162, 175, 178, 193, 225
formula, 221, 222
France, 30, 138, 232, 237
friendship, 160
fruits, viii, 78, 154
fuel prices, 45
funding, 4, 16, 109
funds, 32, 59, 62, 107, 109, 117, 150, 164, 207, 219
furniture manufacturer, 136

G

garment industry, 151
general education, 193, 195
geography, 171
Germany, 30, 93, 138
goods and services, 10, 19, 24, 27, 59, 61, 126, 173, 178, 203, 220, 224, 225
grants, 72
greed, 166
grids, 198
Guangdong, 130
Guinea, 84, 228

H

harbors, 118, 193
harmonization, 55
hazards, 178, 200, 214
high school, 75, 82, 193, 195
Highlands, 228
history, 80
HIV/AIDS, 163, 224
homelessness, 225
homes, 77
Hong Kong, 18, 25, 28, 31, 33, 34, 35, 38, 39, 42, 51, 52, 71, 83, 87, 102, 130, 131, 155, 231
host, 12, 33, 36, 37, 39, 48, 154
hotel, vii, 15, 96, 97, 98
hotels, 47
Hurricane Andrew, 236
hurricanes, 156
husband, 88
hyperinflation, 154
hypothesis, 83, 107, 112, 166, 168, 170, 173, 175, 176, 177, 178, 181, 183, 184, 186, 188, 190, 192, 193, 200, 204, 205, 207, 212, 213, 214, 216

I

identification, 7, 159, 217, 219, 220, 225
idiosyncratic, 158, 212
illiteracy, 214
IMF, 18, 38, 52, 59, 106, 111, 124, 125, 127, 128, 207, 229, 231, 233, 234
immunization, 17
improvements, 53, 56
incidence, 222
independence, 59, 81, 200
India, vii, 1, 4, 18, 19, 22, 23, 27, 28, 33, 36, 38, 51, 52, 94, 100, 103, 105, 106, 126, 131, 232
indirect effect, 3, 8, 61, 62
individuals, 14, 19, 37, 42, 53, 80, 119, 156, 157, 159, 160, 183, 184, 199, 200
Indonesian Employers Association (ASPINDO), 40
Indonesian workers, 34, 35
inequality, 32, 44, 46, 188
infant mortality, 17, 190
inferences, 211
inflation, 2, 8, 9, 10, 11, 12, 14, 22, 58, 66, 78, 80, 110, 118, 163, 164, 166, 175, 178, 203, 205, 206, 207, 208
informal sector, 14, 34, 46, 57, 63, 71, 72, 81, 84, 119, 138, 142, 148, 186, 187, 188
infrastructure, 34, 39, 53, 56, 57, 58, 68, 164, 165, 193, 194, 196, 199

insecurity, 72, 159, 161, 221, 225
inspections, 18
institutions, 58, 93, 104, 109, 127, 193, 202
integration, 22, 27, 44
interbank market, 59
interest rates, 4, 8, 14, 22, 54, 108, 112, 113, 114, 128, 156
intermediaries, 120, 129
investors, 121, 123, 127
iron, 50, 77, 86, 131, 133
irrigation, 53
Islam, 110, 228
islands, viii, 49, 80, 84, 87, 118, 168, 169, 171, 172, 173, 174, 180, 182, 184, 186, 187, 189, 191, 192, 194, 195, 196, 201, 202, 205, 208
isolation, 84, 170
Israel, 11, 155, 178
issues, 1, 64, 73, 82, 84, 85, 103, 228, 230
Italy, 138, 237

J

Jamaica, 72, 233
Japan, vii, 1, 18, 20, 27, 29, 30, 33, 68, 80, 83, 87, 93, 112, 123, 125, 126, 136, 141, 178, 234, 239
Java, 3, 5, 10, 20, 30, 40, 41, 48, 68, 69, 70, 71, 72, 73, 76, 78, 79, 82, 84, 85, 86, 87, 95, 115, 116, 117, 118, 120, 121, 132, 133, 136, 137, 167, 168, 169, 171, 172, 174, 175, 176, 180, 181, 184, 186, 187, 189, 191, 192, 193, 194, 195, 196, 197, 198, 199, 201, 202, 205, 208, 209, 228, 237, 238, 240
joint ventures, 123
junior high school, 193
justification, 208
juvenile delinquency, 76

K

Kenya, 72, 233
kerosene, 65
kinship, 160
Korea, vii, 2, 14, 18, 33, 37, 38, 42, 83, 101, 155
Kuwait, 33

L

large-scale disasters, 159
Latin America, 23, 233
law enforcement, 39, 106
laws, 138
layoffs, 4, 40, 53, 74, 129, 148
lead, 8, 36, 45, 111, 239

learning, 192
lending, 9, 16, 24, 59, 109, 110, 112, 128
level of education, 71, 82, 88, 163, 164, 211, 212
liberalization, 105, 153, 239
life expectancy, 190, 213
lifetime, 80
liquidity, 16, 53, 59, 108, 109
literacy, 163, 188, 189, 213
livestock, 56, 69, 84, 214
living conditions, 73
loans, 10, 24, 38, 39, 54, 59, 72, 94, 108, 122, 128, 148, 151, 207, 214
logging, 136
logistics, 39, 56

M

machinery, 23, 28, 102, 121, 123, 131
magnitude, 73, 117, 159, 209
majority, 65, 68, 70, 71, 77, 81, 83, 84, 86, 88, 89, 90, 96, 97, 99, 100, 101, 104, 106, 113, 115, 129, 131, 138, 141, 142, 143, 148, 151, 154, 174, 178, 181, 184, 188, 222
malaria, 163
Malaysia, 2, 4, 10, 14, 18, 21, 23, 24, 26, 27, 28, 30, 31, 33, 34, 35, 36, 37, 38, 39, 42, 51, 52, 71, 79, 80, 84, 100, 103, 114, 122, 124, 125, 128, 131, 135, 153, 154, 155, 156, 204, 215, 227, 230, 236
malnutrition, 17, 163
man, 70
management, 59, 75, 115, 136, 202
manpower, 119, 168, 183
mapping, 217, 220, 221, 222
marginalization, 170, 203
marital status, 78
market economy, 80
market segment, 105
marketing, 61, 103, 104, 107, 148, 202
married women, 36, 203
Maryland, 230, 235
mass, 120
materials, 9, 55, 61, 103, 117, 118, 119, 133, 136, 141
matrix, 216
matter, 53, 78, 80, 85
measurement, 221, 235
meat, viii, 65, 131, 154
media, 41, 50, 76, 83, 85, 129, 136
median, 214
medical, 75, 193
medicine, 79
merchandise, 125
metals, 131

methodology, 160, 221, 230
Mexico, 236
Miami, 236
middle class, 9, 112
Middle East, 11, 20, 23, 33, 34, 79, 80, 135, 136, 141, 178
migrants, 10, 33, 34, 37, 70, 71, 72, 79, 80, 82, 176
migration, 33, 34, 36, 37, 66, 68, 70, 71, 72, 79, 80, 200, 232
military, 54, 200
Min, Ho Chi, 101
minimum wage, 5, 87, 129, 206
Ministry of Education, 199
mobile phone, 80, 162
models, 159
momentum, 241
monetary policy, 59, 207
monopoly, 207
morbidity, 163
mortality, 17, 163
multiplier, 3, 10, 54, 61, 62, 126, 176, 216, 220
Myanmar, 10, 24, 26, 31, 33, 36, 39, 52, 176

N

Nepal, 31, 33, 36, 103
net exports, 24
Netherlands, 93, 102, 138, 235, 236, 240
NGOs, 17, 72, 73, 164, 200
North Africa, 23
nursing, 37
nutrition, 17, 32, 90, 91, 149

O

obstacles, 106, 235
officials, 18, 73, 79, 137
oil, viii, 7, 11, 33, 45, 48, 49, 56, 65, 77, 78, 87, 97, 99, 100, 119, 135, 154, 155, 175, 177, 178, 183, 207, 217
old age, 156
open economy, 18, 39, 173, 174
openness, 153, 162, 165, 170, 173, 175
operations, 8, 81, 93, 94, 104, 106, 122, 124, 130
opportunities, 4, 37, 70, 74, 76, 78, 83, 102, 115, 117, 119, 120, 122, 138, 159, 203, 231, 233
optimism, 24
organize, 120
outreach, 17
outsourcing, 76, 78
overlap, 68
overtime, 69, 74, 78

ownership, 123, 161, 211

P

Pacific, 22, 23, 34, 154, 222, 227, 228, 230, 231, 236, 238, 239, 240
Pakistan, 22, 23, 28, 33, 36, 100, 102, 103
palm oil, 10, 12, 29, 34, 40, 50, 76, 77, 154, 176, 182, 213, 215, 217
parents, 70, 79, 170
permit, 221
Peru, 210, 232
petroleum, 10, 11, 176, 177
Petroleum, 155
Philippines, vii, 1, 2, 4, 10, 11, 14, 16, 19, 21, 23, 24, 26, 27, 28, 31, 32, 33, 36, 37, 38, 39, 42, 51, 52, 81, 84, 100, 102, 103, 114, 122, 123, 124, 125, 131, 154, 155, 175, 176, 177, 227, 229, 230, 233, 239
Physical Quality of Life Index, 188
pilot study, 72, 154, 233
plants, 105
plastic products, 131
plastics, 131
playing, 30
police, 54
polio, 17
political crisis, 156
political instability, 8
pollution, 104
ponds, 69
positive relationship, 107, 159, 165, 188
potential benefits, 116
poultry, 69, 75
PRC, 23, 103
preferential treatment, 106
price effect, 212
price mechanism, 208
probability, 157, 159, 211
producers, 50, 87, 89, 105, 115, 116, 121, 131, 132, 133, 135, 136, 137, 140, 141, 142, 151, 164, 178, 200, 202, 213, 216, 237
profit, 116, 121, 122, 140
proliferation, 106
prosperity, 178
protection, 56, 57, 72, 76, 105, 110
protectionism, 18, 39, 56
pulp, 30, 41
purchasing power, 182

Q

qualifications, 222
qualitative research, 79
quality improvement, 104
quality of service, 17
questionnaire, 137

R

rating scale, 114
raw materials, 9, 12, 39, 41, 55, 61, 86, 94, 103, 104, 109, 110, 116, 120, 122, 132, 133, 135, 151
reactions, 115
real income, 8, 25, 39, 108, 174, 175, 178, 183
real terms, 69, 116
real wage, 66, 110
reality, 16, 161, 188
recession, vii, 2, 14, 44, 84, 125, 137, 155, 166, 181
reciprocity, 199
recognition, 86
recovery, vii, 29, 39, 51, 54, 55, 57, 77, 119, 123, 159, 160, 178, 188, 203, 207, 209, 213, 214, 231
recovery process, vii, 77
redundancy, 83
regression, 212, 221, 223, 224, 225
regulated economy, 104
regulations, 18, 53, 56, 103, 104, 106, 114, 138
relatives, 66, 75, 94, 104, 106, 107, 150, 200
relief, 56
religion, 78
remittances, viii, 2, 11, 18, 32, 33, 34, 35, 36, 37, 48, 70, 72, 82, 85, 91, 129, 154, 177, 200
rent, 96, 97, 98, 183
repair, 57
reputation, 87
requirements, 86
researchers, 79, 80
reserves, 53, 59
resilience, 2, 4, 21, 39, 54, 94, 113, 114, 117, 119, 122, 128, 159, 160, 161, 166, 170, 183, 184, 188, 190, 193, 200, 203, 204, 206, 207, 208, 210, 212, 213, 214, 222, 237
resistance, 115
resources, 64, 77, 104, 173, 207, 208, 214
response, 4, 9, 10, 11, 14, 18, 46, 47, 53, 54, 55, 56, 58, 60, 63, 64, 65, 108, 122, 123, 124, 159, 178, 200
responsiveness, 159
restaurants, 47, 97, 118, 219
restrictions, 18, 77, 103, 105, 106
retribution, 56
revenue, 54, 104, 141, 204, 205, 207
risk, 60, 64, 109, 156, 157, 158, 200
risks, 86, 156, 158, 159, 175
roots, 78
rubber, 48, 50, 72, 73, 74, 75, 77, 78, 123, 131, 154
rules, 18, 53, 55, 138

S

safety, 17, 18, 57, 72, 117, 138
Saudi Arabia, 34, 35, 155
savings, 9, 36, 37, 60, 62, 63, 66, 94, 104, 106, 183
scaling, 43
scarcity, 135
school, 3, 17, 57, 63, 66, 68, 71, 75, 79, 82, 88, 163, 164, 188, 189, 193, 221
scope, 18
seafood, 129
seasonal factors, 69
seasonality, 65, 66, 69
secondary data, 79, 82, 101, 114, 199
secondary education, 148
security, 9, 73, 106, 160, 188, 212, 225, 228
semiconductor, 28, 95
sensitivity, 159, 160, 161, 170, 177, 184, 188
service provider, 79, 164
services, 10, 15, 21, 31, 37, 47, 50, 57, 58, 61, 69, 81, 86, 97, 101, 112, 126, 129, 135, 153, 176, 182, 193, 202, 217, 219
shape, 59
shareholders, 9
shock, vii, viii, 1, 4, 7, 14, 18, 19, 20, 65, 84, 94, 106, 115, 154, 155, 156, 157, 158, 159, 160, 161, 175, 176, 178, 181, 183, 188, 190, 200, 203, 204, 205, 207, 208, 209, 210, 225
short supply, 107
shortage, 8, 86, 109
showing, 17, 35, 75, 101, 116, 125, 177, 211
shrimp, 106
signals, 7
signs, vii, 77, 155
silver, 132
simulation, 56
simulations, 54
Singapore, 2, 4, 10, 14, 18, 21, 23, 24, 25, 26, 27, 28, 30, 31, 33, 34, 36, 38, 39, 42, 51, 52, 71, 95, 102, 103, 124, 125, 127, 131, 132, 153, 155, 156, 160, 166, 228, 238
skilled workers, 30, 39, 99, 104, 151
small firms, 105, 239
smuggling, 18
society, 190, 193, 200
solution, 63

South Africa, 105, 239
South Asia, 23, 34, 102
South Korea, vii, 1, 2, 14, 16, 25, 28, 41, 79, 81, 113, 155
Southeast Asia, i, iii, vii, 1, 2, 3, 5, 13, 14, 18, 19, 21, 25, 39, 81, 101, 123, 124, 125, 129, 153, 176, 215, 236, 238
Spain, 138
species, 86
specifications, 54
spending, 17, 22, 54, 57, 59, 60, 65, 72, 75, 136
spin, 86
spindle, 105
Sri Lanka, 33, 36, 37, 42
stability, 32, 33, 39, 53, 111, 164, 165, 166, 203
stabilization, 45
stabilizers, 54
stakeholders, 137
standard deviation, 39, 217
standardization, 120
state, 3, 4, 24, 32, 36, 51, 58, 72, 76, 87, 106, 108, 109, 113, 127, 156, 158, 160, 165, 166, 178, 209, 212
statistics, 230
steel, 30, 131
stimulus, 22, 25, 46, 53, 54, 56, 57, 59, 60, 77, 94, 141, 207
stratification, 42
stress, 159
structure, 63, 71, 88, 97, 103, 120, 121, 125, 161, 162, 170, 180, 200, 206, 210, 211, 213, 225
subjectivity, 160, 222, 225
sub-Saharan Africa, 236
subscribers, 162
subsidy, 45
subsistence, 80
substitutes, 118
substitution, 9, 66, 120
supplementation, 17
supplier, 94, 104, 106, 109, 110, 116, 122, 136, 137, 138, 140, 141
supply chain, 18, 27, 101
surplus, 30, 33, 53, 220
survey design, 68
survival, 111, 122
suspensions, 130
sustainability, 178, 204, 205, 212, 228
synthetic fiber, 56

T

Taiwan, 33, 34, 35, 102, 138
tariff, 18, 55, 56, 239

tax cuts, 56
taxation, 210
taxes, 22
teachers, 73, 88
technological progress, 93, 170
technologies, 94
technology, 97, 99, 102, 103, 104, 112, 119, 120, 165, 192
telecommunications, 55
telephone, 162
tenure, 53
tertiary education, 88, 163
textiles, 47, 97, 102, 105, 112, 123, 125, 131
Thailand, vii, 1, 2, 4, 10, 12, 14, 16, 18, 21, 23, 24, 26, 27, 28, 31, 33, 36, 37, 38, 39, 42, 51, 52, 81, 100, 103, 106, 113, 114, 115, 122, 123, 124, 125, 153, 154, 155, 156, 175, 176, 204, 215, 227, 228, 230, 234, 237, 241
theft, 76
time series, 54, 210, 215, 225
tobacco, 50, 68, 100, 131, 142
total energy, 177
total product, 62, 87, 139, 182, 220
total revenue, 138
tourism, 50, 77, 81, 126, 129, 132, 178
Toyota, 97
toys, 4, 18, 55, 102, 130
TPI, 50
training, 142, 148
trajectory, 58
transistor, 41
transmission, viii, 2, 3, 4, 7, 8, 9, 10, 11, 12, 19, 20, 61, 63, 64, 81, 84, 127, 129, 150, 176, 177, 178
transparency, 160, 225
treatment, 163
trial, 225
truck drivers, 73
tuberculosis, 163
tuition, 75
Turkey, 41

U

unemployed individuals, 70
unemployment rate, 14, 42, 46, 110, 164, 188, 205
uniform, 75, 77
uninsured, 157
United Kingdom (UK), 30, 72, 154, 233, 234, 235
United Nations, UN, 99, 100, 188, 222, 225, 229, 231, 232, 235, 236, 238, 239, 240, 241
United States (USA), vii, 1, 27, 41, 83, 87, 136, 227, 235
universities, 164, 193

unstructured interviews, 137
urban, 3, 34, 42, 45, 46, 48, 50, 63, 64, 65, 66, 71, 72, 80, 82, 84, 101, 102, 103, 105, 111, 115, 117, 118, 121, 162, 171, 194, 211, 214, 231

V

valuation, 53
value added tax, 56
variables, 12, 37, 114, 158, 166, 206, 219, 222, 223, 224, 225
variations, 102, 203
VAT, 56
vector, 158, 212
vegetables, viii, 78, 131, 154
vehicles, 22, 131, 195
victims, 82, 135, 216
Vietnam, 10, 26, 28, 33, 51, 52, 100, 103, 124, 131, 135, 177
vocational training, 88, 192
volatility, 39, 53, 223
vulnerability, vii, viii, 2, 5, 7, 82, 154, 155, 156, 157, 158, 159, 160, 161, 166, 167, 169, 170, 173, 175, 176, 178, 188, 189, 193, 200, 204, 209, 210, 212, 213, 214, 215, 217, 220, 221, 222, 223, 224, 225, 230
vulnerable people, 157

W

wage increases, 106
wages, 18, 42, 46, 63, 64, 65, 66, 89, 92, 110, 142, 143, 147, 148, 160, 203
war, 155
Washington, 228, 229, 230, 231, 232, 233, 234, 235, 236, 237, 240
water, 69, 96, 97, 98, 160, 164, 193
weakness, 119
wealth, vii, 1, 17, 183, 207, 214
wearing apparel, 126, 131
web, 21
welfare, 37, 44, 156, 157, 158, 159, 161, 168, 182, 202, 205, 212, 214
welfare loss, 158, 161
well-being, 81, 159, 188, 210
Western Europe, 41, 110
wood, 30, 39, 44, 53, 86, 87, 88, 94, 97, 100, 112, 131, 133, 134, 135, 136, 139, 228
wood products, 44, 86, 87, 97, 131, 136, 139
World Bank, 2, 3, 10, 11, 21, 23, 26, 28, 34, 44, 45, 46, 48, 49, 54, 58, 63, 64, 65, 66, 67, 82, 83, 85, 93, 113, 114, 123, 127, 176, 177, 228, 229, 230, 233, 237, 240, 241
worldwide, vii, 11, 17, 34, 86, 87, 93, 128, 177
WTO, 55

Y

yes/no, 162
yield, 222
young people, 71, 78